Philosophy of Language: the Big Questions

Philosophy: The Big Questions

Series Editor: James P. Sterba, University of Notre Dame, Indiana

Designed to elicit a philosophical response in the mind of the student, this distinctive series of anthologies provides essential classical and contemporary readings that serve to make the central questions of philosophy come alive for today's students. It presents complete coverage of the Anglo-American tradition of philosophy, as well as the kinds of questions and challenges that it confronts today, both from other cultural traditions and from theoretical movements such as feminism and postmodernism.

PHILOSOPHY OF LANGUAGE:

The Big Questions

EDITED BY ANDREA NYE

Blackwell
Publishing

© 1998 by Blackwell Publishing Ltd

BLACKWELL PUBLISHING
350 Main Street, Malden, MA 02148-5020, USA
108 Cowley Road, Oxford OX4 1JF, UK
550 Swanston Street, Carlton, Victoria 3053, Australia

The right of Joe Bloggs to be identified as the Author(s) of the Editorial Material in this Work has been asserted in accordance with the UK Copyright, Designs, and Patents Act 1988.

First published 1998
Reprinted 1999, 2004

Library of Congress Cataloging-in-Publication Data

Philosophy of language : the big questions / edited by Andrea Nye.
    p. cm.— (Philosophy, the big questions ; 5)
  Includes bibliographical references and index.
  ISBN 0–631–20601–9 (hardcover : alk. paper).— ISBN 0–631–20602–7 (pbk. : alk. paper)
  1. Language and languages—Philosophy. I. Nye, Andrea, 1939– . II. Series.
P106.P456 1998
401—dc21   97-45209
                                              CIP

A catalogue record for this title is available from the British Library.

Set in 10½ on 12½ pt Galliard
by Ace Filmsetting Ltd, Frome, Somerset

The publisher's policy is to use permanent paper from mills that operate a sustainable forestry policy, and which has been manufactured from pulp processed using acid-free and elementary chlorine-free practices. Furthermore, the publisher ensures that the text paper and cover board used have met acceptable environmental accreditation standards.

For further information on
Blackwell Publishing, visit our website:
http://www.blackwellpublishing.com

CONTENTS

CONTENTS

PREFACE

Analytic perspectives in philosophy of language form the core of readings in this anthology, as represented in seminal articles by Bertrand Russell, Gottlob Frege, Alfred Tarski, Donald Davidson, and others. In addition, two other sorts of readings are included. First, in order to make philosophy of language accessible to undergraduate students and to place current analytic approaches to language in historical perspective, approaches to language from Plato to the modern era are represented. These place the contemporary emphasis on logical interpretations of language within an explanatory frame. The nature, use, and meaning of language have been understood in very different ways. Without that comparison, it is difficult to isolate the distinguishing features of any theory of language or to accurately assess its strengths and weaknesses.

A second addition to this anthology are materials representing current critical perspectives – feminist, postmodern, and multicultural. English-speaking philosophy of language, with its grounding in logic and linguistics, has often seemed immune to such critique which is fast becoming part of a reconstituted philosophical canon in areas such as ethics and social philosophy. The critical perspectives included here link feminist concerns about sexist language to questions of meaning and truth, poststructural concerns about oppressive discourse to logical form, multicultural experience to theories of translation and reference across cultures.

What results is an approach to philosophy of language that is multidimensional. From a contemporary focus on current analytic theories, the readings allow both a reaching back into the past to better understand current theorizing and a reaching forward to the future for possible new directions of thought.

Tzu-lu asked, "If the prince of Wei were waiting for you to come and administer his country for him, what would be your first measure?"

The master answered, "It would certainly be to rectify names."

Tzu-lu said, "Can I have heard you right? Surely what you say has nothing to do with the matter. Why should names be rectified?"

The Master answered, "Yu! How boorish you are! A civilized person, when things he or she does not understand are mentioned should maintain an attitude of reserve. If names are incorrect, then what is said does not sound reasonable, and if what is said does not sound reasonable, what is to be done cannot be carried out. If what is to be done cannot be carried out, then rituals and music will not flourish. If rituals and music do not flourish, then punishments will not be appropriate to crimes. And if punishments are not appropriate to crimes, then people will not know where to put their hand or their foot. Therefore when the civilized person names something, the name is sure to be proper for speech, and when he says something it is sure to be practical. The civilized person is anything but casual in what he says."

Confucius, *Analects* 13/3

This teaching of the Chinese sage Confucius has puzzled Western philosophers just as it did his student Tzu-lu. What difference can language make? Words are not things; they cannot be used like hammers to drive nails, weapons to harm enemies, police to track down and arrest criminals. Vocal sounds are noises that only by arbitrary convention stand for the things, events, and actions that are the real objects of human concern.

Western commentators have often brushed aside Confucius's remark that Tzu-lu is being a boor. They have called his doctrine of "the rectification of names" an unfortunate reversion to primitive magic. Can a change in language make any real difference? Can the replacing of the traditional "Miss" or "Mrs" with "Ms" bring about equality of the sexes? Does the use of a euphemistic term like "down-sizing" make being laid off from a job less painful? Is a "father" any less a father if he does not care for his children? Surely words are human products; we use them as we wish, to mark objects or actions thought to be important.

Confucius seems to be making a strange claim. If we get the meaning of words wrong, we run the risk of getting our lives wrong. We may not play the proper role in our families, may not fulfill our civic or religious responsibilities, may fail to be fully human. He seems to be saying that instead of words faithfully marking what has already been done, deeds are formed by words. As he puts it in another passage, ". . . when the prince is not a prince, the minister not a minister, the father not a father, the son not a son, one may have a dish of millet in front of one, and yet not know if one will live to eat it" (*Analects* 12/1). In other words, when words are not used according to their proper meanings, all security in life may be lost. Not only will we fail to understand each other, not only will "what is said not accord with what is meant," not only will we not know what to do or be, we may have no way of predicting what will happen in the future and no stable expectation of social continuity.

Unfortunately Confucius did not explain at length the standard by which the meanings of words can be "rectified." If we lose the sense of what it is to be mother or son, citizen or leader, respectful of authority or liberated from oppression, he does not tell us how correct meanings can be restored. Dictionaries are full of words with multiple meanings, meanings that are current and archaic, complementary and contradictory.

Still to our modern ears, there is one thing in Confucius's warning that rings true. Language is important. If we call lust "love," memorization "learning," conformity to public opinion "responsibility," we may be in trouble. To speak meaningfully, reasonably, and truthfully is desirable.

But what is "meaning," what is "rational," and what is "truth"? Questions such as these have taken center stage in twentieth century British and North American analytic philosophy. But concern with language is not new in philosophy. Any discussion of reality, knowledge, or the self must presuppose terms in which what is real, known, or human is understood, terms that may prejudice or distort what is being claimed or argued. In the ancient Greek city-state, where public speaking in the Assembly or law courts was essential to achieving influence and power, language was an instrument of power. Plato, worried about possible deception in politics and law, attempted to anchor the meaning of words to ideal conceptual forms existing independently of any use of language. Aristotle mechanized grammatical and logical structures to provide winning techniques of argument and produce the first formal logic.

In developing sciences in the early modern period and the empirical philosophy that promoted those sciences, language again was an object of concern. In what language can objective scientific descriptions of the world be expressed? Can language be purged of religious or metaphysical meanings with no reference to physical fact? Philosophers looked for a cognitive core of expression that could stand for logically ordered sense perceptions and serve as a faithful representation of physical reality. As the skeptical empiricist David Hume commented, "Does it contain any abstract reasoning concerning quantity or number? Does it contain any experimental reasoning concerning matter of fact and existence? No. Commit it to the flames: For it can contain nothing but sophistry and illusion" (*An Enquiry Concerning Human Understanding*, Section XII, Part III).

By the late nineteenth and early twentieth centuries, some of the enthusiasm about the benefits of science began to dissipate. Wars, industrial pollution, poverty all called into question the uninterrupted progress promised by science. After centuries of colonialism and emigration, a polyglot of different and often warring tongues could be heard in most cities. Even science had taken on a bewildering diversity of paradigms and models. New questions were asked about language. How is it possible to translate from an Indo-European language to a Bantu language? Can the viral theory of disease be translated into terms a Mongolian villager can understand? Can the researches of a medieval alchemist be understood in terms of modern chemistry? Can quantum mechanics be expressed in terms of Newtonian physics? In the face of seemingly intractable failures of communication and commonality, in the face of the apparent relativity even of scientific theory, philosophers looked for structures common to all languages – structural grammars, linguistic universals, logics – that could provide a basis of common meaning and translation between languages.

In the second half of the twentieth century, interest in the logical structure of language took new forms. With the exploding use of computers, artificial intelligence, information nets, data bases, and an expansion of findings in brain research, the dividing line between machine and human began to blur. Faced with a revolution in technology that promised to delegate much human intellectual labor to computers, philosophers worked to develop accounts of natural language that were congruent with "machine languages," that facilitated computer programming, and that bridged the gap between computer and computer user. Other philosophers opposed such a move, pointing to the irreducible biological nature of human language and to differences between natural and machine languages.

In these very different concerns about language are some common themes. If language marks what is distinctively human, then how are we to understand that humanity? Did language arise in the course of hunting and weapon wielding? Or did it develop in conjunction with the cooperative activities of the gathering of plant food? Is language hard-wired into the human brain and to some degree constant through historical times and different cultures, or is it a learned skill? Has language evolved as an aid to evolutionary survival, or is it linked to value judgments and ideals? How these questions are answered, indeed how they are framed, bears on essential questions about human nature. Are humans naturally social or naturally individual? Are humans biological organisms not essentially different from other natural organisms? Does the human brain work like a computer?

Any account of human origins must be highly speculative. More immediate are questions having to do with the nature of the human mind. If language is the very model of thought and the medium of any claim to knowledge, how does the mind process ideas expressed in language? What is the relation between private perceptual experience and what people say in public? How can subjective expressions of feeling be separated from verifiable statements of fact? Human minds do not function in a vacuum. If language represents ideas or things, it is also a medium of communication between people. But which comes first? Are we autonomous consciousnesses who choose to reveal or not reveal our independent minds to other consciousnesses? Or are we essentially social beings who, even when we think to ourselves in isolation, are in a dialogue with ourselves that mimics interpersonal communication? Is it possible to say something without saying something to someone? What part does the person spoken to play in determining the meaning of what is said? These questions bear directly on questions of personal identity, the relation between self and other, and the social or solitary construction of the mind.

Language can also seem the key to understanding what it is to know something. How can we determine what is true? How can we be sure that the objects we talk about are real and not just figments of imagination? How can we know that the logic we use results in valid inferences? The method proposed to achieve knowledge and the terms in which knowledge is communicated must be explained and defended in some language. But how far does that language preform or distort what can be known?

Many philosophers have criticized existent uses of language; some have proposed radical linguistic reforms so that language can better deliver the truth. The apparent inaccessibility of any reality apart from a linguistic description of that reality has led others to argue that there is no truth independent of language but that reality is a projection of linguistic structures which changes depending on the language spoken. Some have gone further to point out ways in which variable grammars and linguistic styles perpetuate and rationalize liberatory or oppressive social practices and institutions.

Out of this ongoing inquiry the "big questions" in philosophy of language emerge.

First, we face the puzzle of the very existence of language. What is language? And what is it for? Why is it necessary? Why do we take it as the mark of humanity?

Second, what is it to say something? Is fitting together a noun with a verb the product of an autonomous human brain, or is it a "speech act" which requires a hearer who reshapes what is said?

Third, how does a word get a meaning, a meaning that can be shared so as to make understanding possible?

Fourth, how do we ensure that we are talking about the same things? What is that mysterious process by which names single out unique individuals on which we can compare views?

Fifth, what is the relation between what we say and reality? Is it possible to align language and reality so that language becomes a duplicate or mirror of what is? Or is there always a discontinuity between the ordered universe of language and the chaotic world of experience?

Sixth, given the diversity of languages and the diversity of peoples who speak those languages, how is understanding possible? In a time of ethnic division, race warfare, and deeply seated historical animosities, Confucius's warning that there is danger in the misunderstanding of words has particular relevance. As he says, at such a time it is important to take matters of language seriously.

PART ONE

LANGUAGE:
WHAT IS IT?

Introduction

Many writers in this first group of readings begin from a sense that language is being misused, misunderstood, or diverted from its proper purpose. Certainly this is true of the opening excerpt from Plato's dialogue *The Sophist*. Here, in one of the earliest attempts to philosophize about language, Socrates explains to a bewildered Theaetetus language's structural complexity. Sophistic philosophers with their facile refutations, Socrates complains, do not understand how language works. In clever and deceitful moves to cut off any attempt to prove an opinion or belief false, they insist that to say "something is not" is an impossibility. But to say something, Socrates argues, is not merely to put together vocal marks or sounds. Although animal signals might be understood this way, human language is complex in structure. In human language, different kinds of words must be "fitted" together, and the correctness of the fit determines whether what is said is true or false. Speaking and thinking is denying or asserting, denying or asserting that is made possible by the grammatical complexity of language. For Socrates, language's primary role is truth-knowing and truth-speaking, not the expression of feeling or the coordination of activities for which animal signals might be sufficient.

In contrast, the French philosopher Rousseau, writing a thousand years later, is concerned to rescue language from any formal articulation of a regime of properly fitting forms. Grammatical and logical relations, he argues, are a later addition which take the life out of the original language of the heart which is the basis for communal social life. Whereas Socrates does not hesitate to speak of the grammatical relations that characterize any meaningful and truthful "logos" or speech, Rousseau points to the diversity of languages. For Rousseau, there is no universal grammar or transcendent forms, but only regional languages suited to different climates and social settings. In these diverse settings, Rousseau distinguishes two different impulses that give rise to language: need and love. The coordination of activities necessary to satisfy physical needs in harsh climates can be accomplished by a language of gesture. In Southern regions, expressive language in which a person communes with another person is born of passion, the felt desire to know and be known by others. In Rousseau's account of linguistic origins, the grammatical "fit" of Socrates' forms is flattened. Strings of preemptory or coordinating signals make up a "gestural" language of need; melodic lines constitute an expressive language of the heart. No longer are "asserting and denying" the essential characteristics of speech, but rather the communicating and expressing which underlie surface linguistic forms.

A hundred years later, with the scientific revolution in full swing, John Locke sees a different danger in embedding Platonic forms in language. The notion that essences such as "matter," "mind," or "substance" are referents that provide meanings for general terms impedes the development of science. For Locke, there are no metaphysical forms, only ideas in individuals' minds, ideas whose origin is the unreliable sense perception which Plato found lacking as a guide to truth. Language's job is not to map eternal forms but to provide external signs for combinations of private sense data. As a result, the relation between linguistic signs and meanings is conventional, without the fit of Plato's grammar or the expressive melodic line of Rousseau's language of passion.

With Locke, a line is drawn down between "real existence" and language, a line that generates many of the problems of philosophy of language in the modern period. If the choice of a sign is conventional and if ideas are private entities accessible only to the person who has them, how is common meaning possible? Given that people with differing experiences, sophistication, and knowledge have different ideas of a thing, how is it possible that they can mean the same thing by a name? If general terms do not mark real existences, if sorts, kinds, and relations are the result of subjective mental processes, how can we know that what we say is true in any objective sense? The latter question marks one of the most difficult questions in philosophy of language: does language create reality, or does language reflect reality? Here Locke straddles the fence. There are no forms or essences that are real existences. But there are real resemblances on which mental processes of abstraction are based.

For other philosophers, simple perceptual ideas gathered into kinds by resemblance are too tenuous an anchor to account for language's ability to represent reality. As science progressed in complexity and diversity and as a variety of mathematical systems were devised in the nineteenth century, philosophers began to worry about the logical foundations of mathematics and the mathematical sciences. The most influential for philosophy of language was the German logician Gottlob Frege.

Since the seventeenth century there had been philosophical concern about whether "natural language," the language we speak in our intimate and social lives, could be made sufficiently precise for the scientific representation of physical reality. Frege explains his invention of a "conceptual notation" as an attempt to correct natural language's ambiguity and fluidity. His proposed new logical idiom for the sciences was to be an amalgam of mathematical function and linguistic predication. In later versions it would become the basis for the "semantic" approach to linguistic meaning adopted by analytic philosophers such as W.V. Quine or Donald Davidson. Frege's mathematicized logical language, updated and revised by Bertrand Russell and others, provides the architecture for a mirroring of the world in Ludwig Wittgenstein's *Tractatus*. In the excerpt reprinted here, Wittgenstein looks to the structural characteristics of a logically ordered language to fit language to the world. The world is the world of "facts," of "things that are the case." Facts are combinations of objects that "fit together like a chain." The "fit" achieved is not between Platonic forms but between configurations of words and configurations of points in the algebraic/geometric space of modern physics. Language is not linked to the world by way of individual sensations which serve as raw material for concepts and theories. Instead, structural correlations between logical forms and facts allow language to picture or model reality. Depending on the accuracy of that picturing, propositions are true or false. Wittgenstein's closing comments puzzled many philosophers:

> My propositions serve as elucidations in the following way: anyone who understands me eventually recognizes them as nonsensical, when he has used them – as

steps – to climb up beyond them. (He must, so to speak, throw away the ladder after he has climbed up on it.)

He must transcend these propositions, and then he will see the world aright. (*Tractatus* 6.54)

In this mysterious pronouncement Wittgenstein raises challenging questions about the logical status of linguistic analysis. Is it possible to get outside language so as to say anything meaningful about it?

John Dewey is also concerned with the language of science, but he takes a more pragmatic view. Language, for Dewey, is the key to the difference between "organic" reflexive behavior and intelligent behavior. This is because language marks the transition between an individual "organism's" thinking activity and agreements made between individuals that confer validity. For Dewey, language is a biological activity continuous with other organic activity, but it also involves a "giant" step of requiring a speaker to take the viewpoint of others. The roots of language are in "shared modes of responsive behavior." Scientific language is only a further development of this tendency in which systems of symbols are further purged of irrelevance and inconsistency.

Dewey introduces two of the problematics that will exercise philosophers in succeeding sections. First, if linguistic meaning depends on shared activities rooted in individual cultures, the diversity of cultures threatens to turn the world into a Tower of Babel, an incomprehensible confusion of tongues. The antidote suggested by Dewey is not, however, the imposition of a master culture or idiom. Instead, he argues, genuine understanding can only come from efforts to initiate activities shared between cultures.

Another problem identified by Dewey has to do with the proper way to philosophize or theorize about language. Philosophy of language and logic is a further and important reflection on language, Dewey says, but he adds a caveat: if logic or theory of language "hypostasizes" logic by imposing on language a canonical form, it can block, just as did Plato's forms and essences, inquiries that deal successfully with practical problems.

Benveniste approaches language from the continental tradition of structural linguistics. Whatever language can be "used for" – whether to model reality, elicit behavior, or regulate concerted attempts to control the environment – its unique essence for Benveniste is its role in communication. Language is not a "tool" that humans invent; it is constitutive of the human subject. The basis of the subjectivity that language constitutes is not in logical structure or relations between concepts or forms, but is inherent in hierarchical and reversible systems of personal pronouns – you, he, I – found in every language. Pronouns establish a relation between self and other that is supported by complementary systems of indexicals: adverbs, demonstratives, and time indicators that position what is said around a speaking human subject.

Some of the political and social implications of this structuralist view of language are explored by the French feminist philosopher Monique Wittig. In French, "I" or "je" seem to be neutral in gender. In fact, Wittig argues, these pronouns mark a masculine position which is reflected in the grammar of the clauses that follow. As a result, women are at a disadvantage as speakers. Again the moral is reform, this time reform of sexism embedded in the grammar of language.

Jerry Fodor's argument for an internal "language of thought" returns to the analytic logicist tradition of Frege and Wittgenstein and contemporary methods of logical analysis. Fodor depends on the following chain of argument: learning a language involves learning the meaning of the predicates of that language; learning the meaning of the predicates of a language involves learning the extensions of those predicates; learning the extensions of predicates is learning "truth rules," and learning truth rules requires a language in which truth rules are represented. Therefore, there must be an internal language of thought that predates the learning of natural language.

To understand this argument, some knowledge of methods of logical analysis is necessary. In contemporary versions of logic descended from Frege's conceptual notation, propositions are "calculated" or combined so as to preserve truth value, using "logical connectives," such as conjunction ("and") and disjunction ("or"). The truth of a complex proposition is understood as a specific "function" of the truth values of the singular propositions out of which it is composed. If a proposition "p" ("John is bald") is true, and another proposition "q" ("John is fat") is also true, then a third proposition, "p & q" ("John is bald and John is fat"), formed by their "conjunction," is also true.

Because there are, in addition, standard logical relations which cannot be handled by a calculus of propositions – for example, if John is bald, and all bald men are fat, then John must be fat – predicate logic is added to deal with the internal structure of propositions. The general form of a proposition is "a is P" or more simply "Pa" where "a" is an object and "P" is a predicate. The meaning of a predicate is its "extension," the "set of things that P is true of." Furthermore, the extensions of sets can be "quantified." Some sets, like unicorn, have *no* members. Similarly, *all* members of some sets are members of other sets. Some members of some sets are members of other sets. These relations can be handled by using "variables" such as "x" or "y" and quantifying expressions "for all x" or "there exists some x." This "logical idiom" allows inferences such as 'if all men are mortal, and all mortals are tall, then all men are tall" to be represented in terms of quantities rather than in terms of concepts. If "for all x, x is male implies x is mortal" and "for all x, x is mortal implies x is tall," then it follows that "for all x, x is male implies x is tall."

To make clearer what is the "generalization" that determines a set, Fodor, like many other contemporary philosophers of language, incorporates the "semantic theory of truth" of Alfred Tarski (see Tarski's article in part V of this volume). Tarski argued that in a given language the meaning of a predicate is determined by a "truth rule" that maps out necessary and sufficient conditions for the truth of any proposition using that predicate. Fodor gives an example of such a truth rule for "is a philosopher" in his note 5.

A semantic approach to language based on this now "standard" logic is further assumed, refined, and analyzed in several of the articles in succeeding sections of this anthology. Fodor points to some of the disputed matters: Is a bare "extensional" aggregate of objects enough to establish a set or is some other sort of "intensional" meaning necessary, perhaps based on logical relations between concepts? Can we know what a name refers to in a "true" singular proposition without some kind of ostensive act external to language? Some of the assumptions common to semantic approaches to language are also evident in Fodor's defense of a language of thought. On the semantic view, language is not a speaking to anyone but the vehicle for the cognitive functioning of an organism. That functioning takes the form of a computational processing of information which, according to Fodor, is "all we have" that can explain the relation between sensory input and behavioral output. Mental processing requires, as does computer function, a medium of representation ordered by logical rules. Fodor's argument is that if knowing a language is having an operational understanding of "truth rules," there must be internal symbolizations in which those rules are represented.

Like Dewey's pragmatic inquiry, the information processing view of language assumes no definitive split between human and animal language. Human cognitive functions and the language that facilitates those functions are further developments of animal cognition and signaling. Omitted in Fodor's language of thought, however, is Dewey's emphasis on intentional goal-seeking that motivates human inquiry and the social role of language in coordinating behavioral response.

1   The Weaving Together of Forms

Plato

[The immediate subject of *The Sophist* is the verbal hunting down and trapping of the "Sophist," practitioner of a style of argument which, in Plato's view, undermined the very possibility of philosophical thought. Armed with Parmenides' claim that what "is not" can have no being of any kind, the Sophists argued that no distinction between truth and falsehood could be made and that no statement could be called "what is not." To refute this claim and make it possible to identify the Sophist as a deceiver, Socrates must first try to make clear the nature of language. Ed.]

Socrates: First, as I was just saying, let us consider saying something (logos[1]) and having an opinion in order to understand better whether not being affects them, whether they are both always true and whether both are never false.
Theaetetus: Good.
Socrates: Let us now, just as before we spoke about ideas and letters, inquire into names. For with these we begin to catch sight of our object.
Theaetetus: What then do we need to understand about names?
Socrates: Whether they all go together with each other or none do, or some do and some do not.
Theaetetus: Clearly it is the last, since some do and some do not.
Socrates: Then perhaps this is what you are saying: those that are spoken in succession and meaningfully do go together, but those that in sequence mean nothing do not go together.
Theaetetus: But what then are you saying by that?
Socrates: What I thought you meant when you agreed with me, because we have two kinds of vocal signs for what is.
Theaetetus: How is that?
Socrates: One kind is called names; the other verbs.
Theaetetus: Explain each.
Socrates: The sign which is about an action we call a verb.
Theaetetus: Yes.
Socrates: And then the vocal sign for those who do these actions we call a noun.
Theaetetus: Precisely.
Socrates: So speaking is never ever of names alone in succession, nor is it of verbs said without nouns.
Theaetetus: That I do not understand.

From *The Sophist*, 261c6–264b3; editor's translation from the Loeb Classical Library Edition. Cambridge, MA: Harvard University Press, 1921.

Socrates: I think you must have been thinking of something else when you agreed just now.

Theaetetus: How is that?

Socrates: For example, "walks," "runs," "sleeps," and all the other verbs which denote actions, even if you said every one of them in succession, it would not amount to saying anything.

Theaetetus: Of course.

Socrates: And again when "lion," "stag," "horse," are spoken and all the other names of things that do those actions are uttered, such a string of words does not amount to saying anything. For in neither case do the words uttered indicate the action or the inaction of anything existing or not existing, not until verbs are mixed with names. Then the words fit and say something which is simply the first combination and really the first and simplest of things that can be said.

Theaetetus: What are you saying?

Socrates: When someone says "A man learns," of things said this is the smallest and the first, is it not?

Theaetetus: Yes.

Socrates: For he signifies when he says that, something about what is, or is coming to be, or has become, or will be, and not only names. He completes what he says, combining verbs with the names. For this reason he speaks, and he does not only say names. To this, to this weaving together of terms, we give the name speaking.

Theaetetus: Right.

Socrates: So then just as some things fit with others and some do not, also among spoken signs some do and do not fit, and those that do fit make up speaking.

Theaetetus: Absolutely.

Socrates: Now something small.

Theaetetus: What?

Socrates: Saying something requires a "what" that is said to be something, otherwise without that "what" saying something is impossible.

Theaetetus: Yes.

Socrates: And isn't it not that this "what" must be something?

Theaetetus: Certainly.

Socrates: Now let us pay attention to each other.

Theaetetus: We should.

Socrates: I will say something to you combining an action and a thing by means of a name and a verb. You tell me what this speech is about.

Theaetetus: I will as best as I can.

Socrates: "Theaetetus sits." The speech is not long, is it?

Theaetetus: No, short.

Socrates: Now your job is to say what it is about and of whom.

Theaetetus: Clearly it is about me and I.

Socrates: Now what about this?

Theaetetus: What?

Socrates: "Theaetetus, with whom I am just now talking, flies."

Theaetetus: What could anyone say but that this is me and about me?

Socrates: We said that it is necessary that each speaking be something.

Theaetetus: Yes.

Socrates: What then is each of these sentences?

Theaetetus: Possibly one is false, one true?

Socrates: The true one of these says what is as it is about you.

Theaetetus: Of course.

Socrates: The false other than what is.

Theaetetus: Yes.

Socrates: It says, that is to say, what is not as it is.

Theaetetus: That's about it.

Socrates: It says then, something is that is other than about you. For we said there are many things that are about each thing, right, and many that are not.

Theaetetus: Yes, this is not at all wrong.

Socrates: Now take the second thing I said about you. First, as we defined what it is to say something, it is by necessity one of the shortest.

Theaetetus: Yes, we did agree on that.

Socrates: But second, it also involves a "what."

Theaetetus: Yes.

Socrates: And if this is not you, then there is no other.

Theaetetus: By no means.

Socrates: And if there is not a "what," it would not be a saying at all, because we proved that it is impossible to speak without whatever it takes to be saying something.

Theaetetus: Right.

Socrates: Now when things are said about you, but these things said are other than these are, and not what is as it is, it appears that when such a combination of verbs and nouns arise we have, in truth, falsehood.

Theaetetus: Yes, for sure.

Socrates: Is it then not clear that thinking and opinion and fantasy, all these arise both falsely and also truly in our minds?

Theaetetus: How?

Socrates: It will be easier for you if you grasp this first: what these are and what are the several differences between them.

Theaetetus: Show me.

Socrates: Thinking and speaking are similar. It is only that one of them, this silent dialogue of the soul with itself, is given the name of thought, no?

Theaetetus: It must be so.

Socrates: But the one which comes from the soul through the mouth by sound is called speaking.

Theaetetus: True.

Socrates: And in speaking we can only . . .

Theaetetus: What?

Socrates: Say and deny.

Theaetetus: We do know that.

Socrates: When in the soul this comes silently in thought, what can you call it but opinion?

Theaetetus: Yes, what can you?

Socrates: And when this state arises, not by anything else but by perception, can it be called anything but fantasy?

Theaetetus: No.

Socrates: Then because speech, we saw, is true and false, and thinking is a dialogue of the mind with itself, and opinion is that completion of thought, and what we say by "it seems" is a combination of perception and opinion, it must be that because all of these are like speech, some thinking and opinion must also sometimes be false.

Theaetetus: It cannot be any other way.

Note

1 "Logos" and its many derivatives from the ordinary Greek word, to speak or say something, is traditionally translated by a variety of contemporary terms depending on the context. In this translation, I have tried to remain faithful to the original discussion in which to say something is at once the most simple and the most puzzling of linguistic acts.

---

2 The Origin of Languages

Jean-Jacques Rousseau

On different ways to communicate our thoughts

Speech singles out man among the animals: language distinguishes one nation from the others. One does not know where a man is from until he has spoken. Usage and need teaches everyone the language of his country, but what is it that makes a particular language that of one country and not another? To explain this it is necessary to go back to an origin that holds locally and which predates even custom. Speech, being the first of social institutions, owes its form only to natural causes.

As soon as a man is recognized by another man as a sentient Being, who thinks and resembles himself, the desire or the need to communicate sentiments and thoughts makes him look for a means. Those means can only come from the senses, which are the sole instruments by which one man can act on another. So you get the institution of sensible signs to express thought. The

From *The Origin of Languages*; editor's translation from *Essai sur l'origine des langues*, text established by Jean Starobinski. Paris: Gallimard, 1990. First published 1781.

11

inventors of language might not have actually reasoned this way, but instinct would have suggested the same conclusion.

The general means by which we can act on the senses of another are limited to two, movement and voice. The action of movement is either immediate by touch, or indirect by gesture. The first, because it has for its limit the length of the arm, cannot be transmitted at a distance; the other reaches as far as visible rays of light. Thus, there is only sight and hearing for receptive organs of language between dispersed men.

Even though the language of gesture and the language of voice are equally natural, always the first is easier and depends less on convention. Because more objects strike the eye than the ear, and figures have more variety than sounds, they are also more expressive and say more in less time. Love, they say, was the inventor of drawing. It could also have invented speech, but with less ease. Little happy with speech, love disdains it; it has more lively matters to express. Would the love which traces with so much pleasure the form of the loved one want to say anything? What sounds could it use to render the rounded movement of that form?

[. . .]

But when it is a question of moving the heart and inflaming the passions, this is a completely different thing: the successive impression of discourse which strikes in repeated beats gives a different emotion than does the actual presence of an object where with one glance you see all. Imagine a painful situation that you know all about; in seeing the person afflicted you will rarely be moved to weep. Leave her the time to tell you all that she feels, and soon you will burst into tears. It is only thus that scenes of tragedy have their effect. Pantomime alone without discourse will leave you almost tranquil. Discourse without gesture draws out tears. Passions have their gestures, but they also have their accents, and these accents, which make us tremble, whose voice cannot be taken away, penetrate to the depth of the heart, carrying there in spite of us the movements which drew them forth and make us actually feel what we understand. Let us conclude that visible signs make imitation more exact, but interest is better excited by sound.

This makes me think that if we had never had anything but physical needs, we might very well never have been able to speak and would make ourselves understood perfectly by a sole language of gesture. We would have been able to establish societies little different than they are today, even which might have achieved their aims better. We would have been able to institute laws, choose rulers, invent arts, establish commerce, and do, in a word, almost as many things as we do with the aid of speech.

[. . .]

How the first invention of speech does not come from need but from passion

One must think, then, that need dictated the first gestures, and passion drew out the first voices. Looking at the facts with these distinctions in mind, perhaps one must theorize about the origins of languages differently than has been done up to now. The genius of oriental languages, the most ancient that are known to us, contradicts absolutely the supposed didactic course of their composition. These languages have nothing methodical or reasoned in them, they are vivid and figurative. One makes the language of the first men the language of geometers, but we see that it was instead the language of Poets.

This must be. One does not begin by reasoning but by feeling. It is argued that men invented speech to express their needs, but this view seems untenable to me. The natural effect of the first needs was to separate men, not bring them together. Needs made it necessary for the species to spread out, that the earth be quickly populated, without which human life would be confined in a corner of the world and the rest would become deserted.

From that alone it follows that the origin of language is not really due to the first needs of men; it would be absurd if the cause which separates them became the means to unite them. From what then could come this beginning? The answer is from moral needs, from the passions. All passions bring closer men driven apart by the necessity of trying to survive. It is not hunger or thirst, but love, hate, pity, anger that draw out the first voices. Fruits do not reject our hands; we can be nourished by them without speech. We follow in silence the prey on which we want to feed, but to move a young heart, to repel an unjust aggressor, for this nature dictates the accents, the cries, the pleas. And so the most ancient words were invented; and so it was that the first languages were musical and passionate before being simple and methodical. . . .

Why the first language had to be figural

Just as the first motives that made men speak were passionate, so his first expressions were Tropes. Figurative language was the first to be born, literal sense was the last. One only calls things by their true name when one sees them under their true form. At first people only talked in poetry; they began to reason a long time after.

But I understand that here the reader will stop me, and ask how it is that an expression can be figurative before it has a literal sense, because the figure is only the translation of that sense. I agree, to understand it is necessary to substitute the idea that passion presents to us for the word which we transpose, for we transpose words only because one transposes ideas also, otherwise the figurative language would mean nothing. I answer with an example.

A primitive man encountering other men will at first be afraid. His fear will make him see men bigger and stronger than himself, and he will give them the name of "Giants." After many experiences, he will come to understand that these supposed Giants are no bigger or stronger than himself, and that their stature does not match at all the idea that he at first attached to the word "Giant." He will then invent another word common to them and himself, for example, such as the name "man," and will leave "Giant" to the false object which struck him during his illusion. So the figurative word is born along

13

with the literal word when passion tricks our eyes and when the first idea that it offers is not of the truth. What I say of words and names works easily also for turns of phrase. The illusory image offered by passion shows itself first; the language which responds to it is also the first. Afterward it becomes metaphorical when the enlightened spirit, recognizing its first error, comes to use expressions for the passion which excited them.

On the distinctive character of the first language and the changes that it must undergo

. . . I do not doubt that independently of vocabulary and syntax, the first language, if it existed still, would not keep the original character which distinguishes it from others. Not only would all the operation of this language have to be in images, in sentiments, in figures, but in its mechanical part it would have to answer to its first object and present to sense, as much as to understanding, the almost inevitable impressions of passion which strives for communication.

As the natural voice is inarticulate, words would have few articulations, some interposed consonants accomplishing enough of a hiatus between vowels to make them fluid and easy to pronounce. On the other hand, sounds would be very varied and the diversity of accents multiply those same voices; quantity and rhythm would be new sources of combination, so that voices, sounds, accent, number, which are in nature, would leave little for articulation, which is conventional, to do. One would sing instead of speak. Most root words would be of imitative sounds, or of the accent of the passions, or from the effect of sensed objects; onomatopoeia would make itself felt continually.

Language would have many synonyms to express the same thing according to its different relations (they say that Arabic has more than a thousand words for a camel and more than a hundred for a sword). It would have few adverbs and abstract words to express those same relations. It would have many augmentatives, diminutives, composite words, and expletive particles to give cadence to periods and roundness to phrases. It would have many irregularities and anomalies, it would neglect grammatical analogy to attach itself to euphony, number, harmony and the beauty of sounds. In the place of arguments, it would have sentences, it would persuade without vanquishing, and please without reasoning; it would resemble the Chinese language in some respects, Greek in others, Arabic in others. Follow these ideas in all their consequences and you will see that Plato's Cratylus is not as ridiculous as it seems.

[. . .]

Formation of the languages of the South

In the beginning, men scattered over the face of the earth have no society but that of the family, no law but that of nature, no language but gesture and some inarticulate sounds. They are not linked by any idea of common brotherhood, and having no other arbiter than force they believe themselves enemies one of another. It was weakness and ignorance which gave them this idea. Knowing nothing, they feared all; they attacked to defend themselves. A man left alone on the face of the earth at the mercy of humankind must be a fierce animal. He is ready to do to others all the evil he feared from them. Fear and weakness are the sources of cruelty.

Social feelings do not develop in us except with enlightenment. Pity, even though natural to the heart of man, remains eternally inactive without the imagination which puts it into play. How do we let ourselves be moved by pity? In transporting ourselves outside of ourselves, in identifying with a suffering being. We only suffer as much as we judge that he suffers; it is not in ourselves but in him that we suffer. Does one really understand how much this transfer presupposes acquired understanding? How am I to imagine evils of which I have no idea? How will I suffer in seeing another suffer if I do not know even that he is suffering, if I ignore what is in common between us? Someone who has never reflected cannot be either forgiving or just or pitying, nor can he be evil or vindictive. He who imagines nothing, feels only himself. He is alone in the midst of the human race.

Reflection is born of compared ideas and it is the plurality of ideas which leads to comparison. He who sees only a single object has no grounds for comparison. He who sees only a small number of things and always the same things from birth does not compare them because the habitude of seeing them dulls the attention necessary to examine them. But in so far as a new object strikes us we want to know it, and among those which we know we look for relations. It is thus that we learn to look at what is under our eyes, and thus that what is strange leads us to examine what affects us.

Apply this to the first men and you will see the reasons for their barbarity. Never having seen anything but what was around them, even what they don't understand, they do not understand themselves. They have the idea of a father, a son, a brother, but not of a man. Their hut contains only those like them; a stranger, an animal, a monster are for them the same thing. Away from their home and their family, the whole universe is nothing to them. . . .

The time of barbary was the golden age not because men were one, but because they were separated. Each, they say, counted himself the master of all. That might be the case, but no one knew or wanted anything that was not to hand: his needs, far from bringing him closer to his counterparts, estranged him. Men, if you wish, attacked at each encounter, but they encountered each other seldom. Everywhere reigned a state of war and all the earth was at peace.

[. . .]

[Rousseau describes at length the beginnings of agriculture and private property, and the formation of social groups, finally arriving at the beginnings of language.]

Then were formed the first links between families, the first meetings of the two sexes. Young girls came to the wells to get water for the household, young men came to water their flocks. Eyes, accustomed to the same objects since childhood, began to see something sweeter. The heart was moved at new objects, an unknown attraction made them less savage, they felt pleasure in no longer being alone. Water became imperceptibly more necessary, the herd was thirsty more often, one arrived in haste and left with regret. In this happy age, when nothing marked the hours, nothing obliged us to count, time had no measure but amusement and boredom. Under the ancient chestnuts, ardent youths forgot by degrees their ferocity and came to know little by little each other. And in forcing themselves to make themselves understood, they learned to explain themselves. . . .

[Rousseau describes the first festivals and the singing and dancing.]

What then! Before this time were not men born on earth? Generations succeeded each other without the sexes being joined and anyone understanding each other. No, there were families, but there were not Nations; there were domestic languages, but there were no popular languages. There were marriages, but there was no love. Each family was sufficient unto itself and was perpetuated by the same blood. Children of these parents grew up together and found ways to explain among themselves, the sexes were distinguished with age, natural inclination was enough to unite them. Instinct took the place of passion, habitude took the place of preference, they became husband and wife without ceasing to be brother and sister. There was not in any of it enough animation to unleash language, nothing which could draw out frequently enough the accents of ardent passion to turn sounds into institutions. One could say as much for the need, rare and not pressing, to get some men to work together at a common task.

One language begins at the well; the other comes afterward, without having had the need of the slightest accord, without even people being face to face. In a word, in mild climates in fertile lands, it requires all the vivacity of agreeable passions to begin to make the inhabitants speak to each other. There the first languages, daughters of pleasure and not of need, carry for a long time the mark of their origin; their seductive accent is not effaced except with the sentiments that are born when new needs begin to force men each to think only of himself and draw his heart back inside himself.

Formation of the languages of the North

In the long term all men are alike, but the order of their progress is not the same. In Southern climates, where nature is bountiful, needs are born from passions; in cold countries where nature is miserly, passions are born from needs. Language, sad daughter of necessity, feels that harsh origin. When man is accustomed to intemperate winds, to cold, sickness, even to hunger, there is nevertheless a point at which nature falls victim to cruel experience. All which is weak perishes; the rest grow strong; there is no middle point between vigor and death.

So it is that Northern peoples are so robust; it is not the climate that makes them so, but those that manage to survive it, and it is not surprising that children retain the constitution of the fathers. Men that are more robust must have organs less delicate, their voices must be ruder and louder. Otherwise, what a difference between the touching inflections which come from the movements of the soul and the cries which are excited by physical need. In these frightful climates all is dead for nine months of the year and the sun heats the air a few weeks only, long enough to teach the inhabitants the good of which they are deprived and prolong their misery. In those places where the earth gives nothing up but by force of work and where the source of life seems more in the arms than in the heart, and men without stopping are occupied with providing subsistence and dream painfully of milder climates, all is limited by physical compulsion. Occasion makes the choice; facility has the preference. The leisure which nourishes the passions gives place to work which represses them. Before dreaming of living happily, it is necessary to dream of living at all. Mutual need uniting men much better than sentiment, society is formed only by industry. The continual danger of perishing does not allow that one limit oneself to a language of gesture, and the first word is not with them "love me" but "help me."

These two phrases, even though they may seem similar, are pronounced in a very different tone. [With the latter] there is nothing to make felt, but everything to make understood. For the accent which the heart does not furnish, one substitutes strong and perceptible articulations, and if there happens to be in the form of the language any natural impression, that too contributes to its harshness.

In effect, Northern men are not without passions, but theirs are of a different kind. Those of warm countries are voluptuous passions which lead to love and softness. Nature does so much for these inhabitants that they have almost nothing to do. As long as an Asiatic has women and repose he is content, but in the North where the inhabitants consume much out of a hostile earth, men who are subject to so many needs are easy to irritate. All that one does around them makes them uneasy. The more they struggle to survive, the more they are poor and the more they hold on to what little they have. To approach them is to make an attempt on their life. For this comes the irascible temperament so prompt to turn in fury against anything that harms them. So are their most natural voices ones of anger and threat, and those voices are always accompanied by strong articulations which make them hard and loud.

3 Of Words

John Locke

Chapter II
Of the Signification of Words

1. *Words are sensible Signs, necessary for Communication of Ideas.* – Man, though he have great variety of thoughts, and such from which others as well as himself might receive profit and delight; yet they are all within his own breast, invisible and hidden from others, nor can of themselves be made to appear. The comfort and advantage of society not being to be had without communication of thoughts, it was necessary that man should find out some external sensible signs, whereof those invisible ideas, which his thoughts are made up of, might be made known to others. For this purpose nothing was so fit, either for plenty or quickness, as those articulate sounds, which with so much ease and variety he found himself able to make. Thus we may conceive how *words*, which were by nature so well adapted to that purpose, came to be made use of by men as the signs of their ideas; not by any natural connexion that there is between particular articulate sounds and certain ideas, for then there would be but one language amongst all men; but by a voluntary imposition, whereby such a word is made arbitrarily the mark of such an idea. The use, then, of words, is to be sensible marks of ideas; and the ideas they stand for are their proper and immediate signification. . . .

3. *Examples of this.* – This is so necessary in the use of language, that in this respect the knowing and the ignorant, the learned and the unlearned, use the words they speak (with any meaning) all alike. They, in every man's mouth, stand for the ideas he has, and which he would express by them. A child having taken notice of nothing in the metal he hears called *gold*, but the bright shining yellow colour, he applies the word gold only to his own idea of that colour, and nothing else; and therefore calls the same colour in a peacock's tail gold. Another that hath better observed, adds to shining yellow great weight: and then the sound gold, when he uses it, stands for a complex idea of a shining yellow and a very weighty substance Another adds to those qualities fusibility: and then the word gold signifies to him a body, bright, yellow, fusible, and very heavy. Another adds malleability. Each of these uses equally the word gold, when they have occasion to express the idea which they have applied it to: but it is evident that each can apply it only to his own idea; nor can he make it stand as a sign of such a complex idea as he has not.

From *An Essay Concerning Human Understanding*, Book III, Chs II–III. First published 1690.

Chapter III
Of General Terms

1. *The greatest Part of Words are general terms.* – All things that exist being particulars, it may perhaps be thought reasonable that words, which ought to be conformed to things, should be so too, – I mean in their signification: but yet we find quite the contrary. The far greatest part of words that make all languages are general terms: which has not been the effect of neglect or chance, but of reason and necessity.

2. *That every particular Thing should have a Name for itself is impossible.* – First, It is impossible that every particular thing should have a distinct peculiar name. For, the signification and use of words depending on that connexion which the mind makes between its ideas and the sounds it uses as signs of them, it is necessary, in the application of names to things, that the mind should have distinct ideas of the things, and retain also the particular name that belongs to every one, with its peculiar appropriation to that idea. But it is beyond the power of human capacity to frame and retain distinct ideas of all the particular things we meet with: every bird and beast men saw; every tree and plant that affected the senses, could not find a place in the most capacious understanding. If it be looked on as an instance of a prodigious memory, that some generals have been able to call every soldier in their army by his proper name, we may easily find a reason why men have never attempted to give names to each sheep in their flock, or crow that flies over their heads; much less to call every leaf of plants, or grain of sand that came in their way, by a peculiar name.

3. *And would be useless, if it were possible.* – Secondly, If it were possible, it would yet be useless; because it would not serve to the chief end of language. Men would in vain heap up names of particular things, that would not serve them to communicate their thoughts. Men learn names, and use them in talk with others, only that they may be understood: which is then only done when, by use or consent, the sound I make by the organs of speech, excites in another man's mind who hears it, the idea I apply it to in mine, when I speak it. This cannot be done by names applied to particular things; whereof I alone having the ideas in my mind, the names of them could not be significant or intelligible to another, who was not acquainted with all those very particular things which had fallen under my notice.

4. *A distinct name for every particular thing, not fitted for enlargement of knowledge.* – Thirdly, But yet, granting this also feasible, (which I think is not,) yet a distinct name for every particular thing would not be of any great use for the improvement of knowledge: which, though founded in particular things, enlarges itself by general views; to which things reduced into sorts, under general names, are properly subservient. These, with the names belonging to them, come within some compass, and do not multiply every moment, beyond what either the mind can contain, or use requires. And therefore, in these, men have for the most part stopped: but yet not so as to hinder themselves from distinguishing particular things by appropriated names, where convenience demands

it. And therefore in their own species, which they have most to do with, and wherein they have often occasion to mention particular persons, they make use of proper names; and there distinct individuals have distinct denominations.

5. *What things have proper Names and why.* – Besides persons, countries also, cities, rivers, mountains, and other the like distinctions of place have usually found peculiar names, and that for the same reason; they being such as men have often an occasion to mark particularly, and, as it were, set before others in their discourses with them. And I doubt not but, if we had reason to mention particular horses as often as we have to mention particular men, we should have proper names for the one, as familiar as for the other, and Bucephalus would be a word as much in use as Alexander. And therefore we see that, amongst jockeys, horses have their proper names to be known and distinguished by, as commonly as their servants: because, amongst them, there is often occasion to mention this or that particular horse when he is out of sight.

6. *How general words are made.* – The next thing to be considered is, – How general words come to be made. For, since all things that exist are only particulars, how come we by general terms; or where find we those general natures they are supposed to stand for? Words become general by being made the signs of general ideas: and ideas become general, by separating from them the circumstances of time and place, and any other ideas that may determine them to this or that particular existence. By this way of abstraction they are made capable of representing more individuals than one; each of which having in it a conformity to that abstract idea, is (as we call it) of that sort.

7. *Shown by the way we enlarge our complex ideas from infancy.* – But, to deduce this a little more distinctly, it will not perhaps be amiss to trace our notions and names from their beginning, and observe by what degrees we proceed, and by what steps we enlarge our ideas from our first infancy. There is nothing more evident, than that the ideas of the persons children converse with (to instance in them alone) are like the persons themselves, only particular. The ideas of the nurse and the mother are well framed in their minds; and, like pictures of them there, represent only those individuals. The names they first gave to them are confined to these individuals; and the names of *nurse* and *mamma*, the child uses, determine themselves to those persons. Afterwards, when time and a larger acquaintance have made them observe that there are a great many other things in the world, that in some common agreements of shape, and several other qualities, resemble their father and mother, and those persons they have been used to, they frame an idea, which they find those many particulars do partake in; and to that they give, with others, the name man, for example. And thus they come to have a general name, and a general idea. Wherein they make nothing new; but only leave out of the complex idea they had of Peter and James, Mary and Jane, that which is peculiar to each, and retain only what is common to them all.

8. *And further enlarge our complex ideas, by still leaving out properties contained in them.* – By the same way that they come by the general name and idea of *man*, they easily advance to more general names and notions. For, observing that several things that differ from their idea of man, and cannot therefore be

comprehended under that name, have yet certain qualities wherein they agree with man, by retaining only those qualities, and uniting them into one idea, they have again another and more general idea; to which having given a name they make a term of a more comprehensive extension: which new idea is made, not by any new addition, but only as before, by leaving out the shape, and some other properties signified by the name man, and retaining only a body, with life, sense, and spontaneous motion, comprehended under the name animal.

9. *General natures are nothing but abstract and partial ideas of more complex ones.* – That this is the way whereby men first formed general ideas, and general names to them, I think is so evident, that there needs no other proof of it but the considering of a man's self, or others, and the ordinary proceedings of their minds in knowledge. And he that thinks *general natures* or *notions* are anything else but such abstract and partial ideas of more complex ones, taken at first from particular existences, will, I fear, be at a loss where to find them. For let any one effect, and then tell me, wherein does his idea of *man* differ from that of *Peter* and *Paul*, or his idea of *horse* from that of *Bucephalus*, but in the leaving out something that is peculiar to each individual, and retaining so much of those particular complex ideas of several particular existences as they are found to agree in? Of the complex ideas signified by the names *man* and *horse*, leaving out but those particulars wherein they differ, and retaining only those wherein they agree, and of those making a new distinct complex idea, and giving the name *animal* to it, one has a more general term, that comprehends with man several other creatures. Leave out of the idea of *animal*, sense and spontaneous motion, and the remaining complex idea, made up of the remaining simple ones of body, life, and nourishment, becomes a more general one, under the more comprehensive term, *vivens*. And, not to dwell longer upon this particular, so evident in itself; by the same way the mind proceeds to *body, substance*, and at last to *being, thing*, and such universal terms, which stand for any of our ideas whatsoever. To conclude: this whole mystery of genera and species, which make such a noise in the schools, and are with justice so little regarded out of them, is nothing else but *abstract ideas*, more or less comprehensive, with names annexed to them. In all which this is constant and unvariable, that every more general term stands for such an idea, and is but a part of any of those contained under it.

10. *Why the Genus is ordinarily made Use of in Definitions.* – This may show us the reason why, in the defining of words, which is nothing but declaring their signification, we make use of the *genus*, or next general word that comprehends it. Which is not out of necessity, but only to save the labour of enumerating the several simple ideas which the next general word or *genus* stands for; or, perhaps, sometime the shame of not being able to do it. But though defining by *genus* and *differentia* (I crave leave to use these terms of art, though originally Latin, since they most properly suit those notions they are applied to), I say, though defining by the *genus* be the shortest way, yet I think it may be doubted whether it be the best. This I am sure, it is not the only, and so not absolutely necessary. For, definition being nothing but making another understand by words what idea the term defined stands for, a definition is best made

by enumerating those simple ideas that are combined in the signification of the term defined: and, if, instead of such an enumeration, men have accustomed themselves to use the next general term, it has not been out of necessity, or for greater clearness, but for quickness and dispatch sake. For I think that, to one who desired to know what idea the word *man* stood for; if it should be said, that man was a solid extended substance, having life, sense, spontaneous motion, and the faculty of reasoning, I doubt not but the meaning of the term man would be as well understood, and the idea it stands for be at least as clearly made known, as when it is defined to be a rational animal: which, by the several definitions of *animal*, *vivens*, and *corpus*, resolves itself into those enumerated ideas. I have, in explaining the term *man*, followed here the ordinary definition of the schools; which, though perhaps not the most exact, yet serves well enough to my present purpose. And one may, in this instance, see what gave occasion to the rule, that a definition must consist of *genus* and *differentia*; and it suffices to show us the little necessity there is of such a rule, or advantage in the strict observing of it. For, definitions, as has been said, being only the explaining of one word by several others, so that the meaning or idea it stands for may be certainly known; language are not always so made according to the rules of logic, that every term can have its signification exactly and clearly expressed by two others. Experience sufficiently satisfies us to the contrary; or else those who have made this rule have done ill, that they have given us so few definitions conformable to it. But of definitions more in the next chapter.

11. *General and Universal are Creatures of the Understanding, and belong not to the Real Existence of things.* – To return to general words: it is plain, by what has been said, that *general* and *universal* belong not to the real existence of things; but are the inventions and creatures of the understanding, made by it for its own use, and concern only signs, whether words or ideas. Words are general, as has been said, when used for signs of general ideas, and so are applicable indifferently to many particular things; and ideas are general when they are set up as the representatives of many particular things: but universality belongs not to things themselves, which are all of them particular in their existence, even those words and ideas which in their signification are general. When therefore we quit particulars, the generals that rest are only creatures of our own making; their general nature being nothing but the capacity they are put into, by the understanding, of signifying or representing many particulars. For the signification they have is nothing but a relation that, by the mind of man, is added to them.

12. *Abstract Ideas are the Essences of Genera and Species.* – The next thing therefore to be considered is, What kind of signification it is that general words have. For, as it is evident that they do not signify barely one particular thing; for then they would not be general terms, but proper names, so, on the other side, it is as evident they do not signify a plurality; for *man* and *men* would then signify the same; and the distinction of numbers (as the grammarians call them) would be superfluous and useless. That then which general words signify is a *sort* of things; and each of them does that, by being a sign of an abstract idea in the mind; to which idea, as things existing are found to agree, so they come to

be ranked under that name, or, which is all one, be of that sort. Whereby it is evident that the *essences* of the sorts, or, if the Latin word pleases better, *species* of things, are nothing else but these abstract ideas. For the having the essence of any species, being that which makes anything to be of that species; and the conformity to the idea to which the name is annexed being that which gives a right to that name; the having the essence, and the having that conformity, must needs be the same thing: since to be of any species, and to have a right to the name of that species, is all one. As, for example, to be a *man*, or of the *species* man, and to have right to the *name* man, is the same thing. Again, to be a man, or of the species man, and have the *essence* of a man, is the same thing. Now, since nothing can be a man, or have a right to the name man, but what has a conformity to the abstract idea the name man stands for, nor anything be a man, or have a right to the species man, but what has the essence of that species; it follows, that the abstract idea for which the name stands, and the essence of the species, is one and the same. From whence it is easy to observe, that the essences of the sorts of things, and, consequently, the sorting of things, is the workmanship of the understanding that abstracts and makes those general ideas.

13. *They are the Workmanship of the Understanding, but have their Foundation in the Similitude of Things.* – I would not here be thought to forget, much less to deny, that Nature, in the production of things, makes several of them alike: there is nothing more obvious, especially in the races of animals, and all things propagated by seed. But yet I think we may say, *the sorting of them under names is the workmanship of the understanding, taking occasion, from the similitude it observes amongst them, to make abstract general ideas*, and set them up in the mind, with names annexed to them, as patterns or forms, (for, in that sense, the word *form* has a very proper signification,) to which as particular things existing are found to agree, so they come to be of that species, have that denomination, or are put into that *classis*. For when we say this is a man, that a horse; this justice, that cruelty; this a watch, that a jack; what do we else but rank things under different specific names, as agreeing to those abstract ideas, of which we have made those names the signs? And what are the essences of those species set out and marked by names, but those abstract ideas in the mind; which are, as it were, the bonds between particular things that exist, and the names they are to be ranked under? And when general names have any connexion with particular beings, these abstract ideas are the medium that unites them: so that the essences of species, as distinguished and denominated by us, neither are nor can be anything but those precise abstract ideas we have in our minds. And therefore the supposed real essences of substances, if different from our abstract ideas, cannot be the essences of the species *we* rank things into. For two species may be one, as rationally as two different essences be the essence of one species: and I demand what are the alterations [which] may, or may not be made in a *horse* or *lead*, without making either of them to be of another species? In determining the species of things by *our* abstract ideas, this is easy to resolve, but if any one will regulate himself herein by supposed *real* essences, he will, I suppose, be at a loss: and he will never be able to know when anything precisely ceases to be of the species of a *horse* or *lead*.

14.   *Each distinct abstract Idea is a distinct Essence.* – Nor will any one wonder that I say these essences, or abstract ideas (which are the measures of name, and the boundaries of species) are the workmanship of the understanding, who considers that at least the complex ones are often, in several men, different collections of simple ideas; and therefore that is *covetousness* to one man, which is not so to another. Nay, even in substances, where their abstract ideas seem to be taken from the things themselves, they are not constantly the same; no, not in that species which is most familiar to us, and with which we have the most intimate acquaintance: it having been more than once doubted, whether the *foetus* born of a woman were a *man*, even so far as that it hath been debated, whether it were or were not to be nourished and baptized: which could not be, if the abstract idea or essence to which the name man belonged were of nature's making; and were not the uncertain and various collection of simple ideas, which the understanding put together, and then, abstracting it, affixed a name to it. So that, in truth, every distinct abstract idea is a distinct essence; and the names that stand for such distinct ideas are the names of things essentially different. Thus a circle is as essentially different from an oval as a sheep from a goat; and rain is as essentially different from snow as water from earth: that abstract idea which is the essence of one being impossible to be communicated to the other. And thus any two abstract ideas, that in any part vary one from another, with two distinct names annexed to them, constitute two distinct sorts, or, if you please, *species*, as essentially different as any two of the most remote or opposite in the world.

---

4   On the Scientific Justification of a Conceptual Notation[1]

Gottlob Frege

Time and again, in the more abstract regions of science, the lack of a means of avoiding misunderstandings on the part of others, and also errors in one's own thought, makes itself felt. Both [shortcomings] have their origin in the imperfection of language, for we do have to use sensible symbols to think.

Our attention is directed by nature to the outside. The vivacity of sense-impressions surpasses that of memory-images {*Erinner-ungsbilder*} to such an extent that, at first, sense-impressions determine almost by themselves the course of our ideas, as is the case in animals. And we would scarcely ever be able to escape this dependency if the outer world were not to some extent dependent upon us.

From *Conceptual Notation and Related Articles*, trans. Terrel Ward Bynum. Oxford: Clarendon Press, 1972, pp. 83–9. First published in German 1882. By permission of the publisher.

Even most animals, through their ability to move about, have an influence on their sense-impressions: they can flee some, seek others. And they can even effect changes in things. Now man has this ability to a much greater degree; but nevertheless, the course of our ideas {*unser Vorstellungsverlauf*} would still not gain its full freedom from this [ability alone]: it would still be limited to that which our hand can fashion, our voice intone, without the great invention of symbols which call to mind {*uns gegenwärtig machen*} that which is absent, invisible, perhaps even beyond the senses {*unsinnlich*}.[2]

I do not deny that even without symbols the perception of a thing can gather about itself {*um sich sammeln*}[3] a group of memory-images {*Erinner-ungsbilder*}; but we could not pursue these further: a new perception would let these images sink into darkness and allow others to emerge. But if we produce the symbol of an idea which a perception has called to mind, we create in this way a firm, new focus about which ideas gather. We then select another [idea] from these in order to elicit *its* symbol. Thus we penetrate step by step into the inner world of our ideas and move about there at will, using the realm of sensibles itself {*das Sinnliche selbst*} to free ourselves from its constraint. Symbols have the same importance for thought that discovering how to use the wind had for navigation. Thus, let no one despise symbols! A great deal depends upon choosing them properly. And their value is not diminished by the fact that, after long practice, we need no longer speak out loud in order to think; for we think in words nevertheless, and if not in words, then in mathematical or other symbols.

Also, without symbols we would scarcely lift ourselves to conceptual thinking. Thus, in applying the same symbol to different but similar things, we actually no longer symbolize the individual thing, but rather what [the similars] have in common: the concept. This concept is first gained by symbolizing it; for since it is, in itself, imperceptible, it requires a perceptible representative in order to appear to us.

This does not exhaust the merits of symbols; but it may suffice to demonstrate their indispensability. Language proves to be deficient, however, when it comes to protecting thought from error. It does not even meet the first requirement which we must place upon it in this respect; namely, being unambiguous. The most dangerous cases [of ambiguity] are those in which the meanings of a word are only slightly different, the subtle and yet not unimportant variations. Of the many examples [of this kind of ambiguity] only one frequently recurring phenomenon may be mentioned here: the same word may serve to designate a concept and a single object which falls under that concept. Generally, no strong distinction is made between concept and individual. "The horse" can denote a single creature; it can also denote the species, as in the sentence: "The horse is an herbivorous animal." Finally, horse[4] can denote a concept,[5] as in the sentence: "This is a horse."

Language is not governed by logical laws in such a way that mere adherence to grammar would guarantee the formal correctness of thought processes {*Gedankenbewegung*}. The forms in which inference is expressed are so varied, so loose and vague, that presuppositions can easily slip in unnoticed and then be overlooked when the necessary conditions for the conclusion are enumerated. In this way, the conclusion obtains a greater generality {*grössere Allgemeinheit*}[6] than it justifiably deserves.

Even such a conscientious and rigorous writer as Euclid often makes tacit use of presuppositions which he specifies neither in his axioms and postulates nor in the premisses of the particular theorem [being proved]. Thus, in the proof of the nineteenth theorem of the first book of *The Elements* (in every triangle, the largest angle lies opposite the largest side), he tacitly uses the statements:

(1) if a line segment is not larger than a second one, the former is equal to or smaller than the latter.

(2) If an angle is the same size as a second one, the former is not larger than the latter.

(3) If an angle is smaller than a second one, the former is not larger than the latter.

Only by paying particular attention, however, can the reader become aware of the omission of these sentences, especially since they seem so close to being as fundamental as the laws of thought that they are used just like those laws themselves.

A strictly defined group of modes of inference is simply not present in [ordinary] language, so that on the basis of linguistic form we cannot distinguish between a "gapless" advance {*lückenloser Fortgang*} [in the argument] and an omission of connecting links. We can even say that the former almost never occurs in [ordinary] language, that it runs against the feel of language because it would involve an insufferable prolixity. In [ordinary] language, logical relations are almost always only hinted at – left to guessing, not actually expressed.

The only advantage that the written word has over the spoken word is permanence: [with the written word], we can review a train of thought many times without fear that it will change; and thus we can test its validity more thoroughly. In this [process of testing], since insufficient security lies in the nature of the word-language itself, the laws of logic are applied externally like a plumbline. But even so, mistakes easily escape the eye of the examiner, especially those which arise from subtle differences in the meanings of a word. That we nevertheless find our way about reasonably well in life as well as in science we owe to the manifold ways of checking that we have at our disposal. Experience and space perception protect us from many errors. Logical rules [, externally applied,] furnish little protection, as is shown by examples from disciplines in which the means of checking begin to fail. These rules have failed to defend even great philosophers from mistakes, and have helped just as little in keeping higher mathematics free from error, because they have always remained external to content.

The shortcomings stressed [here] are rooted in a certain softness {*gewissen Weichheit*} and instability of [ordinary] language, which nevertheless is necessary for its versatility and potential for development. In this respect, [ordinary] language can be compared to the hand, which despite its adaptability to the most diverse tasks is still inadequate.[7] We build for ourselves artificial hands, tools for particular purposes, which work with more accuracy than the hand can provide. And how is this accuracy possible? Through the very stiffness and inflexibility of parts the lack of which makes the hand so dextrous. Word-language is inadequate in a similar way. We need a system of symbols {*Ganzes von Zeichen*}[8] from which every ambiguity is banned, which has a strict logical form from which the content cannot escape.

We may now ask which is preferable, audible symbols or visible ones. The former have, first of all, the advantage that their production is more independent of external circumstances. Furthermore, much can be made in particular of the close kinship of sounds to inner processes {*innere Vorgängen*}. Even their form of appearance {*die Form des Erscheinens*},[9] the temporal sequence, is the same; both are equally fleeting. In particular, sounds have a more intimate relation to the emotions {*das Gemüthsleben*}[10] than shapes and colours do; and the human voice with its boundless flexibility is able to do justice to even the most delicate combinations and variations of feelings. But no matter how valuable these advantages may be for other purposes, they have no importance for the rigour of logical deductions. Perhaps this intimate adaptability of audible symbols to the physical and mental conditions of reason has just the disadvantage of keeping reason more dependent upon these.

It is completely different with visible things, especially shapes. They are generally sharply defined and clearly distinguished. This definiteness of written symbols will tend to make what is signified also more sharply defined; and just such an effect upon ideas {*die Vorstellungen*}[11] must be asked for the rigour of deduction. This can be achieved, however, only if the symbol directly {*unmittelbar*} denotes the thing [symbolized].

A further advantage of the written symbol is greater permanence and immutability. In this way, it is also similar to the concept – as it should be – and thus, of course, the more dissimilar to the restless flow of our actual thought processes {*wirkliche Gedanken-bewegung*}. Written symbols offer the possibility of keeping many things in mind at the same time; and even if, at each moment, we can only concentrate upon a small part of these, we still retain a general impression of what remains, and this is immediately at our disposal whenever we need it.

The spatial relations of written symbols on a two-dimensional writing surface can be employed in far more diverse ways to express inner relationships {*innere Beziehungen*} than the mere following and preceding in one-dimensional time, and this facilitates the apprehension of that to which we wish to direct our attention. In fact, simple sequential ordering in no way corresponds to the diversity of logical relations through which thoughts are interconnected.

Thus, the very properties which set the written symbol further apart [than the spoken word] from the course of our ideas {*der Vorstellungsverlauf*} are most suited to remedy certain shortcomings of our make-up. Therefore, when it is not a question of representing natural thought as it actually took shape in reciprocal action with the word-language, but concerns instead the supplementation of the onesidedness of thinking which results from a close connection with the sense of hearing, then the written symbol will be preferable. Such a notation must be completely different from all word-languages in order to exploit the peculiar advantages of written symbols. It need hardly be mentioned that these advantages scarcely come into play at all in the written word. The relative position of the words with respect to each other on the writing surface depends to a large extent upon the length of the lines [of print] and is, thus, without importance. There are, however, completely different kinds of notation which better exploit these [mentioned] advantages. The arithmetic language of formulas is a conceptual notation since it directly expresses the facts without the intervention of speech. As such, it attains a brevity which allows it to accommodate the content of a simple judgement in one line. Such contents – here equations or inequalities – as they follow from one another are written under one another. If a third follows from two others, we separate the third from the first two with a horizontal stroke, which can be read "therefore". In this way, the two-dimensionality of the writing surface is utilized for the sake of perspicuity. Here the deduction is stereotyped {*sehr einformig*}[12] being almost always based upon identical transformations of identical numbers yielding identical results. Of course, this is by no means the only method of inference in arithmetic; but where the logical progression is different, it is generally necessary to express it in words. Thus, the arithmetic language of formulas lacks expressions for logical connections; and, therefore, it does not merit the name of conceptual notation in the full sense.

Exactly the opposite holds for the symbolism for logical relations originating with Leibniz and revived in modern times by Boole, R. Grassmann, S. Jevons, E. Schröder, and others. Here we do have the logical forms, though not entirely complete; but content is lacking. In these cases, any attempt to replace the single letters with expressions of contents, such as analytic equations, would demonstrate with the resulting imperspicuity, clumsiness – even ambiguity – of the formulas how little suited this kind of symbolism is for the construction of a true conceptual notation.

I would demand the following from a true conceptual notation: it must have simple modes of expression for the logical relations which, limited to the necessary, can be easily and surely mastered. These forms must be suitable for combining most intimately with a content. Also, such brevity must be sought that the two-dimensionality of the writing surface can be exploited for the sake of perspicuity. The symbols for denoting content are less essential. They can be easily created as required, once the general [logical] forms are available. If the analysis of a concept into its ultimate components {*letzte Bestandtheile*} does not succeed or appears unnecessary, we can be content with temporary symbols.

It would be easy to worry unnecessarily about the feasibility of the matter.[13] It is impossible, someone might say to advance science with a conceptual notation, for the invention of the latter already presupposes the completion of the former. Exactly the same apparent difficulty arises for [ordinary] language. This is supposed to have made reason possible, but how could man have invented language without reason? Research into the laws of nature employs physical instruments; but these can be produced only by means of an advanced technology, which again is based upon knowledge of the laws of nature. The [apparently vicious] circle is resolved in each case in the same way: an advance in physics results in an advance in technology, and this makes possible the construction of new instruments by means of which physics is again advanced. The application [of this example] to our case is obvious.

Now I have attempted[14] to supplement the formula language of arithmetic with symbols for the logical relations in order to produce – at first just for arithmetic a conceptual notation of the kind I have presented as desirable. This does not rule out the application of my symbols to other fields. The logical relations occur everywhere, and the symbols for particular contents can be so chosen that they fit the framework of the conceptual notation. Be that as it may, a perspicuous representation of the forms of thought has in any case, significance extending beyond mathematics. May philosophers, then, give some attention to the matter!

Notes

1   [This translation was made independently of the one by J. Bartlett which appeared in *Mind*, 73 (1964), pp. 155–60; and then the two were compared. Wherever Bartlett's interpretation or wording seemed better, it was adopted and duly noted. Wherever important differences of interpretation remained, they were also noted, to give the reader the benefit of both views.]

2   [Bartlett renders this "unseeable", but here it seems to have more the sense of "transcendental". Moving air, for example, is unseeable, but not *unsinnlich*.]

3   [Bartlett renders this "catalyse".]

4   [Frege did not yet use quotation marks to distinguish use from mention. His first systematic use of that convention was in 1892 in "on Sense and Reference", reprinted in this volume. For this reason, the word 'horse' in the above passage is not enclosed in quotation marks.]

5   [Frege is not careful here – as he will be later – to distinguish between '*the* horse', which denotes an individual, and '*a* horse', which denotes a concept.]

6   [Bartlett renders this "greater validity".]

7   [Bartlett's turn of phrase.]

8   [Bartlett's translation.]

9   [Bartlett renders this "the experiential form".]

10 [Bartlett's translation.]

11 [Bartlett renders this "imagery".]

12 [Bartlett's translation.]

13 [Bartlett's turn of phrase.]

14 "Conceptual Notation, a Formula Language of Pure Thought modelled upon the Formula Language of Arithmetic", in *Conceptual Notation and Related Articles*, trans. T. W. Bynum (Oxford: Clarendon Press, 1972); 1st German edition 1879.

5   The Existential Matrix of Inquiry: Cultural

John Dewey

The environment in which human beings live, act and inquire, is not simply physical. It is cultural as well. Problems which induce inquiry grow out of the relations of fellow beings to one another, and the organs for dealing with these relations are not only the eye and ear, but the meanings which have developed in the course of living, together with the ways of forming and transmitting culture with all its constituents of tools, arts, institutions, traditions and customary beliefs.

I. To a very large extent the ways in which human beings respond even to physical conditions are influenced by their cultural environment. Light and fire are physical facts. But the occasions in which a human being responds to things as merely physical in purely physical ways are comparatively rare. Such occasions are the act of jumping when a sudden noise is heard, withdrawing the hand when something hot is touched, blinking in the presence of a sudden increase of light, animal-like basking in sunshine, etc. Such reactions are on the biological plane. But the typical cases of human behavior are not represented by such examples. The *use* of sound in speech and listening to speech, making and enjoying music; the kindling and tending of fire to cook and to keep warm; the production of light to carry on and regulate occupations and social enjoyments: – these things are representative of distinctively human activity.

To indicate the full scope of cultural determination of the conduct of living one would have to follow the behavior of an individual throughout at least a day; whether that of a day laborer, of a professional man, artist or scientist, and whether the individual be a growing child or a parent. For the result would show how thoroughly saturated behavior is with conditions and factors that are of cultural origin and import. Of distinctively human behavior it may be said that the strictly physical environment is so incorporated in a cultural environment that our interactions with the former, the problems that arise with reference to it, and our ways of dealing with these problems, are profoundly affected by incorporation of the physical environment in the cultural.

Man, as Aristotle remarked, is a *social* animal. This fact introduces him into situations and originates problems and ways of solving them that have no precedent upon the organic biological level. For man is social in another sense than the bee and ant, since his activities are encompassed in an environment that is culturally transmitted, so that what man does and how he acts, is determined not by organic structure and physical heredity alone but by the influence of cultural heredity, embedded in traditions, institutions, customs and the pur-

From *Logic: The Theory of Inquiry*, in *The Later Works: 1925–1953*, vol. 12, ed. Jo Ann Boydston. Carbondale, IL: Southern Illinois University Press, 1986, pp. 48–65. Copyright © 1986 by the Board of Trustees, Southern Illinois University. By permission of the publisher.

poses and beliefs they both carry and inspire. Even the neuro-muscular structures of individuals are modified through the influence of the cultural environment upon the activities performed. The acquisition and understanding of language with proficiency in the arts (that are foreign to other animals than men) represent an incorporation within the physical structure of human beings of the effects of cultural conditions, an interpenetration so profound that resulting activities are as direct and seemingly "natural" as are the first reactions of an infant. To speak, to read, to exercise any art, industrial, fine or political, are instances of modifications wrought *within* the biological organism by the cultural environment.

This modification of organic behavior in and by the cultural environment accounts for, or rather is, the transformation of purely organic behavior into behavior marked by intellectual properties with which the present discussion is concerned. Intellectual operations are foreshadowed in behavior of the biological kind, and the latter prepares the way for the former. But to foreshadow is not to exemplify and to prepare is not to fulfil. Any theory that rests upon a naturalistic postulate must face the problem of the extraordinary differences that mark off the activities and achievements of human beings from those of other biological forms. It is these differences that have led to the idea that man is completely separated from other animals by properties that come from a non-natural source. The conception to be developed in the present chapter is that the development of language (in its widest sense) out of prior biological activities is, in its connection with wider cultural forces, the key to this transformation. The problem, so viewed, is not the problem of the transition of organic behavior into something wholly discontinuous with it – as is the case when, for example, Reason, Intuition and the a priori are appealed to for explanation of the difference. It is a special form of the general problem of continuity of change and the emergence of new modes of activity – the problem of development at any level.

Viewing the problem from this angle, its constituents may be reduced to certain heads, three of which will be noted. Organic behavior is centered in *particular* organisms. This statement applies to inferring and reasoning as existential activities. But if inferences made and conclusions reached are to be valid, the subject-matter dealt with and the operations employed must be such as to yield identical results for all who infer and reason. If the same evidence leads different persons to different conclusions, then either the evidence is only speciously the same, or one conclusion (or both) is wrong. The *special* constitution of an individual organism which plays such a role in biological behavior is so irrelevant in controlled inquiry that it has to be discounted and mastered.

Another phase of the problem is brought out by the part played in human judgments by emotion and desire. These *personal* traits cook the evidence and determine the result that is reached. That is, upon the level of organic factors (which are the actively determining forces in the type of cases just mentioned), the individual with his individual peculiarities, whether native or acquired, is an active participant in producing ideas and beliefs, and yet the latter are logically grounded only when such peculiarities are deliberately precluded from taking effect. This point restates what was said in connection with the first point, but it indicates another phase of the matter. If, using accepted terminology, we say that the first difference is that between the singular and the general, the present point may be formulated as the difference between the subjective and the objective. To be intellectually "objective" is to discount and eliminate merely personal factors in the operations by which a conclusion is reached.

Organic behavior is a strictly temporal affair. But when behavior is *intellectually* formulated, in respect both to general ways of behavior and the special environing conditions in which they operate, propositions result and the terms of a proposition do not sustain a temporal relation to one another. It was a temporal event when someone landed on Robinson Crusoe's island. It was a temporal event when Crusoe found the footprint on the sands. It was a temporal event when Crusoe inferred the presence of a possibly dangerous stranger. But while the proposition was about something temporal, the *relation* of the observed fact as evidential to the inference drawn from it is nontemporal. The same holds of every logical relation in and of propositions.

In the following discussion it is maintained that the solution of the problem just stated in some of its phases, is intimately and directly connected with cultural subject-matter. Transformation from organic behavior to intellectual behavior, marked by logical properties, is a product of the fact that individuals live in a cultural environment. Such living compels them to assume in their behavior the standpoint of customs, beliefs, institutions, meanings and projects which are at least relatively general and objective.[1]

II. Language occupies a peculiarly significant place and exercises a peculiarly significant function in the complex that forms the cultural environment. It is itself a cultural institution, and, from one point of view, is but one among many such institutions. But it is (1) the agency by which other institutions and acquired habits are *transmitted*, and (2) it *permeates* both the forms and the contents of all other cultural activities. Moreover, (3) it has its own distinctive structure which is capable of abstraction as a *form*. This structure, when abstracted as a form, had a decisive influence historically upon the formulation of logical theory; the symbols which are appropriate to the form of language as an agency of inquiry (as distinct from its original function as a medium of communication) are still peculiarly relevant to logical theory. Consequently, further discussion will take the wider cultural environment for granted and confine itself to the especial function of language in effecting the transformation of the biological into the intellectual and the potentially logical.

In this further discussion, language is taken in its widest sense, a sense wider than oral and written speech. It includes the latter. But it includes also not only gestures but rites, ceremonies, monuments and the products of industrial and fine arts. A tool or machine, for example, is not simply a simple or complex physical object having its own physical properties and effects, but is also a mode of language. For it *says* something, to those who understand it, about operations of use and their consequences. To the members of a primitive community a loom operated by steam or electricity says nothing. It is composed in a foreign language, and so with most of the mechanical devices of modern civilization. In the present cultural setting, these objects are so intimately bound up with interests, occupations and purposes that they have an eloquent voice.

The importance of language as the necessary, and, in the end, sufficient condition of the existence and transmission of non-purely organic activities and their consequences lies in the fact that, on one side, it is a strictly biological mode of behavior, emerging in natural continuity from earlier organic activities, while, on the other hand, it compels one individual to take the standpoint of other individuals and to see and inquire from a standpoint that is not strictly personal but is common to them as participants or "parties" in a conjoint undertaking. It may be directed by and towards some physical existence. But it first has reference to some other person or persons with whom it institutes *communication* – the making of something common. Hence, to that extent its reference becomes general and "objective."

Language is made up of physical existences; sounds, or marks on paper, or a temple, statue, or loom. But these do not *operate* or function as mere physical things when they are media of communication. They operate in virtue of their *representative* capacity or *meaning*. The particular physical existence which has meaning is, in the case of speech, a conventional matter. But the convention or common consent which sets it apart as a means of recording and communicating meaning is that of agreement in action; of shared modes of responsive behavior and participation in their consequences. The physical sound or mark gets its meaning in and by conjoint community of functional use, not by any explicit convening in a "convention" or by passing resolutions that a certain sound or mark shall have a specified meaning. Even when the meaning of certain legal words is determined by a court, it is not the agreement of the judges which is finally decisive. For such assent does not finish the matter. It occurs for the sake of determining future agreements in associated *behavior*, and it is this subsequent behavior which finally settles the actual meaning of the words in question. Agreement in the proposition arrived at is significant only through this function in promoting agreement in action.

The reason for mentioning these considerations is that they prove that the meaning which a conventional symbol has is not itself conventional. For the meaning is established by agreements of different persons in existential activities having reference to existential consequences. The particular existential sound or mark that stands for *dog* or *justice* in different cultures is arbitrary or conventional in the sense that although it has *causes* there are no *reasons* for it. But *in so far* as it is a medium of communication, its meaning is common, because it is constituted by existential conditions. If a word varies in meaning in intercommunication between different cultural groups, then to that degree communication is blocked and misunderstanding results. Indeed, there ceases to be communication until variations of understanding can be translated, through the meaning of words, into a meaning that is the same to both parties. Whenever communication is blocked and yet is supposed to exist misunderstanding, not merely absence of understanding, is the result. It is an error to suppose that the misunderstanding is about the meaning of the *word* in isolation, just as it is fallacious to suppose that because two persons accept the same dictionary meaning of a word they have therefore come to agreement and understanding. For agreement and disagreement are determined by the consequences of conjoint activities. Harmony or the opposite exists in the effects produced by the several activities that are occasioned by the words used.

III. Reference to concord of consequences as the determinant of the meaning of any sound used as a medium of communication shows that there is no such thing as a *mere* word or *mere* symbol. The physical existence that is the vehicle of meaning may as a particular be called *mere*; the recitation of a number of such sounds or the stringing together of such marks may be called *mere* language. But in fact there is no word in the first case and no language in the second. The activities that occur and the consequences that result which are not determined by meaning, are, by description, only physical. A sound or mark of any physical existence is a part of *language* only in virtue of its *operational* force; that is, as it functions as a means of evoking different activities performed by different persons so as to produce consequences that are shared by all the participants in the conjoint undertaking. This fact is evident and direct in oral communication. It is indirect and disguised in written communication. Where written literature and literacy abound, the conception of language is likely to be framed upon their model. The intrinsic connection of language with community of action is then forgotten. Language is then supposed to be simply a means of expressing or communicating "thoughts" – a means of conveying ideas or meanings that are complete in themselves apart from communal operational force.

Much literature is read, moreover, simply for enjoyment, for esthetic purposes. In this case, language is a means of action only as it leads the reader to build up pictures and scenes to be enjoyed by himself. There ceases to be immediate inherent reference to conjoint activity and to consequences mutually participated in. Such is not the case, however, in reading to get at the meaning of the author; that is, in reading that is emphatically intellectual in distinction from esthetic. In the mere reading of a scientific treatise there is, indeed, no direct overt participation in action with another to produce consequences that are *common* in the sense of being immediately and personally shared. But there must be imaginative construction of the materials and operations which led the author to certain conclusions, and there must be agreement or disagreement with his conclusions as a consequence of following through conditions and operations that are imaginatively reinstated.

Connection with overt activities is in such a case indirect or mediated. But so far as definite grounded agreement or disagreement is reached, an attitude is formed which is a preparatory readiness to act in a responsive way when the conditions in question or others similar to them actually present themselves. The connection with action in question is, in other words, with *possible* ways of operation rather than with those found to be *actually* and immediately required.[2] But preparation for possible action in situations not as yet existent in actuality is an essential condition of, and factor in, all intelligent behavior. When persons meet together in conference to plan in advance of actual occasions and emergencies what shall later be done, or when an individual deliberates in advance regarding his possible behavior in a possible future contingency, something occurs, but more directly, of the same sort as happens in understanding intellectually the meaning of a scientific treatise.

I turn now to the positive implication of the fact that no sound, mark, product of art, is a word or part of language in isolation. Any word or phrase has the meaning which it has only as a member of a constellation of related meanings. Words as representatives are part of an inclusive code. The code may be public or private. A public code is illustrated in any language that is current in a given cultural group. A private code is one agreed upon by members of special groups so as to be unintelligible to those who have not been initiated. Between these two come argots of special groups in a community, and the technical codes invented for a restricted special purpose, like the one used by ships at sea. But in every case, a particular word has its meaning only in relation to the code of which it is one constituent. The distinction just drawn between meanings that are determined respectively in fairly direct connection with action in situations that are present or near at hand, and meanings determined for possible use in remote and contingent situations, provides the basis upon which language codes as systems may be differentiated into two main kinds.

While all language or symbol-meanings are what they are as parts of a system, it does not follow that they have been determined on the basis of their fitness to be such members of a system; much less on the basis of their membership in a comprehensive system. The system may be simply the language in common use. Its meanings hang together not in virtue of their examined relationship to one another, but because they are current in the same set of group habits and expectations. They hang together because of group activities, group interests, customs and institutions. Scientific language, on the other hand, is subject to a test over and above this criterion. Each meaning that enters into the language is expressly determined in its relation to other members of the language system. In all reasoning or ordered discourse this criterion takes precedence over that instituted by connection with cultural habits.

The resulting difference in the two types of language-meanings fundamentally fixes the difference between what is called common sense and what is called science. In the former cases, the customs, the *ethos* and spirit of a group is the decisive factor in determining the system of meanings in use. The system is one in a practical and institutional sense rather than in an intellectual sense. Meanings that are formed on this basis are sure to contain much that is irrelevant and to exclude much that is required for intelligent control of activity. The meanings are coarse, and many of them are inconsistent with each other from a logical point of view. One meaning is appropriate to action under certain institutional group conditions; another, in some other situation, and there is no attempt to relate the different situations to one another in a coherent scheme. In an intellectual sense, there are many languages, though in a social sense there is but one. This multiplicity of language-meaning constellations is also a mark of our existing culture. A word means one thing in relation to a religious institution, still another thing in business, a third thing in law, and so on. This fact is the real Babel of communication. There is an attempt now making to propagate the idea that education which indoctrinates individuals into some special tradition provides the way out of this confusion. Aside from the fact that there are in fact a considerable number of traditions and that selection of some one of them, even though that one be internally consistent and extensively accepted, is arbitrary, the attempt reverses the *theoretical* state of the case. Genuine community of language or symbols can be achieved only through efforts that bring about community of activities under existing conditions. The ideal of scientific-language is construction of a system in which meanings are related to one another in inference and discourse and where the symbols are such as to indicate the relation.

I shall now introduce the word "symbol" giving it its signification as a synonym for a word *as* a word, that is, as a meaning carried by language in a system, whether the system be of the loose or the intellectual rigorous kind.[3] The especial point in the introduction of the word "symbol" is to institute the means by which discrimination between what is designated by it and what is now often designated by *sign* may be instituted. What I have called symbols are often called "artificial signs" in distinction from what are called *natural signs*.

IV. It is by agreement in conjoint action of the kind already described, that the *word* "smoke" stands in the English language for an object of certain qualities. In some other language the same vocable and mark may stand for something different, and an entirely different sound stand for "smoke." To such cases of representation the word "*artificial signs*" applies. When it is said that smoke as an actual existence points to, is evidence of, an existential fire, smoke is said to be a *natural* sign of fire. Similarly, heavy clouds of given qualities are a natural sign of probable rain, and so on. The representative capacity in question is attributed to *things in their connection with one another*, not to marks whose meaning depends upon agreement in social use. There is no doubt of the existence and the importance of the distinction designated by the words "natural" and "artificial" signs. But the fundamentally important difference is not brought out by these words. For reasons now to be given, I prefer to mark the difference by confining the application of *sign* to so-called "natural signs" – employing *symbol* to designate "artificial signs."

The difference just stated is actual. But it fails to note the distinctive intellectual property of what I call symbols. It is, so to speak, an incidental and external fact, logically speaking, that certain things are given representative function by social agreement. The fact becomes logically relevant only because of the possibility of free and independent development of meanings in discourse which arises when once symbols are instituted. A "natural sign," by description, is something that exists in an actual spatial-temporal context. Smoke, as a thing having certain observed qualities, is a sign of fire only when the thing exists and is observed. Its representative capacity, taken by itself, is highly restricted, for it exists only under limited conditions. The situation is very different when the *meaning* "smoke" is embodied in an existence, like a sound or a mark on paper. The actual quality found in existence is then subordinate to a representative office. Not only can the sound be produced practically at will, so that we do not have to wait for the occurrence of the object; but, what is more important, the meaning when embodied in an indifferent or neutral existence is *liberated* with respect to its representative function. It is no longer tied down. It can be related to other meanings in the language-system; not only to that of fire but to such apparently unrelated meanings as friction, changes of temperature, oxygen, molecular constitution, and, by intervening meaning-symbols, to the laws of thermodynamics.

I shall, accordingly, in what follows, connect *sign* and *significance*, *symbol* and *meaning*, respectively, with each other, in order to have terms to designate two different kinds of representative capacity. Linguistically, the choice of terms is more or less arbitrary, although sign and significance have a common verbal root. This consideration is of no importance, however, compared with the necessity of having some words by which to designate the two kinds of representative function. For purposes of theory the important consideration is that existent things, as signs, are *evidence* of the existence of something else, this something being at the time *inferred* rather than observed.

But words, or symbols, provide no *evidence* of any existence. Yet what they lack in this capacity they make up for in creation of another dimension. They make possible ordered discourse or reasoning. For this may be carried on without any of the existences to which symbols apply being actually present: without, indeed, assurance that objects to which they apply anywhere actually exist, and, as in the case of mathematical discourse, without direct reference to existence at all.

Ideas as ideas, hypotheses as hypotheses, would not exist were it not for symbols and meanings as distinct from signs and significances. The greater capacity of symbols for manipulation is of practical importance. But it pales in comparison with the fact that symbols introduce into inquiry a dimension different from that of existence. Clouds of certain shapes, size and color may signify to us the probability of rain; they portend rain. But the *word* cloud when it is brought into connection with other words of a symbol-constellation enable us to relate the meaning of being a cloud with such different matters as differences of temperature and pressures, the rotation of the earth, the laws of motion, and so on.

The difference between sign-significance and symbol-meaning (in the sense defined) is brought out in the following incident.[4] A visitor in a savage tribe wanted on one occasion "the word for Table. There were five or six boys standing round, and tapping the table with my forefinger I asked 'What is this?' One boy said it was *dodela*, another that it was an *etanda*, a third stated that it was *bokali*, a fourth that it was *elamba*, and the fifth said it was *meza*." After congratulating himself on the richness of the vocabulary of the language the visitor found later "that one boy had thought we wanted the word for tapping; another understood we were seeking the word for the material of which the table was made; another had the idea that we required the word for hardness; another thought we wished the name for that which covered the table; and the last . . . gave us the word *meza*, table."

This story might have been quoted earlier as an illustration of the fact that there is not possible any such thing as a direct one-to-one correspondence of names with existential objects; that words mean what they mean in connection with conjoint activities that effect a common, or mutually participated in, consequence. The word sought for was involved in conjoint activities looking to a common end. The act of tapping in the illustration was isolated from any such situation. It was, in consequence, wholly indeterminate in reference; it was no part of *communication*, by which alone acts get significance and accompanying words acquire meaning. For the point in hand, the anecdote illustrates the lack of any evidential status in relation to existence of the symbols or representative values that have been given the name "meanings." Without the intervention of a specific kind of existential operation they cannot indicate or discriminate the *objects* to which they refer. Reasoning or ordered discourse, which is defined by development of symbol-meanings in relation to one another, may (and should) provide a basis for performing these operations, but of itself it determines no existence. This statement holds no matter how comprehensive the meaning-system and no matter how rigorous and cogent the relations of meanings to one another. On the other hand, the story illustrates how, in case the right word had been discovered, the meaning symbolized would have been capable of entering into relations with any number of other meanings independently of the actual presence at any given time of the object *table*. Just as the sign-significance relation defines *inference*, so the relation of meanings that constitutes propositions defines *implication* in discourse, if it satisfies the intellectual conditions for which it is instituted. Unless there are words which mark off the two kinds of relations in their distinctive capacities and offices, with reference to existence, there is danger that two things as logically unlike as inference and implication will be confused. As a matter of fact, the confusion, when inference is treated as identical with implication, has been a powerful agency in creating the doctrinal conception that logic is purely formal – for, as has been said, the relation of meanings (carried by symbols) to one another is, *as such*, independent of existential reference.

V. So far the word "relation" has been rather indiscriminately employed. The discussion has now reached a point where it is necessary to deal with the ambiguity of the word as it is used not merely in ordinary speech but in logical texts. The word "relation" is used to cover three very different matters which in the interest of a coherent logical doctrine must be discriminated. (1) Symbols are "related" directly to one another; (2) they are "related" to existence by the mediating intervention of existential operations; (3) existences are "related" to one another in the evidential sign-signified function. That these three modes of "relation" are different from one another and that the use of one and the same word tends to cover up the difference and thereby create doctrinal confusion, is evident.

In order to avoid, negatively, the disastrous doctrinal confusion that arises from the ambiguity of the word *relation*, and in order to possess, positively, linguistic means of making clear the logical nature of the different subject-matters under discussion, I shall reserve the word *relation* to designate the kind of "relation" which symbol-meanings bear to one another as symbol-meanings. I shall use the term *reference* to designate the kind of relation they sustain to existence; and the words *connection* (and *involvement*) to designate that kind of relation sustained by *things* to one another in virtue of which *infer-ence* is possible.

The differences, when once pointed out, should be so obvious as hardly to require illustration. Consider, however, propositions of mathematical physics. (1) As propositions they form a system of *related* symbol-meanings that may be considered and developed as such. (2) But as propositions of *physics*, not of mere mathematics, they have *reference* to existence; a reference which is realized in operations of *application*. (3) The final test of *valid* reference or applicability resides in the *connections* that exist among things. Existential involvement of things with one another alone warrants inference so as to enable further con-nections among things themselves to be discovered.

The question may be raised whether meaning-relations in discourse arise be-fore or after significance-connections in existence. Did we first infer and then use the results to engage in discourse? Or did relations of meanings, instituted in discourse, enable us to detect the connections in things in virtue of which some things are evidential of other things? The question is rhetorical in that the question of historical priority cannot be settled. The question is asked, how-ever, in order to indicate that in any case ability to treat things as signs would not go far did not symbols enable us to mark and retain just the qualities of things which are the ground of inference. Without, for example, words or sym-bols that discriminate and hold on to the experienced qualities of sight and smell that constitute a thing "smoke," thereby enabling it to serve as a sign of fire, we might react to the qualities in question in animal-like fashion and per-form activities appropriate to them. But no inference could be made that was not blind and blundering. Moreover, since *what* is inferred, namely fire, is not present in observation, any anticipation that could be formed of it would be vague and indefinite, even supposing an anticipation could occur at all. If we compare and contrast the range and the depth of the signifying capacity of existential objects and events in a savage and a civilized group and the corres-ponding power of inference, we find a close correlation between it and the scope and the intimacy of the relations that obtain between symbol-meanings in discourse. Upon the whole, then, it is language, originating as a medium of communication in order to bring about deliberate cooperation and competi-tion in conjoint activities, that has conferred upon existential things their signifying or evidential power.

VI. We are thus brought back to the original problem: namely, transforma-tion of animal activities into intelligent behavior having the properties which, when formulated, are *logical* in nature. Associated behavior is characteristic not only of plants and animals, but of electrons, atoms and molecules; as far as we know of everything that exists in nature. Language did not originate associa-tion, but when it supervened, as a natural emergence from previous forms of animal activity, it reacted to transform prior forms and modes of associated behavior in such a way as to give experience a new dimension.

1. "Culture" and all that culture involves, as distinguished from "nature," is both a condition and a product of language. Since language is the only means

of retaining and transmitting to subsequent generations *acquired* skills, acquired information and acquired habits, it is the latter. Since, however, meanings and the significance of events differ in different cultural groups, it is also the former.

2. Animal activities, such as eating and drinking, searching for food, copulation, etc., acquire new properties. Eating food becomes a group festival and celebration; procuring food, the art of agriculture and exchange; copulation passes into the institution of the family.

3. Apart from the existence of symbol-meanings the results of prior experience are retained only through strictly organic modifications. Moreover, these modifications once made, tend to become so fixed as to retard, if not to prevent, the occurrence of further modifications. The existence of symbols makes possible deliberate recollection and expectation, and thereby the institution of new combinations of selected elements of experiences having an intellectual dimension.

4. Organic biological activities end in overt actions, whose consequences are irretrievable. When an activity and its consequences can be rehearsed by representation in symbolic terms, there is no such final commitment. If the representation of the final consequence is of unwelcome quality, overt activity may be foregone, or the way of acting be replanned in such a way as to avoid the undesired outcome.[5]

These transformations and others which they suggest, are not of themselves equivalent to accrual of logical properties to behavior. But they provide requisite conditions for it. The use of meaning-symbols for institution of purposes or ends-in-view, for deliberation, as a rehearsal through such symbols of the activities by which the ends may be brought into being, is at least a rudimentary form of reasoning in connection with solution of problems. The habit of reasoning once instituted is capable of indefinite development on its own account. The ordered development of meanings in their relations to one another may become an engrossing interest. When this happens, implicit logical conditions are made explicit and then logical theory of some sort is born. It may be imperfect; it will be imperfect from the standpoint of the inquiries and symbol-meanings that later develop. But the first step, the one that costs and counts, was taken when some one began to reflect upon language, upon *logos*, in its syntactical structure and its wealth of meaning contents. Hypostatization of *Logos* was the first result, and it held back for centuries the development of inquiries of a kind that are competent to deal with the problems of the existent world. But the hypostatization was, nevertheless, a tribute to the power of language to generate reasoning and, through application of the meanings contained in it, to confer fuller and more ordered significance upon existence.

In later chapters we shall consider in some detail how a logic of ordered discourse, a logic that gathered in a system the relations which hold meanings consistently together in discourse, was taken to be the final model of logic and thereby obstructed the development of effective modes of inquiry into existence, preventing the necessary reconstruction and expansion of the very meanings that were used in discourse. For when these meanings in their ordered relations to one another were taken to be final in and of themselves, they were directly superimposed upon nature. The necessity of existential operations for application of meanings to natural existence was ignored. This failure reacted into the system of meanings as meanings. The result was the belief that the requirements of rational discourse constitute the measure of natural existence, the criterion of complete Being. It is true that logic emerged as the Greeks became aware of language as Logos with the attendant implication that a system of ordered meanings is involved.

This perception marked an enormous advance. But it suffered from two serious defects. Because of the superior status assigned to forms of rational discourse, they were isolated from the operations by means of which meanings originate, function and are tested. This isolation was equivalent to the hypostatization of Reason. In the second place, the meanings that were recognized were ordered in a gradation derived from and controlled by a class-structure of Greek society. The means, procedures and kinds of organization that arose from active or "practical" participation in natural processes were given a low rank in the hierarchy of Being and Knowing. The scheme of knowledge and of Nature became, without conscious intent, a mirror of a social order in which craftsmen, mechanics, artisans generally, held a low position in comparison with a leisure class. Citizens as citizens were also occupied with doing, a doing instigated by need or lack. While possessed of a freedom denied to the artisan class, they were also taken to fail in completely self-contained and self-sufficient activity. The latter was exemplified only in the exercise of Pure Reason untainted by need for anything outside itself and hence independent of all operations of doing and making. The historic result was to give philosophic, even supposedly ontological, sanction to the cultural conditions which prevented the utilization of the immense potentialities for attainment of knowledge that were resident in the activities of the arts – resident in them because they involve operations of active modification of existing conditions which contain the procedures constituting the experimental method when once they are employed for the sake of obtaining knowledge, instead of being subordinated to a scheme of uses and enjoyments controlled by given socio-cultural conditions.

Notes

1 The non-temporal phase of propositions receives attention later.
2 Literature and literary habits are a strong force in building up a conception of separation of ideas and theories from practical activity.
3 This signification is narrower than the popular usage, according to which anything is a symbol that has representative emotional force even if that force be independent of its intellectual representational force. In this wider sense, a national flag, a crucifix, a mourning garb, etc., are symbols. The definition of the text is in so far arbitrary. But there is nothing arbitrary about the subject-matters to which the limited signification applies.
4 Quoted by and from K. Ogden and I. A. Richards, *The Meaning of Meaning* (New York: Harcourt Brace, 1959), p. 174.
5 Generalizing beyond the strict requirements of the position outlined, I would say

that I am not aware of any so-called merely "mental" activity or result that cannot be described in the objective terms of an organic activity modified and directed by symbols-meaning, or language, in its broad sense.

---

6 Picturing Reality

Ludwig Wittgenstein

1[1]   The world is all that is the case.

1.1   The world is the totality of facts, not of things.

1.11   The world is determined by the facts, and by their being *all* the facts.

1.12   For the totality of facts determines what is the case, and also whatever is not the case.

1.13   The facts in logical space are the world.

1.2   The world divides into facts.

1.21   Each item can be the case or not the case while everything else remains the same.

2   What is the case – a fact – is the existence of states of affairs.

2.01   A state of affairs (a state of things) is a combination of objects (things).

2.011   It is essential to things that they should be possible constituents of states of affairs.

2.012   In logic nothing is accidental: if a thing *can* occur in a state of affairs, the possibility of the state of affairs must be written into the thing itself.

2.0121   It would seem to be a sort of accident, if it turned out that a situation would fit a thing that could already exist entirely on its own.

  If things can occur in states of affairs, this possibility must be in them from the beginning.

  (Nothing in the province of logic can be merely possible. Logic deals with every possibility and all possibilities are its facts.)

  Just as we are quite unable to imagine spatial objects outside space or temporal objects outside time, so too there is *no* object that we can imagine excluded from the possibility of combining with others.

  If I can imagine objects combined in states of affairs, I cannot imagine them excluded from the *possibility* of such combinations.

2.0122   Things are independent in so far as they can occur in all *possible* situations, but this form of independence is a form of connexion with states of affairs, a form of dependence. (It is impossible for words to appear in two different rôles: by themselves, and in propositions.)

From *Tractatus Logico-Philosophicus*. London: Routledge & Kegan Paul, 1961, pp. 7–19. First published in German 1921. By permission of the publisher.

2.0123   If I know an object I also know all its possible occurrences in states of affairs.

(Every one of these possibilities must be part of the nature of the object.)

A new possibility cannot be discovered later.

2.01231 If I am to know an object, though I need not know its external properties, I must know all its internal properties.

2.0124   If all objects are given, then at the same time all *possible* states of affairs are also given.

2.013   Each thing is, as it were, in a space of possible states of affairs. This space I can imagine empty, but I cannot imagine the thing without the space.

2.0131   A spatial object must be situated in infinite space. (A spatial point is an argument-place.)

A speck in the visual field, though it need not be red, must have some colour: it is, so to speak, surrounded by colour-space. Notes must have *some* pitch, objects of the sense of touch *some* degree of hardness, and so on.

2.014   Objects contain the possibility of all situations.

2.0141   The possibility of its occurring in states of affairs is the form of an object.

2.02   Objects are simple.

2.0201   Every statement about complexes can be resolved into a statement about their constituents and into the propositions that describe the complexes completely.

2.021   Objects make up the substance of the world. That is why they cannot be composite.

2.0211   If the world had no substance, then whether a proposition had sense would depend on whether another proposition was true.

2.0212   In that case we could not sketch out any picture of the world (true or false).

2.022   It is obvious that an imagined world, however different it may be from the real one, must have *something* – a form – in common with it.

2.023   Objects are just what constitute this unalterable form.

2.0231   The substance of the world *can* only determine a form, and not any material properties. For it is only by means of propositions that material properties are represented – only by the configuration of objects that they are produced.

2.0232   In a manner of speaking, objects are colourless.

2.0233   If two objects have the same logical form, the only distinction between them, apart from their external properties, is that they are different.

2.02331 Either a thing has properties that nothing else has, in which case we can immediately use a description to distinguish it from the others and refer to it; or, on the other hand, there are several things that have the whole set of their properties in common, in which case it is quite impossible to indicate one of them.

    For if there is nothing to distinguish a thing, I cannot distinguish it, since if I do it will be distinguished after all.

2.024   Substance is what subsists independently of what is the case.

2.025   It is form and content.

2.0251   Space, time and colour (being coloured) are forms of objects.

2.026   There must be objects, if the world is to have an unalterable form.

2.027   Objects, the unalterable, and the subsistent are one and the same.

2.0271   Objects are what is unalterable and subsistent; their configuration is what is changing and unstable.

2.0272   The configuration of objects produces states of affairs.

2.03   In a state of affairs objects fit into one another like the links of a chain.

2.031   In a state of affairs objects stand in a determinate relation to one another.

2.032   The determinate way in which objects are connected in a state of affairs is the structure of the state of affairs.

2.033   Form is the possibility of structure.

2.034   The structure of a fact consists of the structures of states of affairs.

2.04   The totality of existing states of affairs is the world.

2.05   The totality of existing states of affairs also determines which states of affairs do not exist.

2.06   The existence and non-existence of states of affairs is reality.

    (We also call the existence of states of affairs a positive fact, and their non-existence a negative fact.)

2.061   States of affairs are independent of one another.

2.062   From the existence or non-existence of one state of affairs it is impossible to infer the existence or non-existence of another.

2.063   The sum-total of reality is the world.

2.1   We picture facts to ourselves.

2.11   A picture presents a situation in logical space, the existence and non-existence of states of affairs.

2.12   A picture is a model of reality.

2.13   In a picture objects have the elements of the picture corresponding to them.

2.131   In a picture the elements of the picture are the representatives of objects.

2.14   What constitutes a picture is that its elements are related to one another in a determinate way.

2.141   A picture is a fact.

2.15   The fact that the elements of a picture are related to one another in a determinate way represents that things are related to one another in the same way.

    Let us call this connexion of its elements the structure of the picture, and let us call the possibility of this structure the pictorial form of the picture.

2.151   Pictorial form is the possibility that things are related to one another in the same way as the elements of the picture.

2.1511   *That* is how a picture is attached to reality; it reaches right out to it.

2.1512   It is laid against reality like a measure.

2.15121   Only the end-points of the graduating lines actually *touch* the object that is to be measured.

2.1513   So a picture, conceived in this way, also includes the pictorial relationship, which makes it into a picture.

2.1514   The pictorial relationship consists of the correlations of the picture's elements with things.

2.1515   These correlations are, as it were, the feelers of the picture's elements with things.

2.16   If a fact is to be a picture, it must have something in common with what it depicts.

2.161   There must be something identical in a picture and what it depicts, to enable the one to be a picture of the other at all.

2.17   What a picture must have in common with reality, in order to be able to depict it – correctly or incorrectly – in the way it does, is its pictorial form.

2.171   A picture can depict any reality whose form it has.
          A spatial picture can depict anything spatial, a coloured one anything coloured, etc.

2.172   A picture cannot, however, depict its pictorial form: it displays it.

2.173   A picture represents its subject from a position outside it. (Its standpoint is its representational form.) That is why a picture represents its subject correctly or incorrectly.

2.174   A picture cannot, however, place itself outside its representational form.

2.18   What any picture, of whatever form, must have in common with reality, in order to be able to depict it – correctly or incorrectly – in any way at all, is logical form, i.e. the form of reality.

2.181   A picture whose pictorial form is logical form is called a logical picture.

2.182   Every picture is *at the same time* a logical one. (On the other hand, not every picture is, for example, a spatial one.)

2.19   Logical pictures can depict the world.

2.2   A picture has logico-pictorial form in common with what it depicts.

2.201   A picture depicts reality by representing a possibility of existence and of states of affairs.

2.202   A picture represents a possible situation in logical space.

2.203   A picture contains the possibility of the situation that it represents.

2.21   A picture agrees with reality or fails to agree; it is correct or incorrect, true or false.

2.22   What a picture represents it represents independently of its truth or falsity, by means of its pictorial form.

2.221   What a picture represents is its sense.

2.222   The agreement or disagreement of its sense with reality constitutes its truth or falsity.

2.223   In order to tell whether a picture is true or false we must compare it with reality.

2.224   It is impossible to tell from the picture alone whether it is true or false.

2.225   There are no pictures that are true a priori.

Note

1   The decimal numbers assigned to the individual propositions indicate the logical importance of the propositions, the stress laid on them in my exposition. The propositions *n*.1, *n*.2, *n*.3, etc. are comments on proposition no. *n*; the propositions *n.m*1, *n.m*2, etc. are comments on proposition no. *n.m*; and so on.

---

7   Subjectivity in Language[1]

Emile Benveniste

If language is, as they say, the instrument of communication, to what does it owe this property? The question may cause surprise, as does everything that seems to challenge an obvious fact, but it is sometimes useful to require proof of the obvious. Two answers come to mind. The one would be that language is *in fact* employed as the instrument of communication, probably because men have not found a better or more effective way in which to communicate. This amounts to stating what one wishes to understand. One might also think of replying that language has such qualities as make it suited to serve as an instrument; it lends itself to transmitting what I entrust to it – an order, a question, an announcement – and it elicits from the interlocutor a behavior which is adequate each time. Developing a more technical aspect of this idea, one might add that the behavior of language admits of a behaviorist description, in terms of stimulus and response, from which one might draw conclusions as to the intermediary and instrumental nature of language. But is it really language of which we are speaking here? Are we not confusing it with discourse? If we posit that discourse is language put into action, and necessarily between partners, we show amidst the confusion, that we are begging the question, since the nature of this "instrument" is explained by its situation as an "instrument." As for the role of transmission that language plays, one should not fail to observe, on the one

From *Problems in General Linguistics*, trans. Mary Elizabeth Meek. Coral Gables, FL: University of Miami Press, 1971, pp. 223–30. By permission of the publisher.

hand, that this role can devolve upon nonlinguistic means – gestures and mimicry – and, on the other hand, that, in speaking here of an "instrument," we are letting ourselves be deceived by certain processes of transmission which in human societies without exception come after language and imitate its functioning. All systems of signals, rudimentary or complex, are in this situation.

In fact, the comparison of language to an instrument – and it should necessarily be a material instrument for the comparison to even be comprehensible – must fill us with mistrust, as should every simplistic notion about language. To speak of an instrument is to put man and nature in opposition. The pick, the arrow, and the wheel are not in nature. They are fabrications. Language is in the nature of man, and he did not fabricate it. We are always inclined to that naïve concept of a primordial period in which a complete man discovered another one, equally complete, and between the two of them language was worked out little by little. This is pure fiction. We can never get back to man separated from language and we shall never see him inventing it. We shall never get back to man reduced to himself and exercising his wits to conceive of the existence of another. It is a speaking man whom we find in the world, a man speaking to another man, and language provides the very definition of man.

All the characteristics of language, its immaterial nature, its symbolic functioning, its articulated arrangement, the fact that it has content, are in themselves enough to render suspect this comparison of language to an instrument, which tends to dissociate the property of language from man. Certainly in everyday practice the give and take of speaking suggests an exchange, hence a "thing" which we exchange, and speaking seems thus to assume an instrumental or vehicular function which we are quick to hypostasize as an "object." But, once again, this role belongs to the individual act of speech.

Once this function is seen as belonging to the act of speech, it may be asked what predisposition accounts for the fact that the act of speech should have it. In order for speech to be the vehicle of "communication," it must be so enabled by language, of which it is only the actualization. Indeed, it is in language that we must search for the condition of this aptitude. It seems to us that it resides in a property of language barely visible under the evidence that conceals it, which only sketchily can we yet characterize.

It is in and through language that man constitutes himself as a subject, because language alone establishes the concept of "ego" in reality, in its reality which is that of the being.

The "subjectivity" we are discussing here is the capacity of the speaker to posit himself as "subject." It is defined not by the feeling which everyone experiences of being himself (this feeling, to the degree that it can be taken note of, is only a reflection) but as the psychic unity that transcends the totality of the actual experiences it assembles and that makes the permanence of the consciousness. Now we hold that that "subjectivity," whether it is placed in phenomenology or in psychology, as one may wish, is only the emergence in the being of a fundamental property of language. "Ego" is he who *says* "ego." That is where we see the foundation of "subjectivity," which is determined by the linguistic status of "person."

Consciousness of self is only possible if it is experienced by contrast. I use *I* only when I am speaking to someone who will be a *you* in my address. It is this condition of dialogue that is constitutive of *person*, for it implies that reciprocally *I* becomes *you* in the address of the one who in his turn designates himself as *I*. Here we see a principle whose consequences are to spread out in all directions. Language is possible only because each speaker sets himself up as a *subject* by referring to himself as *I* in his discourse. Because of this, *I* posits another person, the one who, being, as he is, completely exterior to "me," becomes my echo to whom I say *you* and who says *you* to me. This polarity of persons is the fundamental condition in language, of which the process of communication, in which we share, is only a mere pragmatic consequence. It is a polarity, moreover, very peculiar in itself, as it offers a type of opposition whose equivalent is encountered nowhere else outside of language. This polarity does not mean either equality or symmetry: "ego" always has a position of transcendence with regard to *you*. Nevertheless, neither of the terms can be conceived of without the other; they are complementary, although according to an "interior/exterior" opposition, and, at the same time, they are reversible. If we seek a parallel to this, we will not find it. The condition of man in language is unique.

And so the old antinomies of "I" and "the other," of the individual and society, fall. It is a duality which it is illegitimate and erroneous to reduce to a single primordial term, whether this unique term be the "I," which must be established in the individual's own consciousness in order to become accessible to that of the fellow human being, or whether it be, on the contrary, society, which as a totality would preexist the individual and from which the individual could only be disengaged gradually, in proportion to his acquisition of self-consciousness. It is in a dialectic reality that will incorporate the two terms and define them by mutual relationship that the linguistic basis of subjectivity is discovered.

But must this basis be linguistic? By what right does language establish the basis of subjectivity?

As a matter of fact, language is responsible for it in all its parts. Language is marked so deeply by the expression of subjectivity that one might ask if it could still function and be called language if it were constructed otherwise. We are of course talking of language in general, not simply of particular languages. But the concordant facts of particular languages give evidence for language. We shall give only a few of the most obvious examples.

The very terms we are using here, *I* and *you*, are not to be taken as figures but as linguistic forms indicating "person." It is a remarkable fact – but who would notice it, since it is so familiar? – that the "personal pronouns" are never missing from among the signs of a language, no matter what its type, epoch, or region may be. A language without the expression of person cannot be imagined. It can only happen that in certain languages, under certain circumstances, these "pronouns" are deliberately omitted; this is the case in most of the Far Eastern societies, in which a convention of politeness imposes the use of periphrases or of special forms between certain groups of individuals in order to replace the direct personal references. But these usages only serve to underline the value of the avoided forms; it is the implicit existence of these pronouns that gives social and cultural value to the substitutes imposed by class relationships.

Now these pronouns are distinguished from all other designations a language articulates in that *they do not refer to a concept or to an individual.*

There is no concept "I" that incorporates all the *I*'s that are uttered at every moment in the mouths of all speakers, in the sense that there is a concept "tree" to which all the individual uses of *tree* refer. The "I," then, does not denominate any lexical entity. Could it then be said that *I* refers to a particular individual? If that were the case, a permanent contradiction would be admitted into language, and anarchy into its use. How could the same term refer indifferently to any individual whatsoever and still at the same time identify him in his individuality? We are in the presence of a class of words, the "personal pronouns," that escape the status of all the other signs of language. Then, what does *I* refer to? To something very peculiar which is exclusively linguistic: *I* refers to the act of individual discourse in which it is pronounced, and by this it designates the speaker. It is a term that cannot be identified except in what we have called elsewhere an instance of discourse and that has only a momentary reference. The reality to which it refers is the reality of the discourse. It is in the instance of discourse in which *I* designates the speaker that the speaker proclaims himself as the "subject." And so it is literally true that the basis of subjectivity is in the exercise of language. If one really thinks about it, one will see that there is no other objective testimony to the identity of the subject except that which he himself thus gives about himself.

Language is so organized that it permits each speaker to *appropriate to himself* an entire language by designating himself as *I.*

The personal pronouns provide the first step in this bringing out of subjectivity in language. Other classes of pronouns that share the same status depend in their turn upon these pronouns. These other classes are the indicators of *deixis,* the demonstratives, adverbs, and adjectives, which organize the spatial and temporal relationships around the "subject" taken as referent: "this, here, now," and their numerous correlatives, "that, yesterday, last year, tomorrow," etc. They have in common the feature of being defined only with respect to the instances of discourse in which they occur, that is, in dependence upon the *I* which is proclaimed in the discourse.

It is easy to see that the domain of subjectivity is further expanded and must take over the expression of temporality. No matter what the type of language, there is everywhere to be observed a certain linguistic organization of the notion of time. It matters little whether this notion is marked in the inflection of the verb or by words of other classes (particles, adverbs, lexical variations, etc.); that is a matter of formal structure. In one way or another, a language always makes a distinction of "tenses"; whether it be a past and a future, separated by a "present," as in French [or English], or, as in various Amerindian languages, of a preterite-present opposed to a future, or a present-future distinguished from a past, these distinctions being in their turn capable of depending on variations of aspect, etc. but the line of separation is always a reference to the "present." Now this "present" in its turn has only a linguistic fact as temporal reference: the coincidence of the event described with the instance of discourse that describes it. The temporal referent of the present can only be internal to the discourse. The *Dictionnaire générale* defines the "present" as "le temps du verbe qui exprime le temps où l'on est." But let us beware of this; there is no other criterion and no other expression by which to indicate "the time at which one is" except to take it as "the time at which one *is speaking*." This is the eternally "present" moment, although it never relates to the same events of an "objective" chronology because it is determined for each speaker by each of the instances of discourse related to it. Linguistic time is *self-referential*. Ultimately, human temporality with all its linguistic apparatus reveals the subjectivity inherent in the very using of language.

Language is accordingly the possibility of subjectivity because it always contains the linguistic forms appropriate to the expression of subjectivity, and discourse provokes the emergence of subjectivity because it consists of discrete instances. In some way language puts forth "empty" forms which each speaker, in the exercise of discourse, appropriates to himself and which he relates to his "person," at the same time defining himself as *I* and a partner as you. The instance of discourse is thus constitutive of all the coordinates that define the subject and of which we have briefly pointed out only the most obvious.

The establishment of "subjectivity" in language creates the category of person – both in language and also, we believe, outside of it as well. Moreover, it has quite varied effects in the very structure of languages, whether it be in the arrangement of the forms or in semantic relationships. Here we must necessarily have particular languages in view in order to illustrate some effects of the change of perspective which "subjectivity" can introduce. We cannot say what the range of the particular phenomena we are pointing out may be in the universe of real languages; for the moment it is less important to delimit them than to reveal them. English provides several convenient examples.

In a general way, when I use the present of a verb with three persons (to use the traditional nomenclature), it seems that the difference in person does not lead to any change of meaning in the conjugated verb form. *I eat, you eat,* and *he eats* have in common and as a constant that the verb form presents a description of an action, attributed respectively and in an identical fashion to "I," "you," and "he." Similarly, *I suffer, you suffer, he suffers* have the description of the same state in common. This gives the impression of being an obvious fact and even the formal alignment in the paradigm of the conjugation implies this.

Now a number of verbs do not have this permanence of meaning in the changing of persons, such as those verbs with which we denote dispositions or mental operations. In saying *I suffer*, I describe my present condition. In saying *I feel (that the weather is going to change)*, I describe an impression which I feel. But what happens if, instead of *I feel (that the weather is going to change)*, I say *I believe (that the weather is going to change)*? The formal symmetry between *I feel* and *I believe* is complete. Is it so for the meaning? Can I consider *I believe* to be a description of myself of the same sort as *I feel*? Am I describing myself believing when I say *I believe (that . . .)*? Surely not. The operation of thought is not at all the object of the utterance; *I believe* (*that* . . .) is equivalent to a mitigated assertion. By saying *I believe* (*that* . . .), I convert into a subjective utterance the fact asserted impersonally, namely, *the weather is going to change*, which is the true proposition.

Let us consider further the following utterances: "You are Mr. X., *I suppose.*" "*I presume* that John received my letter." "He has left the hospital, from which *I conclude* that he is cured." These sentences contain verbs that are verbs of operation: *suppose*, *presume*, and *conclude* are all logical operations. But *suppose*, *presume*, and *conclude*, put in the first person, do not behave the way, for example, *reason* and *reflect* do, which seem, however, to be very close. The forms *I reason* and *I reflect* describe me as reasoning and reflecting. Quite different are *I suppose*, *I presume*, and *I conclude*. In saying *I conclude* (*that* . . .), I do not describe myself as occupied in concluding; what could the activity of "concluding" be? I do not represent myself as being in the process of supposing and presuming when I say *I suppose*, *I presume*. *I conclude* indicates that, in the situation set forth, I extract a relationship of conclusion touching on a given fact. It is this logical relationship which is materialized in a personal verb. Similarly, *I suppose* and *I presume*, are very far from *I suppose* and *I presume*. In *I suppose* and *I presume*, there is an indication of attitude, not a description of an operation. By including *I suppose* and *I presume* in my discourse, I imply that I am taking a certain attitude with regard to the utterance that follows. It will have been noted that all the verbs cited are followed by *that* and a proposition; this proposition is the real utterance, not the personal verb form that governs it. But on the other hand, that personal form is, one might say, the indicator of subjectivity. It gives the assertion that follows the subjective context – doubt, presumption, inference – suited to characterize the attitude of the speaker with respect to the statement he is making. This manifestation of subjectivity does not stand out except in the first person. One can hardly imagine similar verbs in the second person except for taking up an argument again *verbatim*; thus, *you suppose that he has left* is only a way of repeating what "you" has just said: "*I suppose* that he has left." But if one removes the expression of person, leaving only "*he supposes that* . . .," we no longer have, from the point of view of *I* who utters it, anything but a simple statement.

We will perceive the nature of this "subjectivity" even more clearly if we consider the effect on the meaning produced by changing the person of certain verbs of speaking. These are verbs that by their meaning denote an individual act of social import: *swear*, *promise*, *guarantee*, *certify*, with locutional variants like *pledge to* . . ., *commit* (*oneself*) *to* . . . In the social conditions in which a language is exercised, the acts denoted by these verbs are regarded as binding. Now here the difference between the "subjective" utterance and the "nonsubjective" is fully apparent as soon as we notice the nature of the opposition between the "persons" of the verb. We must bear in mind that the "third person" is the form of the verbal (or pronominal) paradigm that does *not* refer to a person because it refers to an object located outside direct address. But it exists and is characterized only by its opposition to the person *I* of the speaker who, in uttering it, situates it as "non-person." Here is its status. The form *he*

. . . takes its value from the fact that it is necessarily part of a discourse uttered by "I."

Now I *swear* is a form of peculiar value in that it places the reality of the oath upon the one who says *I*. This utterance is a *performance*; "to swear" consists exactly of the utterance *I swear*, by which Ego is bound. The utterance *I swear* is the very act which pledges me, not the description of the act that I am performing. In saying *I promise*, *I guarantee*, I am actually making a promise or a guarantee. The consequences (social, judicial, etc.) of my swearing, of my promise, flow from the instance of discourse containing *I swear*, *I promise*. The utterance is identified with the act itself. But this condition is not given in the meaning of the verb, it is the "subjectivity" of discourse which makes it possible. The difference will be seen when *I swear* is replaced by *he swears*. While *I swear* is a pledge, *he swears* is simply a description, on the same plane as *he runs, he smokes*. Here it can be seen that, within the conditions belonging to these expressions, the same verb, according as it is assumed by a "subject" or is placed outside "person," takes on a different value. This is a consequence of the fact that the instance of discourse that contains the verb establishes the act at the same time that it sets up the subject. Hence the act is performed by the instance of the utterance of its "name" (which is "swear") at the same time that the subject is established by the instance of the utterance of its indicator (which is "I").

Many notions in linguistics, perhaps even in psychology, will appear in a different light if one reestablishes them within the framework of discourse. This is language in so far as it is taken over by the man who is speaking and within the condition of intersubjectivity, which alone makes linguistic communication possible.

Note

1   From *Journal de psychologie* 55 (July–September 1958): 267ff.

8   Private Language, Public Languages

Jerry Fodor

The inner is not the outer.

Søren Kierkegaard

Why There Has to Be a Private Language

The discussion thus far might be summarized as follows: One of the essential variables in any theory of higher cognitive processes that we can now imagine is the character of the representation that the organism assigns to features of its environment and to its response options. This is, of course, a very traditional remark to make. Gestalt psychologists, for example, used to emphasize the salience of the *proximal* stimulus in the causation of behavior. Their point was that if you want to know how the organism will respond to an environmental event, you must first find out what properties it takes the event to have.[1] They might, with equal propriety, have emphasized the salience of the proximal response; if you want to know why the organism behaved the way it did, you must first find out what description it intended its behavior to satisfy; what it took itself to be doing. [The previous chapter] sought to make explicit one of the presuppositions of this line of argument: The 'proximal stimulus' is a proximal *representation* of the *distal* stimulus, and the 'proximal response' *stands* for an overt act.

But representation presupposes a medium of representation, and there is no symbolization without symbols. In particular, there is no internal representation without an internal language.

I think, myself, that this conclusion is both true and extremely important. There are, however, ways of construing it which would make it true but not very important. For example, one might argue as follows:

> Of course there is a medium in which we think, and of course it is a language. In fact, it is a natural language: English for English speakers, French for French speakers, Hindi for Hindi speakers, and so on. The argument which seemed to lead to exciting and paradoxical conclusions thus leads only to one's own front door. Your 'traditional remarks' rest, in short, on a traditional confusion. You suppose that natural language is the medium in which we *express* our thoughts; in fact, it is the medium in which we *think* them.

This is a kind of view which has appealed to very many philosophers and psychologists. Indeed, it is appealing, for it allows the theorist both to admit the essential role of computation (and hence of representation) in the

From *The Language of Thought*. Cambridge, MA: Harvard University Press, 1975, pp. 55–64. By permission of the publisher.

production of behavior and to resist the more scarifying implications of the notion of a language of thought. It is, for example, all right for hypothesis formation to be essential to learning, and for hypotheses to presuppose a language to couch them in, so long as the language presupposed is, e.g., English. For English is a representational system to whose existence we are committed independent of our views about cognitive psychology; ask any English speaker. We can, in short, allow that cognitive processes are defined over linguistic objects and we can do so without raising anybody's methodological hackles. All we need to do is assume that the linguistic objects that cognitive processes are defined over are drawn from one of the *public* languages.

The only thing that's wrong with this proposal is that it isn't possible to take it seriously: So far as I can see, the radical consequences of the internal language view will have to be lived with. The obvious (and, I should have thought, sufficient) refutation of the claim that natural languages are the medium of thought is that there are nonverbal organisms that think. I don't propose to quibble about what's to count as thinking, so I shall make the point in terms of the examples discussed in [the previous chapter]. All three of the processes that we examined there – considered action, concept learning, and perceptual integration – are familiar achievements of infrahuman organisms and preverbal children. The least that can be said, therefore, is what we have been saying all along: Computational models of such processes are the only ones we've got. Computational models presuppose representational systems. But the representational systems of preverbal and infrahuman organisms surely cannot be natural languages. So either we abandon such preverbal and infrahuman psychology as we have so far pieced together, or we admit that some thinking, at least, isn't done in English.

Notice that although computation presupposes a representational language, it does *not* presuppose that that language must be one of the ones which function as vehicles of communication between speakers and hearers: e.g., that it must be a natural language. So, on the one hand, there is no internal reason for supposing that our psychology applies only to organisms that talk, and if we do decide to so restrict its application we shall have no model at all for learning, choosing, and perceiving in populations other than fluent human beings. On the other hand, to extend our psychology to infrahuman species is thereby to commit ourselves to cognitive processes mediated by representational systems other than natural languages.

I think many philosophers are unimpressed by these sorts of considerations because they are convinced that it is not a question of fact but, as it were, of linguistic policy whether such psychological predicates as have their paradigmatic applications to fluent human beings ought to be 'extended' to the merely infraverbal. I was once told by a very young philosopher that it is a matter for *decision* whether animals can (can be said to) hear. 'After all,' he said, 'it's *our* word.'

But this sort of conventionalism won't do; the issue isn't whether we ought to be polite to animals. In particular, there are homogeneities between the mental capacities of infraverbal organisms and those of fluent human beings which, so far as anybody knows, are inexplicable except on the assumption that intraverbal psychology is relevantly homogeneous with our psychology.

To take just one example, we remarked in [the previous chapter] that human subjects typically have more trouble mastering disjunctive concepts than they do with conjunctive or negative ones. But we remarked, too, that the notion of the form of a concept needs to be relativized to whatever system of representation the subject employs. For one thing, disjunction is interdefinable with conjunction and negation and, for another, which concepts are disjunctive depends upon which kind terms the vocabulary of the representational system acknowledges. *Color* isn't, I suppose, a disjunctive concept despite the fact that colors come in different colors. Whereas 'red or blue' is a disjunctive concept; i.e., is disjunctively represented in English and, presumably, in whatever system of representation mediates the integration of our visual percepts.

The point is that these remarks apply wholesale to infraverbal concept learning. Animals, too, typically find (what *we* take to be) disjunctive concepts hard to master. We can account for this fact if we assume that the representational system that *they* employ is rele-vantly like the one that *we* employ (e.g., that an animal conditioned to respond positive to either-a-triangle-or-a-square represents the reinforcement contingencies disjunctively, just as the experimenter does).[2] Since no alternative account suggests itself (since, so far as I know, no alternative account has ever been suggested) it would seem to be the behavioral facts, and not our linguistic policies, which require us to hypothesize the relevant homogeneities between our representational system and the ones infraverbal organisms use.[3]

As one might expect, these sorts of issues become critical when we consider the preverbal child learning a first language. The first point to make is that we have no notion at all of how a first language might be learned that does not come down to some version of learning by hypothesis formation and confirmation. This is not surprising since, . . . barring the cases where what is learned is something explicitly taught, we have no notion of how any kind of concept is learned except by hypothesis formation and confirmation. And learning a language L must at least involve learning such concepts as 'sentence of L.'

If, for example, Chomsky is right, then learning a first language involves constructing grammars consonant with some innately specified system of language universals and testing those grammars against a corpus of observed utterances in some order fixed by an innate simplicity metric. And, of course, there must be a language in which the universals, the candidate grammars, and the observed utterances are represented. And, of course, this language cannot be a natural language since, by hypothesis, it is his first language that the child is learning.[4]

In fact, however, for these purposes it doesn't matter whether Chomsky is right, since the same sort of point can be made on the basis of much more modest assumptions about what goes on in language acquisition. I want to discuss this claim in quite considerable detail.

To begin with I am going to take three things for granted: (1) that learning a first language is a matter of hypothesis formation and confirmation in the sense explored in [the previous chapter]; (2) that learning a first language involves at least learning the semantic properties of its predicates; (3) that S learns the semantic properties of P only if S learns some generalization which determines the extension of P (i.e. the set of things that P is true of).

These assumptions are unequally tendentious. Item 1 rests on the arguments reviewed in [the previous chapter]. I take it that item 2 will be granted by anyone who is willing to suppose that there is anything at all to the notion of semantic properties as psychologically real. Item 3 on the other hand is serious; but I shan't argue for it since as will presently become apparent it is assumed primarily for purposes of exposition. Suffice it to remark here that many philosophers have found it plausible that one understands a predicate only if one knows the conditions under which sentences that contain it would be true. But if this is so and if as we have supposed language learning is a matter of testing and confirming hypotheses then among the generalizations about a language that the learner must hypothesize and confirm are some which determine the extensions of the predicates of that language. A generalization that effects such a determination is by stipulation a *truth rule*. I shall henceforth abbreviate all this to 'S learns P only if S learns a truth rule for P.'[5]

Since I propose to work these assumptions very hard, I had better get my caveats in early. There are three. First, though it is, for my purposes, convenient to identify learning the semantic properties of P with learning a truth rule for P, nothing fundamental to the argument I want to give depends on doing so. Readers who object to the identification are free to substitute some other notion of semantic property or to take that notion as unanalyzed. Second, to say that someone has learned a truth rule for a predicate is not to say that he has learned a procedure for determining when the predicate applies, or even that there is such a procedure. Third, if there were anything to dispositional accounts of what is involved in understanding a predicate, we would have an alternative to the theory that learning a predicate involves learning a rule. So the whole discussion will proceed on the assumption that there is, in fact, nothing to be said for dispositional accounts of what is involved in understanding a predicate. I shall expand each of these points at some length before returning to the main argument.

1.   Many philosophers think that truth conditions provide too weak a construal of what we learn when we learn a predicate; e.g., that what we learn must be what sentences containing the predicate entail and are entailed by, not what they materially imply and are materially implied by. I have, in fact, considerable sympathy with such views. But the point I want to stress is that the arguments that follow are entirely neutral so far as those views are concerned. That is, these arguments are neutral vis-à-vis the controversy between extensionalist and intensionalist semantics. If you are an extensionalist, then surely you believe that the semantic properties of a predicate determine its extension. If you are an intensionalist, then presumably you believe that the semantic properties of a predicate determine its *in*tension and that intensions determine extensions. Either way, then, you believe what I have wanted to assume.

Another way of putting it is this: Both intensionalists and extensionalists hold that semantic theories pair object language predicates with their metalinguistic counterparts. Extensionalists hold that the critical condition on the paired expressions is coextensivity. Intensionalists hold that the critical condition is logical equivalence or, perhaps, synonymy. But if either of these latter conditions is satisfied, then the former condition is satisfied too. So, once again, how the extensionalist/intensionalist question is resolved doesn't matter for the purposes I have in mind.

There are, however, philosophers who hold not only that the semantic properties of a predicate don't determine its *in*tension but that they don't determine its *ex*tension either. Such philosophers claim (very roughly) that what we know about the meanings of predicates determine at most their *putative* extensions, but that whether the putative extension of a predicate is in fact its *real* extension is, in the long run, at the mercy of empirical discoveries.

Thus, Putnam argues that when we learn 'gold,' 'cat,' 'water,' etc. we learn socially accepted stereotypes such that it is *reasonable to believe* of things that conform to the stereotypes that they satisfy the predicates. But what it is reasonable to believe need not prove, in the long run, to be true. Perhaps there was a time when only liquid water was known to be water. Perhaps it was then discovered that ice is water in a solid state. (Surely this is ontogenetically plausible even if it's a historical fairy tale.) To discover this would be to discover something about what the extension of 'water' *really* is (viz., that ice is in it). But if it is an empirical discovery that ice is water, then it is hard to see how the fact that 'water' applies to ice could have been determined, in any substantive sense, by what one learns when one learns what 'water' means. And if that is right, then it is hard to see how learning what 'water' means could involve learning something that determines the extension of 'water' in advance of such discoveries. In short, on this view, either the semantic properties of a word aren't what you learn when you learn the word, or the semantic properties of a word don't determine its extension.

I don't want to become involved in assessing these suggestions because, right or wrong, they are largely irrelevant to the main points that I shall make. I will argue, primarily, that you cannot learn a language whose terms express semantic properties not expressed by the terms of some language you are already able to use. In formulating this argument, it is convenient to assume that the semantic properties expressed by a predicate are those which determine its extension, since, whatever its faults may be, that assumption at least yields a sharp sense of identity of semantic properties (two predicates have the same semantic properties if they apply to the same set of things). If, however, that assumption fails, then the same sort of argument can be constructed given any other notion of semantic property, so long as its semantic properties are what you learn when you learn a word. If, for example, what you learn when you learn P is (only) that it would be reasonable to believe that P applies iff S, then, according to my argument, in order to learn the language containing P you must already be able to use some (other) language which contains some (other) term such that it would be reasonable to believe that it applies iff it would be reasonable to believe that P applies. And so on, *mutatis mutandis*, for other construals of *semantic property*.

I shall, then, continue to do what it is convenient to do: take the extension of a predicate to be what its semantic properties primarily determine. But only on the understanding that alternative readings of 'semantic property' may be substituted ad lib.

2. To endorse the view that learning a predicate involves learning a generalization which determines its extension is not to subscribe to any species of verificationism, though the literature has exhibited an occasional tendency to confuse the two doctrines.

Consider the English predicate 'is a chair.' The present view is, roughly, that no one has mastered that predicate unless he has learned that it falls under some such generalization as ⌜*y is a chair*⌝ is true iff Gx. (For a discussion of the notation, see note 5.) But, of course, it does not follow that someone who knows what 'is a chair' means is therefore in command of a general procedure for sorting stimuli into chairs and non-chairs. That *would* follow only on the added assumption that he has a general procedure for sorting stimuli into those which do, and those which do not, satisfy G. But that assumption is no part of the view that learning a language involves learning truth rules for its predicates.

If, e.g., it is true that 'chair' means 'portable seat for one,' then it is plausible that no one has mastered 'is a chair' unless he has learned that it falls under the truth rule ⌜*y is a chair*⌝ is true iff x is a portable seat for one.' But someone might well know this about 'is a chair' and still not be able to tell about some given object (or, for that matter, about any object) whether or not it is a chair. He would be in this situation if, e.g., his way of telling whether a thing is a chair is to find out whether it satisfies the right-hand side of the truth rule, and if he is unable to tell about this (or any) thing whether it is a portable seat for one.

I make these remarks in light of Wittgenstein's observation that many (perhaps all) ordinary language predicates are open-textured; e.g., that there are indefinitely many objects about which we cannot tell whether they are chairs; not just because the lighting is bad or some of the facts aren't in, but because 'is a chair' is, as it were, undefined for objects of those kinds, so that whether they are chairs isn't a question of fact at all (cf. the chair (sic) made of soap bubbles; the packing case that is used as a chair, etc.). This is all true and well taken, but the present point is that it doesn't prejudice the notion that learning truth rules is essential to language learning, or the point that truth rules are expressed by biconditional formulae. All it shows is that if the truth condition on 'is a chair' is expressed by 'is a portable seat for one,' then 'portable seat for one' must be open-textured, undefined, etc., for just those cases where 'is a chair' is.

One can get into no end of trouble by confusing this point. For example, Dreyfus,[6] if I understand him correctly, appears to endorse the following argument against the possibility of machine models of human linguistic capacities: (a) Machine models would presumably employ rules to express the extensions of the predicates they use. (b) Such rules would presumably be biconditionals (e.g., truth rules). But (c) Wittgenstein has shown that the extension of natural language predicates cannot be expressed by such rules because such predicates are inherently fuzzy-edged. So (d) people can't be modeled by machines and (e) a fortiori, people can't *be* machines.

But Wittgenstein showed no such thing. The most that can be inferred from the existence of open texture is that if a formula expresses the truth conditions on P, then its truth value must be indeterminate wherever the truth value of P is indeterminate. To put it slightly differently, if a machine simulates a speaker's use of a predicate, then (the machine ought to be unable to determine whether the predicate applies) iff (the speaker is unable to determine whether the predicate applies). But there is nothing at all in the notion of machines as rule-following devices that suggests that that condition cannot be met. Correspondingly, there is nothing in the notion that people's use of language is rule governed which suggests that every predicate in a language must have a determinate applicability to every object of predication.

3. I have assumed not only that learning a predicate involves learning something which determines its extension, but also that 'learning something which determines the extension of P' should be analyzed as learning that P falls under a certain rule (viz., a truth rule). Now, someone could accept the first assumption while rejecting the second: e.g., by postulating some sort of behavioral analysis of 'S knows the extension of P.' Equivalently for these purposes he could accept both assumptions and postulate a dispositional analysis of knowing a rule. Thus, if the truth rule for P is ⌜Py⌝ is true iff Gx,' then to know the truth rule might be equated with having a disposition to say P just in cases where G applies. Similarly, learning the truth conditions on P would be a matter (not of hypothesizing and confirming that the corresponding truth rule applies, but just) of having one's response dispositions appropriately shaped.

A number of philosophers who ought to know better do, apparently, accept such views. Nevertheless, I shall not bother running through the standard objections since it seems to me that if *anything* is clear it is that understanding a word (predicate, sentence, language) isn't a matter of how one behaves or how one is disposed to behave. Behavior, and behavioral disposition, are determined by the interactions of a variety of psychological variables (what one believes, what one wants, what one remembers, what one is attending to, etc.). Hence, in general, any behavior whatever is compatible with understanding, or failing to understand, any predicate whatever. Pay me enough and I will stand on my head iff you say 'chair.' But I know what 'is a chair' means all the same.

So much for caveats. Now I want to draw the moral. Learning a language (including, of course, a first language) involves learning what the predicates of the language mean. Learning what the predicates of a language mean involves learning a determination of the extension of these predicates. Learning a determination of the extension of the predicates involves learning that they fall under certain rules (i.e., truth rules). But one cannot learn that P falls under R unless one has a language in which P and R can be represented. So one cannot learn a language unless one has a language. In particular, one cannot learn a first language unless one already has a system capable of representing the predicates in that language *and their extensions*. And, on pain of circularity, that system cannot be the language that is being learned. But first languages *are* learned. Hence, at least some cognitive operations are carried out in languages other than natural languages.

Wittgenstein, commenting upon some views of Augustine's, says:

> Augustine describes the learning of human languages as if the child came into a strange country and did not understand the language of the country;[7] that is, as if it already had a language, only not this one. Or again, as if the child could already *think*, only not yet speak. And 'think' would here mean something like 'talk to itself.'[8]

Wittgenstein apparently takes it that such a view is transparently absurd. But the argument that I just sketched suggests, on the contrary, that Augustine was precisely and demonstrably right and that seeing that he was is prerequisite to any serious attempts to understand how first languages are learned.

Notes

1 Not only because behavior is sometimes based on false beliefs (e.g., on misassignments of properties to the stimulus) but also because the behaviorally salient properties of the stimulus are a *selection* from the properties that belong to it: of all the indefinitely many properties the stimulus *does* have, only those can be behaviorally salient which the organism *represents* the stimulus as having. That is why, in practice, it is usually only by attending to the behavior of the organism that we can tell what the (proximal) stimulus is.

2 For an experimental demonstration that preverbal human infants have differential difficulties with disjunctive contingencies of reinforcement, see J. A. Fodor, M. Garrett and S. L. Brill, 'Pe, ka, pu: the perception of speech sounds in prelinguistic infants,' *MIT Quarterly Progress Report*, Jan. 1975.

3 It is worth emphasizing that this example is in no way special. The widespread homogeneity of human and infrahuman mental processes has been the main theme of psychological theorizing since Darwin. The interesting, exciting, and exceptional cases are, in fact, the ones where interspecific differences emerge. Thus, for example, there are situations in which infrahuman organisms treat as homogeneous stimuli which *we* take to be disjunctive. It is very difficult to train *octopus* to discriminate diagonal lines which differ (only) in left-right orientation. The natural assumption is that the representational system the animal employs does not distinguish between (i.e., assigns identical representations to) mirror images. For ingenious elaboration see Sutherland, 'Theories of shape discrimination in octopus,' *Nature*, 186 (1960), 840–4.

4 Chomsky's argument infers the innateness of linguistic information (and hence of the representational system in which it is couched) from the universality of language structure across historically unrelated communities and from the complexity of the information the child must master if he is to become fluent. Versions of this argument can be found in Katz, *The Philosophy of Language* (New York: Harper, 1966), and Vendler, *Res Cogitans* (Ithaca, NY: Cornell University Press, 1972). I think it is a good argument, though it leaves a number of questions pending. Until we know which features of language are universal, it gives us no way of telling which aspects of

the child's representation of his native language are innate. And: *How* complex does learning have to be for the hypothesis of a task-specific innate contribution to be plausible?

The considerations I shall be developing seek to delineate aspects of the child's innate contribution to language learning in ways that avoid these sorts of difficulties. But I shall be assuming what Chomsky et al. have always assumed and what Vendler has made explicit: There is an analogy between learning a second language on the basis of a first and learning a first language on the basis of an innate endowment. In either case, some previously available representational system must be exploited to formulate the generalizations that structure the system that is being learned. Out of nothing nothing comes.

5 I shall, throughout, employ the following format for truth rules. Where P is a predicate in the language to be learned, T is a truth rule for P iff (a) it is of the same form as F, and (b) all of its *substitution instances are true*.

$$F: \ulcorner P_y \urcorner \text{ is true (in L) iff } x \text{ is } G$$

The substitution instances of F are the formulae obtained by:

1. Replacing the angles by quotes. (In effect, variables in angles are taken to range over the expressions of the object language.)
2. Replacing 'P_y' by a sentence whose predicate is P and whose subject is a name or other referring expression.
3. Replacing 'x' by an expression which designates the individual referred to by the subject of the quoted sentence. (This condition yields a nonsyntactic notion of *substitution instance* since whether one formula bears that relation to another will depend, in part, on what their referring expressions refer to. This is, however, both convenient and harmless for our purposes.)

So, suppose that L is English and P is the predicate 'is a philosopher.' Then, a plausible truth rule for P is $\ulcorner y$ *is a philosopher*$\urcorner$ *is true iff x is a philosopher*. Substitution instances of this truth rule would include *'Fred is a philosopher' is true iff Fred is a philosopher; 'the man on the corner is a philosopher' is true iff the man on the corner is a philosopher; and 'Fred is a philosopher' is true iff the man on the corner is a philosopher* (assuming Fred is the man on the corner) . . . etc.

Of course, nothing requires that the expression which forms the right-hand side of a truth rule (or its instances) should be drawn from the same language as the sentence quoted on the left. On the contrary, we shall see that that assumption is quite *im*plausible when *learning* truth rules is assumed to be involved in learning a language. (For a useful introduction to the general program of analyzing meaning in terms of truth, see D. Davidson, 'Truth and meaning,' *Synthese*, 17 (1967), 304–23.)

6 *What Computers Can't Do: A Critique of Artificial Reason* (New York: Harper, 1972).

7 For example, Augustine represents the child as trying to figure out what the adults are referring to when they use the referring expressions of their language. Wittgenstein's point is that this picture could make sense only on the assumption that the child has access to a linguistic system in which the 'figuring out' is carried on.

9 The Mark of Gender

Monique Wittig

The mark of gender, according to grammarians, concerns substantives. They talk about it in terms of function. If they question its meaning, they may joke about it, calling gender a "fictive sex." It is thus that English when compared to French has the reputation of being almost genderless, while French passes for a very gendered language. It is true that, strictly speaking, English does not apply the mark of gender to inanimate objects, to things or nonhuman beings. But as far as the categories of the person are concerned, both languages are bearers of gender to the same extent. Both indeed give way to a primitive ontological concept that enforces in language a division of beings into sexes. The "fictive sex" of nouns or other neuter gender are only accidental developments of this first principle and as such they are relatively harmless.

The manifestation of gender that is identical in English and in French takes place in the dimension of the person. It does not concern only grammarians, although it is a lexical manifestation. As an ontological concept that deals with the nature of Being, along with a whole nebula of other primitive concepts belonging to the same line of thought, gender seems to belong primarily to philosophy. Its *raison d'être* is never questioned in grammar, whose role is to describe forms and functions, not to find a justification for them. It is no longer questioned in philosophy, though, because it belongs to that body of self-evident concepts without which philosophers believe they cannot develop a line of reasoning and which for them go without saying, for they exist prior to any thought, any social order, in nature. So they call gender the lexical delegation of "natural beings," their symbol. Being aware that the notion of gender is not as innocuous as it appears, American feminists use gender as a sociological category, making clear that there is nothing natural about this notion, as sexes have been artificially constructed into political categories – categories of oppression. They have extrapolated the term *gender* from grammar and they tend to superimpose it on the notion of sex. And they are right insofar as gender is the linguistic index of the political opposition between the sexes and of the domination of women. In the same way as sex, man and woman, gender, as a concept, is instrumental in the political discourse of the social contract as heterosexual.

In modern theory, even in the assumptions of disciplines exclusively concerned with language, one remains within the classical division of the concrete world on the one hand, and the abstract one on the other. Physical or social reality and language are disconnected. Abstraction, symbols, signs do not belong to the real. There is on one side the real, the referent, and on the other side language. It is as though the relation to language were a relation of function only and not one of transformation. There is sometimes a confusion between signified and referent, so that they are even used indifferently in certain critical works. Or there is a reduction of the signified to a series of messages, with relays of the referent remaining the only support of the meaning. Among linguists, the Russian Bakhtin, a contemporary of the Russian Formalists whose work has at last been translated, is the only one who seems to me to have a strictly materialist approach to language. In sociolinguistics, there are several developments in this direction, mostly among feminists.[1]

I say that even abstract philosophical categories act upon the real as social. Language casts sheaves of reality upon the social body, stamping it and violently shaping it. For example, the bodies of social actors are fashioned by abstract language as well as by nonabstract language. For there is a plasticity of the real to language: language has a plastic action upon the real. According to Sande Zeig, social gestures are the result of this phenomenon.[2]

About gender, then, it is not only important to dislodge from grammar and linguistics a sociological category that does not speak its name. It is also very important to consider how gender works in language, how gender works upon language, before considering how it works from there upon its users.

Gender takes place in a category of language that is totally unlike any other and which is called the personal pronoun. Personal pronouns are the only linguistic instances that designate the locutors in discourse and their different and successive situations in relationship to that discourse. As such, they are also the pathways and the means of entrance into language. And it is in this sense – that they represent persons – that they interest us here. It is without justification of any kind, without questioning, that personal pronouns somehow engineer gender all through language, taking it along with them quite naturally, so to speak, in any kind of talk, parley, or philosophical treatise. And although they are instrumental in activating the notion of gender, they pass unnoticed. Not being gender-marked themselves in their subjective form (except in one case), they can support the notion of gender while they seem to fulfill another function. In principle, pronouns mark the opposition of gender only in the third person and are not gender bearers, per se, in the other persons. Thus, it is as though gender does not affect them, is not part of their structure, but only a detail in their associated forms. But, in reality, as soon as there is a locutor in discourse, as soon as there is an 'I,' gender manifests itself. There is a kind of suspension of the grammatical form. A direct interpellation of the locutor occurs. The locutor is called upon in person. The locutor intervenes, in the order of the pronouns, without mediation, in *its proper sex* – that is, when the locutor is a sociological woman. One knows that, in French, with *je* ('I'), one must mark the gender as soon as one uses it in relation to past participles and adjectives. In English, where the same kind of obligation does not exist, a locutor, when a sociological woman, must in one way or another, that is, with a certain number of clauses, make her sex public. For gender is the enforcement of sex in language, working in the same way as the declaration of sex in civil status. Gender is not confined within the third person, and the mention of sex in language is not a treatment reserved for the third person. Sex, under the name of gender, permeates the whole body of language and forces every locutor, if she belongs to the oppressed sex, to proclaim it in her speech, that is, to appear in language under her proper physical form and not under the abstract form, which every male locutor has the unquestioned right to use. The abstract form, the general, the universal, this is what the so-called masculine gender means, for the class of men have appropriated the universal for themselves. One must understand that men are not born with a faculty for the universal and that women are not reduced at birth to the particular. The universal has been, and is continually, at every moment, appropriated by men. It does not happen by magic, it must be done. It is an act, a criminal act, perpetrated by one class against another. It is an act carried out at the level of concepts, philosophy, politics. And gender by enforcing upon women a particular category represents a measure of domination. Gender is very harmful to women in the exercise of language. But there is more. Gender is ontologically a total impossibility. For when one becomes a locutor, when one says 'I' and, in so doing, reappropriates language as a whole,[3] proceeding from oneself alone, with the tremendous power to use all language, it is then and there, according to linguists and philosophers, that the supreme act of subjectivity, the advent of subjectivity into consciousness, occurs. It is when starting to speak that one becomes 'I'. This act – the becoming of *the* subject through the exercise of language and through locution – in order to be real, implies that the locutor be an absolute subject. For a relative subject is inconceivable, a relative subject could not speak at all. I mean that in spite of the harsh law of gender and its enforcement upon women, no woman can say 'I' without being for herself a total subject – that is, ungendered, universal, whole. Or, failing this, she is condemned to what I call parrot speech (slaves echoing their masters' talk). Language as a whole gives everyone the same power of becoming an absolute subject through its exercise. But gender, an element of language, works upon this ontological fact to annul it as far as women are concerned and corresponds to a constant attempt to strip them of the most precious thing for a human being – subjectivity. Gender is an ontological impossibility because it tries to accomplish the division of Being. But Being as being is not divided. God or Man as being are One and whole. So what is this divided Being introduced into language through gender? It is an impossible Being, it is a Being that does not exist, an ontological joke, a conceptual maneuver to wrest from women what belongs to them by right: conceiving of oneself as a total subject through the exercise of language. The result of the imposition of gender, acting as a denial at the very moment when one speaks, is to deprive women of the authority of speech, and to force them to make their entrance in a crablike way, particularizing themselves and apologizing profusely. The result is to deny them any claim to the abstract, philosophical, political discourses that give shape to the social body. Gender then must be destroyed. The possibility of its destruction is given through the very exercise of language. For each time I say 'I', I reorganize the world from my point of view and through abstraction I lay claim to universality. This fact holds true for every locutor.

Notes

1   Colette Guillaumin, "The Question of Difference," *Feminist Issues* 2, no. 1 (1982); "The Masculine: Denotations/Connotations," *Feminist Issues* 5, no. 1 (Spring 1985); Nicole-Claude Mathieu, "Masculinity/Femininity," *Feminist Issues* 1, no. 1 (Summer 1980); "Biological Paternity, Social Maternity," *Feminist Issues* 4, no. 1 (Spring 1984).
2   Sande Zeig, "The Actor as Activator," *Feminist Issues* 5, no. 1 (Spring 1985).
3   Cf. Emile Benveniste, *Problems in General Linguistics* (Coral Gables, FL: University of Miami Press, 1971).

PART TWO

MEANING:
HOW DO WORDS GET THEIR SENSE?

Introduction

One of the most enduring puzzles in philosophy of language is the nature of meaning. How can a word point to an object beyond itself? How can a sound or mark have a sense unrelated to its acoustic or written characteristics? Smoke may "mean" fire, but this is because we regularly observe a connection between two physical phenomena, a connection that we are able to explain causally. In contrast, linguistic signs are "nonnatural," indicating something other than themselves through no apparent physical means. Romantics like Rousseau might emphasize the onomatopoiesis of expressive language, logicians like Frege might look to linguistic structure as the form of a proposition, but much of what is said is neither logical nor poetic. Nor does it seem that reference to private ideas can help. Meanings are shared, common to the speakers of a language. Ideas are not. As beings necessarily situated in space and time, we see objects from unique perspectives which make meaning a curious mix of the personal and social. I am the one who means, but what I mean is not only of my own making because if it were I would not be understood.

Meaning has to be common to speakers. But how is that possible? For Plato, a word like "justice" has meaning because it represents a form or essence of justice that is not specific to any speaker but that transcends language. When words are combined and their forms fit, larger units of meaning are created. But once Platonic forms and essences are rejected, there seems to be nothing left to give stable meanings to general terms but personal and indeterminate ideas. Alternatively, if meaning is only in relations internal to language, how can language have any reference to what is not linguistic?

This is the problem addressed by Frege in the classic paper "On Sense and Meaning," which opens this section. In logic, two names for the same object should be substitutable one for the other without change in the truth value of the sentences in which they appear. Nevertheless, in many cases the substitution of a referentially equivalent phrase does affect the truth and falsity of a sentence. A stubborn and logically troublesome residue of "sense," or "mode of presentation," persists and even seems necessary if words are to have a determinate reference and a sentence is to have a truth value. A "sense" seems to lie "in between" an object talked about and an individual's idea of that object, mediating between subjective impression and common reference. Frege argues, however, that these "senses" should not be confused with "ideas" in any "individual mind." Instead, the "sense" of a word is part of a "common store of thoughts transmitted from one generation to another."

"Senses," however, are constantly in danger of reverting to the subjective or the fanciful. In the 1930s, as German metaphysical philosophy mutated into totalitarian ideology and Nazi science began its descent into abuse and horror, the power of words to mystify, befuddle, or cover up the truth became more and more evident. The excesses of Nazi propaganda and idealist philosophy motivated a group of crusading scientists, logicians, and philosophers to promote a new, more rigorous "positivist" theory of meaning. This approach is explained in the excerpt from A. J. Ayer's *Language, Truth and Logic*.

Expressive language, as Ayer summarizes the positivist position, may have a place in religion, ethics, or poetry, but the language of logically ordered empirical science, the only language that can be true or false, is the only language with meaning. The meaning of a term is what it takes to "verify" its application. If the term is not, at least in principle, verifiable, it has no meaning. Others, like Rudolf Carnap, added to the verification theory of meaning updated versions of mathematical logic to provide a well-founded, well-structured architecture for scientific theory that was to guard against the intrusion of religious, mystical, or emotional content.

In the meantime, Wittgenstein, whose *Tractatus* had seemed to many positivists to be the most elegant expression of their point of view, was in the process of making a turn-about in thinking. Here, in an excerpt from a later work, *Philosophical Investigations*, he claims that his early view was mistaken. Words do not have meaning only in that they represent or mirror facts. The uses of words are many, and those varied uses give words meaning. In his new theory of "meaning as use," there are several innovations. First, attention is no longer only on forms of language and the speakers of language. Wittgenstein situates meaning within "forms of life," arguing that language has no sense apart from the social context of its use. Meaning cannot be "private" because there is no way to give common names to private ideas. Meanings cannot be internal to language because formal relations between linguistic elements are by themselves meaningless. Common meaning can only be established in human activities that fix the meaning of words in the way "language games" might be used to teach children new terms.

Second, Wittgenstein points to the essential messiness of meaning. The "sense" that determines the objects to which a predicate can apply is not exact; instead, objects are grouped under concepts according to shifting family resemblances that do not have the rigid determining characteristics necessary for logical inferences.

Several times in the *Investigations* Wittgenstein suggests that linguistic expression might have evolved out of natural vocal or gestural expression. In her "Biosemantics" Ruth Millikan further develops this possibility. She adopts a "quasi-normative" biological function as the basis for a theory of meaning that demystifies meaning and preserves realism. Again language is seen as on a continuum with other animal behavior. On this view, the basis for meaning is neither in semantic structure, nor in a speaker's "ideas," or intentions, but in the "stabilizing" evolutionary function served by particular uses of language. The meaning of a sentence is not the stimulus that provokes it, or what justifies it, but the ways that a sentence relates to the world so as to promote survival.

Millikan makes clear the close connection between theories of meaning and theories of knowledge. A foundational theory of meaning that bases meaning either on logical relations internal to language or in an individual's "sense data" must end in skepticism. When meaning is seen as a biological function, however, language's ties with reality are restored along with the possibility of a theory of truth as "correspondence" with reality.

Connections between language and reality are also the concern of Merrill and Jaakko Hintikka in a ground-breaking article that appeared in one of the first collections of contemporary feminist philosophy, *Discovering Reality*. The Hintikkas argue that the extensional view of meaning – the view that the meaning of a concept is the "extension" of that concept – represents only one way to understand the way individual things are named and characterized in language. Drawing on psychological studies of female and male behavior, they point out that identifying an individual as a discrete autonomous unit may be more natural for men than for women. The semantic approach requires that one be able to identify individuals that make up an extension in this existing world and also in "possible worlds." Among other things, this is because we not only talk of what is and was, but also of what would have been, or might yet be. But, argue the Hintikkas, the identification of similar and discrete individual objects in possible worlds that is necessary in truth-theoretic extensional semantics represents only one way of picking out individuals. Another way, more natural to women than to men, would be to look for relational characteristics. The Hintikkas hint at some of the larger implications of such a finding. Not only may men and women use and understand language differently, but if masculine rather than feminine styles of thinking dominate in philosophizing about language, results may be skewed.

10   On Sense and Meaning

Gottlob Frege

Equality[1] gives rise to challenging questions which are not altogether easy to answer. Is it a relation? A relation between objects, or between names or signs of objects? In my *Begriffsschrift*[2] I assumed the latter. The reasons which seem to favour this are the following: $a = a$ and $a = b$ are obviously statements of differing cognitive value; $a = a$ holds *a priori* and, according to Kant, is to be labelled analytic, while statements of the form $a = b$ often contain very valuable extensions of our knowledge and cannot always be established *a priori*. The discovery that the rising sun is not new every morning, but always the same, was one of the most fertile astronomical discoveries. Even to-day the reidentification of a small planet or a comet is not always a matter of course. Now if we were to regard equality as a relation between that which the names 'a' and 'b' designate, it would seem that $a = b$ could not differ from $a = a$ (i.e. provided $a = b$ is true). A relation would thereby be expressed of a thing to itself, and indeed one in which each thing stands to itself but to no other thing. What we apparently want to state by $a = b$ is that the signs or names 'a' and 'b' designate the same thing, so that those signs themselves would be under discussion; a relation between them would be asserted. But this relation would hold between the names or signs only in so far as they named or designated something. It would be mediated by the connexion of each of the two signs with the same designated thing. But this is arbitrary. Nobody can be forbidden to use any arbitrarily producible event or object as a sign for something. In that case the sentence $a = b$ would no longer refer to the subject matter, but only to its mode of designation; we would express no proper knowledge by its means. But in many cases this is just what we want to do. If the sign 'a' is distinguished from the sign 'b' only as an object (here, by means of its shape), not as a sign (i.e. not by the manner in which it designates something), the cognitive value of $a = a$ becomes essentially equal to that of $a = b$, provided $a = b$ is true. A difference can arise only if the difference between the signs corresponds to a difference in the mode of presentation of the thing designated. Let a, b, c be the lines connecting the vertices of a triangle with the midpoints of the opposite sides. The point of intersection of a and b is then the same as the point of intersection of b and c. So we have different designations for the same point, and these names ('point of intersection of a and b', 'point of intersection of b and c') likewise indicate the mode of presentation; and hence the statement contains actual knowledge.

It is natural, now, to think of there being connected with a sign (name, com-

From *Translations from the Philosophical Writings of Gottlob Frege*, trans. Max Black, 3rd edn. Oxford: Blackwell, 1980, pp. 56–63. First published 1892. By permission of the publisher.

bination of words, written mark), besides that which the sign designates, which may be called the meaning of the sign, also what I should like to call the *sense* of the sign, wherein the mode of presentation is contained. In our example, accordingly, the meaning of the expressions 'the point of intersection of a and b' and 'the point of intersection of b and c' would be the same, but not their sense. The meaning of 'evening star' would be the same as that of 'morning star', but not the sense.

It is clear from the context that by sign and name I have here understood any designation figuring as a proper name, which thus has as its meaning a definite object (this word taken in the widest range), but not a concept or a relation, which shall be discussed further in another article.[3] The designation of a single object can also consist of several words or other signs. For brevity, let every such designation be called a proper name.

The sense of a proper name is grasped by everybody who is sufficiently familiar with the language or totality of designations to which it belongs;[4] but this serves to illuminate only a single aspect of the thing meant, supposing it to have one. Comprehensive knowledge of the thing meant would require us to be able to say immediately whether any given sense attaches to it. To such knowledge we never attain.

The regular connexion between a sign, its sense, and what it means is of such a kind that to the sign there corresponds a definite sense and to that in turn a definite thing meant, while to a given thing meant (an object) there does not belong only a single sign. The same sense has different expressions in different languages or even in the same language. To be sure, exceptions to this regular behaviour occur. To every expression belonging to a complete totality of signs, there should certainly correspond a definite sense; but natural languages often do not satisfy this condition, and one must be content if the same word has the same sense in the same context. It may perhaps be granted that every grammatically well-formed expression figuring as a proper name always has a sense. But this is not to say that to the sense there also corresponds a thing meant. The words 'celestial body most distant from the Earth' have a sense, but it is very doubtful if there is also a thing they mean. The expression 'the least rapidly convergent series' has a sense but demonstrably there is nothing it means, since for every given convergent series, another convergent, but less rapidly convergent, series can be found. In grasping a sense, one is not certainly assured of meaning anything.

If words are used in the ordinary way, what one intends to speak of is what they mean. It can also happen, however, that one wishes to talk about the words themselves or their sense. This happens, for instance, when the words of another are quoted. One's own words then first designate words of the other speaker, and only the latter have their usual meaning. We then have signs of signs. In writing, the words are in this case enclosed in quotation marks. Accordingly, a word standing between quotation marks must not be taken as having its ordinary meaning.

In order to speak of the sense of an expression 'A' one may simply use the phrase 'the sense of the expression "A"'. In indirect speech one talks about the sense, e.g., of another person's remarks. It is quite clear that in this way of speaking words do not have their customary meaning but designate what is usually their sense. In order to have a short expression, we will say: In indirect speech, words are used *indirectly* or have their *indirect* meaning. We distinguish accordingly the *customary* from the *indirect* meaning of a word; and its *customary* sense from its *indirect* sense. The indirect meaning of a word is accordingly its customary sense. Such exceptions must always be borne in mind if the mode of connexion between sign, sense, and meaning in particular cases is to be correctly understood.

The meaning and sense of a sign are to be distinguished from the associated idea. If what a sign means is an object perceivable by the senses, my idea of it is an internal image,[5] arising from memories of sense impressions which I have had and acts, both internal and external, which I have performed. Such an idea is often imbued with feeling; the clarity of its separate parts varies and oscillates. The same sense is not always connected, even in the same man, with the same idea. The idea is subjective: one man's idea is not that of another. There result, as a matter of course, a variety of differences in the ideas associated with the same sense. A painter, a horseman, and a zoologist will probably connect different ideas with the name 'Bucephalus'. This constitutes an essential distinction between the idea and the sign's sense, which may be the common property of many people and therefore is not a part or a mode of the individual mind. For one can hardly deny that mankind has a common store of thoughts which is transmitted from one generation to another.[6]

In the light of this, one need have no scruples in speaking simply of *the* sense, whereas in the case of an idea one must, strictly speaking, add whom it belongs to and at what time. It might perhaps be said: Just as one man connects this idea, and another that idea, with the same word, so also one man can associate this sense and another that sense. But there still remains a difference in the mode of connexion. They are not prevented from grasping the same sense; but they cannot have the same idea. *Si duo idem faciunt, non est idem.* If two persons picture the same thing, each still has his own idea. It is indeed sometimes possible to establish differences in the ideas, or even in the sensations, of different men; but an exact comparison is not possible, because we cannot have both ideas together in the same consciousness.

The meaning of a proper name is the object itself which we designate by using it; the idea, which we have in that case is wholly subjective; in between lies the sense, which is indeed no longer subjective like the idea, but is yet not the object itself. The following analogy will perhaps clarify these relationships. Somebody observes the Moon through a telescope. I compare the Moon itself to the meaning; it is the object of the observation mediated by the real image projected by the object glass in the interior of the telescope, and by the retinal image of the observer. The former I compare to the sense, the latter is like the idea or experience. The optical image in the telescope is indeed one-sided and dependent upon the standpoint of observation; but it is still objective, inasmuch as it can be used by several observers. At any rate it could be arranged for several to use it simultaneously. But each one would have his own retinal image. On account of the diverse shapes of the observers' eyes, even a geometrical congruence could hardly be achieved, and an actual coincidence would be out of the question. This analogy might be developed still further, by assuming A's retinal image made visible to B; or A might also see his own retinal image in a mirror. In this way we might perhaps show how an idea can itself be taken as an object, but as such is not for the observer what it directly is for the person having the idea. But to pursue this would take us too far afield.

We can now recognize three levels of difference between words, expressions, or whole sentences. The difference may concern at most the ideas, or the sense but not the meaning, or, finally, the meaning as well. With respect to the first level, it is to be noted that, on account of the uncertain connexion of ideas with words, a difference may hold for one person, which another does not find. The difference between a translation and the original text should properly not overstep the first level. To the possible differences here belong also the colouring and shading which poetic eloquence seeks to give to the sense. Such colouring and shading are not objective, and must be evoked by each hearer or reader according to the hints of the poet or the speaker. Without some affinity in human ideas art would certainly be impossible; but it can never be exactly determined how far the intentions of the poet are realized.

In what follows there will be no further discussion of ideas and experiences; they have been mentioned here only to ensure that the idea aroused in the hearer by a word shall not be confused with its sense or its meaning.

To make short and exact expressions possible, let the following phraseology be established:

A proper name (word, sign, sign combination, expression) *expresses* its sense, *means* or *designates* its meaning. By employing a sign we express its sense and designate its meaning.

Idealists or sceptics will perhaps long since have objected: 'You talk, without further ado, of the Moon as an object; but how do you know that the name "the Moon" has any meaning? How do you know that anything whatsoever has a meaning?' I reply that when we say 'the Moon', we do not intend to speak of our idea of the Moon, nor are we satisfied with the sense alone, but we presuppose a meaning. To assume that in the sentence 'The Moon is smaller than the Earth' the idea of the Moon is in question, would be flatly to misunderstand the sense. If this is what the speaker wanted, he would use the phrase 'my idea of the Moon'. Now we can of course be mistaken in the presupposition, and such mistakes have indeed occurred. But the question whether the presupposition is perhaps always mistaken need not be answered here; in order to justify mention of that which a sign means it is enough, at first, to point out our intention in speaking or thinking. (We must then add the reservation: provided such a meaning exists.)

So far we have considered the sense and meaning only of such expressions, words, or signs as we have called proper names. We now inquire concerning the sense and meaning of an entire assertoric sentence. Such a sentence contains a thought.[7] Is this thought, now, to be regarded as its sense or its meaning? Let us assume for the time being that the sentence does mean something. If we now replace one word of the sentence by another having the same meaning, but a different sense, this can have no effect upon the meaning of the sentence. Yet we can see that in such a case the thought changes; since, e.g., the thought in the sentence 'The morning star is a body illuminated by the Sun' differs from that in the sentence 'The evening star is a body illuminated by the Sun.' Anybody who did not know that the evening star is the morning star might hold the one thought to be true, the other false. The thought, accordingly, cannot be what is meant by the sentence, but must rather be considered as its sense. What is the position now with regard to the meaning? Have we a right even to inquire about it? Is it possible that a sentence as a whole has only a sense, but no meaning? At any rate, one might expect that such sentences occur, just as there are parts of sentences having sense but no meaning. And sentences which contain proper names without meaning will be of this kind. The sentence 'Odysseus was set ashore at Ithaca while sound asleep' obviously has a sense. But since it is doubtful whether the name 'Odysseus', occurring therein, means anything, it is also doubtful whether the whole sentence does. Yet it is certain, nevertheless, that anyone who seriously took the sentence to be true or false would ascribe to the name 'Odysseus' a meaning, not merely a sense; for it is of what the name means that the predicate is affirmed or denied. Whoever does not admit the name has meaning can neither apply nor withhold the predicate. But in that case it would be superfluous to advance to what the name means; one could be satisfied with the sense, if one wanted to go no further than the thought. If it were a question only of the sense of the sentence, the thought, it would be needless to bother with what is meant by a part of the sentence; only the sense, not the meaning, of the part is relevant to the sense of the whole sentence. The thought remains the same whether 'Odysseus' means something or not. The fact that we concern ourselves at all about what is meant by a part of the sentence indicates that we generally recognize and expect a meaning for the sentence itself. The thought loses value for us as soon as we recognize that the meaning of one of its parts is missing. We are therefore justified in not being satisfied with the sense of a sentence, and in inquiring also as to its meaning. But now why do we want every proper name to have not only a sense, but also a meaning? Why is the thought not enough for us? Because, and to the extent that, we are concerned with its truth-value. This is not always the case. In hearing an epic poem, for instance, apart from the euphony of the language we are interested only in the sense of the sentences and the images and feelings thereby aroused. The question of truth would cause us to abandon aesthetic delight for an attitude of scientific investigation. Hence it is a matter of no concern to us whether the name 'Odysseus', for instance, has meaning, so long as we accept the poem as a work of art.[8] It is the striving for truth that drives us always to advance from the sense to the thing meant.

Notes

1   I use this word in the sense of identity and understand '$a = b$' to have the sense of 'a is the same as b' or 'a and b coincide'.

2 [The reference is to Frege's *Begriffsschrift, eine der arithmetischen nachgebildete Formelsprache des reinen Denkens* (Halle, 1879).]

3 [See his 'Ueber Begriff und Gegenstand' (*Vierteljahrsschrift für wissenschaftliche Philosophie* XVI [1892]. 192–205): pp. 42–55 of this volume.]

4 In the case of an actual proper name such as 'Aristotle' opinions as to the sense may differ. It might, for instance, be taken to be the following: the pupil of Plato and teacher of Alexander the Great. Anybody who does this will attach another sense to the sentence 'Aristotle was born in Stagira' than will a man who takes as the sense of the name: the teacher of Alexander the Great who was born in Stagira. So long as the thing meant remains the same, such variations of sense may be tolerated, although they are to be avoided in the theoretical structure of a demonstrative science and ought not to occur in a perfect language.

5 We may include with ideas direct experiences: here, sense-impressions and acts themselves take the place of the traces which they have left in the mind. The distinction is unimportant for our purpose, especially since memories of sense-impressions and acts always go along with such impressions and acts themselves to complete the perceptual image. One may on the other hand understand direct experience as including any object, in so far as it is sensibly perceptible or spatial.

6 Hence it is inadvisable to use the word 'idea' to designate something so basically different.

7 By a thought I understand not the subjective performance of thinking but its objective content, which is capable of being the common property of several thinkers.

8 It would be desirable to have a special term for signs having only sense. If we name them, say, representations, the words of the actors on the stage would be representations; indeed the actor himself would be a representation.

---

11 The Principle of Verification

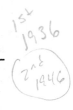

A. J. Ayer

The principle of verification is supposed to furnish a criterion by which it can be determined whether or not a sentence is literally meaningful. A simple way to formulate it would be to say that a sentence had literal meaning if and only if the proposition it expressed was either analytic or empirically verifiable. To this, however, it might be objected that unless a sentence was literally meaningful it would not express a proposition;[1] for it is commonly assumed that every proposition is either true or false, and to say that a sentence expressed what was either true or false would entail saying that it was literally meaningful. Accordingly, if the principle of verification were formulated in this way, it might be argued not only that it was incomplete as a criterion of meaning, since it would not cover

From *Language, Truth and Logic*. London: Victor Gollancz, 1936. By permission of the publisher.

the case of sentences which did not express any propositions at all, but also that it was otiose, on the ground that the question which it was designed to answer must already have been answered before the principle could be applied. It will be seen that when I introduce the principle in this book I try to avoid this difficulty by speaking of "putative propositions" and of the proposition which a sentence "purports to express"; but this device is not satisfactory. For, in the first place, the use of words like "putative" and "purports" seems to bring in psychological considerations into which I do not wish to enter, and secondly, in the case where the "putative proposition" is neither analytic nor empirically verifiable, there would, according to this way of speaking, appear to be nothing that the sentence in question could properly be said to express. But if a sentence expresses nothing there seems to be a contradiction in saying that what it expresses is empirically unverifiable; for even if the sentence is adjudged on this ground to be meaningless, the reference to "what it expresses" appears still to imply that something is expressed.

This is, however, no more than a terminological difficulty, and there are various ways in which it might be met. One of them would be to make the criterion of verifiability apply directly to sentences, and so eliminate the reference to propositions altogether. This would, indeed, run counter to ordinary usage, since one would not normally say of a sentence, as opposed to a proposition, that it was capable of being verified, or, for that matter, that it was either true or false; but it might be argued that such a departure from ordinary usage was justified, if it could be shown to have some practical advantage. The fact is, however, that the practical advantage seems to lie on the other side. For while it is true that the use of the word "proposition" does not enable us to say anything that we could not, in principle, say without it, it does fulfil an important function; for it makes it possible to express what is valid not merely for a particular sentence s but for any sentence to which s is logically equivalent. Thus, if I assert, for example, that the proposition p is entailed by the proposition q I am indeed claiming implicitly that the English sentence s which expresses p can be validly derived from the English sentence r which expresses q, but this is not the whole of my claim. For, if I am right, it will also follow that any sentence, whether of the English or any other language, that is equivalent to s can be validly derived, in the language in question, from any sentence that is equivalent to r; and it is this that my use of the word "proposition" indicates. Admittedly, we could decide to use the word "sentence" in the way in which we now use the word "proposition," but this would not be conducive to clarity, particularly as the word "sentence" is already ambiguous. Thus, in a case of repetition, it can be said either that there are two different sentences or that the same sentence has been formulated twice. It is in the latter sense that I have so far been using the word, but the other usage is equally legitimate. In either usage, a sentence which was expressed in English would be accounted a different sentence from its French equivalent, but this would not hold good for the new usage of the word "sentence" that we should be introducing if we substituted "sentence" for "proposition." For in that case we should have to say that the English expression and its French equivalent were different formulations of the same sentence. We might indeed be justified in increasing the ambiguity of the word "sentence" in this way if we thereby avoided any of the difficulties that have been thought to be attached to the use of the word "proposition"; but I do not think that this is to be achieved by the mere substitution of one verbal token for another. Accordingly, I conclude that this technical use of the word "sentence," though legitimate in itself, would be likely to promote confusion, without securing us any compensatory advantage.

A second way of meeting our original difficulty would be to extend the use of the word "proposition," so that anything that could properly be called a sentence would be said to express a proposition, whether or not the sentence was literally meaningful. This course would have the advantage of simplicity, but it is open to two objections. The first is that it would involve a departure from current philosophical usage; and the second is that it would oblige us to give up the rule that every proposition is to be accounted either true or false. For while, if we adopted this new usage, we should still be able to say that anything that was either true or false was a proposition, the converse would no longer hold good; for a proposition would be neither true nor false if it was expressed by a sentence which was literally meaningless. I do not myself think that these objections are very serious, but they are perhaps sufficiently so to make it advisable to solve our terminological problem in some other way.

The solution that I prefer is to introduce a new technical term; and for this purpose I shall make use of the familiar word "statement," though I shall perhaps be using it in a slightly unfamiliar sense. Thus I propose that any form of words that is grammatically significant shall be held to constitute a sentence, and that every indicative sentence, whether it is literally meaningful or not, shall be regarded as expressing a statement. Furthermore, any two sentences which are mutually translatable will be said to express the same statement. The word "proposition," on the other hand, will be reserved for what is expressed by sentences which are literally meaningful. Thus, the class of propositions becomes, in this usage, a sub-class of the class of statements, and one way of describing the use of the principle of verification would be to say that it provided a means of determining when an indicative sentence expressed a proposition, or, in other words, of distinguishing the statements that belonged to the class of propositions from those that did not.

It should be remarked that this decision to say that sentences express statements involves nothing more than the adoption of a verbal convention; and the proof of this is that the question, "What do sentences express?" to which it provides an answer is not a factual question. To ask of any particular sentence what it is that it expresses may, indeed, be to put a factual question; and one way of answering it would be to produce another sentence which was a translation of the first. But if the general question, "What do sentences express?" is to be interpreted factually, all that can be said in answer is that, since it is not the case that all sentences are equivalent, there is not any one thing that they all express. At the same time, it is useful to have a means of referring indefinitely to "what sentences express" in cases where the sentences themselves are not particularly specified; and this purpose is served by the introduction of the word "statement" as a technical term. Accordingly, in saying that sentences express statements, we are indicating how this technical term is to be understood, but we are not thereby conveying any factual information in the sense in which we should be conveying factual information if the question we were answering was empirical. This may, indeed, seem a point too obvious to be worth making; but the question, "What do sentences express?" is closely analogous to the question, "What do sentences mean?" and, as I have tried to show elsewhere,[2] the question, "What do sentences mean?" has been a source of confusion to philosophers because they have mistakenly thought it to be factual. To say that indicative sentences mean propositions is indeed legitimate, just as it is legitimate to say that they express statements. But what we are doing, in giving answers of this kind, is to lay down conventional definitions; and it is important that these conventional definitions should not be confused with statements of empirical fact.

Returning now to the principle of verification, we may, for the sake of brevity, apply it directly to statements rather than to the sentences which express them, and we can then reformulate it by saying that a statement is held to be literally meaningful if and only if it is either analytic or empirically verifiable. But what is to be understood in this context by the term "verifiable"? I do indeed attempt to answer this question in the first chapter of this book; but I have to acknowledge that my answer is not very satisfactory.

To begin with, it will be seen that I distinguish between a "strong" and a "weak" sense of the term "verifiable," and that I explain this distinction by saying that "a proposition is said to be verifiable in the strong sense of the term, if and only if its truth could be conclusively established in experience," but that "it is verifiable, in the weak sense, if it is possible for experience to render it probable." And I then give reasons for deciding that it is only the weak sense of the term that is required by my principle of verification. What I seem, however, to have overlooked is that, as I represent them, these are not two genuine alternatives.[3] For I subsequently go on to argue that all empirical propositions are hypotheses which are continually subject to the test of further experience; and from this it would follow not merely that the truth of any such proposition never was conclusively established but that it never could be; for however strong the evidence in its favour, there would never be a point at which it was impossible for further experience to go against it. But this would mean that my "strong" sense of the term "verifiable" had no possible application, and in that case there was no need for me to qualify the other sense of "verifiable" as weak; for on my own showing it was the only sense in which any proposition could conceivably be verified.

If I do not now draw this conclusion, it is because I have come to think that there is a class of empirical propositions of which it is permissible to say that they can be verified conclusively. It is characteristic of these propositions, which I have elsewhere[4] called "basic propositions," that they refer solely to the content of a single experience, and what may be said to verify them conclusively is the occurrence of the experience to which they uniquely refer. Furthermore, I should now agree with those who say that propositions of this kind are "incorrigible," assuming that what is meant by their being incorrigible is that it is impossible to be mistaken about them except in a verbal sense. In a verbal sense, indeed, it is always possible to misdescribe one's experience; but if one intends to do no more than record what is experienced without relating it to anything else, it is not possible to be factually mistaken; and the reason for this is that one is making no claim that any further fact could confute. It is, in short, a case of "nothing venture, nothing lose." It is, however, equally a case of "nothing venture, nothing win," since the mere recording of one's present experience does not serve to convey any information either to any other person or indeed to oneself; for in knowing a basic proposition to be true one obtains no further knowledge than what is already afforded by the occurrence of the relevant experience. Admittedly, the form of words that is used to express a basic proposition may be understood to express something that is informative both to another person and to oneself, but when it is so understood it no longer expresses a basic proposition. It was for this reason, indeed, that I maintained that there could not be such things as basic propositions, in the sense in which I am now using the term; for the burden of my argument was that no synthetic proposition could be purely ostensive. My reasoning on this point was not in itself incorrect, but I think that I mistook its purport. For I seem not to have perceived that what I was really doing was to suggest a motive for refusing to apply the term "prop-osition" to statements that "directly recorded an immediate experience"; and this is a terminological point which is not of any great importance.

Whether or not one chooses to include basic statements in the class of empirical propositions, and so to admit that some empirical propositions can be conclusively verified, it will remain true that the vast majority of the propositions that people actually express are neither themselves basic statements, nor deducible from any finite set of basic statements. Consequently, if the principle of verification is to be seriously considered as a criterion of meaning, it must be interpreted in such a way as to admit statements that are not so strongly verifiable as basic statements are supposed to be. But how then is the word "verifiable" to be understood?

It will be seen that, in this book, I begin by suggesting that a statement is "weakly" verifiable, and therefore meaningful, according to my criterion, if "some possible sense-experience would be relevant to the determination of its truth or falsehood." But, as I recognize, this itself requires interpretation; for the word "relevant" is uncomfortably vague. Accordingly, I put forward a second version of my principle, which I shall restate here in slightly different terms, using the phrase "observation-statement," in place of "experiential proposition," to designate a statement "which records an actual or possible observation." In this version, then, the principle is that a statement is verifiable, and consequently meaningful, if some observation-statement can be deduced from it in conjunction with certain other premises, without being deducible from those other premises alone.

I say of this criterion that it "seems liberal enough," but in fact it is far too liberal, since it allows meaning to any statement whatsoever. For, given any statement "*S*" and an observation-statement "*O*," "*O*" follows from "*S*" and "if *S* then *O*" without following from "if *S* then *O*" alone. Thus, the statements "the Absolute is lazy" and "if the Absolute is lazy, this is white" jointly entail the observation-statement "this is white," and since "this is white" does not follow from either of these premises, taken by itself, both of them satisfy my criterion of meaning. Furthermore, this would hold good for any other piece of nonsense that one cared to put, as an example, in place of "the Absolute is lazy," provided only that it had the grammatical form of an indicative sentence. But a criterion of meaning that allows such latitude as this is evidently unacceptable.[5]

It may be remarked that the same objection applies to the proposal that we should take the possibility of falsification as our criterion. For, given any statement "*S*" and any observation; statement "*O*", "*O*" will be incompatible with the conjunction of "*S*" and "if *S* then not *O*." We could indeed avoid the difficulty, in either case, by leaving out the stipulation about the other premises. But as this would involve the exclusion of all hypotheticals from the class of empirical propositions, we should escape from making our criteria too liberal only at the cost of making them too stringent.

Another difficulty which I overlooked in my original attempt to formulate the principle of verification is that most empirical propositions are in some degree vague. Thus, as I have remarked elsewhere,[6] what is required to verify a statement about a material thing is never the occurrence of precisely this or precisely that sense-content, but only the occurrence of one or other of the sense-contents that fall within a fairly indefinite range. We do indeed test any such statement by making observations which consist in the occurrence of particular sense-contents; but, for any test that we actually carry out, there is always an indefinite number of other tests, differing to some extent in respect either of their conditions or their results, that would have served the same purpose. And this means that there is never any set of observation-statements of which it can truly be said that precisely they are entailed by any given statement about a material thing.

Nevertheless, it is only by the occurrence of some sense-content, and consequently by the truth of some observation-statement, that any statement about a material thing is actually verified; and from this it follows that every significant statement about a material thing can be represented as entailing a disjunction of observation-statements, although the terms of this disjunction, being infinite, can not be enumerated in detail. Consequently, I do not think that we need be troubled by the difficulty about vagueness, so long as it is understood that when we speak of the "entailment" of observation-statements, what we are considering to be deducible from the premises in question is not any particular observation-statement, but only one or other of a set of such statements, where the defining characteristic of the set is that all its members refer to sense-contents that fall within a certain specifiable range.

There remains the more serious objection that my criterion, as it stands, allows meaning to any indicative statement whatsoever. To meet this, I shall emend it as follows. I propose to say that a statement is directly verifiable if it is either itself an observation-statement, or is such that in conjunction with one or more observation-statements it entails at least one observation-statement which is not deducible from these other premises alone; and I propose to say that a statement is indirectly verifiable if it satisfies the following conditions: first, that in conjunction with certain other premises it entails one or more directly verifiable statements which are not deducible from these other premises alone; and secondly, that these other premises do not include any statement that is not either analytic, or directly verifiable, or capable of being independently established as indirectly verifiable. And I can now reformulate the principle of verification as requiring of a literally meaningful statement, which is not analytic, that it should be either directly or indirectly verifiable, in the foregoing sense.

It may be remarked that in giving my account of the conditions in which a statement is to be considered indirectly verifiable, I have explicitly put in the proviso that the "other premises" may include analytic statements; and my reason for doing this is that I intend in this way to allow for the case of scientific theories which are expressed in terms that do not themselves designate anything observable. For while the statements that contain these terms may not appear to describe anything that anyone could ever observe, a "dictionary" may be provided by means of which they can be transformed into statements that are verifiable; and the statements which constitute the dictionary can be regarded as analytic. Were this not so, there would be nothing to choose between such scientific theories and those that I should dismiss as metaphysical; but I take it to be characteristic of the metaphysician, in my somewhat pejorative sense of the term, not only that his statements do not describe anything that is capable, even in principle, of being observed, but also that no dictionary is provided by means of which they can be transformed into statements that are directly or indirectly verifiable.

Metaphysical statements, in my sense of the term, are excluded also by the older empiricist principle that no statement is literally meaningful unless it describes what could be experienced, where the criterion of what could be experienced is that it should be something of the same kind as actually has been experienced.[7] But, apart from its lack of precision, this empiricist principle has, to my mind, the defect of imposing too harsh a condition upon the form of scientific theories; for it would seem to imply that it was illegitimate to introduce any term that did not itself designate something observable. The principle of verification, on the other hand, is, as I have tried to show, more liberal in this respect, and in view of the use that is actually made of scientific theories which the other would rule out, I think that the more liberal criterion is to be preferred.

It has sometimes been assumed by my critics that I take the principle of verification to imply that no statement can be evidence for another unless it is a part of its meaning; but this is not the case. Thus, to make use of a simple illustration, the statement that I have blood on my coat may, in certain circumstances, confirm the hypothesis that I have committed a murder, but it is not part of the meaning of the statement that I have committed a murder that I should have blood upon my coat, nor, as I understand it, does the principle of verification imply that it is. For one statement may be evidence for another, and still neither itself express a necessary condition of the truth of this other statement, nor belong to any set of statements which determines a range within which such a necessary condition falls; and it is only in these cases that the principle of verification yields the conclusion that the one statement is part of the meaning of the other. Thus, from the fact that it is only by the making of some observation that any statement about a material thing can be directly verified it follows, according to the principle of verification, that every such statement contains some observation-statement or other as part of its meaning, and it follows also that, although its generality may prevent any finite set of observation-statements from exhausting its meaning, it does not contain anything as part of its meaning that cannot be represented as an observation-statement; but there may still be many observation-statements that are relevant to its truth or falsehood without being part of its meaning at all. Again, a person who affirms the existence of a deity may try to support his contention by appealing to the facts of religious experience; but it does not follow from this that the factual meaning of his statement is wholly contained in the propositions by which these religious experiences are described. For there may be other empirical facts that he would also consider to be relevant; and it is possible that the descriptions of these other empirical facts can more properly be regarded as containing the factual meaning of his statement than the descriptions of the religious experiences. At the same time, if one accepts the principle of verification, one must hold that his statement does not have any other factual meaning than what is contained in at least some of the relevant empirical propositions; and that if it is so interpreted that no possible experience could go to verify it, it does not have any factual meaning at all.

In putting forward the principle of verification as a criterion of meaning, I do not overlook the fact that the word "meaning" is commonly used in a variety of senses, and I do not wish to deny that in some of these senses a statement may properly be said to be meaningful even though it is neither analytic nor empirically verifiable. I should, however, claim that there was at least one proper use of the word "meaning" in which it would be incorrect to say that a statement was meaningful unless it satisfied the principle of verification; and I have, perhaps tendentiously, used the expression "literal meaning" to distinguish this use from the others, while applying the expression "factual meaning" to the case of statements which satisfy my criterion without being analytic. Furthermore, I suggest that it is only if it is literally meaningful, in this sense, that a statement can properly be said to be either true or false. Thus, while I wish the principle of verification itself to be regarded, not as an empirical hypothesis,[8] but as a definition, it is not supposed to be entirely arbitrary. It is indeed open to anyone to adopt a different criterion of meaning and so to produce an alternative definition which may very well correspond to one of the ways in which the word "meaning" is commonly used. And if a statement satisfied such a criterion, there is, no doubt, some proper use of the word "understanding" in which it would be capable of being understood. Nevertheless, I think that, unless it satisfied the principle of verification, it would not be capable of being understood in the sense in which either scientific hypotheses or common-sense statements are habitually understood. I confess, however, that it now seems to me unlikely that any metaphysician would yield to a claim of this kind; and although I should still defend the use of the criterion of verifiability as a methodological principle, I realize that for the effective elimination of metaphysics it needs to be supported by detailed analyses of particular metaphysical arguments.

Notes

1 *Vide* M. Lazerowitz, "The Principle of Verifiability," *Mind*, 1937, pp. 372–8.
2 In *The Foundations of Empirical Knowledge*, pp. 92–104.
3 *Vide* M. Lazerowitz, "Strong and Weak Verification," *Mind*, 1939, pp. 202–13.
4 "Verification and Experience," *Proceedings of the Aristotelian Society*, Vol. XXXVII; cf. also *The Foundations of Empirical Knowledge*, pp. 80–4.
5 *Vide* I. Berlin, "Verifiability in Principle," *Proceedings of the Aristotelian Society*, Vol. XXXIX.
6 *The Foundations of Empirical Knowledge*, pp. 240–1.
7 cf. Bertrand Russell, *The Problems of Philosophy*, p. 91: "Every proposition which we can understand must be composed wholly of constituents with which we are acquainted." And, if I understand him correctly, this is what Professor W. T. Stace has in mind when he speaks of a "Principle of Observable Kinds." *Vide* his "Positivism," *Mind*, 1944. Stace argues that the principle of verification "rests upon" the principle of observable kinds, but this is a mistake. It is true that every statement that is allowed to be meaningful by the principle of observable kinds is also allowed to be meaningful by the principle of verification: but the converse does not hold.
8 Both A. C. Ewing, "Meaninglessness," *Mind*, 1937, pp. 347–64, and W. T. Stace, "Positivism," *Mind*, 1944, take it as an empirical hypothesis.

---

12 Meaning as Use

Ludwig Wittgenstein

1. "Cum ipsi (majores homines) appellabant rem aliquam, et cum secundum eam vocem corpus ad aliquid movebant, videbam, et tenebam hoc ab eis vocari rem illam, quod sonabant, cum eam vellent ostendere. Hoc autem eos velle ex motu corporis aperiebatur: tamquam verbis naturalibus omnium gentium, quae fiunt vultu et nutu oculorum, ceterorumque membrorum actu, et sonitu vocis indicante affectionem animi in petendis, habendis, rejiciendis, fugiendisve rebus. Ita verba in variis sententiis locis suis posita, et crebro audita, quarum rerum signa essent, paulatim colligebam, measque jam voluntates, edomito in eis signis ore, per haec enuntiabam." (Augustine, *Confessions*, I. 8.)[1]

From *Philosophical Investigations*, trans. G. E. M. Anscombe. Oxford: Blackwell, 1958, pp. 2–12. By permission of the publisher.

These words, it seems to me, give us a particular picture of the essence of human language. It is this: the individual words in language name objects – sentences are combinations of such names. – In this picture of language we find the roots of the following idea: Every word has a meaning. This meaning is correlated with the word. It is the object for which the word stands.

Augustine does not speak of there being any difference between kinds of word. If you describe the learning of language in this way you are, I believe, thinking primarily of nouns like "table", "chair", "bread", and of people's names, and only secondarily of the names of certain actions and properties; and of the remaining kinds of word as something that will take care of itself.

Now think of the following use of language: I send someone shopping. I give him a slip marked "five red apples". He takes the slip to the shopkeeper, who opens the drawer marked "apples"; then he looks up the word "red" in a table and finds a colour sample opposite it; then he says the series of cardinal numbers – I assume that he knows them by heart – up to the word "five" and for each number he takes an apple of the same colour as the sample out of the drawer. – It is in this and similar ways that one operates with words. – "But how does he know where and how he is to look up the word 'red' and what he is to do with the word 'five'?" – Well, I assume that he *acts* as I have described. Explanations come to an end somewhere. – But what is the meaning of the word "five"? – No such thing was in question here, only how the word "five" is used.

2. That philosophical concept of meaning has its place in a primitive idea of the way language functions. But one can also say that it is the idea of a language more primitive than ours.

Let us imagine a language for which the description given by Augustine is right. The language is meant to serve for communication between a builder A and an assistant B. A is building with building-stones: there are blocks, pillars, slabs and beams. B has to pass the stones, and that in the order in which A needs them. For this purpose they use a language consisting of the words "block", "pillar", "slab", "beam". A calls them out; – B brings the stone which he has learnt to bring at such-and-such a call. – Conceive this as a complete primitive language.

3. Augustine, we might say, does describe a system of communication; only not everything that we call language is this system. And one has to say this in many cases where the question arises "Is this an appropriate description or not?" The answer is: "Yes, it is appropriate, but only for this narrowly circumscribed region, not for the whole of what you were claiming to describe."

It is as if someone were to say: "A game consists in moving objects about on a surface according to certain rules . . ." – and we replied: You seem to be thinking of board games, but there are others. You can make your definition correct by expressly restricting it to those games.

4. Imagine a script in which the letters were used to stand for sounds, and also as signs of emphasis and punctuation. (A script can be conceived as a language for describing sound-patterns.) Now imagine someone interpreting that script as if there were simply a correspondence of letters to sounds and as if the

letters had not also completely different functions. Augustine's conception of language is like such an over-simple conception of the script.

5. If we look at the example in §1, we may perhaps get an inkling how much this general notion of the meaning of a word surrounds the working of language with a haze which makes clear vision impossible. It disperses the fog to study the phenomena of language in primitive kinds of application in which one can command a clear view of the aim and functioning of the words.

A child uses such primitive forms of language when it learns to talk. Here the teaching of language is not explanation, but training.

6. We could imagine that the language of §2 was the *whole* language of A and B; even the whole language of a tribe. The children are brought up to perform *these* actions, to use *these* words as they do so, and to react in *this* way to the words of others.

An important part of the training will consist in the teacher's pointing to the objects, directing the child's attention to them, and at the same time uttering a word; for instance, the word "slab" as he points to that shape. (I do not want to call this "ostensive definition", because the child cannot as yet *ask* what the name is. I will call it "ostensive teaching of words". – I say that it will form an important part of the training, because it is so with human beings; not because it could not be imagined otherwise.) This ostensive teaching of words can be said to establish an association between the word and the thing. But what does this mean? Well, it can mean various things; but one very likely thinks first of all that a picture of the object comes before the child's mind when it hears the word. But now, if this does happen – is it the purpose of the word? – Yes, it *can* be the purpose. – I can imagine such a use of words (of series of sounds). (Uttering a word is like striking a note on the keyboard of the imagination.) But in the language of §2 it is *not* the purpose of the words to evoke images. (It may, of course, be discovered that that helps to attain the actual purpose.)

But if the ostensive teaching has this effect, – am I to say that it effects an understanding of the word? Don't you understand the call "Slab!" if you act upon it in such-and-such a way? – Doubtless the ostensive teaching helped to bring this about; but only together with a particular training. With different training the same ostensive teaching of these words would have effected a quite different understanding.

"I set the brake up by connecting up rod and lever." – Yes, given the whole of the rest of the mechanism. Only in conjunction with that is it a brake-lever, and separated from its support it is not even a lever; it may be anything, or nothing.

7. In the practice of the use of language (2) one party calls out the words, the other acts on them. In instruction in the language the following process will occur: the learner *names* the objects; that is, he utters the word when the teacher points to the stone. – And there will be this still simpler exercise: the pupil repeats the words after the teacher – both of these being processes resembling language.

We can also think of the whole process of using words in (2) as one of those games by means of which children learn their native language. I will call these games "language-games" and will sometimes speak of a primitive language as a language-game.

And the processes of naming the stones and of repeating words after someone might also be called language-games. Think of much of the use of words in games like ring-a-ring-a-roses.

I shall also call the whole, consisting of language and the actions into which it is woven, the "language-game".

8. Let us now look at an expansion of language (2). Besides the four words "block", "pillar", etc., let it contain a series of words used as the shopkeeper in (1) used the numerals (it can be the series of letters of the alphabet); further, let there be two words, which may as well be "there" and "this" (because this roughly indicates their purpose), that are used in connexion with a pointing gesture; and finally a number of colour samples. A gives an order like: "d–slab–there". At the same time he shews the assistant a colour sample, and when he says "there" he points to a place on the building site. From the stock of slabs B takes one for each letter of the alphabet up to "d", of the same colour as the sample, and brings them to the place indicated by A. – On other occasions A gives the order "this–there". At "this" he points to a building stone. And so on.

9. When a child learns this language, it has to learn the series of 'numerals' a, b, c, . . . by heart. And it has to learn their use. – Will this training include ostensive teaching of the words? – Well, people will, for example, point to slabs and count: "a, b, c slabs". – Something more like the ostensive teaching of the words "block", "pillar", etc. would be the ostensive teaching of numerals that serve not to count but to refer to groups of objects that can be taken in at a glance. Children do learn the use of the first five or six cardinal numerals in this way.

Are "there" and "this" also taught ostensively? – Imagine how one might perhaps teach their use. One will point to places and things – but in this case the pointing occurs in the *use* of the words too and not merely in learning the use. –

10. Now what do the words of this language *signify*? – What is supposed to shew what they signify, if not the kind of use they have? And we have already described that. So we are asking for the expression "This word signifies this" to be made a part of the description. In other words the description ought to take the form: "The word . . . signifies . . .".

Of course, one can reduce the description of the use of the word "slab" to the statement that this word signifies this object. This will be done when, for example, it is merely a matter of removing the mistaken idea that the word "slab" refers to the shape of building-stone that we in fact call a "block" – but the kind of '*referring*' this is, that is to say the use of these words for the rest, is already known.

Equally one can say that the signs "a", "b", etc. signify numbers; when, for example, this removes the mistaken idea that "a", "b", "c", play the part actually played in language by "block", "slab", "pillar". And one can also say that "c" means this number and not that one; when, for example, this serves to explain that the letters are to be used in the order a, b, c, d, etc. and not in the order a, b, d, c.

But assimilating the descriptions of the uses of words in this way cannot make the uses themselves any more like one another. For, as we see, they are absolutely unlike.

11.   Think of the tools in a tool-box: there is a hammer, pliers, a saw, a screw-driver, a rule, a glue-pot, glue, nails and screws. – The functions of words are as diverse as the functions of these objects. (And in both cases there are similarities.)

Of course, what confuses us is the uniform appearance of words when we hear them spoken or meet them in script and print. For their *application* is not presented to us so clearly. Especially when we are doing philosophy!

12.   It is like looking into the cabin of a locomotive. We see handles all looking more or less alike. (Naturally, since they are all supposed to be handled.) But one is the handle of a crank which can be moved continuously (it regulates the opening of a valve); another is the handle of a switch, which has only two effective positions, it is either off or on; a third is the handle of a brake-lever, the harder one pulls on it, the harder it brakes; a fourth, the handle of a pump: it has an effect only so long as it is moved to and fro.

13.   When we say: "Every word in language signifies something" we have so far said *nothing whatever*, unless we have explained exactly *what* distinction we wish to make. (It might be, of course, that we wanted to distinguish the words of language (8) from words 'without meaning' such as occur in Lewis Carroll's poems, or words like "Lilliburlero" in songs.)

14.   Imagine someone's saying: "*All* tools serve to modify something. Thus the hammer modifies the position of the nail, the saw the shape of the board, and so on." – And what is modified by the rule, the glue-pot, the nails? – "Our knowledge of a thing's length, the temperature of the glue, and the solidity of the box." – Would anything be gained by this assimilation of expressions? –

15.   The word "to signify" is perhaps used in the most straightforward way when the object signified is marked with the sign. Suppose that the tools A uses in building bear certain marks. When A shews his assistant such a mark, he brings the tool that has that mark on it.

It is in this and more or less similar ways that a name means and is given to a thing. – It will often prove useful in philosophy to say to ourselves: naming something is like attaching a label to a thing.

16.   What about the colour samples that A shews to B: are they part of the *language*? Well, it is as you please. They do not belong among the words; yet when I say to someone: "Pronounce the word 'the'", you will count the second "the" as part of the sentence. Yet it has a role just like that of a colour-sample in language-game (8); that is, it is a sample of what the other is meant to say.

It is most natural, and causes least confusion, to reckon the samples among the instruments of the language.

((Remark on the reflexive pronoun "*this* sentence".))

17.   It will be possible to say: In language (8) we have different *kinds of word*. For the functions of the word "slab" and the word "block" are more alike

than those of "slab" and "d". But how we group words into kinds will depend on the aim of the classification, – and on our own inclination.

Think of the different points of view from which one can classify tools or chess-men.

18. Do not be troubled by the fact that languages (2) and (8) consist only of orders. If you want to say that this shows them to be incomplete, ask yourself whether our language is complete; – whether it was so before the symbolism of chemistry and the notation of the infinitesimal calculus were incorporated in it; for these are, so to speak, suburbs of our language. (And how many houses or streets does it take before a town begins to be a town?) Our language can be seen as an ancient city: a maze of little streets and squares, of old and new houses, and of houses with additions from various periods; and this surrounded by a multitude of new boroughs with straight regular streets and uniform houses.

19. It is easy to imagine a language consisting only of orders and reports in battle. – Or a language consisting only of questions and expressions for answering yes and no. And innumerable others. – And to imagine a language means to imagine a form of life.

But what about this: is the call "Slab!" in example (2) a sentence or a word? – If a word, surely it has not the same meaning as the like-sounding word of our ordinary language, for in §2 it is a call. But if a sentence, it is surely not the elliptical sentence: "Slab!" of our language. – As far as the first question goes you can call "Slab!" a word and also a sentence; perhaps it could be appropriately called a 'degenerate sentence' (as one speaks of a degenerate hyperbola); in fact it *is* our 'elliptical' sentence. – But that is surely only a shortened form of the sentence "Bring me a slab", and there is no such sentence in example (2). – But why should I not on the contrary have called the sentence "Bring me a slab" a *lengthening* of the sentence "Slab!"? – Because if you shout "Slab!" you really mean: "Bring me a slab". – But how do you do this: how do you *mean that* while you *say* "Slab!"? Do you say the unshortened sentence to yourself? And why should I translate the call "Slab!" into a different expression in order to say what someone means by it? And if they mean the same thing – why should I not say: "When he says 'Slab!' he means 'Slab!'? Again, if you can mean "Bring me the slab", why should you not be able to mean "Slab!"? – But when I call "Slab!", then what I want is, *that he should bring me a slab*! – Certainly, but does 'wanting this' consist in thinking in some form or other a different sentence from the one you utter? –

20. But now it looks as if when someone says "Bring me a slab" he could mean this expression as *one* long word corresponding to the single word "Slab!" – Then can one mean it sometimes as one word and sometimes as four? And how does one usually mean it? – I think we shall be inclined to say: we mean the sentence as *four* words when we use it in contrast with other sentences such as "*Hand* me a slab", "Bring *him* a slab", "Bring *two* slabs", etc.; that is, in contrast with sentences containing the separate words of our command in other combinations. – But what does using one sentence in contrast with others consist in? Do the others, perhaps, hover before one's mind? *All* of them? And

while one is saying the one sentence, or before, or afterwards? – No. Even if such an explanation rather tempts us, we need only think for a moment of what actually happens in order to see that we are going astray here. We say that we use the command in contrast with other sentences because *our language* contains the possibility of those other sentences. Someone who did not understand our language, a foreigner, who had fairly often heard someone giving the order: "Bring me a slab!", might believe that this whole series of sounds was one word corresponding perhaps to the word for "building-stone" in his language. If he himself had then given this order perhaps he would have pronounced it differently, and we should say: he pronounces it so oddly because he takes it for a single word. – But then, is there not also something different going on in him when he pronounces it, – something corresponding to the fact that he conceives the sentence as a *single* word? – Either the same thing may go on in him, or something different. For what goes on in you when you give such an order? Are you conscious of its consisting of four words *while* you are uttering it? Of course you have a *mastery* of this language – which contains those other sentences as well – but is this having a mastery something that *happens* while you are uttering the sentence? – And I have admitted that the foreigner will probably pronounce a sentence differently if he conceives it differently; but what we call his wrong conception *need* not lie in anything that accompanies the utterance of the command.

The sentence is "elliptical" not because it leaves out something that we think when we utter it, but because it is shortened – in comparison with a particular paradigm of our grammar. – Of course one might object here: "You grant that the shortened and the unshortened sentence have the same sense. – What is this sense, then? Isn't there a verbal expression for this sense?" – But doesn't the fact that sentences have the same sense consist in their having the same *use*? – (In Russian one says "stone red" instead of "the stone is red"; do they feel the copula to be missing in the sense, or attach it in *thought*?)

21. Imagine a language-game in which A asks and B reports the number of slabs or blocks in a pile, or the colours and shapes of the building-stones that are stacked in such-and-such a place. – Such a report might run: "Five slabs". Now what is the difference between the report or statement "Five slabs" and the order "Five slabs!"? – Well, it is the part which uttering these words plays in the language-game. No doubt the tone of voice and the look with which they are uttered, and much else besides, will also be different But we could also imagine the tone's being the same—for an order and a report can be spoken in a *variety* of tones of voice and with various expressions of face – the difference being only in the application. (Of course, we might use the words "statement" and "command" to stand for grammatical forms of sentence and intonations; we do in fact call "Isn't the weather glorious to-day?" a question, although it is used as a statement.) We could imagine a language in which *all* statements had the form and tone of rhetorical questions; or every command the form of the question "Would you like to . . . ?". Perhaps it will then be said: "What he says has the form of a question but is really a command", – that is, has the function of a command in the technique of using the language. (Similarly one says "You

will do this" not as a prophecy but as a command. What makes it the one or the other?)

22.   Frege's idea that every assertion contains an assumption, which is the thing that is asserted, really rests on the possibility found in our language of writing every statement in the form: "It is asserted that such-and-such is the case." – But "that such-and-such is the case" is *not* a sentence in our language – so far it is not a *move* in the language-game. And if I write, not "It is asserted that . . .", but "It is asserted: such-and-such is the case", the words "It is as-serted" simply become superfluous.

We might very well also write every statement in the form of a question fol-lowed by a "Yes"; for instance: "Is it raining? Yes!" Would this shew that every statement contained a question?

Of course we have the right to use an assertion sign in contrast with a ques-tion-mark, for example, or if we want to distinguish an assertion from a fiction or a supposition. It is only a mistake if one thinks that the assertion consists of two actions, entertaining and asserting (assigning the truth-value, or something of the kind), and that in performing these actions we follow the propositional sign roughly as we sing from the musical score. Reading the written sentence loud or soft is indeed comparable with singing from a musical score, but '*mean-ing*' (thinking) the sentence that is read is not.

Frege's assertion sign marks the *beginning of the sentence*. Thus its function is like that of the full-stop. It distinguishes the whole period from a clause *within* the period. If I hear someone say "it's raining" but do not know whether I have heard the beginning and end of the period, so far this sentence does not serve to tell me anything.

23.   But how many kinds of sentence are there? Say assertion, question, and command? – There are *countless* kinds: countless different kinds of use of what we call "symbols", "words", "sentences". And this multiplicity is not something fixed, given once for all; but new types of language, new lan-guage-games, as we may say, come into existence, and others become obso-lete and get forgotten. (We can get a *rough picture* of this from the changes in mathematics.)

Here the term "language-*game*" is meant to bring into prominence the fact that the *speaking* of language is part of an activity, or of a form of life.

Review the multiplicity of language-games in the following examples, and in others:

Giving orders, and obeying them –
Describing the appearance of an object, or giving its measurements –
Constructing an object from a description (a drawing) –
Reporting an event –
Speculating about an event –
Forming and testing a hypothesis –
Presenting the results of an experiment in tables and diagrams –
Making up a story; and reading it –
Play-acting –

Singing catches –
Guessing riddles –
Making a joke; telling it –
Solving a problem in practical arithmetic –
Translating from one language into another –
Asking, thanking, cursing, greeting, praying.

– It is interesting to compare the multiplicity of the tools in language and of the ways they are used, the multiplicity of kinds of word and sentence, with what logicians have said about the structure of language. (Including the author of the *Tractatus Logico-Philosophicus.*)

Note

1   "When they (my elders) named some object, and accordingly moved towards something, I saw this and I grasped that the thing was called by the sound they uttered when they meant to point it out. Their intention was shewn by their bodily movements, as it were the natural language of all peoples: the expression of the face, the play of the eyes, the movement of other parts of the body, and the tone of voice which expresses our state of mind in seeking, having, rejecting, or avoiding something. Thus, as I heard words repeatedly used in their proper places in various sentences, I gradually learnt to understand what objects they signified; and after I had trained my mouth to form these signs, I used them to express my own desires."

---

13   Biosemantics

Ruth Millikan

In the early pages of *Philosophical Investigations*, Wittgenstein compares words to tools. "Think of the tools in a tool box: there is a hammer, pliers, a saw, a screwdriver, a gluepot, nails and screws. – The functions of words are as diverse as the functions of these objects" (para. 11). Surely he would have said the same about the functions of language devices generally – words, surface syntactic forms, tonal inflections, etc. We might try to carry Wittgenstein's analogy further.

1.   Tools "have functions" but do not always serve these functions. Although the function of the screwdriver is driving screws, it sometimes fails in this task.

From *Language, Thought and Other Biological Categories.* Cambridge, MA: MIT Press, 1984, pp. 1–11. Copyright © 1984 by the Massachusetts Institute of Technology. By permission of the publisher.

Moreover it is not always used even with the intention of driving a screw but, say, for prying or for poking holes. Language devices "have functions" but do not always serve these functions. Although the function of the imperative mood is to produce action, it sometimes fails in this task. Moreover it is not always used even with the intention of producing action but, say, insincerely, sarcastically, jokingly.

2.   It is true that whereas the physical constitution of a tool is usually directly relevant to its function, the physical forms of language devices usually appear to be arbitrary in relation to their functions. There is no sense in which the household screwdriver might have served the pliers function, but "dog" might have served the "and" function and vice versa. But there are exceptions to this observation, most clearly in the case of tools. The key to my front door has a shape that is quite arbitrary within limits in relation to its function of opening my front door. Almost any shape would have done – provided that the lock on my door was adjusted accordingly. And it is in just this sense that almost any sound could have served the "dog" function – provided that the mechanisms within hearers that respond to tokens of this sound were adjusted accordingly.

3.   Although the functions of tools are extremely various, there is a uniform manner in which any tool may be described as such: (a) describe the purpose of the tool; (b) describe how the tool works, hence also the constitution of the tool, the method of operating or handling the tool, and other conditions normally requisite for the tool to perform its function. Is there a uniform manner in which any language device may be described as such?

The Tarski–Davidson tradition of semantics talks about certain kinds of words, describing these in terms of their effects upon the truth conditions of sentences in which they occur. The Austin–Searle tradition talks about other words and devices, "performatives" and "illocutionary force indicating devices," describing these in terms of conventional rules governing their use. The Grice–Schiffer–Lewis tradition talks about (speaking here very roughly) indicatives and imperatives, describing these in terms of nested speaker intentions. At least it is clear that no accepted manner of description applicable to every language device has yet emerged. But why should there be a problem about a uniform manner of description in the case of language devices when there is none in the case of tools? Where does the analogy with tools break down?

When we say that a tool has a certain function, its "own" or "proper" function, which can be distinguished from (1) its actual functions – what in fact it succeeds in doing on various occasions of use – and (2) the functions that various users intend it to perform on various occasions, we are referring to a function, roughly, that the tool type was designed by someone to serve. Natural language devices are not (at least literally) devices once "designed by someone" to serve certain functions. "The function of language device A is to F" does not bear the same analysis as does "the function of tool A is to F."

Consider another analogy. Body organs and instinctive behaviors also "have functions." As is the case with both tools and language devices, not every token of such a device succeeds in serving its "own" or "proper" function. And we can also imagine a person intentionally using such a natural device, say one of his own organs or reflexes, to serve a purpose that does not accord with its proper function. For example, people usually use their hands and arms "as Nature intended" for grasping, manipulating, pushing or pulling, etc. But a person can also use these members as matter upon which to draw, as subjects for physiological experimentation, as objects of aesthetic contemplation, etc. Moreover, some of these natural devices appear, as do all language devices and some tools, to have forms that are relatively arbitrary in relation to their functions. For example, instinctive mating displays, bird songs, and (other) ways of marking out territory are quite specific for the various species yet arbitrary in form within broad limits. And, as is the case with language devices but not with tools, these natural devices have not literally been "designed" by someone to serve their functions. The "functions" of these natural devices are, roughly, the functions upon which their continued reproduction or survival has depended.

Do language devices "have functions" that admit of the same kind of analysis? The functions of body organs and instinctive behaviors are radically diversified, yet when known can be described in the same sort of uniform manner in which the functions of tools can be described. Could a similar manner of description be used for language devices?

By "language devices" I mean words, surface syntactic forms, tonal inflections, stress patterns, punctuations, and any other significant surface elements that a natural spoken or written language may contain. We begin with two speculations. First, as is the case with other natural devices that are regularly reproduced by biological systems (e.g., body organs and instinctive behaviors), we suppose that normally a natural-language device has continued to be proliferated only because it has served a describable, stable function or set of functions. Second, as is the case, for example, with mating displays, speaker utterances of a language device presumably are proliferated only insofar as stable overt or covert reactions by cooperating partners (the female, the hearer) are also proliferated. The device type in each normal case, we speculate, should have at least one function – perhaps simple, perhaps complex – that accounts for the continued proliferation *both* of tokens of the device and of corresponding cooperative hearer reactions.

The language device performs this function in cooperation not with a specific hearer's response mechanism but with a random hearer, and the hearer's cooperative response mechanism performs its function in cooperation with a random speaker's utterance. Hence it is necessary that both the language device and its cooperative hearer mechanism be "standardized." Similarly, the mating dance of the male stickleback fish must perform its proper function in cooperation with the response mechanism built into a random female stickleback and vice versa. So the male dance and the female response must be standardized throughout the species if these devices are to perform their proper functions, hence survive. But stabilization of the function of a given language form and standardization within a language community of the form and cooperating response that serve that function must be two sides of a coin. For this reason I will use both "stabilizing (proper) function" and "standardizing (proper) function" for the hypothesized function of a given language device that accounts for the continued proliferation both of speaker utterances and of stable cooperative (overt or covert) hearer responses.

Language devices are often used in secondary or parasitic ways, as in metaphor, sarcasm, or lying. And even when used literally and felicitously, they may still fail to perform standardly. For example, the hearer may not hear, or though having heard may still fail to reply with the proper overt or covert response. Further, speakers sometimes misuse language, as when a speaker says "temerity" but means timidity. The standardizing and stabilizing function of a language device should be thought of not as an invariable function or as an average function but as a function that accords with a critical mass of cases of actual use, forming a center of gravity to which wayward speakers and hearers tend to return after departures. It is because a language device has such a stabilizing and standardizing proper function, which it performs in such a critical mass of actual cases, that it can *survive* incidents in which this stabilizing function fails to be performed, without extinction or change of function.

These speculations are of course extremely vague. Many points will need to be clarified in order to evaluate them. But what they *suggest* is that there is a level upon which the "functions" of language devices can be analyzed that is not found either by averaging over idiolects or by examining speaker intentions. I will argue that public language is to the idiolect rather as the biological species is to the individual. The business of the biological species of staying in business determines standards for individuals of that species, standards which, though they often correspond to averages, are not defined in terms of mere averages over the species. Consider, for example, how few sperm or immature members of most species actually manage to perform all the functions that nonetheless are proper to them – that help account for the survival of the kind. Similarly, the proper functions of natural language devices, considered as elements of public languages such as French or German, are not derived by averaging over the actual functions of these devices within idiolects. The idiolect is not the basic unit of analysis here. The business of the language species of staying in business imposes a standard of correctness upon idiolects that is not a matter of mere averages.

In order to press this analogy, a definition of "function" or "proper function" is needed that is broad enough to encompass both the functions of language devices and the functions of biological devices. Producing a definition that will do the work required of it efficiently is a task of medium difficulty, but the rewards are many. One reward will be that human purposes, looked at from a naturalist's viewpoint, turn out to correspond to proper functions of a certain kind, so that a connection between human purposes and the natural purposes of body organs and instinctive behaviors will be established that does not rest on mere metaphor. The purposes or functions of tools and the unconscious purposes or functions of customs will also turn out to correspond to (different kinds of) proper functions. But the main point of developing the theory of proper functions is to use it as a tool for understanding language and other representations, inner and outer.

One result will be an analysis of sentence and word meaning that does not take speaker meaning as base, and an analysis of speaker meaning that does not take sentence or word meaning as base. These two kinds of meaning are entwined to be sure, but neither is the root in terms of which the other is to be explicated. Compatibly, I will argue that the meaningfulness of sentences can be described without making reference to the fact that sentences are typically used to express and transmit thoughts, and that what beliefs and desires and intentions are can be explained without making reference to language.

[...]

The key notion that is needed in order to discuss intentionality ("of-ness," "aboutness") will be, in a way, only a by-product of the notion "proper function." This is a quasi-normative (roughly, the biological or medical) notion "Normal." (I will capitalize the technical term "Normal" routinely. Possibly this is unnecessary, but in such contexts as "hence, Normally, such and such happens" it may be too easy to forget that it is not statistics or averages that are referred to but a specific sort of quasi-norm, and often a false reading would prove disastrous.) I will argue that looking for stabilizing proper functions of various language devices – roughly, for functions that explain the survival or proliferation of these devices together with their characteristic cooperative hearer responses – can lend a sharp focus to questions about what language devices *do*. But looking to the conditions under which these devices work when they work in accordance with historically Normal explanations is what reveals the representing or intentional side of language. These conditions are conditions that sentences Normally map. Thus the exact nature of the relation between two traditional kinds of investigations of language forms, the first of which concentrates upon use, performance, speech acts, etc., the second upon semantic value, will also be clarified. Stabilizing proper function, I will argue, is the first aspect of public-language meaning; something more like "semantic value" or "intentional content" or "propositional content," explicated by reference to the notion Normal and by reference to mapping functions, is the second and most important aspect.

I will call this second aspect of meaning "Fregean sense" (to distinguish it from "dictionary sense") or just "sense," various connections with Frege's notion *Sinn* being recognizable. *Fregean sense* is the most basic stuff of "meaning," and in some contexts it will be clarifying just to call it that. Using the notion *Fregean sense*, I will develop a "general theory of signs" roughly in the sense C. S. Peirce envisioned – a theory that covers conventional signs and also thoughts (as well as some other things).

This theory of signs and thoughts has an important consequence. Sense, the basic intentional or semantic feature, is neither reference nor intension. Moreover it is not determined by intension. Because it is not determined by intension there is an epistemological problem associated with intentionality. It turns out that we cannot know a priori either *that* we think or what we think *about*, just as we do not know a priori whether what we think is true. But, I will argue, facing up to this disturbing result saves realism.

Just how it saves realism will come out slowly as we proceed to the end of the book. But readers who are philosophers are likely to be impatient here. So let me say some words to these readers, hoping that others will catch the drift if not every detail.

A very striking theme of mid-twentieth century philosophers was that it is possible to reject the notion that our knowledge rests upon a foundation of "givens." It is possible reasonably to deny that incorrigible knowledge of things directly experienced (pains, perceived red patches) is a given; it is possible to deny that there are infallible observations of any sort that come epistemologically first, the rest of our knowledge logically following after. It is also possible to deny that there are any truths of reason or even any analytic truths known infallibly to be true. From this discovery there has emerged a movement that not only rejects the tarnished ideal of Cartesian certainty for knowledge[1] but rejects any attempt to ground our knowledge by stratifying it into layers, some of which serve irreversibly as foundations for others. The movement says of itself that it rejects "foundationalism" in epistemology.

A rejection of foundationalism goes hand in hand with rejection of correspondence as a test of truth for any level of judgment. No longer are there thought to be experiences or sensations or sense data with which one compares protocol sentences to see if these sentences are mapping truly, any more than one compares sentences about genes directly with genes to see if these sentences are mapping truly.

So described, the movement against foundationalism seems to me to be not only challenging but, in essence, right. But certain *conclusions* have been drawn from these new axioms, drawn almost universally, that seem to me to be unhelpful, indeed, dead wrong. The dominant view seems to be that acceptance of these new axioms entails rejection of correspondence (using Brand Blanshard's terms) not only as the "test of truth" but also as the "nature of truth" – that realism, in one rough sense of "realism," must go. It is argued stoutly – indeed, almost all of the most commanding arguments have been on this side – that reference cannot be thought of as a correspondence relation between a word and a thing, and that truth is not the mapping of a sentence onto what the sentence is about. Rather, truth must be understood as a redundant notion ("'p' is true" just equals "p"), or it must be the same as rational assertability, or semantic assertability, or even just as socially respectable assertability – "what our peers will, *ceteris paribus*, let us get away with saying."[2] The dominant view is also that, once foundationalism has been abandoned, epistemological holism is the only alternative. If our beliefs are not tied and stabilized by a base of incorrigible observation judgments on the bottom and a skyhook of analytic judgments on the top, it must be that they are stabilized only by adhering to one another – by the coherence of the whole.

These popular views are not without paradox. Indeed, there are many problems. One is how to avoid on the one side a wholesale and incomprehensible relativism[3] concerning truth while avoiding on the other the conclusion that we have not yet got any knowledge at all (though we might in some most unlikely but conceivable future time when "our total theory of the world" is complete and consistent and we all agree on it). Another is how to deal with the paradoxes concerning indeterminacy of meaning and translation[4] that grow out of this viewpoint. But the problem to which I wish to draw attention is that of reconciling this view with our view of man as a natural creature and a product of evolution.

If man is a natural creature and a product of evolution, it is reasonable to suppose that man's capacities as a knower are also a product of evolution. If we are capable of believing and knowing things, it must be because these capacities, and the organs in us or organization of us that are responsible for these capacities, *historically* performed a service that helped us to proliferate. Knowing must then be something that man has been doing all along – certainly not something he might get to some day when the Peircean end of inquiry arrives. Knowing must also be something that man has been doing *in the world*, and that has adapted him to that world, by contrast with which not knowing, being ignorant, is something objectively different and less advantageous.

From this standpoint it seems clear that man's knowing must be some kind of natural relation that he often bears to his world. Hence true sentences, being direct vehicles for conveying knowledge, must also bear some kind of natural relation (presumably a relation routed through man) to man's world. If we can understand why singing fancy songs helps song birds, why emitting ultrasonic sounds helps bats, why having a seventeen-year cycle helps seventeen-year locusts, why having ceremonial fights helps mountain sheep, and why dancing figure eights helps bees, surely it is mere cowardice to refuse even to wonder why uttering, in particular, *subject-predicate sentences, subject to negation*, helps man. Surely there is some explanation for this helping that is quite general and not magical. Nodding one's head and saying how it is wonderful that using subject-predicate sentences, subject to negation, helps us creatively-to-develop-evolving-forms-of-social-behavior-and-life while at the same time (mysteriously) adapting us to the environment will not do. Nor will it do to claim that coherence in a set of beliefs is the test of truth without at the same time attempting some explanation of why having a coherent set of beliefs rather than an incoherent set has anything to do with adapting to the world – that is, without explaining what coherence is *for*, how it helps. And, if we wanted to remain holists, it would have to be explained how man could have been doing so well for all these eons *without* having an overall coherent set of beliefs – without a consistent, let alone total, "theory of the world."

One more observation. A very tempting theory of man's knowledge is that it consists in part of inner "maps" of sorts or of inner "representations" that model man's outside world inside him. It is hard to see how any a priori or metaphysical argument, such as those of Quine, Putnam, and Rorty, could have established that this is *not* how man does it. So it is hard to see how realism could be so obviously out of the question as is being claimed.[5]

These are not sharply focused difficulties, but I suggest they add to the general feeling that something *has* gone wrong with the newest of the empiricisms.

The main thing that has gone wrong, I will argue, is that the new empiricists have accomplished only half of their own revolution. They have failed to drop the foundationalist theory of *meaning* embedded in the tradition they reject along with the foundationalist theory of truth embedded there.

How simple and watertight the argument against realism can seem:

> To find the meaning of a word or sentence, look to what would justify its applica-
> tion or assertion or, if you prefer the causal to the logical order, look to what
> would cause it to be uttered. Now consider the meaning of " 'p' is true." Its
> assertion is justified on the grounds that p, or on grounds that would justify as-
> serting that p; its assertion is caused by prior beliefs and/or stimulations of the
> afferent nerves. That "p" corresponds to anything obviously plays no role in the
> justification of " 'p' is true" or in the causal derivation of its utterance. Hence
> correspondence has nothing to do with the meaning of "true," and certainly it
> cannot be, as has been claimed by the realists, the very essence or nature of truth.

But suppose we run this argument in reverse, taking the realist claim as premise:

> Correspondence is the very nature of truth and is of course involved in the very
> meaning of "true." For a sentence to be true is for it to correspond in a certain
> way to some part of the world. Now consider the sentence " 'p' is true." That "p"
> should correspond to anything clearly plays no role in the justification of " 'p' is
> true" or in the causal derivation of its utterance. Hence the meaning of " 'p' is
> true" has nothing to do with the justification or with the causal derivation of the
> utterance of " 'p' is true." Generalizing this, there seems to be good reason to
> think that meaning in other cases may also have nothing to do with justification or
> causal derivation.

But what could meaning be if it had nothing directly to do with justification or causal derivation? It would be nice, of course, if it were something such that terms and sentences in your idiolect might have the same meanings as same-sounding terms and sentences in my idiolect, despite the fact that our ways of justifying applications and the causal paths that lead to our utterances of these terms and sentences were different. That would help toward soothing our "in-determinacy of meaning and translation" anxieties. And making a *start* in this direction is not too hard.

Assume that what makes a sentence true is that there is something in the world onto which it maps in accordance with certain mapping functions (The status of these mapping functions would need, of course, to be explained.) Now the *meaning* of a sentence is something which, having itself been made determinate, in turn determines the conditions under which the sentence is true. But, we have said, the sentence will be true under the condition that there *is* something in the world onto which it maps in accordance with certain map-ping functions. What determines the meaning of a sentence is then what deter-mines the mapping functions in accordance with which it must map onto something in the world in order to be true. Put roughly, the meaning of a sentence is its own special mapping functions – those in accordance with which it "should" or "is supposed to" map onto the world. (Sentences are supposed to be true, aren't they?) *But* we are rejecting correspondence as the test of truth on any level. So these mapping functions cannot be rules that the *user* of the sentence somehow has in his head and applies. It cannot be the user who "supposes" that his sentences map so. Similarly, the "supposed to" that determines the meaning must be of a different kind from that in which a person is "supposed" in accordance with the expectations of *others* to conform to certain rules when applying a certain sentence or justifying its application.

The *beginning* was not too hard. But now the difficulties are piling up. What kinds of "things" in the world do sentences map onto? What kinds of mapping functions are involved? More crucial, what kind of "supposed to" *is* this? What *does* determine which mapping function goes with a sentence – what the meaning is? Further, if something else than the way I justify my assertions or the way they are causally derived determined my meaning, how on earth could I ever *grasp my own meaning* – know what I or the sentences I used meant? Or teach my children to mean the same as I mean when they used the same English words and sentences?

These questions I will try to answer, step by step and with loving care. At the same time I will place meaning and, in general, intentionality (aboutness, of-ness) in nature alongside sentences and the people who utter sentences. In so doing I will also try to show why sentences that exhibit subject-predicate structure, subject to negation, are of use to man, and how the law of noncontradiction (the essence of coherence) fits into nature. The notion *Fregean sense* is the basic tool that I will use in this construction.

We should not expect the results of dropping a foundationalist theory of meaning to be any less unsettling than those of dropping a foundationalist theory of knowledge have been. True, the results of dropping both together will leave us without the paradoxes that resulted from dropping only one. But ancient dogmas, permeating our philosophical instincts and every traditional and familiar argument, are not easy to rout. In particular, though it will not be comfortable, we must be willing to give up what are perhaps the most cherished of all our dogmas – dogmas that I will lump under the heading Meaning Rationalism. We must be willing to discover that, just as we cannot know a priori or with Cartesian certainty whether any particular thing we think or say is true, so we cannot know a priori or with Cartesian certainty that in seeming to think or talk about something we are thinking or talking about – *anything at all*. We cannot know a priori *that we mean*. Nor can we know a priori or with Cartesian certainty *what* it is that we are thinking or talking about. Further, we cannot tell just by armchair reflection whether or not two terms in our idiolect are synonymous, whether a single term is ambiguous, or whether any particular state of affairs is or is not "logically possible" in any interesting or useful sense of that idiom. As man can fail in knowing, so he can fail in meaning; success is not on any level a "given." Putting this another way, our meanings are as much theoretical items as are any other items. Should we have expected to be able to give up all the other givens (including, in accordance with Sellarsian insight, the givenness of knowledge of sensations) while keeping the givenness of meanings?

After this final parting with Descartes we must also be willing to embark on new ventures in epistemology – the adventure of trying to construct a nonfoundational empiricist epistemology of meaning alongside the more traditional sort of empiricist epistemology – epistemology of judgment and truth. I will do this in such a way as to bypass holism. Then we will be able to understand how man, before the dawn of history, (before the dawn of full scale "theories") could still have proceeded in his piece-meal way genuinely to know, in bits and snatches, some things about his world.

The result will be a position that, though the starkest possible antithesis of rationalism, will still be close to Aristotelian realism. Properties and kinds will show up only in the actual world. Nominalism will be denied.[6] (If one cannot tell by armchair reflection whether a seeming thought is a thought – is of anything at all – then those universals that are *mere* "objects of thought" need not really "be" at all – and certainly need not be somewhere outside of nature.) Also, logic will take an Aristotelian place as, in its way, the first of the *natural* sciences.

Notes

1 I use "Cartesian certainty" throughout this essay to denote that final sort of certainty that Descartes yearned for but, it seems, did not actually claim was possible. See his *Replies to Objections II*, *Philosophical Works of Descartes*, Vol. II, trans. E. Haldane and J. R. T. Ross, Dover, New York, 1955. (Richard Lee pointed this passage out to me.)

2 Richard Rorty, *Philosophy and the Mirror of Nature*, Princeton University Press, Princeton, N.J., 1979, p. 176.

3 For a clear statement of this problem, see Hilary Putnam, "Why Reason Can't Be Naturalized," *Synthese* 52 (1982), pp. 3–23.

4 Would the history of recent philosophy have been different if Quine had discovered "the paradox of the indeterminacy of meaning and translation" while Goodman had offered "the theory of the irrationality of induction"?

5 The relation of the question asked in this paragraph to Putnam's distinction between "metaphysical realism" and "internal realism" is addressed in the Epilogue. There I maintain that the distinction cannot be maintained without retreating to a position that puts theories themselves someplace other than in the world, thus reintroducing the veil of ideas in the form of a veil of theories.

6 More accurately, most forms of nominalism will be denied. If all it takes to be a nominalist is that one refuses to allow properties *in re* to be independent *objects*, then I have no quarrel with nominalism.

14   How Can Language Be Sexist?

Merrill B. Hintikka and Jaakko Hintikka

Prima facie, our title question may seem pointless. Barring bigots, virtually everybody will agree that language is frequently used in a sexist way. Why, then, the question?

We are formulating the title of the paper in this way because it serves to call attention to a general predicament of feminist philosophy as a serious theoretical enterprise. The sexist uses of language which first come to most people's minds are likely to instantiate relatively uninteresting aspects of language. Examples are offered by sexism expressed through purely emotive meaning and by those sexist uses of language which directly reflect sexist customs and institutions, for instance the different ways of addressing a person in Japanese. There is no problem as to how such sexism is possible in language; nor is there any interesting intellectual problem as to how such sexist usages can be diagnosed and cured. Once we have our emotions in line and our institutions and customs freed from sexism, no residual problem remains. Or so it seems.

This discussion illustrates certain criticisms which are often leveled in general at feminist philosophy. While the social problems addressed by feminist philosophy are usually acknowledged to be real and important, it is frequently denied that their diagnosis and solution requires or leads us to any new philosophical, methodological, or other theoretical insights. Hence feminist philosophy comes to seem a misnomer. The problems with which it deals do not appear to have a sufficiently important theoretical component to be labeled philosophical; hence the analyses and solutions it offers are thought not worthy of the designation "philosophy".

This is a view we are trying to combat by means of a case study. We suggest that a number of sexist uses of language illustrate interesting general theoretical problems. The diagnosis of such sexist uses hence involves serious problems of theoretical semantics. Even though there is in some cases no question as to how sexist language is possible, in others the very mechanism through which it comes about presents an interesting problem. In this paper, we are less anxious to solve this general theoretical problem we see raising its head here – it is too large for one paper anyway – than to recognize it, and less concerned with the details of instances of sexist language and sexist language use than with their connection with the general problem we are posing. Through pointing out this connection, we are trying to give a concrete

From *Discovering Reality*, ed. Sandra Harding and Merrill B. Hintikka. Dordrecht: D. Reidel, 1983, pp. 139–48. Copyright © 1983 by D. Reidel Publishing Company. By permission of Kluwer Academic Publishers.

example of the *theoretical* interest of problems naturally arising from feminist concerns.

The theoretical problem we are posing is the following: In virtually every important current logical or philosophical approach to semantics, a set of representative relations between language and the world it deals with is taken for granted. For instance, in Tarski-type truth definitions, the valuation of nonlogical constants is taken for granted.[1] In Montague semantics, the meaning functions associated with primitive words are likewise taken for granted.[2] And in approaches which rely on translation to some privileged "language of thought", the semantics of the target language is likewise left largely unanalyzed.[3]

What we wish to suggest is, first, that the principles according to which these basic representative relations between language and reality are determined need much more attention than they are now given and that awareness of these principles is vital even for the understanding of and for the applications of contemporary formal semantics. We are tempted to speak of a subsystem of language (a subset of the totality of rules governing language) which is in some sense more fundamental than the subsystem studied in present-day formal semantics. For reasons which emerge somewhat more fully in what follows, we call the latter the *structural* system and the former the *referential* system.[4]

This formulation is somewhat oversimplified, however, in that there is more interplay between the two systems than our schematic first statement leads one to expect. Furthermore, it is not clear that all the phenomena we have in mind are connected closely enough with each other on either side of the fence to justify us in speaking of a real (sub)system. Hence the preliminary formulation of our theme and the term "referential system" must be taken with a grain of salt, and must be considered as being tentative and exploratory in nature. In any case, we shall illustrate the general thesis by means of discussions of a few narrower problems. We shall also indicate how a couple of specific manifestations of sexism of language exemplify our general theoretical problem.

Some aspects of the referential system are sometimes classified as belonging to pragmatics rather than to semantics. Such labels are harmless as long as they do not mislead us into expecting that such "pragmatic" phenomena are somehow intrinsically related to the many other items also relegated to "the pragmatic wastebasket", to use Yehoshua Bar-Hillel's expression. For instance, we do not see any interesting connection between what we call the referential system and discourse-theoretical (e.g., conversational) phenomena.

As long as the referential system works and does not vary contextually, it remains relatively inconspicuous. (By "working", we mean here sufficing as the sole or main input into the structural system.) This inconspicuousness is one of the reasons why so little attention has been paid to it. For the same reason, the occasions when some aspect of the referential system varies, or proves insufficient for the purpose of understanding the semantics of some natural-language expression, are likely to offer the best quick illustrations of our theses.

We shall first try to give an example where the referential system does not by itself supply enough information to enable the structural system to operate in the way it is in these days usually expected to operate. This example is offered by a word whose force has perhaps been discussed more than that of any other single word: the word "good". Of course we cannot here exhaustively discuss the problems connected with it. We shall simply suggest that the way it operates is to rely on some evaluation principle but to leave it for the context to settle which one this evaluation principle is. On some occasions, the speaker may, e.g., rely on some set of values he or she shares with the audience or at least assumes to be familiar to the audience, whether or not its members actively subscribe to them. But on other occasions, the speaker – who could then be, for instance, a moral reformer – might use the same words to announce a new valuation principle. Preexisting valuations are typically determined by some-one's *interests*.[5] But when Socrates claims to be a virtuous man, an *agathos*, while refusing to participate in public life and neglecting his family's welfare, he is not only not relying on an existing valuation principle for one's actions. He is also not relying on any known interest to express his point. He was proclaiming a *new* morality by making judgments which presuppose it (i.e., presuppose the valuation principles which constitute the proclaimed new morality).[6]

The reason why we have classified this context-dependence of "good" as belonging to the referential subsystem of language should be obvious. What is at issue is which cases the predicate "good" can be correctly applied to, i.e., which extension (reference) it has. Since such extensions of our primitive terms are what is assumed to be given prior to the usual (structural) analysis of the semantics of natural language, which is the currently favored type of semantical analysis of any notion, a single evaluation principle would be needed in order for this word to be capable of being handled in the usual approach. However, it is part and parcel of how the referential system operates that in the case of this word no unique scale or principle is forthcoming.

This implies that one's actual use of "good" (in the several constructions into which it can enter) may rely on tacit evaluations or interests. These can be present without our noticing their presence. A small but subtle instance is of-fered by the difference in meaning between the English expression *a good man* and its literal counterparts in other languages, e.g., German, Swedish and Finn-ish. The difference is strikingly illustrated by comparing a passage from G. E. Moore's autobiography (in the *Library of Living Philosophers* volume devoted to him)[7] with Yrjö Hirn's essay (originally written in Swedish) on "Voltaire's heart".[8] Moore tells of one of his schoolteachers that he was not only a *good* man but also a benevolent man. Moore's words indicate clearly that he takes benevolence not to be a component of goodness, which has to do with such things as being conscientious and high-principled. In contrast, Hirn describes at some length Voltaire's noble efforts on behalf of oppressed and persecuted individuals, and goes on to argue that these good works were not only reflec-tions of Voltaire's high humanitarian principles and of his efficiency in putting them into practice. They show, Hirn argues, that Voltaire was a genuinely hu-mane, caring person, in brief, *en god människa* (a good man).

What is going on here is of course that the ambiguity of the English word *man* between a human being and a male of the species has led to the use of *a good man* where the tacitly presupposed interests are not those we presumably have in all our fellow human beings but those which we are likely to have in fellow citizens, business partners and colleagues, who are clearly presumed to be males. The former include primarily at least a minimum of concern with the basic welfare of other human beings. A good man would by this be a *humane* man, a good representative of mankind, i.e., a kindly or kind man. (Interestingly, these two uses of *kind* are in fact etymologically related.)[9] Indeed, this is precisely what happens in several of those languages which do not exhibit the same ambiguity as English. For instance, for a German *ein guter Mensch* is, well, not unlike a *Mensch* in the colloquial Yiddish sense.

In contrast, the interests of the other kind are what have lent the English words *a good man* their customary force. They signal the virtues a fellow citizen or colleague is expected to exhibit. What of the woman who is citizen and colleague? Can she be a good man? That closely analogous phenomenon has pervaded the psychological concept of a healthy adult: in so far as a human being is a healthy woman, she fails to be a healthy adult, and in so far as she is a healthy adult, she fails to be a healthy woman.[10] Such unwitting sexism cuts much deeper, it seems to us, than e.g., any emotively sexist uses of language.

This diagnosis is supported by the observation that the same ambiguity and the same sexist presupposition is found with vengeance in the ancient Greek.[11] There the relevant interests were predominantly interests in another citizen-soldier, i.e., the military interests, however defensive, that all citizens of a *polis* presumably had.

A much more general part of the referential system are the principles which determine the individuation of the particular entities we talk about in our language. Jaakko Hintikka has argued elsewhere that the best way of conceptualizing these principles is in terms of what is usually (and misleadingly) called possible-worlds semantics, i.e., by considering what the "embodiments" or "roles" of our individuals were in a range of possible situations or possible courses of events.[12] Whatever one can say of this approach in the last analysis, it serves to clarify several aspects of the central conceptual problems in this area. For instance, it leads to the insight that a major role in identifications across the boundaries of possible worlds is played by re-identification, i.e., by the principles which enable us to speak of the same entities as (often) existing at different stages of one and the same course of events. It is characteristic of the state of the art that many of the very best philosophers flatly refuse to consider the details of these principles. W. V. O. Quine doesn't think that any reasonable, theoretically respectable principles can be discovered,[13] while Saul Kripke claims that we have to postulate temporally persistent individuals as a primitive, unanalyzable presupposition.[14] Notwithstanding such views, we believe that a further analysis of the re-identification and cross-identification principles has a tremendous philosophical and possibly also psychological and automation-theoretical interest. As the basic theoretical situation remains almost completely uncharted, we cannot survey it here. Instead we will discuss some of the related issues.

One pertinent observation here is the following: On the possible-worlds model, the referential system has to include two partly independent components.[15] On the one hand, the references of our primitive nonlogical constants such as singular terms, predicates, function symbols, etc. in each possible world have to be specified. On the other hand, the imaginary "world lines" (which connect the roles of the same particulars in different worlds) have to be drawn. Each of these is a part of the objective foundation of ordinary (structural) semantics. The relative independence of these two tasks, the interpretation of nonlogical constants world by world and the drawing of the world lines (which span several worlds), implies that the corresponding two ingredients of the referential system can to some extent be varied independently. This does in fact happen, and such a variation of a part of the referential system is one of the phenomena in our language that can awaken philosophers' and linguists' interest in (or at least attention to) the referential system.

In order to see what such a variation might amount to, we must note a few facts here. In many typical cases, we are dealing with the possible worlds compatible with someone's knowledge, belief, or other propositional attitude. For example, let us consider what Jane knows. This is specified by the set of all possible worlds compatible with what she knows, called Jane's epistemic alternatives or her "knowledge worlds". Whatever is true in all these epistemic alternatives is known by Jane, and *vice versa*. Hence a singular term, say "b", picks out the same individual in all of Jane's epistemic alternatives (goes together with a world line) if and only if it is true that

$$(1) \qquad (\exists x) \text{ Jane knows that } (b = x).$$

More colloquially, (1) obviously say the same as

$$(2) \qquad \text{Jane knows who } b \text{ is.}$$

Now the ways in which world lines are drawn can vary without changing the evaluation principles which affect one world at a time. Hence the truth conditions of (1) and (2) can be varied accordingly without affecting the rest of the referential system. More generally, it is (among other things) in the variation of the force of phrases of the form *knows + an indirect question* that the variation of world lines can be "seen".

Possible-worlds semantics show what the cash value of such variation is. It is a question of what the person in question would consider as the same individual in different actual and possible situations, what he or she would "count as" the same individual. Not surprisingly, sexism can rear its head occasionally here, too. The diaries of that inveterate male chauvinist, Evelyn Waugh, offer an example. He quotes there the old saw worthy of Polonius: "Be kind to young ladies. You never know who they will be." The possible-worlds framework instantly reveals the mechanism of Waugh's sexism: Waugh is in effect treating women married to the same gent as being interchangeable, formally speaking, as nodes of one and the same "world line" connecting individuals in future courses of events.

Such variation has been taken by Quine to indicate that something is wrong with the possible-worlds semantics of sentences like (1) and (2). All the variation is in the referential system, however. The structural system, which is the subject matter Quine was in effect commenting on,[16] is of course completely unaffected by this variation.

One of the central problems in this area is how the world lines are drawn, i.e., how we as a matter of fact handle cross-identification in our conceptual system. We are in the process of developing a theory of actual cross-identification.[17] Unfortunately the subject is too large to be expounded here, and we must hence confine ourselves to a promissory note as far as the general problems of identification and individuation are concerned. Instead, let us consider a couple of the many interesting narrower issues involved in the general problem of cross-identification.

David Lewis has in effect claimed that cross-identification takes place according to similarity: those individuals in different possible worlds are as it were declared identical ("counterparts" in Lewis' terminology) which are most closely similar to each other.[18] "Similarity" is not intended to be a primitive notion in this approach. Rather, the relevant comparison may involve several different and differently weighted similarity considerations.

This is not the only a priori possibility, however. Instead of comparing individuals one by one, we may try to compare the structures of the two possible worlds in question at large and try to match them. Individuals corresponding to each other in the closest match we can achieve would be Lewisian counterparts. Such possible cross-world comparisons obviously depend much more on the relational and functional characteristics of the denizens of the different scenarios ("possible worlds") we are envisaging than on the essential properties of the entities involved in the comparison. For instance, these non-essentialist modes of cross-identification may depend on the continuity properties of the entities in question, which are of course relational rather than essential properties.

What is striking here is that certain psychological studies suggest that there may be sex-linked differences (whether innate or culturally conditioned does not matter for our purposes) in the very matter of such assimilation comparisons. For instance, some studies seem to show that boys tend to bracket together objects (or pictures of objects) whose intrinsic characteristics are similar, whereas girls weight more heavily the functional and relational characteristics of the entities to be compared.[19] For instance, boys frequently bracketed together such entities as a truck, a car, and an ambulance, while girls bracketed such entities as a doctor, a hospital bed, and an ambulance. More generally, women are generally more sensitive to, and likely to assign more importance to, relational characteristics (e.g., interdependencies) than males, and less likely to think in terms of independent discrete units. Conversely, males generally prefer what is separable and manipulatable.[20] If we put a premium on the former features, we are likely to end up with one kind of cross-identification and one kind of ontology; if we follow the guidance of the latter considerations, we end up with a different one. Moreover, it is not hard to see what the difference between the two will be. All identification which turns on essential properties, weighted similarities, or suchlike, presupposes a predetermined set of discrete individuals, the bearers of those essential properties as similarity relations, and focuses our attention on them. In contrast, an emphasis on relational characteristics of our individuals encourages comparisons of different worlds in terms of their total structure, which leads to entirely different identification methods, which are much more holistic and relational.

The suggestion – and we do not intend it to be more than a suggestion – we make here is now clear: it is not just possible, but quite likely, that there are sex-linked differences in our processes of cross-identification. The differences are such as not to be manifested either very frequently or very blatantly. But in the more refined areas of speculative thought, such differences might very well have their consequences. Indeed, cross identification methods are in an obvious sense constitutive of our ontology. Hence, what we are suggesting is that language could perhaps be, if not sexist, then at least sexually biased and sensitive to sex differences in the very respects that are most closely related to the structure of our ontology.

Lest this suggestion strike the reader as unrealistic, let us note some of its consequences and ramifications. Quite independently of the perspective from which we are here viewing the problems of ontology and cross-identification, it is arguable that Western philosophical thought has been overemphasizing such ontological models as postulate a given fixed supply of discrete individuals, individuated by their instrinsic or essential (non-relational) properties. These models are unfavorably disposed towards cross-identification by means of functional or other relational considerations. Is it to go too far to suspect a bias here? It seems to us that a bias is unmistakable in recent philosophical semantics and ontology. There we find almost everyone postulating a given domain of discrete individuals whose identity from one model (world) to another is unproblematic. An especially blatant example of this trend is Kripke's notion of a rigid designator,[21] which becomes virtually useless as soon as cross-identification is recognized as a problem. (No wonder Kripke has been led to argue that the re-identification of temporally persisting physical objects must be taken for granted.) Another conspicuous part of the same syndrome is philosophers' surprising slowness in appreciating Jaakko Hintikka's discovery of the duality of cross-identification methods (the descriptive and the perspectival one),[22] which breaks the hegemony of neat prefabricated individuals in philosophical ontology. It is hard not to see in this strong tendency a preference of independent but manipulative units similar to the sex-linked preference several psychologists have noted.

Similar points can be made about earlier history of philosophical ontology. Separability and "thisness" were the characteristic marks of Aristotelian substances,[23] which are historically the most important proposed ontological units of the world. Conversely, we may very well ask whether Leibniz' ontology of monads, whose identity lies in their reflecting the whole universe, has really been given its due.[24] Even though firm documentation is extremely hard in these matters, at the very least we obtain here a challenging perspective on the history of philosophical ontology. At the same time, our questions illustrate the systematic interest within language theory of the referential system we have tentatively postulated. For it is problems of individuation and identification which constitute perhaps the most important ingredient of any serious study of the referential system at large, and hence of philosophical ontology.

Notes

1 Cf. Alfred Tarski, 'The concept of truth in formalized languages', in Alfred Tarski, *Logic, Semantics, Metamathematics*, Clarendon Press, Oxford, 1956, pp. 152–278. [See Tarski, this volume.]

2 Cf. Richmond H. Thomason (ed.), *Formal Philosophy: Selected Papers of Richard Montague*, Yale University Press, New Haven, 1974; D. R. Dowty, R. E. Wall, and S. Peters, *Introduction to Montague Semantics*, D. Reidel, Dordrecht, 1981.

3 Cf., e.g., Jerry A. Fodor, *The Language of Thought*, Thomas Y. Crowell, New York, 1975. [See Fodor, this volume.]

4 Further observations concerning this distinction are made in Jaakko Hintikka and Merrill B. Hintikka, 'Towards a general theory of individuation and identification', in the proceedings of the Sixth International Wittgenstein Symposium, Hölder-Pichler-Tempsky, Vienna, 1982.

5 This point is well argued in the seminal last chapter 'The word "good" ' of Paul Ziff, *Semantic Analysis*, Cornell University Press, Ithaca, N.Y., 1960.

6 Cf. here A. Adkins, *Merit and Responsibility*, Clarendon Press, Oxford, 1960.

7 P. A. Schilpp (ed.), *The Philosophy of G. E. Moore* (The Library of Living Philosophers), Tudor, New York, 1952, pp. 3–39, especially p. 9.

8 Yrjö Hirn, 'Voltaires hjärta, in Yrjö Hirn, *De lagerkrönta skoplaggen*, Söderström & Co., Helsinki, 1951.

9 For an interesting discussion, see chapter 2 of C. S. Lewis, *Studies in Words*, second edn, Cambridge University Press, Cambridge, 1967.

10 Cf. Inge K. Broverman, Donald M. Broverman, et. al., 'Sex-role stereotypes and clinical judgments of mental health', *Journal of Consulting and Clinical Psychology* 34, no. 1 (1970), 1–7.

11 Cf. Adkins, op. cit. (note 6 above), especially chapter 3.

12 See his books *Models for Modalities*, D. Reidel, Dordrecht, 1969, and *The Intentions of Intentionality*, D. Reidel, Dordrecht, 1975.

13 Cf. W. V. Quine, 'Worlds away', *Journal of Philosophy* 73 (1976), 859–63. [See Quine, this volume.]

14 Cf. Saul Kripke, 'Identity through time', paper delivered at the Seventy-Sixth Annual Meeting of APA Eastern Division, New York, December 27-30, 1979. [See Kripke, this volume.]

15 This point has been implicit in Jaakko Hintikka's work ever since the last chapter of *Knowledge and Belief*, Cornell University Press, Ithaca, N.Y., 1962.

16 Op. cit (note 12 above).

17 'Towards a general theory of individuation and identification' (note 4 above).

18 David Lewis, 'Counterpart theory and quantified modal logic', *Journal of Philosophy* 65 (1968), 113–26.

19 Cf., e.g., J. Kagan, H. A. Moss and I. E. Sigel, 'The psychological significance of styles of conceptualization', in J. C. Wright and J. Kagan (eds.), *Basic Cognitive Processes in Children* (Society for Research in Child Development Monograph 28, no. 2), 1963.

20 Cf., e.g., Eleanor E. Maccoby, 'Sex differences in intellectual fuctioning', in Eleanor E. Maccoby (ed.), *The Development of Sex Differences*, Stanford University Press, Stanford, Calif., 1966, pp. 25–55.

21 Saul Kripke, *Naming and Necessity*, Harvard University Press, Cambridge, Mass., 1980.

22 Cf. 'On the logic of perception', in *Models for Modalities* (note 12 above); 'Know-

ledge by acquaintance – individuation by acquaintance', in Jaakko Hintikka, *Knowledge and the Known*, D. Reidel, Dordrecht, 1974.

23 Cf. Aristotle, *Categories*, ch. 5.

24 Cf. Jaakko Hintikka, 'Leibniz on plenitude, relations, and the "Reign of Law" ', in Simo Knuuttila (ed.), *Reforging the Great Chain of Being*, D. Reidel, Dordrecht, 1981, pp. 259–86.

PART THREE

SPEAKING:
WHAT IS IT TO SAY SOMETHING?

Introduction

In many of the previous readings, language is treated more as artifact than activity. The examples are often from technical languages removed from ordinary contexts of speaking, conversation, and deliberation. Structured meanings are studied that are independent of what an individual speaker or hearer might wish or intend. A semantic account of meaning, as exemplified by the reading by Fodor in part I, is a "theory" that uses a technical "metalanguage" to explain what language must be regardless of possibly deviant use. But can language be understood apart from its ordinary use in speech? And can speech be understood apart from individual speakers' intentions to communicate something to someone?

By the second half of the twentieth century, Wittgenstein's arguments against the possibility of a private language had convinced many English-speaking philosophers that what is communicated in language cannot be a speaker's private ideas or sensations as Locke and other empiricists had claimed. The criteria of meaning for words must be public and observable. Given a prevailing suspicion of "mentalism" as unscientific, a speaker's meaning cannot be explained with reference to mental states or ideas. The problem, however, is that simple behavioral accounts of speaking – a word has meaning because it has a tendency to be uttered by a speaker in certain circumstances and a tendency to elicit from a hearer certain behavior – do not seem to account for the gap between stimulus and reaction that characterizes speech.

It is that gap that H. P. Grice tries to close in his classic paper on speakers' intentions. To mean something linguistically is to intend to induce a belief or other attitude in a hearer, but it is to do so by means of the hearer's recognition of that intention. In this twist of interlocking intentions, Grice argues, is the essence of communication in language. Speech does not involve natural signs that cause or trigger a response. The apparently nonnatural meaning inherent in speaking is a peculiar kind of intention. The conventionality of language allows a speaker to induce a belief or other attitude in a hearer not by any physical means but by the hearer's recognition of a speaker's intention. With this formula, Grice hoped to give a naturalistic explanation of meaning. The intentions which figure in his explanation, he assures his readers, are garden-variety intentions, seldom conscious or explicit, inferable from the normal consequences of human actions.

John Austin also focuses on the pragmatics of language use. Although positivists might have correctly laid out truth conditions for the cognitive content of any meaningful assertion, in many, if not most, uses of language, we do not assert anything. Instead, Austin argues, we do something. With the idea of a performative utterance and a careful cataloging of "infelicities" in the execution of "speech acts," it is possible to put the "skids under our metaphysical feet" and maintain philosophical rigor and exactitude. After Austin, the study of the pragmatics of speech acts became a growth industry, increasingly articulated and formalized by philosophers such as John Searle.

In contrast to the semantic view, both Grice and Austin see a dual relation between philosophy of language and "ordinary" language. Spoken language is the subject matter of philosophy of language, and it is also the means of philosophizing about language. In his article "Meaning," Grice gives a definition of what the word "meaning" means, a definition that is discovered in careful consideration of examples and attention to "what one would say" in ordinary contexts. Once a preliminary definition is given, counter-examples are used to test the accuracy of that definition. Austin's work is characterized by the same careful attention to examples and to subtle shifts in wording that change the force of what one can "do with words."

The remaining three articles in this section challenge analytic accounts of language from three different perspectives: Marxist theory, the Indian tradition of philosophy of language, and feminism. Although Marx said little about language, in *Marxism and the Philosophy of Language* Volosinov marks out the direction he thinks a Marxist philosophy of language would have to take. In the excerpt included in this volume, he explains the social matrix of a continual creation/recreation of linguistic meaning. There can be no solitary meaning. To say something is always to say something to someone. Even in silent rumination or writing a projected audience is addressed. Speaking is "shared territory" between speaker and hearer, territory not rigidly mapped with conventional or logical rules. Nor is one speaker in the driver's seat, as Grice seems to suggest, striving to manipulate hearers' beliefs and attitudes. For Volosinov, the relationship between speaker and hearer is "reciprocal." The form and style of what is said is shaped by social relations but also subject to innovation in continued dialogue.

Chakrabarti, writing out of the Nyāya school of Indian philosophy, challenges the solipsism that is the basis for many philosophies of language. When it is assumed that an individual has access only to his own perceptions, memories, intuitions, or inferences, language must play a subsidiary role as evidence of knowledge-producing operations. On the Nyāya view, however, testimony, or "being told" something by someone who has not been discredited, is an independent source of knowledge and one of the primary functions of language. Chakrabarti's "being told" requires neither the manipulations of Grice's interlocking intentions, nor Austin's separation of performative illocutionary force from propositional content. For Chakrabarti, the logician's propositional content apart from truth or falsity is an artificial overlay on a natural and direct "seeing" of what someone is saying in which understanding and truth are fused.

Luce Irigaray also contrasts the reality of speaking with the abstraction of a body of "codified mediations" which allow exchange between men within a Fregean "common store of thoughts." Benveniste's subject "I" ordering a world around his own presence easily mutates into the neutral voice of objective science in which personal pronouns are suppressed. Like the Hintikkas, Irigaray points to the gender specificity of both language use and language theory. In contrast to the semantic model, women think and speak in relational rather than solipsistic terms. Women seek dialogue rather than assertion, telling, or commanding. The unified and dominant subject position is not a position women comfortably assume, which means that they often feel alienated from practices of monological assertion and theories of language that privilege that assertion.

As is often the case in theorizing about language, Irigaray's analysis is both descriptive and prescriptive. Given that men and women relate to language in different ways, they seldom are able to communicate. If a primary dialogical "speaking to someone" could be recovered, however, real reciprocity might result based on the "recognition" of another speaking subject.

15 Meaning

H. P. Grice

Consider the following sentences:

"Those spots mean (meant) measles."
"Those spots didn't mean anything to me, but to the doctor they meant measles."
"The recent budget means that we shall have a hard year."

1.   I cannot say, "Those spots meant measles, but he hadn't got measles," and I cannot say, "The recent budget means that we shall have a hard year, but we shan't have." That is to say, in cases like the above, *x meant that p* and *x means that p* entail *p*.

2.   I cannot argue from "Those spots mean (meant) measles" to any conclusion about "what is (was) meant by those spots"; for example, I am not entitled to say, "What was meant by those spots was that he had measles." Equally I cannot draw from the statement about the recent budget the conclusion "What is meant by the recent budget is that we shall have a hard year."

3.   I cannot argue from "Those spots meant measles" to any conclusion to the effect that somebody or other meant by those spots so-and-so. *Mutatis mutandis*, the same is true of the sentence about the recent budget.

4.   For none of the above examples can a restatement be found in which the verb "mean" is followed by a sentence or phrase in inverted commas. Thus "Those spots meant measles" cannot be reformulated as "Those spots meant 'measles' " or as "Those spots meant 'he has measles.' "

5.   On the other hand, for all these examples an approximate restatement can be found beginning with the phrase "The fact that . . ."; for example, "The fact that he had those spots meant that he had measles" and "The fact that the recent budget was as it was means that we shall have a hard year."

Now contrast the above sentences with the following:

"Those three rings on the bell (of the bus) mean that the 'bus is full.' "
"That remark, 'Smith couldn't get on without his trouble and strife,' meant that Smith found his wife indispensable."

1.   I can use the first of these and go on to say, "But it isn't in fact full – the conductor has made a mistake"; and I can use the second and go on, "But in

From *The Philosophical Review*, 66 (1957), pp. 251–9. By permission of the publisher.

fact Smith deserted her seven years ago." That is to say, here *x means that P* and *x meant that p* do not entail *p*.

2. I can argue from the first to some statement about "what is (was) meant" by the rings on the bell and from the second to some statement about "what is (was) meant" by the quoted remark.

3. I can argue from the first sentence to the conclusion that somebody (viz., the conductor) meant, or at any rate should have meant, by the rings that the bus is full, and I can argue analogously for the second sentence.

4. The first sentence can be restated in a form in which the verb "mean" is followed by a phrase in inverted commas, that is, "Those three rings on the bell mean 'the bus is full.' "

5. Such a sentence as "The fact that the bell has been rung three times means that the bus is full" is not a restatement of the meaning of the first sentence. Both may be true, but they do not have, even approximately, the same meaning.

When the expressions "means," "means something," "means that" are used in the kind of way in which they are used in the first set of sentences, I shall speak of the sense, or senses, in which they are used, as the *natural* sense, or senses, of the expressions in question. When the expressions are used in the kind of way in which they are used in the second set of sentences, I shall speak of the sense, or senses, in which they are used, as the *nonnatural* sense, or senses, of the expressions in question. I shall use the abbreviation "means$_{NN}$" to distinguish the nonnatural sense or senses.

I propose, for convenience, also to include under the head of natural senses of "mean" such senses of "mean" as may be exemplified in sentences of the pattern "*A* means (meant) *to do* so-and-so (by *x*)," where *A* is a human agent. By contrast, as the previous examples show, I include under the head of nonnatural senses of "mean" any senses of "mean" found in sentences of the patterns "*A* means (meant) something by *x*" or *A* means (meant) by *x* that . . ." (This is overrigid; but it will serve as an indication.)

I do not want to maintain that *all* our uses of "mean" fall easily, obviously, and tidily into one of the two groups I have distinguished; but I think that in most cases we should be at least fairly strongly inclined to assimilate a use of "mean" to one group rather than to the other. The question which now arises is this: "What more can be said about the distinction between the cases where we should say that the word is applied in a natural sense and the cases where we should say that the word is applied in a nonnatural sense?" Asking this question will not of course prohibit us from trying to give an explanation of "meaning$_{NN}$" in terms of one or another natural sense of "mean."

This question about the distinction between natural and nonnatural meaning is, I think, what people are getting at when they display an interest in a distinction between "natural" and "conventional" signs. But I think my formulation is better. For some things which can mean$_{NN}$ something are not signs (e.g., words are not), and some are not conventional in any ordinary sense (e.g., certain gestures); while some things which mean naturally are not signs of what they mean (cf. the recent budget example).

I want first to consider briefly, and reject, what I might term a casual type of answer to the question, "What is meaning$_{NN}$?" We might try to say, for instance, more or less with C. L. Stevenson,[1] that for x to mean$_{NN}$ something, x must have (roughly) a tendency to produce in an audience some attitude (cognitive or otherwise) and a tendency, in the case of a speaker, to *be* produced *by* that attitude, these tendencies being dependent on "an elaborate process of conditioning attending the use of the sign in communication."[2] This clearly will not do.

1. Let us consider a case where an utterance, if it qualifies at all as meaning$_{NN}$ something, will be of a descriptive or informative kind and the relevant attitude, therefore, will be a cognitive one, for example, a belief. (I use "utterance" as a neutral word to apply to any candidate for meaning$_{NN}$; it has a convenient act-object ambiguity.) It is no doubt the case that many people have a tendency to put on a tail coat when they think they are about to go to a dance, and it is no doubt also the case that many people, on seeing someone put on a tail coat, would conclude that the person in question was about to go to a dance. Does this satisfy us that putting on a tail coat means$_{NN}$ that one is about to go to a dance (or indeed means$_{NN}$ anything at all)? Obviously not. It is no help to refer to the qualifying phrase "dependent on an elaborate process of conditioning . . . ." For if all this means is that the response to the sight of a tail coat being put on is in some way learned or acquired, it will not exclude the present case from being one of meaning$_{NN}$. But if we have to take seriously the second part of the qualifying phrase ("attending the use of the sign in communication"), then the account of meaning$_{NN}$ is obviously circular. We might just as well say, "X has meaning$_{NN}$ if is used in communication," which, though true, is not helpful.

2. If this is not enough, there is a difficulty – really the same difficulty, I think – which Stevenson recognizes: how we are to avoid saying, for example, that "Jones is tall" is part of what is meant by "Jones is an athlete," since to tell someone that Jones is an athlete would tend to make him believe that Jones is tall. Stevenson here resorts to invoking linguistic rules, namely, a permissive rule of language that "athletes may be nontall." This amounts to saying that we are not prohibited by rule from speaking of "nontall athletes." But why are we not prohibited? Not because it is not bad grammar, or is not impolite, and so on, but presumably because it is not meaningless (or, if this is too strong, does not in any way violate the rules of meaning for the expressions concerned). But this seems to involve us in another circle. Moreover, one wants to ask why, if it is legitimate to appeal here to rules to distinguish what is meant from what is suggested, this appeal was not made earlier, in the case of groans, for example, to deal with which Stevenson originally introduced the qualifying phrase about dependence on conditioning.

A further deficiency in a causal theory of the type just expounded seems to be that, even if we accept it as it stands, we are furnished with an analysis only of statements about the *standard* meaning, or the meaning in general, of a "sign." No provision is made for dealing with statements about what a particular speaker or writer means by a sign on a particular occasion (which may well diverge from the standard meaning of the sign); nor is it obvious how the theory could be adapted to make such provision. One might even go further in criticism and maintain that the causal theory ignores the fact that the meaning (in general) of a sign needs to be explained in terms of what users of the sign do (or should) mean by it on particular occasions; and so the latter notion, which is unexplained by the causal theory, is in fact the fundamental one. I am sympathetic to this more radical criticism, though I am aware that the point is controversial.

I do not propose to consider any further theories of the "causal-tendency" type. I suspect no such theory could avoid difficulties analogous to those I have outlined without utterly losing its claim to rank as a theory of this type.

I will now try a different and, I hope, more promising line. If we can elucidate the meaning of

"x meant$_{NN}$ something (on a particular occasion)" and
"x meant$_{NN}$ that so-and-so (on a particular occasion)"

and of

"A meant$_{NN}$ something by x (on a particular occasion)" and
"A meant$_{NN}$ by x that so-and-so (on a particular occasion),"

this might reasonably be expected to help us with

"x means$_{NN}$ (timeless) something (that so-and-so),"
"A means$_{NN}$ (timeless) by x something (that so-and-so),"

and with the explication of "means the same as," "understands," "entails," and so on. Let us for the moment pretend that we have to deal only with utterances which might be informative or descriptive.

A first shot would be to suggest that "x meant$_{NN}$ something" would be true if x was intended by its utterer to induce a belief in some "audience" and that to say what the belief was would be to say what x meant$_{NN}$. This will not do. I might leave B's handkerchief near the scene of a murder in order to induce the detective to believe that B was the murderer; but we should not want to say that the handkerchief (or my leaving it there) meant$_{NN}$ anything or that I had meant$_{NN}$ by leaving it that B was the murderer. Clearly, we must at least add that, for x to have meant$_{NN}$ anything, not merely must it have been "uttered" with the intention of inducing a certain belief but also the utterer must have intended an "audience" to recognize the intention behind the utterance.

This, though perhaps better, is not good enough. Consider the following cases:

(1) Herod presents Salome with the head of St. John the Baptist on a charger.
(2) Feeling faint, a child lets its mother see how pale it is (hoping that she may draw her own conclusions and help).

(3) I leave the china my daughter has broken lying around for my wife to see.

Here we seem to have cases which satisfy the conditions so far given for meaning$_{NN}$. For example, Herod intended to make Salome believe that St. John the Baptist was dead and no doubt also intended Salome to recognize that he intended her to believe that St. John the Baptist was dead. Similarly for the other cases. Yet I certainly do not think that we should want to say that we have here cases of meaning$_{NN}$.

What we want to find is the difference between, for example, "deliberately and openly letting someone know" and "telling" and between "getting someone to think" and "telling."

The way out is perhaps as follows. Compare the following two cases:

(1) I show Mr. X a photograph of Mr. Y displaying undue familiarity to Mrs. X.
(2) I draw a picture of Mr. Y behaving in this manner and show it to Mr. X.

I find that I want to deny that in (1) the photograph (or my showing it to Mr. X) meant$_{NN}$ anything at all; while I want to assert that in (2) the picture (or my drawing and showing it) meant$_{NN}$ something (that Mr. Y had been unduly familiar), or at least that I had meant$_{NN}$ by it that Mr. Y had been unduly familiar. What is the difference between the two cases? Surely that in case 1. Mr. X's recognition of my intention to make him believe that there is something between Mr. Y and Mrs. X is (more or less) irrelevant to the production of this effect by the photograph. Mr. X would be led by the photograph at least to suspect Mrs. X even if instead of showing it to him I had left it in his room by accident; and I (the photograph shower) would not be unaware of this. But it will make a difference to the effect of my picture on Mr. X whether or not he takes me to be intending to inform him (make him believe something) about Mrs. X, and not to be just doodling or trying to produce a work of art.

But now we seem to be landed in a further difficulty if we accept this account. For consider now, say, frowning. If I frown spontaneously, in the ordinary course of events, someone looking at me may well treat the frown as a natural sign of displeasure. But if I frown deliberately (to convey my displeasure), an onlooker may be expected, provided he recognizes my intention, *still* to conclude that I am displeased. Ought we not then to say, since it could not be expected to make any difference to the onlooker's reaction whether he regards my frown as spontaneous or as intended to be informative, that my frown (deliberate) does *not* mean$_{NN}$ anything? I think this difficulty can be met; for though in general a deliberate frown may have the same effect (as regards inducing belief in my displeasure) as a spontaneous frown, it can be expected to have the same effect only *provided* the audience takes it as intended to convey displeasure. That is, if we take away the recognition of intention, leaving the other circumstances (including the recognition of the frown as deliberate), the belief-producing tendency of the frown must be regarded as being impaired or destroyed.

Perhaps we may sum up what is necessary for A to mean$_{NN}$ something by x as follows. A must intend to induce by x a belief in an audience, and he must also intend his utterance to be recognized as so intended. But these intentions are not independent; the recognition is intended by A to play its part in inducing the belief, and if it does not do so something will have gone wrong with the fulfillment of A's intentions. Moreover, A's intending that the recognition should play this part implies, I think, that he assumes that there is some chance that it will in fact play this part, that he does not regard it as a foregone conclusion that the belief will be induced in the audience whether or not the intention behind the utterance is recognized. Shortly, perhaps, we may say that "A meant$_{NN}$ something by x" is roughly equivalent to "A uttered x with the intention of inducing a belief by means of the recognition of this intention." (This seems to involve a reflexive paradox, but it does not really do so.)

Now perhaps it is time to drop the pretence that we have to deal only with "informative" cases. Let us start with some examples of imperatives or quasi-imperatives. I have a very avaricious man in my room, and I want him to go; so I throw a pound note out of the window. Is there here any utterance with a meaning$_{NN}$? No, because in behaving as I did, I did not intend his recognition of my purpose to be in any way effective in getting him to go. This is parallel to the photograph case. If on the other hand I had pointed to the door or given him a little push, then my behavior might well be held to constitute a meaningful$_{NN}$ utterance, just because the recognition of my intention would be intended by me to be effective in speeding his departure. Another pair of cases would be (1) a policeman who stops a car by standing in its way and (2) a policeman who stops a car by waving.

Or, to turn briefly to another type of case, if as an examiner I fail a man, I may well cause him distress or indignation or humiliation; and if I am vindictive, I may intend this effect and even intend him to recognize my intention. But I should not be inclined to say that my failing him meant$_{NN}$ anything. On the other hand, if I cut someone in the street I do feel inclined to assimilate this to the cases of meaning$_{NN}$, and this inclination seems to be dependent on the fact that I could not reasonably expect him to be distressed (indignant, humiliated) unless he recognized my intention to affect him in this way. (Cf., if my college stopped my salary altogether I should accuse them of ruining me; if they cut it by 2/6^d I might accuse them of insulting me; with some intermediate amounts I might not know what to say.)

Perhaps then we may make the following generalizations.

1.   "A meant$_{NN}$ something by x" is (roughly) equivalent to "A intended the utterance of x to produce some effect in an audience by means of the recognition of this intention"; and we may add that to ask what A meant is to ask for a specification of the intended effect (though, of course, it may not always be possible to get a straight answer involving a "that" clause, for example, "a belief that . . .")

2.   "x meant something" is (roughly) equivalent to "Somebody meant$_{NN}$ something by x." Here again there will be cases where this will not quite work.

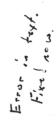

I feel inclined to say that (as regards traffic lights) the change to red meant$_{NN}$ that the traffic was to stop; but it would be very unnatural to say, "Somebody (e.g., the Corporation) meant$_{NN}$ by the red-light change that the traffic was to stop." Nevertheless, there seems to be *some* sort of reference to somebody's intentions.

3. "*x* means$_{NN}$ (timeless) that so-and-so" might as a first shot be equated with some statement or disjunction of statements about what "people" (vague) intend (with qualifications about "recognition") to effect by *x*. I shall have a word to say about this.

Will any kind of intended effect do, or may there be cases where an effect is intended (with the required qualifications) and yet we should not want to talk of meaning$_{NN}$? Suppose I discovered some person so constituted that, when I told him that whenever I grunted in a special way I wanted him to blush or to incur some physical malady, thereafter whenever he recognized the grunt (and with it my intention), he did blush or incur the malady. Should we then want to say that the grunt meant$_{NN}$ something? I do not think so. This points to the fact that for *x* to have meaning$_{NN}$, the intended effect must be something which in some sense is within the control of the audience, or that in some sense of "reason" the recognition of the intention behind *x* is for the audience a reason and not merely a cause. It might look as if there is a sort of pun here ("reason for believing" and "reason for doing"), but I do not think this is serious. For though no doubt from one point of view questions about reasons for believing are questions about evidence and so quite different from questions about reasons for doing, nevertheless to recognize an utterer's intention in uttering *x* (descriptive utterance), to have a reason for believing that so-and-so, is at least quite like "having a motive for" accepting so-and-so. Decisions "that" seem to involve decisions "to" (and this is why we can "refuse to believe" and also be "compelled to believe"). (The "cutting" case needs slightly different treatment, for one cannot in any straightforward sense "decide" to be offended; but one can refuse to be offended.) It looks then as if the intended effect must be something within the control of the audience, or at least the *sort* of thing which is within its control.

One point before passing to an objection or two. I think it follows that from what I have said about the connection between meaning$_{NN}$ and recognition of intention that (insofar as I am right) only what I may call the primary intention of an utterer is relevant to the meaning$_{NN}$ of an utterance. For if I utter *x*, intending (with the aid of the recognition of this intention) to induce an effect *E*, and intend this effect *E* to lead to a further effect *F*, then insofar as the occurrence of *F* is thought to be dependent solely on *E*, I cannot regard *F* as in the least dependent on recognition of my intention to induce *E*. That is, if (say) I intend to get a man to do something by giving him some information, it cannot be regarded as relevant to the meaning$_{NN}$ of my utterance to describe what I intended to do.

Now some question may be raised about my use, fairly free, of such words as "intention" and "recognition." I must disclaim any intention of peopling all our talking life with armies of complicated psychological occurrences. I do not hope to solve any philosophical puzzles about intending, but I do want briefly to argue that no special difficulties are raised by my use of the word "intention" in connection with meaning. First, there will be cases where an utterance is accompanied or preceded by a conscious "plan," or explicit formulation of intention (e.g., I declare how I am going to use *x* or ask myself how to "get something across"). The presence of such an explicit "plan" obviously counts fairly heavily in favor of the utterer's intention (meaning) being as "planned"; though it is not, I think, conclusive; for example, a speaker who has declared an intention to use a familiar expression in an unfamiliar way may slip into the familiar use. Similarly in nonlinguistic cases: if we are asking about an agent's intention, a previous expression counts heavily; nevertheless, a man might plan to throw a letter in the dustbin and yet take it to the post; when lifting his hand he might "come to" and say *either* "I didn't intend to do this at all" *or* "I suppose I must have been intending to put it in."

Explicitly formulated linguistic (or quasi-linguistic) intentions are no doubt comparatively rare. In their absence we would seem to rely on very much the same kinds of criteria as we do in the case of nonlinguistic intentions where there is a general usage. An utterer is held to intend to convey what is normally conveyed (or normally intended to be conveyed), and we require the general usage (e.g., he never knew or had forgotten the general usage). Similarly in nonlinguistic cases: we are presumed to intend the normal consequences of our actions.

Again, in cases where there is doubt, say, about which of two or more things an utterer intends to convey, we tend to refer to the context (linguistic or otherwise) of the utterance and ask which of the alternatives would be relevant to other things he is saying or doing, or which intention in a particular situation would fit in with some purpose he obviously has (e.g., a man who calls for a "pump" at a fire would not want a bicycle pump). Nonlinguistic parallels are obvious: context is a criterion in settling the question of why a man who has just put a cigarette in his mouth has put his hand in his pocket; relevance to an obvious end is a criterion in settling why a man is running away from a bull.

In certain linguistic cases we ask the utterer afterward about his intention, and in a few of these cases (the very difficult ones, like a philosopher asked to explain the meaning of an unclear passage in one of his works), the answer is not based on what he remembers but is more like a decision, a decision about how what he said is to be taken. I cannot find a nonlinguistic parallel here; but the case is so special as not to seem to contribute a vital difference.

All this is very obvious; but surely to show that the criteria for judging linguistic intentions are very like the criteria for judging nonlinguistic intentions is to show that linguistic intentions are very like nonlinguistic intentions.

Notes

1 *Ethics and Language* (New Haven, 1944), ch. 3.
2 Ibid., p. 57.

16   Performative Utterances

John Austin

You are more than entitled not to know what the word 'performative' means. It is a new word and an ugly word, and perhaps it does not mean anything very much. But at any rate there is one thing in its favour, it is not a profound word. I remember once when I had been talking on this subject that somebody afterwards said: 'You know, I haven't the least idea what he means, unless it could be that he simply means what he says'. Well, that is what I should like to mean.

Let us consider first how this affair arises. We have not got to go very far back in the history of philosophy to find philosophers assuming more or less as a matter of course that the sole business, the sole interesting business, of any utterance – that is, of anything we say – is to be true or at least false. Of course they had always known that there are other kinds of things which we say – things like imperatives, the expressions of wishes, and exclamations – some of which had even been classified by grammarians, though it wasn't perhaps too easy to tell always which was which. But still philosophers have assumed that the only things that they are interested in are utterances which report facts or which describe situations truly or falsely. In recent times this kind of approach has been questioned – in two stages, I think. First of all people began to say: 'Well, if these things are true or false it ought to be possible to decide which they are, and if we can't decide which they are they aren't any good but are, in short, nonsense'. And this new approach did a great deal of good; a great many things which probably are nonsense were found to be such. It is not the case, I think, that all kinds of nonsense have been adequately classified yet, and perhaps some things have been dismissed as nonsense which really are not; but still this movement, the verification movement, was, in its way, excellent.

However, we then come to the second stage. After all, we set some limits to the amount of nonsense that we talk, or at least the amount of nonsense that we are prepared to admit we talk; and so people began to ask whether after all some of those things which, treated as statements, were in danger of being dismissed as nonsense did after all really set out to be statements at all. Mightn't they perhaps be intended not to report facts but to influence people in this way or that, or to let off steam in this way or that? Or perhaps at any rate some elements in these utterances performed such functions, or, for example, drew attention in some way (without actually reporting it) to some important feature of the circumstances in which the utterance was being made. On these lines people have now adopted a new slogan, the slogan of the 'different uses of

From *Philosophical Papers*, ed. J. O. Urmson and G. J. Warnock. Oxford: Clarendon Press, 1970, pp. 233–41. By permission of the publisher.

language'. The old approach, the old statemental approach, is sometimes called even a fallacy, the descriptive fallacy.

Certainly there are a great many uses of language. It's rather a pity that people are apt to invoke a new use of language whenever they feel so inclined, to help them out of this, that, or the other well-known philosophical tangle; we need more of a framework in which to discuss these uses of language; and also I think we should not despair too easily and talk, as people are apt to do, about the *infinite* uses of language. Philosophers will do this when they have listed as many, let us say, as seventeen; but even if there were something like ten thousand uses of language, surely we could list them all in time. This, after all, is no larger than the number of species of beetle that entomologists have taken the pains to list. But whatever the defects of either of these movements – the 'verification' movement or the 'use of language' movement – at any rate they have effected, nobody could deny, a great revolution in philosophy and, many would say, the most salutary in its history. (Not, if you come to think of it, a very immodest claim.)

Now it is one such sort of use of language that I want to examine here. I want to discuss a kind of utterance which looks like a statement and grammatically, I suppose, would be classed as a statement, which is not nonsensical, and yet is not true or false. These are not going to be utterances which contain curious 'verbs like 'could' or 'might', or curious words like 'good', which many philosophers regard nowadays simply as danger signals. They will be perfectly straightforward utterances, with ordinary verbs in the first person singular present indicative active, and yet we shall see at once that they couldn't possibly be true or false. Furthermore, if a person makes an utterance of this sort we should say that he is *doing* something rather than merely *saying* something. This may sound a little odd, but the examples I shall give will in fact not be odd at all, and may even seem decidedly dull. Here are three or four. Suppose, for example, that in the course of a marriage ceremony I say, as people will, 'I do' – (sc. take this woman to be my lawful wedded wife). Or again, suppose that I tread on your toe and say 'I apologize'. Or again, suppose that I have the bottle of champagne in my hand and say 'I name this ship the *Queen Elizabeth*'. Or suppose I say 'I bet you sixpence it will rain tomorrow'. In all these cases it would be absurd to regard the thing that I say as a report of the performance of the action which is undoubtedly done – the action of betting, or christening, or apologizing. We should say rather that, in saying what I do, I actually perform that action. When I say 'I name this ship the *Queen Elizabeth*' I do not describe the christening ceremony, I actually perform the christening; and when I say 'I do' (sc. take this woman to be my lawful wedded wife), I am not reporting on a marriage, I am indulging in it.

Now these kinds of utterance are the ones that we call *performative* utterances. This is rather an ugly word, and a new word, but there seems to be no word already in existence to do the job. The nearest approach that I can think of is the word 'operative', as used by lawyers. Lawyers when talking about legal instruments will distinguish between the preamble, which recites the circumstances in which a transaction is effected, and on the other hand the operative part – the part of it which actually performs the legal act which it is the purpose of the instrument to perform. So the word 'operative' is very near to what we want. 'I give and bequeath my watch to my brother' would be an operative clause and is a performative utterance. However, the word 'operative' has other uses, and it seems preferable to have a word specially designed for the use we want.

Now at this point one might protest, perhaps even with some alarm, that I seem to be suggesting that marrying is simply saying a few words, that just saying a few words *is* marrying. Well, that certainly is not the case. The words have to be said in the appropriate circumstances, and this is a matter that will come up again later. But the one thing we must not suppose is that what is needed in addition to the saying of the words in such cases is the performance of some internal spiritual act, of which the words then are to be the report. It's very easy to slip into this view at least in difficult, portentous cases, though perhaps not so easy in simple cases like apologizing. In the case of promising – for example, 'I promise to be there tomorrow' – it's very easy to think that the utterance is simply the outward and visible (that is, verbal) sign of the perform-ance of some inward spiritual act of promising, and this view has certainly been expressed in many classic places. There is the case of Euripides' Hippolytus, who said 'My tongue swore to, but my heart did not' – perhaps it should be 'mind' or 'spirit' rather than 'heart', but at any rate some kind of backstage artiste. Now it is clear from this sort of example that, if we slip into thinking that such utterances are reports, true or false, of the performance of inward and spiritual acts, we open a loop-hole to perjurers and welshers and bigamists and so on, so that there are disadvantages in being excessively solemn in this way. It is better, perhaps, to stick to the old saying that our word is our bond.

However, although these utterances do not themselves report facts and are not themselves true or false, saying these things does very often *imply* that cer-tain things are true and not false, in some sense at least of that rather woolly word 'imply'. For example, when I say 'I do take this woman to be my lawful wedded wife', or some other formula in the marriage ceremony, I do imply that I'm not already married, with wife living, sane, undivorced, and the rest of it. But still it is very important to realize that to imply that something or other is true, is not at all the same as saying something which is true itself.

These performative utterances are not true or false, then. But they do suffer from certain disabilities of their own. They can fail to come off in special ways, and that is what I want to consider next. The various ways in which a performa-tive utterance may be unsatisfactory we call, for the sake of a name, the infelici-ties; and an infelicity arises – that is to say, the utterance is unhappy – if certain rules, transparently simple rules, are broken. I will mention some of these rules and then give examples of some infringements.

First of all, it is obvious that the conventional procedure which by our utter-ance we are purporting to use must actually exist. In the examples given here this procedure will be a verbal one, a verbal procedure for marrying or giving or whatever it may be; but it should be borne in mind that there are many non-verbal procedures by which we can perform exactly the same acts as we perform by these verbal means. It's worth remembering too that a great many of the things we do are at least in part of this conventional kind. Philosophers at least are too apt to assume that an action is always in the last resort the making of a physical movement, whereas it's usually, at least in part, a matter of convention.

The first rule is, then, that the convention invoked must exist and be accepted. And the second rule, also a very obvious one, is that the circumstances in which we purport to invoke this procedure must be appropriate for its invocation. If this is not observed, then the act that we purport to perform would not come off – it will be, one might say, a misfire. This will also be the case if, for example, we do not carry through the procedure – whatever it may be – correctly and completely, without a flaw and without a hitch. If any of these rules are not observed, we say that the act which we purported to perform is void, without effect. If, for example, the purported act was an act of marrying, then we should say that we 'went through a form' of marriage, but we did not actually succeed in marrying.

Here are some examples of this kind of misfire. Suppose that, living in a country like our own, we wish to divorce our wife. We may try standing her in front of us squarely in the room and saying, in a voice loud enough for all to hear, 'I divorce you'. Now this procedure is not accepted. We shall not thereby have succeeded in divorcing our wife, at least in this country and others like it. This is a case where the convention, we should say, does not exist or is not accepted. Again, suppose that, picking sides at a children's party, I say 'I pick George'. But George turns red in the face and says 'Not playing'. In that case I plainly, for some reason or another, have not picked George – whether because there is no convention that you can pick people who aren't playing, or because George in the circumstances is an inappropriate object for the procedure of picking. Or consider the case in which I say 'I appoint you Consul', and it turns out that you have been appointed already – or perhaps it may even transpire that you are a horse; here again we have the infelicity of inappropriate circumstances, inappropriate objects, or what not. Examples of flaws and hitches are perhaps scarcely necessary – one party in the marriage ceremony says 'I will', the other says 'I won't'; I say 'I bet sixpence', but nobody says 'Done', nobody takes up the offer. In all these and other such cases, the act which we purport to perform, or set out to perform, is not achieved.

But there is another and a rather different way in which this kind of utterance may go wrong. A good many of these verbal procedures are designed for use by people who hold certain beliefs or have certain feelings or intentions. And if you use one of these formulae when you do not have the requisite thoughts or feelings or intentions then there is an abuse of the procedure, there is insincerity. Take, for example, the expression, 'I congratulate you'. This is designed for use by people who are glad that the person addressed has achieved a certain feat, believe that he was personally responsible for the success, and so on. If I say 'I congratulate you' when I'm not pleased or when I don't believe that the credit was yours, then there is insincerity. Likewise if I say I promise to do something, without having the least intention of doing it or without believing it feasible. In these cases there is something wrong certainly, but it is not like a misfire. We should not say that I didn't in fact promise, but rather that I did promise but promised insincerely; I did congratulate you but the congratulations were hollow. And there may be an infelicity of a somewhat similar kind when the performative utterance commits the speaker to future conduct of a certain description and then in the future he does not in fact behave in the expected way. This is very obvious, of course, if I promise to do something and then break my promise, but there are many kinds of commitment of a rather less tangible form than that in the case of promising. For instance, I may say 'I welcome you', bidding you welcome to my home or wherever it may be, but then I proceed to treat you as though you were exceedingly unwelcome. In this case the procedure of saying 'I welcome you' has been abused in a way rather different from that of simple insincerity.

Now we might ask whether this list of infelicities is complete, whether the kinds of infelicity are mutually exclusive, and so forth. Well, it is not complete, and they are not mutually exclusive; they never are. Suppose that you are just about to name the ship, you have been appointed to name it, and you are just about to bang the bottle against the stem; but at that very moment some low type comes up, snatches the bottle out of your hand, breaks it on the stem, shouts out 'I name this ship the *Generalissimo Stalin*', and then for good measure kicks away the chocks. Well, we agree of course on several things. We agree that the ship certainly isn't now named the *Generalissimo Stalin*, and we agree that it's an infernal shame and so on and so forth. But we may not agree as to how we should classify the particular infelicity in this case. We might say that here is a case of a perfectly legitimate and agreed procedure which, however, has been invoked in the wrong circumstances, namely by the wrong person, this low type instead of the person appointed to do it. But on the other hand we might look at it differently and say that this is a case where the procedure has not as a whole been gone through correctly, because part of the procedure for naming a ship is that you should first of all get yourself appointed as the person to do the naming and that's what this fellow did not do. Thus the way we should classify infelicities in different cases will be perhaps rather a difficult matter, and may even in the last resort be a bit arbitrary. But of course lawyers, who have to deal very much with this kind of thing, have invented all kinds of technical terms and have made numerous rules about different kinds of cases, which enable them to classify fairly rapidly what in particular is wrong in any given case.

As for whether this list is complete, it certainly is not. One further way in which things may go wrong is, for example, through what in general may be called misunderstanding. You may not hear what I say, or you may understand me to refer to something different from what I intended to refer to, and so on. And apart from further additions which we might make to the list, there is the general over-riding consideration that, as we are performing an act when we issue these performative utterances, we may of course be doing so under duress or in some other circumstances which make us not entirely responsible for doing what we are doing. That would certainly be an unhappiness of a kind – any kind of nonresponsibility might be called an unhappiness; but of course it is a quite different kind of thing from what we have been talking about. And I might mention that, quite differently again, we could be issuing any of these utterances, as we can issue an utterance of any kind whatsoever, in the course, for example, of acting a play or making a joke or writing a poem – in which case of course it would not be seriously meant and we shall not be able to say that we seriously performed the act concerned. If the poet says 'Go and catch a falling star' or whatever it may be, he doesn't seriously issue an order. Considerations of this kind apply to any utterance at all, not merely to performatives.

That, then, is perhaps enough to be going on with. We have discussed the performative utterance and its infelicities. That equips us, we may suppose, with two shining new tools to crack the crib of reality maybe. It also equips us – it always does – with two shining new skids under our metaphysical feet. The question is how we use them.

17   Verbal Interaction

V. N. Volosinov

Indeed, from whichever aspect we consider it, expression-utterance is determined by the actual conditions of the given utterance – above all, by its *immediate social situation*.

Utterance, as we know, is constructed between two socially organized persons, and in the absence of a real addressee, an addressee is presupposed in the person, so to speak, of a normal representative of the social group to which the speaker belongs. The *word is oriented toward an addressee*, toward *who* that addressee might be: a fellow-member or not of the same social group, of higher or lower standing (the addressee's hierarchical status), someone connected with the speaker by close social ties (father, brother, husband, and so on) or not. There can be no such thing as an abstract addressee, a man unto himself, so to speak. With such a person, we would indeed have no language in common, literally and figuratively. Even though we sometimes have pretensions to experiencing and saying things *urbi et orbi*, actually, of course, we envision this "world at large" through the prism of the concrete social milieu surrounding us. In the majority of cases, we presuppose a certain typical and stabilized *social purview* toward which the ideological creativity of our own social group and time is oriented, i.e., we assume as our addressee a contemporary of our literature, our science, our moral and legal codes.

Each person's inner world and thought has its stabilized *social audience* that

From *Marxism and the Philosophy of Language*, trans. L. Matejka and I. R. Titunik. New York: Seminar Press, 1973, pp. 85–90. By permission of Academic Press Inc., Orlando.

comprises the environment in which reasons, motives, values, and so on are fashioned. The more cultured a person, the more closely his inner audience will approximate the normal audience of ideological creativity; but, in any case, specific class and specific era are limits that the ideal of addressee cannot go beyond.

Orientation of the word toward the addressee has an extremely high significance. In point of fact, *word is a two-sided act*. It is determined equally by *whose* word it is and *for whom* it is meant. As word, *it is precisely the product of the reciprocal relationship between speaker and listener, addresser and addressee*. Each and every word expresses the "one" in relation to the "other." I give myself verbal shape from another's point of view, ultimately, from the point of view of the community to which I belong. A word is a bridge thrown between myself and another. If one end of the bridge depends on me, then the other depends on my addressee. A word is territory shared by both addresser and addressee, by the speaker and his interlocutor.

But what does being the speaker mean? Even if a word is not entirely his, constituting, as it were, the border zone between himself and his addressee – still, it does in part belong to him.

There is one instance of the situation wherein the speaker is the undoubted possessor of the word and to which, in this instance, he has full rights. This instance is the physiological act of implementing the word. But insofar as the act is taken in purely physiological terms, the category of possession does not apply.

If, instead of the physiological act of implementing sound, we take the implementation of word as sign, then the question of proprietorship becomes extremely complicated. Aside from the fact that word as sign is a borrowing on the speaker's part from the social stock of available signs, the very individual manipulation of this social sign in a concrete utterance is wholly determined by social relations. The stylistic individualization of an utterance that the Vosslerites speak about represents a reflection of social interrelationships that constitute the atmosphere in which an utterance is formed. *The immediate social situation and the broader social milieu wholly determine – and determine from within, so to speak – the structure of an utterance.*

Indeed, take whatever kind of utterance we will, even the kind of utterance that is not a referential message (communication in the narrow sense) but the verbal expression of some need – for instance, hunger – we may be certain that it is socially oriented in its entirety. Above all, it is determined immediately and directly by the participants of the speech event, both explicit and implicit participants, in connection with a specific situation. That situation shapes the utterance, dictating that it sound one way and not another – like a demand or request, insistence on one's rights or a plea for mercy, in a style flowery or plain, in a confident or hesitant manner, and so on.

The immediate social situation and its immediate social participants determine the "occasional" form and style of an utterance. The deeper layers of its structure are determined by more sustained and more basic social connections with which the speaker is in contact.

Even if we were to take an utterance still in process of generation "in the soul," it would not change the essence of the matter, since the structure of experience is just as social as is the structure of its outward objectification. The degree to which an experience is perceptible, distinct, and formulated is directly proportional to the degree to which it is socially oriented.

In fact, not even the simplest, dimmest apprehension of a feeling – say, the feeling of hunger not outwardly expressed – can dispense with some kind of ideological form. Any apprehension, after all, must have inner speech, inner intonation and the rudiments of inner style: one can apprehend one's hunger apologetically, irritably, angrily, indignantly, etc. We have indicated, of course, only the grosser, more egregious directions that inner intonation may take; actually, there is an extremely subtle and complex set of possibilities for intoning an experience. Outward expression in most cases only continues and makes more distinct the direction already taken by inner speech and the intonation already embedded in it.

Which way the intoning of the inner sensation of hunger will go depends upon the hungry person's general social standing as well as upon the immediate circumstances of the experience. These are, after all, the circumstances that determine in what evaluative context, within what social purview, the experience of hunger will be apprehended. The immediate social context will determine possible addressees, friends or foes, toward whom the consciousness and the experience of hunger will be oriented: whether it will involve dis-satisfaction with cruel Nature, with oneself, with society, with a specific group within society, with a specific person, and so on. Of course, various degrees of perceptibility, distinctiveness, and differentiation in the social orientation of an experience are possible; but without some kind of evaluative social orientation there is no experience. Even the cry of a nursing infant is "oriented" toward its mother. There is the possibility that the experience of hunger may take on political coloring, in which case its structure will be determined along the lines of a potential political appeal or a reason for political agitation. It may be apprehended as a form of protest, and so on.

With regard to the potential (and sometimes even distinctly sensed) addressee, a distinction can be made between two poles, two extremes between which an experience can be apprehended and ideologically structured, tending now toward the one, now toward the other. Let us label these two extremes the "*I-experience*" and the "*we-experience*."

The "I-experience" actually tends toward extermination: the nearer it approaches its extreme limit, the more it loses its ideological structuredness and, hence, its apprehensible quality, reverting to the physiological reaction of the animal. In its course toward this extreme, the experience relinquishes all its potentialities, all outcroppings of social orientation, and, therefore, also loses its verbal delineation. Single experiences or whole groups of experiences can approach this extreme, relinquishing, in doing so, their ideological clarity and structuredness and testifying to the inability of the consciousness to strike social roots.[1]

The "we-experience" is not by any means a nebulous herd experience; it is differentiated. Moreover, ideological differentiation, the growth of consciousness, is in direct proportion to the firmness and reliability of the social orientation. The stronger, the more organized, the more differentiated the collective in which an individual orients himself, the more vivid and complex his inner world will be.

The "we-experience" allows of different degrees and different types of ideological structuring.

Let us suppose a case where hunger is apprehended by one of a disparate set of hungry persons whose hunger is a matter of chance (the man down on his luck, the beggar, or the like). The experience of such a declassé loner will be colored in some specific way and will gravitate toward certain particular ideological forms with a range potentially quite broad: humility, shame, enviousness, and other evaluative tones will color his experience. The ideological forms along the lines of which the experience would develop would be either the individualistic protest of a vagabond or repentant, mystical resignation.

Let us now suppose a case in which the hungry person belongs to a collective where hunger is not haphazard and does bear a collective character – but the collective of these hungry people is not itself tightly bound together by material ties, each of its members experiencing hunger on his own. This is the situation most peasants are in. Hunger is experienced "at large," but under conditions of material disparateness, in the absence of a unifying economic coalition, each person suffers hunger in the small, enclosed world of his own individual economy. Such a collective lacks the unitary material frame necessary for united action. A resigned but unashamed and undemeaning apprehension of one's hunger will be the rule under such conditions – "everyone bears it, you must bear it, too." Here grounds are furnished for the development of the philosophical and religious systems of the nonresistor or fatalist type (early Christianity, Tolstoyanism).

A completely different experience of hunger applies to a member of an objectively and materially aligned and united collective (a regiment of solders; workers in their association within the walls of a factory; hired hands on a large-scale, capitalist farm; finally, a whole class once it has matured to the point of "class unto itself"). The experience of hunger this time will be marked predominantly by overtones of active and self-confident protest with no basis for humble and submissive intonation. These are the most favorable grounds for an experience to achieve ideological clarity and structuredness.[2]

All these types of expression, each with its basic intonations, come rife with corresponding terms and corresponding forms of possible utterances. The social situation in all cases determines which term, which metaphor, and which form may develop in an utterance expressing hunger out of the particular intonational bearings of the experience.

A special kind of character marks the individualistic *self-experience*. It does not belong to the "I-experience" in the strict sense of the term as defined above. The individualistic experience is fully differentiated and structured. Individualism is a special ideological form of the "we-experience" of the bourgeois class (there is also an analogous type of individualistic self-experience for the feudal aristocratic class). The individualistic type of experience derives from a steadfast and confident social orientation. Individualistic confidence in oneself, one's sense of personal value, is drawn not from within, not from the depths of one's personality, but from the outside world. It is the ideological interpretation of one's social recognizance and tenability by rights, and of the objective security and tenability provided by the whole social order, of one's individual livelihood. The structure of the conscious, individual personality is just as social a structure as is the collective type of experience. It is a particular kind of interpretation, projected into the individual soul, of a complex and sustained socioeconomic situation. But there resides in this type of individualistic "we-experience," and also in the very order to which it corresponds, an inner contradiction that sooner or later will demolish its ideological structuredness.

An analogous structure is presented in solitary self-experience ("the ability and strength to stand alone in one's rectitude"), a type cultivated by Romain Rolland and, to some extent, by Tolstoj. The pride involved in this solitude also depends upon "we." It is a variant of the "we-experience" characteristic of the modern-day West European intelligentsia. Tolstoj's remarks about there being different kinds of thinking – "for oneself" and "for the public" – merely juxtapose two different conceptions of "public." Tolstoj's "for oneself" actually signifies only another social conception of addressee peculiar to himself. There is no such thing as thinking outside orientation toward possible expression and, hence, outside the social orientation of that expression and of the thinking involved.

Thus the personality of the speaker, taken from within, so to speak, turns out to be wholly a product of social interrelations. Not only its outward expression but also its inner experience are social territory. Consequently, the whole route between inner experience (the "expressible") and its outward objectification (the "utterance") lies entirely across social territory. When an experience reaches the stage of actualization in a full-fledged utterance, its social orientation acquires added complexity by focusing on the immediate social circumstances of discourse and, above all, upon actual addressees.

Notes

1   On the possibility of a set of human sexual experiences falling out of social context with concomitant loss of verbal cognizance, see our book, *Frejdizm* [Freudianism] (1927), pp. 135–6.
2   Interesting material about expressions of hunger can be found in Leo Spitzer's books, *Italienische Kriegs-gefangenenbriefe* and *Die Umschreibungen des Begriffes Hunger*. The basic concern in these studies is the adaptability of word and image to the conditions of an exceptional situation. The author does not, however, operate with a genuine sociological approach.

18   Telling as Letting Know

Arindam Chakrabarti

Claims and Caveats

We often find out facts about distant times and places from the words of unexamined authorities. Francis Bacon was fined £40,000 nearly 400 years ago for taking bribes while in public office. Some of us know this just by reading popular books on the history of philosophy, not necessarily written by great historians whose strength of documentary evidence we have cared to establish first. I also know that I was born on the 16th of September. My mother told me so. Thus parents, books, teachers, newspapers, the radio, historians, eye-witnesses, laboratory-technicians and specialists *tell* us that *p*, and as a result, on many occasions – though not on all – we come to *know* that *p*.

Such knowledge depends upon and is comparable to knowledge by sense-perception, memory or inference on the basis of personal observation, but is not reducible to, i.e., not just another case of these above-mentioned varieties of knowledge.

Surely, when my mother uttered the words (in which she reported my date of birth) I had to hear them, both in the sense of hearing the noises she made and in the culturally conditioned sense of perceptually discriminating which words of her language she was using by making these noises. I also had – however automatically – to remember which word meant what in the language she spoke. In some even larger sense of "perceiving" or "seeing" I even had to *perceive* or *see* that she was seriously asserting what her sentence meant on that occasion of its use and recognize perceptually or inferentially her intention to inform me. I might have had to exercise other inferential skills to eliminate from the context any possibility of a joke just as I inferred from the rest of the sentences of the book that that remark about Bacon was not meant as an exaggeration or as an unasserted merely got-up philosophical example-sentence. (One could utter the sentence: "Some empiricists took bribes from every janitor of the Tower of London" as an example-sentence in Elementary Logic without telling one's audience that some empiricists did that.)

But the end-product, namely my knowledge of Bacon's public disgrace or my date of birth, is not *reducible* to just an amalgam of such sense-perception, memory, or inference. It is word-generated knowledge or knowledge by testimony (K.T. for short) – a *sui generis*. That is going to be the central claim of this paper.

From *Knowing from Words*, ed. B. K. Matilal and A. Chakrabarti. Dordrecht: Kluwer Academic Publishers, 1994, pp. 99–109. Copyright © 1994 Kluwer Academic Publishers. By permission of the publisher.

Upon the received view or standard account of linguistic communication, comprehension and credence fall apart. A trust-less understanding of the uttered sentence is taken as epistemically prior to and simpler than getting informed by the utterance. Even where we swallow information unquestioningly, uptake and acceptance might not be psychologically distinguishable but the standard account insists that they should be conceptually distinguished. Of course it will be perverse to argue in the following fashion:

Premise 1: I understand an utterance of the sentence "Bush is angry" only if I know what it means.
Premise 2: What it means is that Bush is angry.

Conclusion: I understand an utterance of the sentence "Bush is angry" only if I know that Bush is angry.

However, it is not so very obvious what is wrong with this argument. I shall not argue that any one who distrusts a particular utterance fails to understand it, because it goes without saying that you need to grasp the meaning of an utterance just as clearly in order to have disbelief in it as you need to do if you have to rely on it. But I think the standard separation of knowing what S said and knowing that what S said is the case tends to encourage an inferential account of the latter kind of knowing or K.T. It also tends to promote an ontology of abstract contents insofar as it requires us to come up with an answer to the question: what is knowledge of meaning (falling short of knowledge of a fact) knowledge of? One exciting and unorthodox consequence of accepting the irreducibility thesis about K.T. might be that trustless uptake or mere understanding should be regarded as the more complicated attitude (necessary, for instance, for accounting for our appreciation of fictional utterances or jokes) rather than as the simpler core compared to direct derivation of knowledge that p from an honest and informed utterance to the effect that p. The picture suggested would be that the so-called beliefless grasp of the content of an assertion is *K.T. minus trust*, rather than K.T. being *understanding plus trust*.

Since Hume argued (*Enquiry*, Chapter X) that our reliance on Testimony is just a garden case of inductive reasoning on the basis of the observed trustworthiness of the source of information, it has become the received view in Western philosophy that such knowledge from telling is reducible to inference, at least in principle. Of course, there is the other, more individualistic streak in Western Epistemology which refuses to give the status of knowledge at all to correct information gathered from a trusted teller. Explicitly stated by Locke, and perhaps traceable back to the passage in Plato's *Theaetetus* (201C) which dismisses true judgments on the basis of reliable hearsay as non-knowledge, this view would look upon the enterprise of knowledge as a task to be performed single-handedly. Thus Locke seems to suggest that only what one has oneself found out by personal contact with reality or through hard epistemic toil of other sorts counts as knowledge:

The floating of other men's opinions in our brains makes us not one jot the more knowing, though they happen to be true. What in them was science is in us by Opiniatretry . . . Such borrowed wealth like Fairy-money, though it were Gold in the hand from which he received it will be but Leaves and dust when it comes to use. (*Essay*, I, iv, #23)

I shall not try in this paper to combat such an extreme dismissal of K.T. The social character of knowledge, which Locke's kind of epistemological individualism tends to overlook becomes more and more inescapable with the progress and sophistication of Science. Dependence on authority goes deeper than just the level of learning details of scientific data from the specialist. As Quinton points out

> . . . the instruments of criticism in whose possession cognitive autonomy consists are themselves provided by authority.

Imagine a meticulous seeker of knowledge refusing to believe a laboratory report on a certain specimen, wishing to first examine it herself under a microscope. Insofar as she takes the accuracy of the microscope on trust her claim of complete cognitive autonomy would be self-refuting.

Let me bluntly state at this point that I think every competent user of language can on many occasions pass on knowledge and receive genuine knowledge through telling and being told. To think otherwise is to make the scope of the term "knowledge" unrealistically narrow and to be blind to one vital function of language, namely, the function of spreading or instilling well-grounded information. So I shall take the knowledge-hood of K.T. for granted and then only try to resist the reductive pressures by defending K.T.'s independence.

In the history of classical Indian epistemology, and about a thousand years before Hume, K.T.'s independence was threatened by Carvaka materialists, Buddhists and Vaisesikas who tried to reduce our alleged knowledge from the trusted words of an honest knowledgeable informant to either perception, or memory or inference. The Nyaya school tried to refute all these reductionistic proposals by insisting that the hearer's process of retrieving the very piece of knowledge which normally causes the speaker's utterance of a sentence is a unique "means of knowing" on a par with but never fully subsumable under sense-perception, introspection, memory, or inference. Trying often to express insights emerging out of Sanskrit texts dealing with this issue in the idiom of contemporary analytic epistemology, I shall defend K.T.'s independence in my own way.

To start with, some caveats. Although in what follows I shall be talking only about "speakers" and "hearers," I hope my arguments can be extended *mutatis mutandis* to cover the cases of writers and readers. There are, to be sure, additional problems in the case of written, type-written or printed words because ink-marks on paper need not be generated by the writer's (if there is any writer at all) intention to communicate knowledge. But I shall not deal with those additional issues here.

Secondly, although to avoid confusion I shall only discuss indicative utterances and our knowledge of truths about the world derived from them, I envisage the possibility of a general theory of knowing by being told which will also cover imperative utterances and our knowledge of what or how to do. We surely make claims of practical knowledge, both in the sense of learning technical know-hows and finding out morally correct or prudentially wise courses of action. And some of these knowledge-claims are made on the basis of what we are instructed, asked or advised to do.

A request or a command can be an instance of telling as much as an account or an assertion can be. Correspondingly, by listening to my instructor, or reading the manual or following a religious text we can *know* what to do or how to act. Spelling out the content of such knowledge constitutes a hard task for any theory which takes *truth* as a crucial feature of knowledge, but I don't want to speak to that issue at this stage.

Thirdly, I mentioned knowledge of the remote past or faraway places as impressive cases of knowledge by testimony because in such cases testimony seems to be irreplaceable or not easily replaceable by any other source of knowledge. But in numerous day-to-day contexts we actually rely on spoken or written words even if it concerns something happening very close by or even here at the present time. Thus our knowledge of train or plane-schedules, knowledge of the data, knowledge of what the person next to me is feeling or thinking, etc., are samples of knowledge which we standardly derive from words we hear or read. So, such knowledge does not have to be about distant places and times. Take the case of a person introducing herself at a social gathering. "I am Anita," says the stranger at a party and I come to know that she is Anita. If I am asked later on in the evening how I knew that *that* very person is Anita, I can perfectly rationally respond: "Because I was told by her" (in spite of the possibility that she was misleading me or joking with me).

This brings me to the fourth caveat. I introduced the topic as knowledge from the words of the authority. But the term "authority" need not be taken too seriously. Especially, we should not smell any theological deference to some privileged custodians of authority or elitism here. A thief can be an "authority" in this sense if he speaks from knowledge, speaks sincerely and without any wish to deceive. A murderer's words can give us knowledge when he is confessing in court. Usually, only such utterances count as knowledge-generating as are themselves *actually* caused by the speaker's knowledge of the very same fact. But sometimes even this requirement can be relaxed. A tape-recorder, a telephone-answering machine, a child parroting its elders can make us know valuable facts. Nevertheless, we do not need first to establish the general trustworthiness of the speaker in each case. Sometimes, of course, a topic-specific authority of the speaker is *presumed*. If my mother tells me about the time and circumstances of my birth I tend to have justified beliefs, rather than if strangers tell me about it. Notice that a presumption is not a premise. Unless we have good reason to doubt someone's version, it is natural for us to believe, and we even have the right to be sure, so that if what was said turns out to be true our belief counts as knowledge.

Finally, I said I shall be claiming that such knowledge is comparable but not reducible to perception, inference or memory. What did I mean by "comparable" and "not reducible"? Let me make that a bit clearer.

Obviously, I am not claiming that whenever someone tells me that *p*, I come to know that *p*. Like truths, jokes, stories and lies are told as well, and often we find out sooner or later that what was told is a lie, a joke, or a piece of fiction. Apart from such deliberately non-true utterances, some utterances spring from the speaker's own mistakes or fantasies. Not all spreaders of rumor know that they are not imparting knowledge. If we believe in such an utterance we end up being in the same error. So our claims of knowledge from others' words run the risk of misunderstanding, deception, and honestly transmitted false belief. But this testimony is in the same position as inductive inference or perception or memory. We can be deceived by the senses, misinterpret their message, go wrong in our generalization, and can misremember past experiences. But just as in spite of this defeasibility we can offer as justification for our knowledge-claim "I saw it with my own eyes" or "it follows from widely corroborated generalizations" or "I remember it clearly" – we can also offer "I was told by an eyewitness or an authority on the subject" – as an answer deserving equal epistemic prestige. So, when I say "comparable" I mean comparable in epistemic risk and respectability.

Now for the meaning of "not reducible." There is a trivial sense in which all knowledge could be reduced to inference. A claimant of knowledge as distinguished from a mere possessor of true belief, we agree, must be ready to provide a proof, a ground, an evidence, or a justification. If giving reasons for a belief automatically counts as "reasoning" and justifications are understood as arguments then we could call even our perceptual knowledge *inferential*. One could distinguish between two levels here. Suppose the alleged knowledge in question is *knowledge that p*. Is our demand for justification (which is relevant for the knowledgehood of the belief) a demand for evidence supporting the proposition *p*, or a demand for evidence for the proposition that the subject knows that *p*?

Consider first the case of perceptually obtained knowledge. When on the basis of sense experience I claim to know that this liquid is bitter, I could be asked to justify my belief. In response, I could just say, "I can taste the bitterness in it." This constitutes first-level justification of the proposition believed in. But one could press me further and ask: "Why do you believe what you taste (on this occasion or generally)?" My answer to that, if not naturalistically causal or statistically reliabilistic – could be inevitably inferential. For instance, I could justify my trust in perception by an inference on the basis of the empirical fact that false beliefs usually lead to practical failures or frustrations whereas trust upon the verdict of my senses has led me generally to success and satisfaction. This will be a second-level justification or a meta-justification for my originally perceptual – justifying ground. Similarly (to take Austin's example), when in answer to the question: "How do you know the Persians were defeated at Marathon?" – I say "Herodotus expressly states that they were" – that does constitute adequate first-level justification. Of course, we have to assume that I am ready to add "and I have no reason to suspect deliberate distortion or lack of correct information or ambiguity or insincerity in that part of Herodotus." But, parallelly, in the perceptual case we have to assume the perceiver's preparedness to add "and I have no reason to suspect that my sense-organs were defective, or that I was dreaming, or that my brain was being manipulated by a malevolent demon or was in a vat, etc." Now, one can go on to ask at the second level – either about this particular occasion or generally – "Why do you believe what you are told?" My answer to that distinct query will be an appeal to some sort of non-deductive inference from pragmatic success or survival-value or from people's general veracity-commitment: unless I answer naturalistically that I cannot help it or more strongly that since I use language to communicate I have to be generally disposed to accept people's say-so on pain of pragmatic self-stultification. If an analogous inferential answer or transcendental argument at the second level of justification does *not* tend to reduce all perception to inference, then I do not see why necessity of a similar inferential legitimization should brand our knowledge from people's words as *inferential* knowledge. At most it shows my knowledge *that I know that p* to be inferential; my knowledge *that p* still remains knowing by being told – good old K.T. – pristine in its irreducibility.

As I have admitted at the very outset K.T. has to depend on perception, e.g., of the noises the speaker makes or of the ink-marks the writer leaves on paper, on a dispositional memory of the entire socio-linguistic training which we call language-mastery, on inferential techniques of contextual disambiguation. But such dependence can be shown in the reverse direction as well. Most of us admit that perceptions like recognizing a particular flower or bush as Rhododendron typically depend upon usually uncritical acceptance of some testimony or other. That does not make such identificatory observations *reducible* to knowledge by testimony!

Suppose someone in this room points to a notebook and says, "This notebook was bought in Cambridge." I need to look at the notebook to find out the demonstrated referent of "This" and also perhaps *inferentially* to eliminate Cambridge, England, from the range of possible speaker-intended meanings. Still – if I end up getting certain that the notebook was indeed bought in Cambridge, Massachusetts, and the certainty turns out to have been knowledge, I cannot call my knowledge just a mixture of visual and auditory perception, guessing and remembering, etc. I knew by being told. The epistemic process can perhaps be *resolved* into bits of those other kinds of knowledge but the integrated end-product cannot be *reduced* to them.

So – I hope I have made my central claim clear. Let me now formulate it once again in a fuller form by enriching the simple-looking notion of "telling" a little more:

1. When S utters a sentence of the form "Fa" in a language that H has mastery of, it is natural for H's correct understanding of the sentence to take the form of the *awareness that Fa*, unless the context warrants the suspicion that S is lying, joking, speaking hypothetically, merely quoting non-committally, or is himself mis-informed.

2. If S's utterance of "Fa" is caused by knowledge that Fa then H's belief generated by a comprehending audition of the utterance also, on most

occasions, deserves the title of knowledge. To use the words of Michael Welbourne, "Knowledge is never denatured" when it travels in the vehicle of understood words. (See Welbourne, 1986, p. 49.)

3.   Our beliefless uptake of the so-called bare propositional content of an utterance (e.g., when we understand as an example given in a Grammar or Logic class the sentence "Socrates envied Plato for his nose") is a more sophisticated and complex cognitive event than our straightforward trusting intake of information. Just as lying or storytelling is a more sophisticated or artificial activity than speaking the truth (compare Reid, "Truth . . . requires no art or training"), understanding with a pinch or lump of salt is more complicated than a believing grasp of meaning where the characterizing tie between the qualifier (F) and the qualificand (a) itself works as the tie of commitment or assertion. Reception of the other person's message *naturally* comes unsalted.

4.   Even the message decoded from a command or request, i.e. what one is told to be or when or how one is told to do something, can be represented as something *known* from words with adequate care. Of course, one cannot claim to derive knowledge that the addressee *has* the property of bringing the chair from the request "Bring the chair please." Since commands cannot be assessed as *true* or *false*, Dummett has suggested using the neutral terms *correct* and *incorrect* for them. The command "Bring the chair" – issued to John – is correct just in case it is John who is asked to bring the chair. Bringing the chair can, as it were, be known to qualify John in two distinct ways – actually and commandedly. To get the message of an imperative is to grasp who is *required*, *desired* or *obligated* to bring about what, just as to get the message of an indicative is to grasp what or who is *asserted* to be of what sort. This uniform account of knowledge from telling surely avoids the problem of the standard Fregean sense-force model.

Is K.T. Perception or Memory

Colloquially we often describe understanding or even believing someone's statements as "seeing." We wait till we *see* someone's point and as long as the statement sounds too bizarre we do not quite *see* it making sense. Along with the words even the information is sometimes spoken of as having been "heard." This usage is not confined to English. Building up on similar usage the materialistic empiricist Cārvāka school of heterodox Indian philosophy had apparently tried to reduce knowing from words into a kind of perception. Now, informative utterances which transmit knowledge hitherto unattained by the auditor usually concern items which are outside his current perceptual range. No one can seriously insist that through trusted words we actually see or touch or taste or smell the objects spoken of. To listen to an eye-witness's account of a past incident vould then have to be like the experience of watching a *feelie* as imagined by Huxley in *A Brave New World*. But sometimes through the assistance of vividly remembered perceptual correlates of words we *perceive* things in a broader sense, as it were in our mind's eye. Could the information-intake be said to be perceptual in that sense? But the phenomeno-logical evidence seems to go against this suggestion. Every doubtfree comprehension of an utterance describing an unperceived situation does not take the form of even imagining what it would be for one to perceive it oneself. There is a broader sense in which we are said to perceptually identify speech-acts, i.e., know whether someone is committedly asserting or just entertaining a hypothesis or telling a tale or cracking a joke. But to perceive that someone is seriously and with authority saying that *p* is not to perceive that *p*. Two technical difficulties for the perceptualist reduction have been pointed out by Jagadīśa, a sixteenth-century Indian philosopher of the new Nyāya school.

In perception, one is typically at the mercy of the senses. Sometimes the sensory data are touched up or processed through memory (which might include previous linguistic training) and recognitional capabilities. Once we rely upon memory-assisted perception we have to include within the content of our allegedly sentence-generated knowledge *all that I perceptually recognize* at the time of listening to the utterance of the sentence. We might be reminded of some special feature of the speaker by the special accent or intonation which we cannot help noticing while we hear the utterance and as a result my perceptually obtained belief might be the belief that a certain Californian believes that Oxford is a boring city when the utterance was simply "Oxford is a boring city." So the perceptualist reduction will let in a lot of extra content which we don't want to include into exactly what I learn *from* the words. I might see and hear lots of nuances and other recognizable features of the utterance, knowledge of which could not be equated with what I *learn* from the utterance itself.

Secondly, in a speech-propagated belief the exact structure of the content is uniquely determined by the speaker's choice of words, word-order, and the speaker-intended mode of presentation of the objects of reference. From the utterance "The cat is on the mat" we learn that the cat is on the mat and not that the mat is under the cat, even if the two descriptions are extensionally equivalent. Had it been a perceptual experience – we could play around with the order of quantification or predication without falsifying the claim of knowledge. If I saw Bush drinking vodka without realizing that it was Bush and it was vodka that he was drinking – I can still be said (in a *de re* idiom) to have seen Bush drinking vodka. But if somebody told me "An important American statesman was drinking the favorite Russian drink" – I cannot know-by-being-told (because I was not told) that Bush was drinking vodka; even if I rightly guessed or otherwise visualized that very situation and even if that were the situation which prompted the speakers' description. Thus K.T. is not perception.

Memory, of course, plays a very vital role in K.T. We have to call up the meanings of individual words and store our general syntactial training in our memory. But if the end-knowledge as a whole had to be merely reproductive then we could only be informed about situations which we have ourselves previously observed. Surely, in this sense, not all knowledge-imparting tellings are *remindings*. The major point of using language is to extend our fellow-beings' stock *beyond* their personal observations and reminiscences. By understanding *new* sentences in a trusting manner we most certainly come to know facts which we did not ourselves witness and hence could not be reminded of. K.T. might be similar to remembering and some verbal reports when well-understood may create the illusion in a hearer that she is just recalling what she in fact never observed; yet that does not make the resulting sentence-generated knowledge a case of mere memory. From testimony I *can* but from memory I *cannot* retrieve information which I have not myself stored observationally into my own system.

It was Thomas Reid who suggested the comparison between receiving information about our surroundings from our senses and receiving information through language used by our fellow creatures. Reid could not have meant that listening to a report (which you trust) *is* a case of sensory acquaintance with the reported state of affairs. By this comparison he was mainly stressing the *directness* of our knowledge from words as against the inferential account given by Hume who not only called it "reasoning" from testimony but explicitly reduced the process to drawing conclusions from the trustworthiness of the source, etc.

References

Quinton, A., *Thoughts and Thinkers* (London: Duckworth, 1982).

Reid, T., *Inquiry on the Human Mind*, section XXIV (Edinburgh and London: Neill, 1814).

Welbourne, M., *The Community of Knowledge* (Aberdeen: Aberdeen University Press, 1986).

19   He I Sought but Did Not Find

Luce Irigaray

Relationships between people, and the desire for and use of communication, are more typical of women, as I have shown in numerous examples. Yet, these interpersonal relations are deprived of sexed identity, of I_{she} and of relations to one or to several partners of the same gender. In the responses given during linguistic research in various languages, few utterances make manifest a relationship between women.[1] A woman almost has to be both an active feminist, aware of her cultural alienation, and someone who has thought about her dependence upon language for her to make sentences that manage not to rule out a relation between women, although, to repeat, the percentage of sentences expressing a relation between women or a relationship of the subject of enunciation to a woman or to several women is very low, barely a few percent.

Women therefore speak unaware of their I_{she} and without communicating with a *you*she whether by direct or indirect communication: *I*she speak to *you*she – direct communication, or, *I*she speak about *her* – indirect communication. In those cases where it does appear, the woman's *I* is left to relations with *you*he, *he* or *He* and to *they*he (*ils*).

In this situation – one created by culture and language – dialogue becomes difficult, indeed impossible, particularly between daughter and mother. Yet women still desire to communicate, the results of linguistic research show that. In their responses women set the stage for two people; they represent them in a situation of communication; they use many verbs, prepositions and adverbs which describe dialogue and communication – not always possible but almost always sought after. In view of this, it is quite right to say that women are the guardians of communication, even if this communication is in many ways stultified and lacking real partners at present. Women would appear to be the guardians of love not only as mothers but also as speaking subjects whose message is above all to communicate.

With the loss of their *I*she and *you* she, their desire or intention to communicate is almost exclusively oriented toward *he*/they (*il[s]*). Intentionality thus artificially remains turned in a privileged direction: toward *he/they*, and with no return to the female self nor between female selves. The *he/they* becomes a pseudo-transcendence to which *she* is oriented, losing her subjectivity on the way, and thus the possibility of real communication.

Communication, exchange between people, intersubjectivity – the privileged loci of the least alienated female identity – are thus held back from appropriation by the female gender and from reciprocity between the sexes. With no return to the self, woman/women cannot truly engage in dialogue. They concern themselves with men – especially fathers and sons – situate themselves in familiar surroundings, hope for the future and continually try to communicate, particularly in the form of a question that might actually be a hope of being returned to themselves through the response they receive. And so in various ways they ask: Do you love me? The question really means: What am I for you? Or, Who am I? or, How can I return to myself?

More often than not the man gives no response. And in this order romantic courtship is not really a response since the woman is desired bodily, not spiritually and energetically and in the respect for her mother, her first transcendence. Libido is masculine, or neuter, so Freud claims. Yet there is a specific feminine energy, related more to communication, to growth, and not just to reproduction. A fairly common representation of the carnal act, and again a Freudian one, presents it as an immolation of energy – especially feminine energy. Energy is to be sacrificed by man for the sake of his return to the serious matters of public life, culture, science – activities that, it would seem, need to be cleansed of every aspect of affectivity and sexuality by returning to a zero degree of libidinal tension. As far as the woman is concerned, it has to be sacrificed in order to annul her own existence and the problems she poses. Energy is not to be cultivated in accordance with two modalities, two realities or truths, two measures (in the sense of rhythm as well as rationality), two temporalities, two tonalities, two voices, two colors. It is to be sacrificed on the cross – writes Hegel – rising towards a so-called neutral truth, devoid of perceptive and sensorial qualities, an everlasting truth, alien to our bodies living in the here and now.

The Western tradition typically represents living energy as sacrificed to spirit, to a truth assimilated to immutable ideals, beyond growth, beyond corporeality; celestial ideals imposed as models so that we all become alike – our sensible, natural and historical differences neutralized.

In this sense, the demand for equality for all, between all men and all women, is indeed faithful to our secular metaphysical ideal, an ideal aimed at universality, totality, the absolute, and essence by reducing distinctions and dissimilarities. This ideal intends to neutralize the specific energy of living beings in a puppet pantomime with one master – be it profit, technology, or a civil or religious master – pulling the strings.[2]

At the other extreme of this ideal becoming – not in terms of a destiny proper to the subject but in terms of an abstract model – nature carries out its generative fertile task: woman produces children. This act is also universally idealized, not as the culture of the woman's psychological energy, but rather as the exaltation of a natural act required by the public realm. Energy is utilized, on the one hand, to transform man, the citizen, into a slave to preconceived notions and, on the other hand, to venerate procreation which in itself is but a natural act. Our tradition thus lives on in an unresolved contradiction between an abstract ideal, split off from concerns for growth and sensible qualities, and a veneration of life in its raw state. With this contradiction, the culture of energy is paralyzed and destroyed. Humanity remains suspended between the contemplation of certain natural phenomena and the marvels or disasters of technological energy without being able to manage its own human energy.

In this context, war still fascinates as a sort of energetic debauchery or potlatch. Whether the energy is engendered by living beings or is manufactured, notably by technology, there is sacrifice, killing and destruction. Once this excessive expenditure is over, order is more or less restored on a temporary basis but nothing has actually been resolved. Energy between human beings does not operate any better, quite the opposite. War brings with it hatred, resentment, grief, and anguish, which takes years, centuries even, to redress. And the question, "Why", always remains, a question it seems impossible to answer.

If we are to regulate and cultivate energy between human beings, we need language. But not just denotative language, language that names, declares the reality or truth of things and transmits information; we also and especially need language that facilitates and maintains communication. And it is not just the lexicon we are talking about, but a syntax appropriate to intersubjectivity. This also calls into question why we speak – the very purpose of speech.

Regarding exchange, we have seen that women seek communication and especially dialogue. This quest, which, owing to culture, language, and to some extent, desire, is especially addressed to *he/they* (*il[s]*), does not meet with reciprocity. For men's teleology implies rather an abandonment of immediate communication – of intersubjectivity and dialogue – in order to set off in quest of an *oeuvre* (in which they usually alienate themselves) and, among other things, a spiritual journey compelled by a transcendence appropriate to their ego.

Hegel clearly points to this in the development of the dialectic: the individual is estranged from natural, sensible immediacy for the sake of a spiritual becoming in which reciprocal communication is never considered a goal of spirituality. This development works through the forward projections of an in-itself that becomes for-itself through reflection. Spirit is increasingly estranged from nature and in this movement supposedly assimilates all the in-itself and spiritualizes it.

Man is only able to communicate with other men by means of mediation: in the public realm, at work, in religion and so forth. But these mediations are already *his*. Men communicate in a public realm constructed in accordance with their model of identity, in accordance with their laws. However, their culture emphasizes property and abstract ideal values rather than relations between people. The community of men is generally an aggregate of one + one + one . . . whose individuation is abolished in the construction of a whole defined by geography, history, language, property or capital, opinions or beliefs, leaders or representatives, either elected or imposed, and so on.

Such are the persons who make up the whole but they are no longer persons explicitly related to their generic identity, as in the family. And what's more, they do not communicate among themselves except through already codified mediations: language, law, and religion, relations which leave little room for speaking subjects in the here and now. Among themselves, men hardly say a word to each other. They talk about the incidental aspects of daily life, they argue, but they do not communicate. They pass on news, and comment upon it. The fact that we neither realize that men and women do not talk in the same way nor appreciate what the differences are between their discourses is a sign, or symptom, of the absence of communication in the public realm of men. To say that men speak more objectively, women more emotionally, proves to be very much an approximation of the truth and is, in any case, partially wrong.

On the other hand, it would seem that women do communicate more and that men use language in order to denote reality or to produce and establish their truths rather than to communicate (immediately or mediately) among themselves.

How, then, can women and men be brought together if they each follow such different intentions? I believe that the process Hegel named recognition is one means of putting them face to face with each other again, one with the other, man and woman. Recognition is the act that could enable the hierarchical domination between the sexes to be overcome, which could restore woman and man, women and men to their respective identity and dignity, and which should bring about relations that are cultured, spiritual and not merely natural; relations founded upon a form of indirection or intransitivity. And so: I love to you, rather than: I love you.[3]

Notes

1   Cf. *Sexes et genres à travers les langues*, trans. G. Gill (Ithaca, N.Y.: Cornell University Press, 1985).

2 Plato's allegory of the cave was, during his time, a staging of such a pantomime (cf. *Speculum of the Other Woman*).

3 Here and in the following chapters Irigaray transforms verbs in their transitive form (that is, a verb that customarily or in a given occurrence requires a direct object). The verb *aimer*, to love or to like, is a transitive verb in French as in English. With *je t'aime* (I love you), the pronoun, *te* (you) is not only the direct object of the subject, *je* (I), but in French precedes the verb, so that the *te*, the potential other, is spatially 'assimilated' between the subject and his/her action. Irigaray intends the other to be positioned as subject not object, thus 'you' (*toi*) is not to be considered an indirect object of the verb as such. Introducing the preposition *à* syntactically separates the 'you' (*toi*) from the action of the 'I', and is intended to suggest a movement toward the other subject rather than the constitution of this latter by the action of the 'I', and is intended to suggest a movement toward the other subject rather than the constitution of this latter by the action of the 'I'. Thus, *j'aime à toi*. I have chosen to translate *à* as 'to', since I consider it best conveys this sense of movement toward the other as subject while not deviating from the relative simplicity of the transformed grammatical structure in French. Except where explicitly stated, the *à toi, à moi*, etc., although used as possessive pronouns in French (yours, mine), are not intended to function as such here.

PART FOUR

REFERENCE:
WHAT DO WE TALK ABOUT?

Introduction

Reference is at once one of the most technical problems in philosophy of language and one of the most common in everyday language use. If I am to tell you something in Chakrabarti's sense, or if we are to have a meaningful dialogue in Irigaray's sense, then I must know what you are talking about. If we are not referring to the same object, there is no engagement between what you say and I say, and therefore no possibility of understanding or agreement. We are locked in solipsistic universes of discourse, often misinterpreting what we are told.

Problems with reference are particularly difficult in semantic accounts of language. Truth-functional logic requires a base of singular and true predications, such as "Bill Clinton is from Arkansas," out of which complex truths are compiled. As Socrates observed to Theaetetus, singular predication is the simplest of linguistic units and it always requires a "what" (in this case Clinton) about which something is said. But how is that reference to a singular unique object to be accomplished. Even if ostension – the direct pointing out of an object – can be rescued from Wittgenstein's claim that pointing alone cannot indicate what is meant, we have direct acquaintance with very few of the things that we talk about. We know most things indirectly only by description. For most of us who have not met him in person, Clinton is "the present President of the United States."

Propositions containing denoting or referring expressions, whether names or singular descriptions, have caused special difficulty in logic where propositions must have a determinate truth value. What is one to make of a name or description that refers to no one, like "the present King of France"? What is one to make of the truth or falsity of a proposition about a fictional object, like "Unicorns have one horn." An even more daunting problem comes with application of the logical principle of substitutivity that challenged Frege to produce his theory of sense and reference. If two expressions mean the same thing, then they should be substitutable for each other without any change in truth value. But when different descriptions indicating the same person are substituted, the truth of a proposition may change. I may know that the present President of the United States is from Arkansas, but I may not know that the husband of Hillary Rodham is from Arkansas, even though the President of the United States is the same as the husband of Hillary. The two phrases refer to the same man, but in the context of the belief statement cannot be substituted for one another without possibly changing the truth value of the statement.

In his classic paper "On Denoting," Russell rejects both Frege's and Meinong's ways of dealing with these problems. Meinong posited an object for every denoting word or phrase no matter whether that object "subsists" in reality or not. Frege divided meaning into "sense" which indicates an object in a specific way, and "reference" which directly designates an object. Both solutions, Russell argues, create logical contradictions. His solution is "analytic." Puzzles about reference can be solved by the correct logical "reduction" or translation of propositions that include denoting phrases. The proper logical form of the denoting phrase, "The present President of the US" is: "It is not always false of x that x is President and that x is from Arkansas, and, if y is President, y is always identical with x." Denoting phrases do not themselves have reference to an object, either directly or as picked out by a sense, but are descriptions of a particular logical form, that is descriptions that are true of only one thing.

Does this mean that a body of truths like science is only a tissue of description, not anchored firmly to reality and true only relative to a given theory or set of descriptions? It is worries of this sort that motivate a rival "causal theory of reference," represented here by a selection from Saul Kripke. Whatever the logical advantages of Russell's reduction, Kripke argues, it does not capture the way we actually use words. In a complex series of counter-examples, Kripke shows that people often use names without knowing any uniquely identifying description at all. Furthermore, if it turns out that the usual identifying description is mistaken, the reference does not change. The solution is to see that proper names, and also some natural kind words, are "rigid designators." They attach directly to things or kinds of things without the intervention of senses or descriptions. Names are given in an initial "baptism" and passed on in causal chains of use. The implications for science are heartening. Once the substance "water" is fixed as an object of scientific interest, scientists can proceed to discover true things about water. They can determine that previous theories about water are false; they can also hope to establish water's necessary characteristics.

The examples that Kripke and other defenders of a "causal theory of reference" relied on were names for either individuals or natural kinds like water or gold. In contrast, the examples used by Foucault in his *Archeology of Knowledge* are objects of social scientific interest that emerged in a period of intellectual and social change. At the beginning of the nineteenth century, new social practices of incarceration and medicine were instituted along with new sets of objects of research in sciences such as psychology and sociology. These included psychiatric conditions like paranoia and neurosis, "delinquencies" like homosexuality, racial categories, and intelligence quotients. In Foucault's detailed account of the institutional, social, and political conditions for the appearance of these entities, there is no rigid designation. Objects of scientific interest are not discovered, baptized, and then studied in a chain of related researches. Nor are they simply the values of variables relevant to various new theories. Instead, they emerge out of a complex weave of historically specific discourses, uses of words, practices, authorities, and institutions that mark and often maim physical bodies.

The oppressive power of such references was not lost on Foucault or on those who studied his work. In her article "Critically Queer," Judith Butler speculates as to how the use of derogatory terms, in many cases historically related to scientific categories such as those studied by Foucault, can be undermined. Butler draws on historical studies of the nexus of institutional, discursive, and social authorities and also on the speech act theory of John Austin to understand the "force" of "naming" someone "queer" or "nigger." These are not labels for preexisting entities, she argues, but performative utterances that place individuals within certain categorizations or roles. Because an "I" is the "you" in someone else's address, a name can become a "paralyzing slur." And even when there is an attempt to consciously "resignify" names like "queer" or "black" in a positive way, a history of oppression can distort the result and must be continually reevaluated.

Butler's postmodern speaker does not claim the autonomy of the labeling and quantifying logician, nor is she complacent about performative rules that determine what she "can do with words." Initial baptisms, as well as speech acts, may create oppressive relations between husband and wife, heterosexual and straight, black and white, which make a speaker a rigidly designated object of oppression. But Butler also cites the dialogical malleability of language. A resignified "I am a queer" or "I am a black" in appropriate political contexts can change what it is to be queer or black.

Another critical perspective is that of the Hispanic philosopher, María Lugones. Not everyone, Lugones argues, lives in one universe of discourse. People of color often must travel between worlds of sense that are actual and not merely possible. In those worlds they may be different persons, identified by different descriptions. In postmodern literature much has been made of the oppressive force of the linguistic and conceptual systems within which a subject must take an identity. But in the possibility of identity across worlds, Lugones finds a basis for an intersubjectivity that makes common reference and the understanding of others possible.

20   On Denoting

Bertrand Russell

By a 'denoting phrase' I mean a phrase such as any one of the following: a man,
some man, any man, every man, all men, the present King of England, the
present King of France, the center of mass in the solar system at the first instant
of the twentieth century, the revolution of the earth round the sun, the revolution of the sun round the earth. Thus a phrase is denoting solely in virtue of its
form. We may distinguish three cases: (1) A phrase may be denoting, and yet
not denote anything; e.g., 'the present King of France.' (2) A phrase may denote one definite object; e.g., 'the present King of England' denotes a certain
man. (3) A phrase may denote ambiguously; e.g., 'a man' denotes not many
men, but an ambiguous man. The interpretation of such phrases is a matter of
considerable difficulty: indeed, it is very hard to frame any theory not susceptible of formal refutation. All the difficulties with which I am acquainted are
met, so far as I can discover, by the theory which I am about to explain.

The subject of denoting is of very great importance, not only in logic and
mathematics, but also in theory of knowledge. For example, we know that the
center of mass of the solar system at a definite instant is some definite point, and
we can affirm a number of propositions about it: but we have no immediate
acquaintance with this point, which is only known to us by description. The
distinction between *acquaintance* and *knowledge about* is the distinction between
the things we have presentations of, and the things we only reach by denoting
phrases. It often happens that we know that a certain phrase denotes unambiguously, although we have no acquaintance with what it denotes: this occurs in the
above case of the center of mass. In perception we have acquaintance with the
objects of perception, and in thought we have acquaintance with objects of a
more abstract logical character: but we do not necessarily have acquaintance with
the objects denoted by phrases composed of words with whose meanings we are
acquainted. To take a very important instance: there seems no reason to believe
that we are ever acquainted with other people's minds, seeing that these are not
directly perceived: hence what we know about them is obtained through denoting. All thinking has to start from acquaintance, but it succeeds in thinking *about*
many things with which we have no acquaintance.

The course of my argument will be as follows. I shall begin by stating the
theory I intend to advocate;[1] I shall then discuss the theories of Frege and
Meinong, showing why neither of them satisfies me; then I shall give the grounds
in favor of my theory; and finally I shall briefly indicate the philosophical consequences of my theory.

From *Mind* , 14 (1905), pp. 479–93. By permission of the Bertrand Russell Archives, Hamilton,
Canada.

My theory, briefly, is as follows. I take the notion of the *variable* as fundamental; I use '$C(x)$' to mean a proposition[2] in which x is a constituent, where x, the variable, is essentially and wholly undetermined. Then we can consider the two notions '$C(x)$ is always true' and '$C(x)$ is sometimes true.'[3] Then *everything* and *nothing* and *something* (which are the most primitive of denoting phrases) are to be interpreted as follows:

C (everything) means '$C(x)$ is always true';
C (nothing) means ' "$C(x)$ is false" is always true';
C (something) means 'It is false that "$C(x)$ is false" is always true.'[4]

Here the notion '$C(x)$ is always true' is taken as ultimate and indefinable, and others are defined by means of it. *Everything, nothing* and *something* are not assumed to have any meaning in isolation, but a meaning is assigned to *every* proposition in which they occur. This is the principle of the theory of denoting I wish to advocate: that denoting phrases never have any meaning in themselves, but that every proposition in whose verbal expression they occur has a meaning. The difficulties concerning denoting are, I believe, all the result of a wrong analysis of propositions whose verbal expressions contain denoting phrases. The proper analysis, if I am not mistaken, may be further set forth as follows.

Suppose now we wish to interpret the proposition, 'I met a man.' If this is true, I met some definite man; but that is not what I affirm. What I affirm is, according to the theory I advocate:

' "I met x, and x is human" is not always false.'

Generally, defining the class of men as the class of objects having the predicate *human*, we say that:

'C (a man)' means ' "$C(x)$ and x is human" is not always false.'

This leaves 'a man,' by itself, wholly destitute of meaning, but gives a meaning to every proposition in whose verbal expression 'a man' occurs.

Consider next the proposition 'all men are mortal.' This proposition[5] is really hypothetical and states that *if* anything is a man, it is mortal. That is, it states that if x is a man, x is mortal, whatever x may be. Hence, substituting 'x is human' for 'x is a man', we find:

'All men are mortal' means ' "If x is human, x is mortal" is always true.'

This is what is expressed in symbolic logic by saying that 'all men are mortal' means ' "x is human" implies "x is mortal" for all values of x.' More generally, we say:

'C (all men)' means ' "If x is human, then $C(x)$ is true" is always true.'

Similarly

'C (no men)' means ' "If x is human, then $C(x)$ is false" is always true.'
'C (some men)' will mean the same as 'C (a man),'[6] and
'C (a man)' means 'It is false that "$C(x)$ and x is human" is always false.'
'C (every man)' will mean the same as 'C (all men).'

It remains to interpret phrases containing *the*. These are by far the most interesting and difficult of denoting phrases. Take as an example 'the father of Charles II was executed.' This asserts that there was an x who was the father of Charles II and was executed.' Now, *the*, when it is strictly used, involves uniqueness; we do, it is true, speak of '*the son* of So-and-so' even when So-and-so has several sons, but it would be more correct to say 'a son of So-and-so.' Thus for our purposes we take *the* as involving uniqueness. Thus when we say 'x was the father of Charles II' we not only assert that x had a certain relation to Charles II, but also that nothing else had this relation. The relation in question, without the assumption of uniqueness, and without any denoting phrases, is expressed by 'x begat Charles II.' To get an equivalent of 'x was the father of Charles II,' we must add, 'If y is other than x, y did not beget Charles II,' or what is equivalent, 'If y begat Charles II, y is identical with x.' Hence, 'x is the father of Charles II' becomes: 'x begat Charles II; and "if y begat Charles II y is identical with x" is always true of y.'

Thus 'the father of Charles II was executed' becomes:

'It is not always false of x that x begat Charles II and that x was executed and that "if y begat Charles II, y is identical with x" is always true of y.'

This may seem a somewhat incredible interpretation; but I am not at present giving reasons, I am merely *stating* the theory.

To interpret 'C (the father of Charles II),' where C stands for any statement about him, we have only to substitute $C(x)$ *for* 'x was executed' in the above. Observe that, according to the above interpretation, 'C (the father of Charles II)' implies:

'It is not always false of x that "if y begat Charles II, y is identical with x" is always true of y,'

which is what is expressed in common language by 'Charles II had one father and no more.' Consequently if this condition fails, *every* proposition of the form 'C (the father of Charles II)' is false. Thus e.g. every proposition of the form 'C (the present King of France)' is false. This is a great advantage in the present theory. I shall show later that it is not contrary to the law of contradiction, as might be at first supposed.

The above gives a reduction of all propositions in which denoting phrases occur to forms in which no such phrases occur. Why it is imperative to effect such a reduction, the subsequent discussion will endeavor to show.

The evidence for the above theory is derived from the difficulties which seem unavoidable if we regard denoting phrases as standing for genuine constituents of the propositions in whose verbal expressions they occur. Of the possible theories which admit such constituents the simplest is that of Meinong.[7] This theory regards any grammatically correct denoting phrase as standing for an *object*. Thus 'the present King of France,' 'the round square,' etc., are supposed to be genuine objects. It is admitted that such objects do not *subsist*, but nevertheless they are supposed to be objects. This is in itself a difficult view; but the chief objection is that such objects, admittedly, are apt to infringe the law of contradiction. It is contended, for example, that the existent present King of France exists, and also does not exist, that the round square is round, and also not round, etc. But this is intolerable, and if any theory can be found to avoid this result, it is surely to be preferred.

The above breach of the law of contradiction is avoided by Frege's theory. He distinguishes, in a denoting phrase, two elements, which we may call the *meaning* and the *denotation*.[8] Thus 'the center of mass of the solar system at the beginning of the twentieth century' is highly complex in *meaning*, but its *denotation* is a certain point, which is simple. The solar system, the twentieth century, etc., are constituents of the *meaning;* but the denotation has no constituents at all.[9] One advantage of this distinction is that it shows why it is often worthwhile to assert identity. If we say 'Scott is the author of *Waverley*,' we assert an identity of denotation with a difference of meaning. I shall, however, not repeat the grounds in favor of this theory, as I have urged its claims elsewhere, and am now concerned to dispute those claims.

One of the first difficulties that confronts us, when we adopt the view that denoting phrases *express* a meaning and *denote* a denotation,[10] concerns the cases in which the denotation appears to be absent. If we say 'the King of England is bald,' that is, it would seem, not a statement about the complex *meaning* 'the King of England,' but about the actual man denoted by the meaning. But now consider 'the King of France is bald.' By parity of form, this also ought to be about the denotation of the phrase 'the King of France.' But this phrase, though it has a *meaning* provided 'the King of England' has a meaning, has certainly no denotation, at least in any obvious sense. Hence one would suppose that 'the King of France is bald' ought to be nonsense; but it is not nonsense, since it is plainly false. Or again consider such a proposition as the following: 'If u is a class which has only one member, then that one member is a member of u,' or, *as we may state it*, 'If u is a unit class, the u is a u.' This proposition ought to be *always* true, since the conclusion is true whenever the hypothesis is true. But 'the u' is a denoting phrase, and it is the denotation, not the meaning, that is said to be a u. Now if u is *not* a unit class, 'the u' seems to denote nothing; hence our proposition would seem to become nonsense as soon as u is not a unit class.

Now it is plain that such propositions do *not* become nonsense merely because their hypotheses are false. The king in *The Tempest* might say, 'If Ferdinand is not drowned, Ferdinand is my only son.' Now 'my only son' is a denoting phrase, which, on the face of it, has a denotation when, and only when, I have exactly one son. But the above statement would nevertheless have remained true if Ferdinand had been in fact drowned. Thus we must either provide a denotation in cases in which it is at first sight absent, or we must abandon the view that the denotation is what is concerned in propositions which contain denotating phrases. The latter is the course that I advocate. The former course may be taken, as by Meinong, by admitting objects which do not subsist, and denying that they obey the law of contradiction; this, however, is to be avoided if possible. Another way of taking the same course (so far as our present alternative is concerned) is adopted by Frege, who provides by definition some purely conventional denotations for the cases in which otherwise there would be none. Thus 'the King of France,' is to denote the null-class; 'the only son of Mr. So-and-so' (who has a fine family of ten), is to denote the class of all his sons; and so on. But this procedure, though it may not lead to actual logical error, is plainly artificial, and does not give an exact analysis of the matter. Thus if we allow that denoting phrases, in general, have the two sides of meaning and denotation, the cases where there seems to be no denotation cause difficulties both on the assumption that there really is a denotation and on the assumption that there really is none.

Notes

1   I have discussed this subject in *Principles of Mathematics*, Chap. V and § 476. The theory there advocated is very nearly the same as Frege's, and is quite different from the theory to be advocated in what follows.
2   More exactly, a propositional function.
3   The second of these can be defined by means of the first, if we take it to mean, 'It is not true that "$C(x)$ is false" is always true.'
4   I shall sometimes use, instead of this complicated phrase, the phrase '$C(x)$ is not always false,' or '$C(x)$ is sometimes true,' supposedly *defined* to mean the same as the complicated phrase.
5   As has been ably argued in Mr. Bradley's *Logic*, Book I, Chap. II.
6   Psychologically 'C (a man)' has a suggestion of only one, and 'C (some men)' has a suggestion of *more than one*, but we may neglect these suggestions in a preliminary sketch.
7   See *Untersuchungen zur Gegenstandstheorie und Psychologie* (Leipzig, 1904), the first three articles (by Meinong, Ameseder, and Mally respectively).
8   [See his "On Sense and Reference," reprinted in this volume.]
9   Frege distinguishes the two elements of meaning and denotation everywhere, and not only in complex denoting phrases. Thus it is the *meanings* of the constituents of a denoting complex that enter into its *meaning*, not their *denotation*. In the proposition 'Mont Blanc is over 1,000 metres high,' it is according to him the *meaning* of 'Mont Blanc,' not the actual mountain, that is a constituent of the *meaning* of the proposition.
10   In this theory, we shall say that the denoting phrase *expresses* a meaning; and we shall say both of the phrase and of the meaning that they *denote* a denotation. In the other theory, which I advocate, there is no *meaning*, and only sometimes a *denotation*.

21   Naming and Necessity

Saul Kripke

There is a well known doctrine of John Stuart Mill, in his book *A System of Logic*, that names have denotation but not connotation. To use one of his examples, when we use the name 'Dartmouth' to describe a certain locality in England it may be so called because it lies at the mouth of the Dart. But even, he says, had the Dart (that's a river) changed its course so that Dartmouth no longer lay at the mouth of the Dart, we could still with propriety call this place 'Dartmouth,' even though the name may suggest that it lies at the mouth of the Dart. Changing Mill's terminology, perhaps we should say that a name such as 'Dartmouth' does have a 'connotation' to some people, namely, it does connote (not to me – I never thought of this) that any place called 'Dartmouth' lies at the mouth of the Dart. But then in some way it doesn't have a 'sense.' At least it is not part of the meaning of the name 'Dartmouth' that the town so named lies at the mouth of the Dart. Someone who said that Dartmouth did not lie at the Dart's mouth would not contradict himself.

It should not be thought that every phrase of the form 'the *x* such that *Fx*' is always used in English as a description rather than a name. I guess everyone has heard about The Holy Roman Empire, which was neither holy, Roman nor an empire. Today we have The United Nations. Here it would seem that since these things can be so-called even though they are not Holy Roman United Nations, these phrases should be regarded not as definite descriptions but as names. In the case of some terms, people might have doubts as to whether they're names or descriptions; like 'God' – does it describe God as the unique divine being or is it a name of God? But such cases needn't necessarily bother us.

Now here I am making a distinction which is certainly made in language. But the classical tradition of modern logic has gone very strongly against Mill's view. Frege and Russell both thought, and seemed to arrive at these conclusions independently of each other, that Mill was wrong in a very strong sense: really a proper name, properly used, simply was a definite description abbreviated or disguised. Frege specifically said that such a description gave the sense of the name.[1]

Now the reasons against Mill's view and in favor of the alternative view adopted by Frege and Russell are really very powerful; and it is hard to see – though one may be suspicious of this view because names don't seem to be disguised descriptions – how the Frege–Russell view, or some suitable variant, can fail to be the case.

Let me give an example of some of the arguments which seem conclusive in favor of the view of Frege and Russell. The basic problem for any view such as Mill's is how we can determine what the referent of a name, as used by a given speaker, is. According to the description view, the answer is clear. If 'Joe Doakes' is just short for 'the man who corrupted Hadleyburg,' then whoever corrupted Hadleyburg uniquely is the referent of the name 'Joe Doakes.' However, if there is *not* such a descriptive content to the name, then how do people ever use names to refer to things at all? Well, they may be in a position to point to some things and thus determine the references of certain names ostensively. This was Russell's doctrine of acquaintance, which he thought the so-called genuine or proper names satisfied. But of course ordinary names refer to all sorts of people, like Walter Scott, to whom we can't possibly point. And our reference here seems to be determined by our knowledge of them. Whatever we know about them determines the referent of the name as the unique thing satisfying those properties. For example, if I use the name 'Napoleon,' and someone asks, 'To whom are you referring?', I will answer something like, 'Napoleon was emperor of the French in the early part of the nineteenth century; he was eventually defeated at Waterloo,' thus giving a uniquely identifying description to determine the referent of the name. Frege and Russell, then, appear to give the natural account of how reference is determined here; Mill appears to give none.

There are subsidiary arguments which, though they are based on more specialized problems, are also motivations for accepting the view. One is that sometimes we may discover that two names have the same referent, and express this by an identity statement. So, for example (I guess this is a hackneyed example), you see a star in the evening and it's called Hesperus.' (That's what we call it in the evening, is that right? – I hope it's not the other way around.) We see a star in the morning and call it 'Phosphorus.' Well, then, in fact we find that it's not a star, but is the planet Venus and that Hesperus and Phosphorus are in fact the same. So we express this by 'Hesperus is Phosphorus.' Here we're certainly not just saying of an object that it's identical with itself. This is something that we discovered. A very natural thing to say is that the real content [is that] the star which we saw in the evening is the star which we saw in the morning (or, more accurately, that the thing which we saw in the evening is the thing which we saw in the morning). This, then, gives the real meaning of the identity statement in question; and the analysis in terms of descriptions does this.

Also we may raise the question whether a name has any reference at all when we ask, e.g., whether Aristotle ever existed. It seems natural here to think that what is questioned is not whether this *thing* (man) existed. Once we've *got* the thing, we know that it existed. What really is queried is whether anything answers to the properties we associate with the name – in the case of Aristotle, whether any one Greek philosopher produced certain works, or at least a suitable number of them.

It would be nice to answer all of these arguments. I am not entirely able to see my way clear through every problem of this sort that can be raised. Furthermore, I'm pretty sure that I won't have time to discuss all these questions in these lectures. Nevertheless, I think it's pretty certain that the view of Frege and Russell is false.[2]

[. . .]

According to the view I advocate, then, terms for natural kinds are much closer to proper names than is ordinarily supposed. The old term 'common name' is thus quite appropriate for predicates marking out species or natural kinds, such as 'cow' or 'tiger.' My considerations apply also, however, to certain mass terms for natural kinds, such as 'gold,' 'water,' and the like. It is interesting to compare my views to those of Mill. Mill counts both predicates like 'cow,' definite descriptions, and proper names as names. He says of 'singular' names that they are connotative if they are definite descriptions but non-connotative if they are proper names. On the other hand, Mill says that *all* 'general' names are connotative; such a predicate as 'human being' is defined as the conjunction of certain properties which give necessary and sufficient conditions for humanity – rationality, animality, and certain physical features.[3] The modern logical tradition, as represented by Frege and Russell, seems to hold that Mill was wrong about singular names, but right about general names. More recent philosophy has followed suit, except that, in the case of both proper names and natural kind terms, it often replaces the notion of defining properties by that of a cluster of properties, only some of which need to be satisfied in each particular case. My own view, on the other hand, regards Mill as more-or-less right about 'singular' names, but wrong about 'general' names. *Perhaps* some 'general' names ('foolish,' 'fat,' 'yellow') express properties.[4] In a significant sense, such general names as 'cow' and 'tiger' do not, unless *being a cow* counts trivially as a property. Certainly 'cow' and 'tiger' are *not* short for the conjunction of properties a dictionary would take to define them, as Mill thought. Whether science can discover empirically that certain properties are *necessary* of cows, or of tigers, is another question, which I answer affirmatively.

Let's consider how this applies to the types of identity statements expressing scientific discoveries that I talked about before – say, that water is H_2O. It certainly represents a discovery that water is H_2O. We identified water originally by its characteristic feel, appearance, and perhaps taste (though the taste may usually be due to the impurities). If there were a substance, even actually, which had a completely different atomic structure from that of water, but resembled water in these respects, would we say that some water wasn't H_2O? I think not. We would say instead that just as there is a fool's gold there could be a fool's water; a substance which, though having the properties by which we originally identified water, would not in fact be water. And this, I think, applies not only to the actual world but even when we talk about counterfactual situations. If there had been a substance, which was a fool's water, it would then be fool's water and not water. On the other hand if this substance can take another form – such as the polywater allegedly discovered in the Soviet Union, with very different identifying marks from that of what we now call water – it is a form of water because it is the same substance, even though it doesn't have the appearances by which we originally identified water.

Let's consider the statement 'Light is a stream of photons' or 'Heat is the motion of molecules.' By referring to light, of course, I mean something which we have some of in this room. When I refer to heat, I refer not to an internal sensation that someone may have, but to an external phenomenon which we perceive through the sense of feeling; it produces a characteristic sensation which we call the sensation of heat. Heat *is* the motion of molecules. We have also discovered that increasing heat corresponds to increasing motion of molecules, or, strictly speaking, increasing average kinetic energy of molecules. So temperature is identified with mean molecular kinetic energy. However, I won't talk about temperature because there is the question of how the actual scale is to be set. It might just be set in terms of the mean molecular kinetic energy.[5] But what represents an interesting phenomenological discovery is that when it's hotter the molecules are moving faster. We have also discovered about light that light is a stream of photons; alternatively it is a form of electromagnetic radiation. Originally we identified light by the characteristic internal visual impressions it can produce in us, that make us able to see. Heat, on the other hand, we originally identified by the characteristic effect on one aspect of our nerve endings or our sense of touch.

Imagine a situation in which human beings were blind or their eyes didn't work. They were unaffected by light. Would that have been a situation in which light did not exist? It seems to me that it would not. It would have been a situation in which our eyes were not sensitive to light. Some creatures may have eyes not sensitive to light. Among such creatures are unfortunately some people, of course: they are called 'blind.' Even if all people had had awful vestigial growths and just couldn't see a thing, the light might have been around; but it would not have been able to affect people's eyes in the proper way. So it seems to me that such a situation would be a situation in which there was light, but people could not see it. So, though we may identify light by the characteristic visual impressions it produces in us, this seems to be a good example of fixing a reference. We fix what light is by the fact that it is whatever, out in the world, affects our eyes in a certain way. But now, talking about counterfactual situations in which, let's say, people were blind, we would not then say that since, in such situations, nothing could affect their eyes, light would not exist; rather we would say that that would be a situation in which light – the thing we have identified as that which in fact enables us to see – existed but did not manage to help us see due to some defect in us.

Perhaps we can imagine that, by some miracle, sound waves somehow enabled some creature to see. I mean, they gave him visual impressions just as we have, maybe exactly the same color sense. We can also imagine the same creature to be completely *insensitive* to light (photons). Who knows what subtle undreamt of possibilities there may be? Would we say that in such a possible world, it was sound which was light, that these wave motions in the air were light? It seems to me that, given our concept of light, we should describe the situation differently. It would be a situation in which certain creatures, maybe even those who were called 'people' and inhabited this planet, were sensitive not to light but to sound waves, sensitive to them in exactly the same way that we are sensitive to light. If this is so, once we have found out what light is, when we talk about other possible worlds we are talking about *this* phenomenon in the world, and not using 'light' as a phrase *synonymous* with 'whatever gives us the visual impression – whatever helps us to see'; for there might have been light and it not helped us to see; and even something else might have helped us to see. The way we identified light *fixed a reference*.

And similarly for other such phrases, such as 'heat'. Here heat is something which we have identified (and fixed the reference of its name) by its giving a certain sensation, which we call 'the sensation of heat.' We don't have a special name for this sensation other than as a sensation of heat. It's interesting that the language is this way. Whereas you might suppose it, from what I am saying, to have been the other way. At any rate, we identify heat and are able to sense it by the fact that it produces in us a sensation of heat. It might here be so important to the concept that its reference is fixed in this way, that if someone else detects heat by some sort of instrument, but is unable to feel it, we might want to say, if we like, that the concept of heat is not the same even though the referent is the same.

Nevertheless, the term 'heat' doesn't *mean* 'whatever gives people these sensations.' For first, people might not have been sensitive to heat, and yet the heat still have existed in the external world. Secondly, let us suppose that somehow light rays, because of some difference in their nerve endings, *did* give them these sensations. It would not then be heat but light which gave people the sensation which we call the sensation of heat.

Can we then imagine a possible world in which heat was not molecular motion? We can imagine, of course, having discovered that it was not. It seems to me that any case which someone will think of, which he thinks at first is a case in which heat – contrary to what is actually the case – would have been something other than molecular motion, would actually be a case in which some creatures with different nerve endings from ours inhabit this planet (maybe even we, if it's a contingent fact about us that we have this particular neural structure), and in which these creatures were sensitive to that something else, say light, in such a ways that they felt the same thing that we feel when we feel heat. But this is not a situation in which, say, light would have been heat, but a situation in which a stream of photons would have produced the characteristic sensations which *we* call 'sensations of heat.'

Similarly for many other such identifications, say, that lightning is electricity. Flashes of lightning are flashes of electricity. Lightning is an electrical discharge. We can imagine, of course, I suppose, other ways in which the sky might be illuminated at night with the same sort of flash without any electrical discharge being present. Here too, I am inclined to say, when we imagine this, we imagine something with all the visual appearances of lightning but which is not, in fact, lightning. One could be told: this appeared to be lightning but it was not. I suppose this might even happen now. Someone might, by a clever sort of apparatus, produce some phenomenon in the sky which would fool people into thinking that there was lightning even though in fact no lightning was present. And you wouldn't say that that phenomenon, because it looks like lightning, was in fact lightning. It was a different phenomenon from lightning, which is the phenomenon of an electrical discharge; and this is not lightning but just something that deceives us into thinking that there is lightning.

What characteristically goes on in these cases of, let's say, 'heat is molecular motion'? There is a certain referent which we have fixed, for the real world and for all possible worlds, by a contingent property of it, namely the property that it's able to produce such and such sensations in us. Let's say it's a contingent property of heat that it produces such and such sensations in people. It's after all contingent that there should ever have been people on this planet at all. So one doesn't know a priori what physical phenomenon, described in other terms – in basic terms of physical theory – is the phenomenon which produces these sensations. We don't know this, and we've discovered eventually that this phenomenon is in fact molecular motion. When we have discovered this, we've discovered an identification which gives us an essential property of this phenomenon. We have discovered a phenomeon which in all possible worlds will be molecular motion – which could not have failed to be molecular motion, because that's what the phenomenon *is*.[6] On the other hand, the property by which we identify it originally, that of producing such and such a sensation in us, is not a necessary property but a contingent one. This very phenomenon could have existed, but due to differences in our neural structures and so on, have failed to be felt as heat. Actually, when I say *our* neural structures, as those of human beings, I'm really hedging a point which I made earlier; because of course, it might be part of the very nature of human beings that they have a neural structure which is sensitive to heat. Therefore this too could turn out to be necessary if enough investigation showed it. This I'm just ignoring, for the purpose of simplyfying the discussion. At any rate it's not necessary, I suppose that this planet should have been inhabited by creatures sensitive to heat in this way.

Notes

1   Strictly speaking, of course, Russell says that the names don't abbreviate descriptions and don't have any sense; but then he also says that, just because the things that we call 'names' do abbreviate descriptions, they're not really names. So, since 'Walter Scott,' according to Russell, does abbreviate a description, 'Walter Scott' is not a name; and the only names that really exist in ordinary language are, perhaps, demonstratives such as 'this' or 'that,' used on a particular occasion to refer to an object with which the speller is 'acquainted' in Russell's sense. Though we won't put things the way Russell does, we could describe Russell as saying that names, as they are ordinarily called, *do* have sense. They have sense in a strong way, namely, we should be able to give a definite description such that the referent of the name, by definition, is the object satisfying the description. Russell himself, since he eliminates descriptions from his primitive notation, seems to hold in 'On Denoting' that the notion of 'sense' is illusory. In reporting Russell's views, we thus deviate from him in two respects. First, we stipulate that names shall be names as ordinarily conceived, not Russell's 'logically proper names'; second, we regard descriptions, and their abbreviations, as having sense.

2   When I speak of the Frege–Russell view and its variants, I include only those versions which give a substantive theory of the reference of names. In particular, Quine's proposal that in a 'canonical notation' a name such as 'Socrates' should be replaced by a description 'the Socratizer' (where 'Socratizes' is an invented predicate), and that the description should then be eliminated by Russell's method, was not intended as a theory of reference for names but as a proposed reform of language with certain advantages. The problems discussed here will all apply, *mutatis mutandis*, to the reformed language; in particular, the question, 'How is the reference of "Socrates" determined?' yields to the question, 'How is the extension of "Socratizes" determined?' Of course I do not suggest that Quine has ever claimed the contrary.

3   Mill, *A System of Logic* (New York: Longman, 1961).

4   I am not going to give any criterion for what I mean by a 'pure property,' or Fregean intension. It is hard to find unquestionable examples of what is meant. Yellowness certainly expresses a manifest physical property of an object and, relative to the discussion of gold above, can be regarded as a property in the required sense. Actually, however, it is not without a certain referential element of its own, for on the present view yellowness is picked out and rigidly designated as that external physical property of the object which we sense by means of the *visual impression of yellowness*. It does in this respect resemble the natural kind terms. The phenomenological quality of the sensation itself, on the other hand, can be regarded as a *quale* in some pure sense. Perhaps I am rather vague about these questions, but further precision seems unnecessary here.

5   Of course, there is the question of the relation of the statistical mechanical notion of temperature to, for example, the thermodynamic notion. I wish to leave such questions aside in this discussion.

6   Some people have been inclined to argue that although certainly we cannot say that sound waves 'would have been heat' if they had been felt by the sensation which we feel when we feel heat, the situation is different with respect to a possible phenomenon, not present in the actual world, and distinct from molecular motion. Perhaps, it is suggested, there might be another form of heat other than 'our heat,' which was not molecular motion; though no actual phenomenon other than molecular motion, such as sound, would qualify. Similar claims have been made for gold and for light. Although I am disinclined to accept these views, they would make relatively little difference to the substance of the present lectures. Someone who is inclined to hold these views can simply replace the terms 'light,' 'heat,' 'pain,' etc., in the examples by 'our light,' 'our heat,' 'our pain,' and the like. I therefore will not take the space to discuss this issue here.

22   The Formation of Objects

Michel Foucault

We must now list the various directions that lie open to us, and see whether this notion of 'rules of formation' – of which little more than a rough sketch has so far been provided – can be given real content. Let us look first at the formation of objects. And in order to facilitate our analysis, let us take as an example the discourse of psychopathology from the nineteenth century onwards – a chronological break that is easy enough to accept in a first approach to the subject. There are enough signs to indicate it, but let us take just two of these: the establishment at the beginning of the century of a new mode of exclusion and confinement of the madman in a psychiatric hospital; and the possibility of tracing certain present-day notions back to Esquirol, Heinroth, or Pinel (paranoia can be traced back to monomania, the intelligence quotient to the initial notion of imbecility, general paralysis to chronic encephalitis, character neurosis to non-delirious madness); whereas if we try to trace the development of psychopathology beyond the nineteenth century, we soon lose our way, the path becomes confused, and the projection of Du Laurens or even Van Swieten on the pathology of Kraepelin or Bleuler provides no more than chance coincidences. The objects with which psychopathology has dealt since this break in time are very numerous, mostly very new, but also very precarious, subject to change and, in some cases, to rapid disappearance: in addition to motor disturbances, hallucinations, and speech disorders (which were already regarded as manifestations of madness, although they were recognized, delimited, described, and analysed in a different way), objects appeared that belonged to hitherto unused registers: minor behavioural disorders, sexual aberrations and disturbances, the phenomena of suggestion and hypnosis, lesions of the central nervous system, deficiencies of intellectual or motor adaptation, criminality. And on the basis of each of these registers a variety of objects were named, circumscribed, analysed, then rectified, re-defined, challenged, erased. Is it possible to lay down the rule to which their appearance was subject? Is it possible to discover according to which non-deductive system these objects could be juxtaposed and placed in succession to form the fragmented field – showing at certain points great gaps, at others a plethora of information – of psychopathology? What has ruled their existence as objects of discourse?

(a)   First we must map the first *surfaces* of their *emergence*: show where these individual differences, which, according to the degrees of rationalization, con-

From *The Archeology of Knowledge*, trans. A. M. Sheridan Smith. New York: Pantheon Books, 1972, pp. 40–6. Copyright © Éditions Gallimard 1969. By permission of Georges Borchardt, Inc. and Routledge, London.

ceptual codes, and types of theory, will be accorded the status of disease, alienation, anomaly, dementia, neurosis or psychosis, degeneration, etc., may emerge,
and then be designated and analysed. These surfaces of emergence are not the
same for different societies, at different periods, and in different forms of discourse. In the case of nineteenth-century psychopathology, they were probably
constituted by the family, the immediate social group, the work situation, the
religious community (which are all normative, which are all susceptible to deviation, which all have a margin of tolerance and a threshold beyond which
exclusion is demanded, which all have a mode of designation and a mode of
rejecting madness, which all transfer to medicine if not the responsibility for
treatment and cure, at least the burden of explanation); although organized
according to a specific mode, these surfaces of emergence were not new in the
nineteenth century. On the other hand, it was no doubt at this period that new
surfaces of appearance began to function: art with its own normativity, sexuality
(its deviations in relation to customary prohibitions become for the first time an
object of observation, description, and analysis for psychiatric discourse), penality
(whereas in previous periods madness was carefully distinguished from criminal
conduct and was regarded as an excuse, criminality itself becomes – and subsequent to the celebrated 'homicidal monomanias' – a form of deviance more or
less related to madness). In these fields of initial differentiation, in the distances,
the discontinuities, and the thresholds that appear within it, psychiatric discourse
finds a way of limiting its domain, of defining what it is talking about, of giving it
the status of an object – and therefore of making it manifest, nameable, and
describable.

(b) We must also describe the authorities of delimitation: in the nineteenth
century, medicine (as an institution possessing its own rules, as a group of individuals constituting the medical profession, as a body of knowledge and practice, as an authority recognized by public opinion, the law, and government)
became the major authority in society that delimited, designated, named, and
established madness as an object; but it was not alone in this: the law and penal
law in particular (with the definitions of excuse, non-responsibility, extenuating
circumstances, and with the application of such notions as the *crime passionel*,
heredity, danger to society), the religious authority (in so far as it set itself up as
the authority that divided the mystical from the pathological, the spiritual from
the corporeal, the supernatural from the abnormal, and in so far as it practised
the direction of conscience with a view to understanding individuals rather than
carrying out a casuistical classification of actions and circumstances), literary
and art criticism (which in the nineteenth century treated the work less and less
as an object of taste that had to be judged, and more and more as a language
that had to be interpreted and in which the author's tricks of expression had to
be recognized).

(c) Lastly, we must analyse the *grids of specification*: these are the systems
according to which the different 'kinds of madness' are divided, contrasted, related, regrouped, classified, derived from one another as objects of psychiatric
discourse (in the nineteenth century, these grids of differentiation were: the soul,
as a group of hierarchized, related, and more or less interpenetrable faculties; the

body, as a three-dimensional volume of organs linked together by networks of dependence and communication; the life and history of individuals, as a linear succession of phases, a tangle of traces, a group of potential reactivations, cyclical repetitions; the interplays of neuropsychological correlations as systems of reciprocal projections, and as a field of circular causality).

Such a description is still in itself inadequate. And for two reasons. These planes of emergence, authorities of delimitation, or forms of specification do not provide objects, fully formed and armed, that the discourse of psychopathology has then merely to list, classify, name, select, and cover with a network of words and sentences: it is not the families – with their norms, their prohibitions, their sensitivity thresholds – that decide who is mad, and present the 'patients' to the psychiatrists for analysis and judgement; it is not the legal system itself that hands over certain criminals to psychiatry, that sees paranoia beyond a particular murder, or a neurosis behind a sexual offence. It would be quite wrong to see discourse as a place where previously established objects are laid one after another like words on a page. But the above enumeration is inadequate for a second reason. It has located, one after another, several planes of differentiation in which the objects of discourse may appear. But what relations exist between them? Why this enumeration rather than another? What defined and closed group does one imagine one is circumscribing in this way? And how can one speak of a 'system of formation' if one knows only a series of different, heterogeneous determinations, lacking attributable links and relations?

In fact, these two series of questions refer back to the same point. In order to locate that point, let us re-examine the previous example. In the sphere with which psychopathology dealt in the nineteenth century, one sees the very early appearance (as early as Esquirol) of a whole series of objects belonging to the category of delinquency: homicide (and suicide), *crimes passionels*, sexual offences, certain forms of theft, vagrancy – and then, through them, heredity, the neurogenic environment, aggressive or self-punishing behaviour, perversions, criminal impulses, suggestibility, etc. It would be inadequate to say that one was dealing here with the consequences of a discovery: of the sudden discovery by a psychiatrist of a resemblance between criminal and pathological behaviour, a discovery of the presence in certain delinquents of the classical signs of alienation, or mental derangement. Such facts lie beyond the grasp of contemporary research: indeed, the problem is how to decide what made them possible, and how these 'discoveries' could lead to others that took them up, rectified them, modified them, or even disproved them. Similarly, it would be irrelevant to attribute the appearance of these new objects to the norms of nineteenth-century bourgeois society, to a reinforced police and penal framework, to the establishment of a new code of criminal justice, to the introduction and use of extenuating circumstances, to the increase in crime. No doubt, all these processes were at work; but they could not of themselves form objects for psychiatric discourse; to pursue the description at this level one would fall short of what one was seeking.

If, in a particular period in the history of our society, the delinquent was psychologized and pathologized, if criminal behaviour could give rise to a whole series of objects of knowledge, this was because a group of particular relations was adopted for use in psychiatric discourse. The relation between planes of specification like penal categories and degrees of diminished responsibility, and planes of psychological characterization (faculties, aptitudes, degrees of development or involution, different ways of reacting to the environment, character types, whether acquired, innate, or hereditary). The relation between the authority of medical decision and the authority of judicial decision (a really complex relation since medical decision recognizes absolutely the authority of the judiciary to define crime, to determine the circumstances in which it is committed, and the punishment that it deserves; but reserves the right to analyse its origin and to determine the degree of responsibility involved). The relation between the filter formed by judicial interrogation, police information, investigation, and the whole machinery of judicial information, and the filter formed by the medical questionnaire, clinical examinations, the search for antecedents, and biographical accounts. The relation between the family, sexual and penal norms of the behaviour of individuals, and the table of pathological symptoms and diseases of which they are the signs. The relation between therapeutic confinement in hospital (with its own thresholds, its criteria of cure, its way of distinguishing the normal from the pathological) and punitive confinement in prison (with its system of punishment and pedagogy, its criteria of good conduct, improvement, and freedom). These are the relations that, operating in psychiatric discourse, have made possible the formation of a whole group of various objects.

Let us generalize: in the nineteenth century, psychiatric discourse is characterized not by privileged objects, but by the way in which it forms objects that are in fact highly dispersed. This formation is made possible by a group of relations established between authorities of emergence, delimitation, and specification. One might say, then, that a discursive formation is defined (as far as its objects are concerned, at least) if one can establish such a group; if one can show how any particular object of discourse finds in it its place and law of emergence; if one can show that it may give birth simultaneously or successively to mutually exclusive objects, without having to modify itself.

Hence a certain number of remarks and consequences.

1.   The conditions necessary for the appearance of an object of discourse, the historical conditions required if one is to 'say anything' about it, and if several people are to say different things about it, the conditions necessary if it is to exist in relation to other objects, if it is to establish with them relations of resemblance, proximity, distance, difference, transformation – as we can see, these conditions are many and imposing. Which means that one cannot speak of anything at any time; it is not easy to say something new; it is not enough for us to open our eyes, to pay attention, or to be aware, for new objects suddenly to light up and emerge out of the ground. But this difficulty is not only a negative one; it must not be attached to some obstacle whose power appears to be, exclusively, to blind, to hinder, to prevent discovery, to conceal the purity of the evidence or the dumb obstinacy of the things themselves; the object does

not await in limbo the order that will free it and enable it to become embodied in a visible and prolix objectivity; it does not pre-exist itself, held back by some obstacle at the first edges of light. It exists under the positive conditions of a complex group of relations.

2.   These relations are established between institutions, economic and social processes, behavioural patterns, systems of norms, techniques, types of classification, modes of characterization; and these relations are not present in the object; it is not they that are deployed when the object is being analysed; they do not indicate the web, the immanent rationality, that ideal nervure that reappears totally or in part when one conceives of the object in the truth of its concept. They do not define its internal constitution, but what enables it to appear, to juxtapose itself with other objects, to situate itself in relation to them, to define its difference, its irreducibility, and even perhaps its heterogeneity, in short, to be placed in a field of exteriority.

3.   These relations must be distinguished first from what we might call 'primary' relations, and which, independently of all discourse or all object of discourse, may be described between institutions, techniques, social forms, etc. After all, we know very well that relations existed between the bourgeois family and the functioning of judicial authorities and categories in the nineteenth century that can be analysed in their own right. They cannot always be superposed upon the relations that go to form objects: the relations of dependence that may be assigned to this primary level are not necessarily expressed in the formation of relations that makes discursive objects possible. But we must also distinguish the secondary relations that are formulated in discourse itself: what, for example, the psychiatrists of the nineteenth century could say about the relations between the family and criminality does not reproduce, as we know, the interplay of real dependencies; but neither does it reproduce the interplay of relations that make possible and sustain the objects of psychiatric discourse; Thus a space unfolds articulated with possible discourses: a system of *real* or *primary relations*, a system of *reflexive* or *secondary relations*, and a system of relations that might properly be called *discursive*. The problem is to reveal the specificity of these discursive relations, and their interplay with the other two kinds.

4.   Discursive relations are not, as we can see, internal to discourse: they do not connect concepts or words with one another; they do not establish a deductive or rhetorical structure between propositions or sentences. Yet they are not relations exterior to discourse, relations that might limit it, or impose certain forms upon it, or force it, in certain circumstances, to state certain things. They are, in a sense, at the limit of discourse: they offer it objects of which it can speak, or rather (for this image of offering presupposes that objects are formed independently of discourse), they determine the group of relations that discourse must establish in order to speak of this or that object, in order to deal with them, name them, analyse them, classify them, explain them, etc. These relations characterize not the language (*langue*) used by discourse, nor the circumstances in which it is deployed, but discourse itself as a practice.

23   Critically Queer

Judith Butler

> Discourse is not life; its time is not yours.
> Michel Foucault, *Politics and the Study of Discourse*

The risk of offering a final chapter on "queer" is that the term will be taken as the summary moment, but I want to make a case that it is perhaps only the most recent. In fact, the temporality of the term is precisely what concerns me here: how is it that a term that signaled degradation has been turned – "refunctioned" in the Brechtian sense – to signify a new and affirmative set of meanings? Is this a simple reversal of valuations such that "queer" means either a past degradation or a present or future affirmation? Is this a reversal that retains and reiterates the abjected history of the term? When the term has been used as a paralyzing slur, as the mundane interpellation of pathologized sexuality, it has produced the user of the term as the emblem and vehicle of normalization; the occasion of its utterance, as the discursive regulation of the boundaries of sexual legitimacy. Much of the straight world has always needed the queers it has sought to repudiate through the performative force of the term. If the term is now subject to a reappropriation, what are the conditions and limits of that significant reversal? Does the reversal reiterate the logic of repudiation by which it was spawned? Can the term overcome its constitutive history of injury? Does it present the discursive occasion for a powerful and compelling fantasy of historical reparation? When and how does a term like "queer" become subject to an affirmative resignification for some when a term like "nigger," despite some recent efforts at reclamation, appears capable of only reinscribing its pain? How and where does discourse reiterate injury such that the various efforts to recontextualize and resignify a given term meet their limit in this other, more brutal, and relentless form of repetition?[1]

In *On the Genealogy of Morals*, Nietzsche introduces the notion of the "sign-chain" in which one might read a utopian investment in discourse, one that reemerges within Foucault's conception of discursive power. Nietzsche writes, "the entire history of a 'thing,' an organ, a custom can be a continuous sign-chain of ever new interpretations and adaptations whose causes do not even have to be related to one another but, on the contrary, in some cases succeed and alternate with one another in a purely chance fashion"(77). The "ever new" possibilities of resignification are derived from the postulated historical discontinuity of the term. But is this postulation itself suspect? Can resignifiability be

From *Bodies that Matter*. New York and London: Routledge, 1993, pp. 223–30. Copyright © 1993 by Routledge. By permission of the publisher and author.

derived from a pure historicity of "signs"? Or must there be a way to think about the constraints on and in resignification that takes account of its propensity to return to the "ever old" in relations of social power? And can Foucault help us here or does he, rather, reiterate Nietzschean hopefulness within the discourse of power? Investing power with a kind of vitalism, Foucault echoes Nietzsche as he refers to power as "ceaseless struggles and confrontations . . . produced from one moment to the next, at every point, or rather in every relation from one point to another."[2]

Neither power nor discourse is rendered anew at every moment; they are not as weightless as the utopics of radical resignification might imply. And yet how are we to understand their convergent force as an accumulated effect of usage that both constrains and enables their reworking? How is it that the apparently injurious effects of discourse become the painful resources by which a resignifying practice is wrought? Here it is not only a question of how discourse injures bodies, but how certain injuries establish certain bodies at the limits of available ontologies, available schemes of intelligibility. And further, how is it that the abjected come to make their claim through and against the discourses that have sought their repudiation?

Performative Power

Eve Sedgwick's recent reflections on queer per-formativity ask us not only to consider how a certain theory of speech acts applies to queer practices, but how it is that "queering" persists as a defining moment of performativity.[3] The centrality of the marriage ceremony in J. L. Austin's examples of performativity suggests that the heterosexualization of the social bond is the paradigmatic form for those speech acts which bring about what they name. "I pronounce you . . ." puts into effect the relation that it names. But from where and when does such a performative draw its force, and what happens to the performative when its purpose is precisely to undo the presumptive force of the heterosexual ceremonial?

Performative acts are forms of authoritative speech: most performatives, for instance, are statements that, in the uttering, also perform a certain action and exercise a binding power.[4] Implicated in a network of authorization and punishment, performatives tend to include legal sentences, baptisms, inaugurations, declarations of ownership, statements which not only perform an action, but confer a binding power on the action performed. If the power of discourse to produce that which it names is linked with the question of performativity, then the performative is one domain in which power acts *as* discourse.

Importantly, however, there is no power, construed as a subject, that acts, but only, to repeat an earlier phrase, a reiterated acting that *is* power in its persistence and instability. This is less an "act," singular and deliberate, than a nexus of power and discourse that repeats or mimes the discursive gestures of power. Hence, the judge who authorizes and installs the situation he names invariably *cites* the law that he applies, and it is the power of this citation that gives the performative its binding or conferring power. And though it may appear that the binding power of his words is derived from the force of his will or from a prior authority, the opposite is more true: it is *through* the citation of the law that the figure of the judge's "will" is produced and that the "priority" of textual authority is established.[5] Indeed, it is through the invocation of convention that the speech act of the judge derives its binding power; that binding power is to be found neither in the subject of the judge nor in his will, but in the citational legacy by which a contemporary "act" emerges in the context of a chain of binding conventions.

Where there is an "I" who utters or speaks and thereby produces an effect in discourse, there is first a discourse which precedes and enables that "I" and forms in language the constraining trajectory of its will. Thus there is no "I" who stands *behind* discourse and executes its volition or will *through* discourse. On the contrary, the "I" only comes into being through being called, named, interpellated, to use the Althusserian term, and this discursive constitution takes place prior to the "I"; it is the transitive invocation of the "I". Indeed, I can only say "I" to the extent that I have first been addressed, and that address has mobilized my place in speech; paradoxically, the discursive condition of social recognition *precedes and conditions* the formation of the subject: recognition is not conferred on a subject, but forms that subject. Further, the impossibility of a full recognition, that is, of ever fully in-habiting the name by which one's social identity is inaugurated and mobilized, implies the instability and incompleteness of subject-formation. The "I" is thus a citation of the place of the "I" in speech, where that place has a certain priority and anonymity with respect to the life it animates: it is the historically revisable possibility of a name that precedes and exceeds me, but without which I cannot speak.

Queer Trouble

The term "queer" emerges as an interpellation that raises the question of the status of force and opposition, of stability and variability, *within* performativity. The term "queer" has operated as one linguistic practice whose purpose has been the shaming of the subject it names or, rather, the producing of a subject *through* that shaming interpellation. "Queer" derives its force precisely through the repeated invocation by which it has become linked to accusation, pathologization, insult. This is an invocation by which a social bond among homophobic communities is formed through time. The interpellation echoes past interpellations, and binds the speakers, as if they spoke in unison across time. In this sense, it is always an imaginary chorus that taunts "queer!" To what extent, then, has the performative "queer" operated alongside, as a deformation of, the "I pronounce you . . ." of the marriage ceremony? If the performative operates as the sanction that performs the heterosexualization of the social bond, perhaps it also comes into play precisely as the shaming taboo which "queers" those who resist or oppose that social form as well as those who occupy it without hegemonic social sanction.

On that note, let us remember that reiterations are never simply replicas of the same. And the "act" by which a name authorizes or deauthorizes a set of social or sexual relations is, of necessity, *a repetition*. "Could a performative succeed," asks Derrida, "if its formulation did not repeat a 'coded' or iterable utterance . . . if it were not identifiable in some way as a 'citation'?"[6] If a performative provisionally succeeds (and I will suggest that "success" is always and only provisional), then it is not because an intention successfully governs the action of speech, but only because that action echoes prior actions, and *accumulates the force of authority through the repetition or citation of a prior, authoritative set of practices*. What this means, then, is that a performative "works" to the extent that *it draws on and covers over* the constitutive conventions by which it is mobilized. In this sense, no term or statement can function performatively without the accumulating and dissimulating historicity of force.

This view of performatitivity implies that discourse has a history[7] that not only precedes but conditions its contemporary usages, and that this history effectively decenters the presentist view of the subject as the exclusive origin or owner of what is said.[8] What it also means is that the terms to which we do, nevertheless, lay claim, the terms through which we insist on politicizing identity and desire, often demand a turn *against* this constitutive historicity. Those of us who have questioned the presentist assumptions in contemporary identity categories are, therefore, sometimes charged with depoliticizing theory. And yet, if the genealogical critique of the subject is the interrogation of those constitutive and exclusionary relations of power through which contemporary discursive resources are formed, then it follows that the critique of the queer subject is crucial to the continuing *democratization* of queer politics. As much as identity terms must be used, as much as "outness" is to be affirmed, these same notions must become subject to a critique of the exclusionary operations of their own production: for whom is outness a historically available and affordable option? Is there an unmarked class character to the demand for universal "outness"? Who is represented by *which* use of the term, and who is excluded? For whom does the term present an impossible conflict between racial, ethnic, or religious affiliation and sexual politics? What kinds of policies are enabled by what kinds of usages, and which are backgrounded or erased from view? In this sense, the genealogical critique of the queer subject will be central to queer politics to the extent that it constitutes a self-critical dimension within activism, a persistent reminder to take the time to consider the exclusionary force of one of activism's most treasured contemporary premises.

As much as it is necessary to assert political demands through recourse to identity categories, and to lay claim to the power to name oneself and determine the conditions under which that name is used, it is also impossible to sustain that kind of mastery over the trajectory of those categories within discourse. This is not an argument *against* using identity categories, but it is a reminder of the risk that attends every such use. The expectation of self-determination that self-naming arouses is paradoxically contested by the historicity of the name itself: by the history of the usages that one never controlled, but that constrain the very usage that now emblematizes autonomy; by the future efforts to deploy the term against the grain of the current ones, and that will exceed the control of those who seek to set the course of the terms in the present.

If the term "queer" is to be a site of collective contestation, the point of departure for a set of historical reflections and futural imaginings, it will have to remain that which is, in the present, never fully owned, but always and only redeployed, twisted, queered from a prior usage and in the direction of urgent and expanding political purposes. This also means that it will doubtless have to be yielded in favor of terms that do that political work more effectively. Such a yielding may well become necessary in order to accommodate – without domesticating – democratizing contestations that have and will redraw the contours of the movement in ways that can never be fully anticipated in advance.

It may be that the conceit of autonomy implied by self-naming is the paradigmatically presentist conceit, that is, the belief that there is a one who arrives in the world, in discourse, without a history, that this one makes oneself in and through the magic of the name, that language expresses a "will" or a "choice" rather than a complex and constitutive history of discourse and power which compose the invariably ambivalent resources through which a queer and queering agency is forged and reworked. To recast queer agency in this chain of historicity is thus to avow a set of constraints on the past and the future that mark at once the *limits* of agency and its most *enabling conditions*. As expansive as the term "queer" is meant to be, it is used in ways that enforce a set of overlapping divisions: in some contexts, the term appeals to a younger generation who want to resist the more institutionalized and reformist politics sometimes signified by "lesbian and gay"; in some contexts, sometimes the same, it has marked a predominantly white movement that has not fully addressed the way in which "queer" plays – or fails to play – within non-white communities; and whereas in some instances it has mobilized a lesbian activism,[9] in others the term represents a false unity of women and men. Indeed, it may be that the critique of the term will initiate a resurgence of both feminist and anti-racist mobilization within lesbian and gay politics or open up new possibilities for coalitional alliances that do not presume that these constituencies are radically distinct from one another. The term will be revised, dispelled, rendered obsolete to the extent that it yields to the demands which resist the term precisely because of the exclusions by which it is mobilized.

We no more create from nothing the political terms that come to represent our "freedom" than we are responsible for the terms that carry the pain of social injury. And yet, neither of those terms are as a result any less necessary to work and rework within political discourse.

In this sense, it remains politically necessary to lay claim to "women," "queer," "gay," and "lesbian," precisely because of the way these terms, as it were, lay their claim on us prior to our full knowing. Laying claim to such terms in reverse will be necessary to refute homophobic deployments of the terms in law, public policy, on the street, in "private" life. But the necessity to mobilize the necessary error of identity (Spivak's term) will always be in tension with the democratic contestation of the term which works against its deployments in racist and misogynist discursive regimes. If "queer" politics postures independently of these other modalities of power, it will lose its democratizing force. The political deconstruction of "queer" ought not to paralyze the use of such terms, but, ideally, to extend its range, to make us consider at what expense and for what purposes the terms are used, and through what relations of power such categories have been wrought. Some recent race theory has underscored the use of "race" in the service of "racism," and proposed a politically informed inquiry into the process of *racialization*, the formation of race.[10] Such an inquiry does not suspend or ban the term, although it does insist that an inquiry into formation is linked to the contemporary question of what is at stake in the term. The point may be taken for queer studies as well, such that "queering" might signal an inquiry into (a) the *formation* of homosexualities (a historical inquiry which cannot take the stability of the term for granted, despite the political pressure to do so) and (b) the *deformative* and *misappropriative* power that the term currently enjoys. At stake in such a history will be the differential formation of homosexuality across racial boundaries, including the question of how racial and reproductive relations become articulated through one another.

One might be tempted to say that identity categories are insufficient because every subject position is the site of converging relations of power that are not univocal. But such a formulation underestimates the radical challenge to the subject that such converging relations imply. For there is no self-identical subject who houses or bears these relations, no site at which such relations converge. This converging and inter-articulation *is* the contemporary fate of the subject. In other words, the subject as a self-identical entity is no more.

It is in this sense that the temporary totalization performed by identity categories is a necessary error. And if identity is a necessary error, then the assertion of "queer" will be necessary as a term of affiliation, but it will not fully describe those it purports to represent. As a result, it will be necessary to affirm the contingency of the term: to let it be vanquished by those who are excluded by the term but who justifiably expect representation by it, to let it take on meanings that cannot now be anticipated by a younger generation whose political vocabulary may well carry a very different set of investments. Indeed, the term "queer" itself has been precisely the discursive rallying point for younger lesbians and gay men and in yet other contexts, for lesbian interventions and, in yet other contexts, for bisexuals and straights for whom the term expresses an affiliation with anti-homophobic politics. That it can become such a discursive site whose uses are not fully constrained in advance ought to be safeguarded not only for the purposes of continuing to democratize queer politics, but also to expose, affirm, and rework the specific historicity of the term.

Notes

This essay was originally published in *GLQ*, vol. 1, no. 1 (Fall 1993). I thank David Halperin and Carolyn Dinshaw for their useful editorial suggestions. This chapter is an altered version of that essay.

1   This is a question that pertains most urgently to recent questions of "hate speech."

2   Foucault, *History of Sexuality, Volume One,* pp.93–3

3   See Eve Kosofsky Sedgwick's "Queer Performativity" in *GLQ,* vol. 1, no. 1 (Spring 1993). I am indebted to her provocative work and for prompting me to rethink the relationship between gender and performativity.

4   It is, of course, never quite right to say that language or discourse "performs," since it is unclear that language is primarily constituted as a set of "acts". After all, this description of an "act" cannot be sustained through the trope that established the act as a singular event, for the act will turn out to refer to prior acts and to a reiteration of "acts" that is perhaps more suitably described as a citational chain. Paul de Man points out in "Rhetoric of Persuasion" that the distinction between constative and performative utterances is confounded by the fictional status of both ". . . the possibility for language to perform is just as fictional as the possibility for language to assert" (p.129). Further, he writes, "considered as persuasion, rhetoric is performative, but considered as a system of tropes, it deconstructs its own performance" (pp.130–1, in *Allegories of Reading* [New Haven: Yale University Press, 1987]).

5   In what follows, that set of performatives that Austin terms illocutionary will be at issue, those in which the binding power of the act *appears* to be derived from the intention or will of the speaker. In "Signature, Event, Context," Derrida argues that the binding power that Austin attributes to the speaker's intention in such illocutionary acts is more properly attributable to a citational force of the speaking, the iterability that establishes the authority of the speech act, but which establishes the non-singular character of that act. In this sense, every "act" is an echo or citational chain, and it is its citationality that constitutes its performative force.

6   "Signature, Event, Context," p.18.

7   The historicity of discourse implies the way in which history is constitutive of discourse itself. It is not simply that discourses are located *in* histories, but that they have their own constitutive historical character. Historicity is a term which directly implies the constitutive character of history in discursive practice, that is, a condition in which a "practice" could not exist apart from the sedimentation of conventions by which it is produced and becomes legible.

8   My understanding of the charge of presentism is that an inquiry is presentist to the extent that it (a) universalizes a set of claims regardless of historical and cultural challenges to that universalization or (b) takes a historically specific set of terms and universalizes them falsely. It may be that both gestures in a given instance are the same. It would, however, be a mistake to claim that all conceptual language or philosophical language is "presentist," a claim which would be tantamount to prescribing that all philosophy become history. My understanding of Foucault's notion of genealogy is that it is a specifically philosophical exercise in exposing and tracing the installation and operation of false universals. My thanks to Mary Poovey and Joan W. Scott for explaining this concept to me.

9   See Cherry Smith, *Lesbians Talk Queer Notions* (London: Scarlet Press, 1992).

10   See Omi and Winant, *Racial Formation in the United States: From the 1960s to the 1980s.*

24 "Worlds" and "World"-Traveling

María Lugones

Some time ago I came to be in a state of profound confusion as I experienced myself as both having and not having a particular attribute. I was sure I had the attribute in question and, on the other hand, I was sure that I did not have it. I remain convinced that I both have and do not have this attribute. The attribute is playfulness. I am sure that I am a playful person. On the other hand, I can say, painfully, that I am not a playful person. I am not a playful person in certain worlds. One of the things I did as I became confused was to call my friends, far away people who knew me well, to see whether or not I was playful. Maybe they could help me out of my confusion. They said to me, "Of course you are playful" and they said it with the same conviction that I had about it. Of course I am playful. Those people who were around me said to me, "No, you are not playful. You are a serious woman. You just take everything seriously." They were just as sure about what they said to me and could offer me every bit of evidence that one could need to conclude that they were right. So I said to myself: "Okay, maybe what's happening here is that there is an attribute that I do have but there are certain worlds in which I am not at ease and it is because I'm not at ease in those worlds that I don't have that attribute in those worlds. But what does that mean?" I was worried both about what I meant by "worlds" when I said "in some worlds I do not have the attribute" and what I meant by saying that lack of ease was what led me not to be playful in those worlds. Because you see, if it was just a matter of lack of ease, I could work on it.

I can explain some of what I mean by a "world." I do not want the fixity of a definition at this point, because I think the term is suggestive and I do not want to close the suggestiveness of it too soon. I can offer some characteristics that serve to distinguish between a "world," a utopia, a possible world in the philosophical sense, and a world-view. By a "world" I do not mean a utopia at all. A utopia does not count as a world in my sense. The "worlds" that I am talking about are possible. But a possible world is not what I mean by a "world" and I do not mean a world-view, though something like a world-view is involved here.

For something to be a "world" in my sense it has to be inhabited at present by some flesh and blood people. That is why it cannot be a utopia. It may also be inhabited by some imaginary people. It may be inhabited by people who are dead or people that the inhabitants of this "world" met in some other "world" and now have in this "world" in imagination.

From "Playfulness, 'World'-Traveling, and Loving Perception." *Hypatia*, 2:2 (Summer 1987), pp. 9–18. Copyright © 1987 by María Lugones. By permission of the author.

A "world" in my sense may be an actual society given its dominant culture's description and construction of life, including a construction of the relationships of production, of gender, race, etc. But a "world" can also be such a society given a non-dominant construction, or it can be such a society or *a* society given an idiosyncratic construction. As we will see it is problematic to say that these are all constructions of the same society. But they are different "worlds."

A "world" need not be a construction of a whole society. It may be a construction of a tiny portion of a particular society. It may be inhabited by just a few people. Some "worlds" are bigger than others.

A "world" may be incomplete in that things in it may not be altogether constructed or some things may be constructed negatively (they are not what "they" are in some other "world.") Or the "world" may be incomplete because it may have references to things that do not quite exist in it, references to things like Brazil, where Brazil is not quite part of that "world." Given lesbian feminism, the construction of "lesbian" is purposefully and healthily still up in the air, in the process of becoming. What it is to be a Hispanic in this country is, in a dominant Anglo construction purposefully incomplete. Thus one can not really answer questions of the sort "What is a Hispanic?", "Who counts as a Hispanic?", "Are Latinos, Chicanos, Hispanos, black Dominicans, white Cubans, Korean-Colombians, Italian-Argentinians Hispanic?" What it is to be a "Hispanic" in the varied so-called Hispanic communities in the U.S. is also yet up in the air. We have not yet decided whether there is something like a "Hispanic" in our varied "worlds." So, a "world" may be an incomplete visionary non-utopian construction of life or it may be a traditional construction of life. A traditional Hispano construction of Northern New Mexican life is a "world." Such a traditional construction, in the face of a racist, ethnocentrist, money-centered Anglo construction of Northern New Mexican life is highly unstable because Anglos have the means for imperialist destruction of traditional Hispano "worlds."

In a "world" some of the inhabitants may not understand or hold the particular construction of them that constructs them in that "world." So, there may be "worlds" that construct me in ways that I do not even understand. Or it may be that I understand the construction, but do not hold it of myself. I may not accept it as an account of myself, a construction of myself. And yet, I may be animating such a construction.

One can "travel" between these "worlds" and one can inhabit more than one of these "worlds" at the very same time. I think that most of us who are outside the mainstream of, for example, the U.S. dominant construction or organization of life are "world travelers" as a matter of necessity and of survival. It seems to me that inhabiting more than one "world" at the same time and "traveling" between "worlds" is part and parcel of our experience and our situation. One can be at the same time in a "world" that constructs one as stereotypically Latin, for example, and in a "world" that constructs one as Latin. Being stereotypically Latin and being simply Latin are different simultaneous constructions of persons that are part of different "worlds." One animates one or the other or both at the same time without necessarily confusing them, though simultaneous enactment can be confusing if one is not on one's guard.

In describing my sense of a "world," I mean to be offering a description of experience, something that is true to experience even if it is ontologically problematic. Though I would think that any account of identity that could not be true to this experience of outsiders to the mainstream would be faulty even if ontologically unproblematic. Its ease would constrain, erase, or deem aberrant experience that has within it significant insights into non-imperialistic understanding between people.

Those of us who are "world"-travellers have the distinct experience of being different in different "worlds" and of having the capacity to remember other "worlds" and ourselves in them. We can say "That is me there, and I am happy in that 'world'." So, the experience is of being a different person in different "worlds" and yet of having memory of oneself as different without quite having the sense of there being any underlying "I." So I can say "That is me there and I am so playful in that 'world'." I say "That is *me* in that 'world'" not because I recognize myself in that person, rather the first person statement is non-inferential. I may well recognize that that person has abilities that I do not have and yet the having or not having of the abilities is always an "I have . . ." and "I do not have . . .", i.e. it is always experienced in the first person.

The shift from being one person to being a different person is what I call "travel." This shift may not be willful or even conscious, and one may be completely unaware of being different than one is in a different "world," and may not recognize that one is in a different "world." Even though the shift can be done willfully, it is not a matter of acting. One does not pose as someone else, one does not pretend to be, for example, someone of a different personality or character or someone who uses space or language differently than the other person. Rather one is someone who has that personality or character or uses space and language in that particular way. The "one" here does not refer to some underlying "I." One does not *experience* any underlying "I."

Being at Ease in a "World"

In investigating what I mean by "being at ease in a 'world'," I will describe different ways of being at ease. One may be at ease in one or in all of these ways. There is a maximal way of being at ease, viz. being at ease in all of these ways. I take this maximal way of being at ease to be somewhat dangerous because it tends to produce people who have no inclination to travel across "worlds" or have no experience of "world" traveling.

The first way of being at ease in a particular "world" is by being a fluent speaker in that "world." I know all the norms that there are to be followed, I know all the words that there are to be spoken. I know all the moves. I am confident.

Another way of being at ease is by being normatively happy. I agree with all the norms, I could not love any norms better. I am asked to do just what I want to do or what I think I should do. At ease.

Another way of being at ease in a "world" is by being humanly bonded. I am with those I love and they love me too. It should be noticed that I may be with those I love and be at ease because of them in a "world" that is otherwise as hostile to me as "worlds" get.

Finally one may be at ease because one has a history with others that is shared, especially daily history, the kind of shared history that one sees exemplified by the response to the "Do you remember poodle skirts?" question. There you are, with people you do not know at all. The question is posed and then they all begin talking about their poodle skirt stories. I have been in such situations without knowing what poodle skirts, for example, were and I felt so ill at ease because it was not *my* history. The other people did not particularly know each other. It is not that they were humanly bonded. Probably they did not have much politically in common either. But poodle skirts were in their shared history.

One may be at ease in one of these ways or in all of them. Notice that when one says meaningfully "This is *my* world," one may not be at ease in it. Or one may be at ease in it only in some of these respects and not in others. To say of some "world" that it is "*my* world" is to make an evaluation. One may privilege one or more "worlds" in this way for a variety of reasons: for example because one experiences oneself as an agent in a fuller sense than one experiences "oneself" in other "worlds." One may disown a "world" because one has first person memories of a person who is so thoroughly dominated that she has no sense of exercising her own will or has a sense of having serious difficulties in performing actions that are willed by herself and no difficulty in performing actions willed by others. One may say of a "world" that it is "my world" because one is at ease in it, i.e. being at ease in a "world" may be the basis for the evaluation.

Given the clarification of what I mean by a "world," "world"-travel, and being at ease in a "world," we are in a position to return to my problematic attribute, playfulness. It may be that in this "world" in which I am so unplayful, I am a different person than in the "world" in which I am playful. Or it may be that the "world" in which I am unplayful is constructed in such a way that I could be playful in it. I could practice, even though that "world" is constructed in such a way that my being playful in it is kind of hard. In describing what I take a "world" to be, I emphasized the first possibility as both the one that is truest to the experience of "outsiders" to the mainstream and as ontologically problematic because the "I" is identified in some sense as one and in some sense as a plurality. I identify myself as myself through memory and I retain myself as different in memory. When I travel from one "world" to another, I have this image, this memory of myself as playful in this other "world." I can then be in a particular "world" and have a double image of myself as, for example, playful and as not playful. But this is a very familiar and recognizable phenomenon to the outsider to the mainstream in some central cases: when in one "world" I animate, for example, that "world's" caricature of the person I am in the other "world." I can have both images of myself and to the extent that I can materialize or animate both images at the same time I become an ambiguous being. This is very much a part of trickery and foolery. It is worth remembering that the trickster and the fool are significant characters in many non-dominant or outsider cultures. One then sees any particular "world" with these double edges and sees absurdity in them and so inhabits oneself differently. Given that Latins are constructed in Anglo "worlds" as stereotypically intense – intensity being a central characteristic of at least one of the Anglo stereotypes of Latins – and given that many Latins, myself included, are genuinely intense, I can say to myself "I am intense" and take a hold of the double meaning. And further-more, I can be stereotypically intense or be the real thing and, if you are Anglo, you do not know when I am which *because* I am Latin-American. As Latin-American I am an ambiguous being, a two-imaged self: I can see that gringos see me as stereotypically intense because I am, as a Latin-American, constructed that way but I may or may not *intentionally* animate the stereotype or the real thing knowing that you may not see it in anything other than in the stereotypi-cal construction. This ambiguity is funny and is not just funny, it is survival-rich. We can also make the picture of those who dominate us funny precisely because we can see the double edge, we can see them doubly constructed, we can see the plurality in them. So we know truths that only the fool can speak and only the trickster can play out without harm. We inhabit "worlds" and travel across them and keep all the memories.

Sometimes the "world"-traveler has a double image of herself and each self includes as important ingredients of itself one or more attributes that are *incom-patible* with one or more of the attributes of the other self: for example being playful and being unplayful. To the extent that the attribute is an important ingredient of the self she is in that "world" i.e., to the extent that there is a particularly good fit between that "world" and her having that attribute in it and to the extent that the attribute is personality or character central, that "world" would have to be changed if she is to be playful in it. It is not the case that if she could come to be at ease in it, she would be her own playful self. Because the attribute is personality or character central and there is such a good fit between that "world" and her being constructed with that attribute as central, *she* can-not become playful, she is unplayful. To become playful would be for her to become a contradictory being. So I am suggesting that the lack of ease solution cannot be a solution to my problematic case. My problem is not one of lack of ease. I am suggesting that I can understand my confusion about whether I am or am not playful by saying that I am both and that I am different persons in different "worlds" and can remember myself in both as I am in the other. I am a plurality of selves. This is to understand my confusion because *it is to come to see it as a piece* with much of the rest of my experience as an outsider in some of the "worlds" that I inhabit and of a piece with significant aspects of the experi-ence of non-dominant people in the "worlds" of their dominators.

So though I may not be at ease in the "worlds" in which I am not con-structed playful, it is not that I am not playful *because* I am not at ease. The two are compatible. But lack of playfulness is not caused by lack of ease. Lack of playfulness is not symptomatic of lack of ease but of lack of health. I am not a healthy being in the "worlds" that construct me unplayful.

Playfulness

I had a very personal stake in investigating this topic. Playfulness is not only the attribute that was the source of my confusion and the attitude that I recommend as the loving attitude in traveling across "worlds," I am also scared of ending up a serious human being, someone with no multi-dimensionality, with no fun in life, someone who is just someone who has had the fun constructed out of her. I am seriously scared of getting stuck in a "world" that constructs me that way. A world that I have no escape from and in which I cannot be playful.

I thought about what it is to be playful and what it is to play and I did this thinking in a "world" in which I only remember myself as playful and in which all of those who know me as playful are imaginary beings. A "world" in which I am scared of losing my memories of myself as playful or have them erased from me. Because I live in such a "world," after I formulated my own sense of what it is to be playful and to play I decided that I needed to "go to the literature." I read two classics on the subject: Johan Huizinga's *Homo Ludens* and Hans-Georg Gadamer's chapter on the concept of play in his *Truth and Method*. I discovered, to my amazement, that what I thought about play and playfulness, if they were right, was absolutely wrong. Though I will not provide the arguments for this interpretation of Gadamer and Huizinga here, I understood that both of them have an agonistic sense of "play." Play and playfulness have, ultimately, to do with contest, with winning, losing, battling. The sense of playfulness that I have in mind has nothing to do with those things. So, I tried to elucidate both senses of play and playfulness by contrasting them to each other. The contrast helped me see the attitude that I have in mind as the loving attitude in traveling across "worlds" more clearly.

An agonistic sense of playfulness is one in which *competence* is supreme. You better know the rules of the game. In agonistic play there is risk, there is *uncertainty*, but the uncertainty is about who is going to win and who is going to lose. There are rules that inspire hostility. The attitude of *playfulness is conceived as secondary to or derivative from play*. Since play is agon, then the only conceivable playful attitude is an agonistic one (the attitude does not turn an activity into play but rather presupposes an activity that is play). One of the paradigmatic ways of playing for both Gadamer and Huizinga is role-playing. In role-playing, the person who is a participant in the game has a *fixed conception of him or herself*. I also think that the players are imbued with *self-importance* in agonistic play since they are so keen on winning given their own merits, their very own competence.

When considering the value of "world"-traveling and whether playfulness is the loving attitude to have while traveling, I recognized the agonistic attitude as inimical to traveling across "worlds." The agonistic traveler is a conqueror, an imperialist. Huizinga, in his classic book on play, interprets western civilization as play. That is an interesting thing for Third World people to think about. Western civilization has been interpreted by a white western man as play in the agonistic sense of play. Huizinga reviews western law, art, and many other aspects of western culture and sees agon in all of them. Agonistic playfulness leads those who attempt to travel to another "world" with this attitude to failure. Agonistic travelers fail consistently in their attempt to travel because what they do is to try to conquer the other "world." The attempt is not an attempt to try to erase the other "world." That is what assimilation is all about. Assimilation is the destruction of other people's "worlds." So, the agonistic attitude, the playful attitude given western man's construction of playfulness, is not a healthy, loving attitude to have in travelling across "worlds." Notice that given the agonistic attitude one *cannot* travel across "worlds," though one can kill other "worlds" with it. So for people who are interested in crossing racial and ethnic boundaries, an arrogant western man's construction of playfulness is deadly. One cannot cross the boundaries with it. One needs to give up such an attitude if one wants to travel.

So then, what is the loving playfulness that I have in mind? Let me begin with one example: We are by the river bank. The river is very, very low. Almost dry. Bits of water here and there. Little pools with a few trout hiding under the rocks. But mostly is wet stones, grey on the outside. We walk on the stones for awhile. You pick up a stone and crash it onto the others. As it breaks, it is quite wet inside and it is very colorful, very pretty. I pick up a stone and break it and run toward the pieces to see the colors. They are beautiful. I laugh and bring the pieces back to you and you are doing the same with your pieces. We keep on crashing stones for hours, anxious to see the beautiful new colors. We are playing. The playfulness of our activity does not presuppose that there is something like "crashing stones" that is a particular form of play with its own rules. Rather *the attitude that carries us through the activity, a playful attitude, turns the activity into play.* Our activity has no rules, though it is certainly intentional activity and we both understand what we are doing. The playfulness that gives meaning to our activity includes uncertainty but in this case the uncertainty is an *openness to surprise.* This is a particular metaphysical attitude that does not expect the world to be neatly packaged. Rules may fail to explain what we are doing. We are not self-important, we are not fixed in particular constructions of ourselves, which is part of saying that we are *open to self-construction.* We may not have rules, and when we do have rules, *there are no rules that are to us sacred.* We are not worried about competence. We are not wedded to a particular way of doing things. While playful we have not abandoned ourselves to, nor are we stuck in, any particular "world." We *are there creatively.* We are not passive.

Playfulness is, in part, an openness to being a fool, which is a combination of not worrying about competence, not being self-important, not taking norms as sacred and finding ambiguity and double edges a source of wisdom and delight.

So, positively, the playful attitude involves openness to surprise, openness to being a fool, openness to self-construction or reconstruction and to construction or reconstruction of the "worlds" we inhabit playfully. Negatively, playfulness is characterized by uncertainty, lack of self-importance, absence of rules or a not taking rules as sacred, a not worrying about competence and a lack of abandonment to a particular construction of oneself, others and one's relation to them. In attempting to take a hold of oneself and of one's relation to others in a particular "world," one may study, examine and come to understand oneself. One may then see what the possibilities for play are for the being one is in that "world." One may even decide to inhabit that self fully in order to understand it better and find its creative possibilities. All of this is just self-reflection and it is quite different from resigning or abandoning oneself to the particular construction of oneself that one is attempting to take a hold of.

Conclusion

There are "worlds" we enter at our own risk, "worlds" that have agon, conquest, and arrogance as the main ingredients in their ethos. These are "worlds" that we enter out of necessity and which would be foolish to enter playfully in either the agonistic sense or in my sense. In such "worlds" we are not playful.

But there are "worlds" that we can travel to lovingly and traveling to them is part of loving at least some of their inhabitants. The reason why I think that traveling to someone's "world" is a way of identifying with them is because by traveling to their "world" we can understand *what it is to be them and what it is to be ourselves in their eyes.* Only when we have traveled to each other's "worlds" are we fully subjects to each other (I agree with Hegel that self-recognition requires other subjects, but I disagree with his claim that it requires tension or hostility).

Knowing other women's "worlds" is part of knowing them and knowing them is part of loving them. Notice that the knowing can be done in greater or lesser depth, as can the loving. Also notice that traveling to another's "world" is not the same as becoming intimate with them. Intimacy is constituted in part by a very deep knowledge of the other self and "world" traveling is only part of having this knowledge. Also notice that some people, in particular those who are outsiders to the mainstream, can be known only to the extent that they are known in several "worlds" and as "world"-travelers.

Without knowing the other's "world " one does not know the other and without knowing the other one is really alone in the other's presence because the other is only dimly present to one.

Through traveling to other people's "worlds" we discover that there are "worlds" in which those who are the victims of arrogant perception are really subjects, lively beings, resistors, constructors of visions even though in the mainstream construction they are animated only by the arrogant perceiver and are pliable, foldable, file-awayable, classifiable. I always imagine the Aristotelian slave as pliable and foldable at night or after he or she cannot work anymore (when he or she dies as a tool). Aristotle tells us nothing about the slave *apart from the master.* We know the slave only through the master. The slave is a tool of the master. After working hours he or she is folded and placed in a drawer till the next morning. My mother was apparent to me mostly as a victim of arrogant perception. I was loyal to the arrogant perceiver's construction of her and thus disloyal to her in assuming that she was exhausted by that construction. I was unwilling to be like her and thought that identifying with her, seeing myself in her necessitated that I become like her. I was wrong both in assuming that she was exhausted by the arrogant perceiver's construction of her and in my understanding of identification, though I was not wrong in thinking that identification was part of loving and that it involved in part my seeing myself in her. I came to realize through traveling to her "world" that she is not foldable and pliable, that she is not exhausted by the mainstream Argentinian patriarchal construction of her. I came to realize that there are "worlds" in which she shines as a creative being. Seeing myself in her through traveling to her "world" has meant seeing how different from her I am in her "world."

So in recommending "world"-traveling and identification through "world"-traveling as part of loving other women, I am suggesting disloyalty to arrogant perceivers, including the arrogant perceiver in ourselves, and to their constructions of women. In revealing agonistic playfulness as incompatible with "world"-traveling, I am revealing both its affinity with imperialism and arrogant perception and its incompatibility with loving and loving perception.

References

Gadamer, Hans-George. 1975. *Truth and method*. New York: Seabury Press.
Huizinga, Johan. 1968. *Homo ludens*. Buenos Aires, Argentina: Emecé Editores.

PART FIVE

TRUTH:
WHAT IS THE RELATION BETWEEN LANGUAGE AND REALITY?

Introduction

Truth has come up many times in previous readings. Analyses of meaning often make clear the relation of meaning and truth. Theories of reference explain how words pick out an object so something true or false can be said about that object. Wittgenstein's mirror theory of language asserts that a proposition is true depending on the fit between its structure and the structure of a state of affairs. For Dewey, truth is the successful use of a representation to further human aims. The positivist's verification theory of meaning depends on the assumption that a proposition is true when it can be verified.

But as positivism spread in the wake of Nazism from Germany to Britain and then to the United States, theories of truth began to come under fire. What exactly are these verified kernels of truth that are combined according to the rules of logic to yield true theories in science? Is a pure ideologically untainted empirical perception that can decisively verify propositions possible? Any communicable "sense data" or raw experience, it would seem, is shaped by ideas or Fregean "senses."

Traditionally two alternatives divided the field of truth theory. A philosopher defended either some version of a correspondence theory of truth or some version of a coherence theory of truth. A linguistic expression is true either when it matches reality, or – on the reasoning that any extralinguistic reality is inaccessible – when the expression coheres with other accepted beliefs. Both theories often have been refuted. The consistency of a statement with other statements seems to be no truth at all unless those other statements are proven to be true. On the other hand, the more intuitively acceptable correspondence theory also runs into difficulty. Any reality that is specifiable must be specifiable in some language, making it impossible to see how one could match language up with brute fact. For these and other reasons, in the 1930s the concept of truth, along with other "semantic" notions such as "meaning" and "designation," was charged with being unscientific. Statements about truth or meaning were not "verifiable" in any straightforward way, nor did it seem they could be understood as logical truths that needed no verification. At the same time, it was hard to see how they could be eliminated along with other suspect "metaphysical" concepts. Certainly one wanted the theories of science to be "true," but in what sense true was unclear.

The first selection in this section is the landmark paper by Alfred Tarski which professed to solve these problems. In Tarski's hands, the study of meaning and truth is reconstituted as a "modest and sober" enterprise with no encumbering metaphysical baggage. His innovations become the starting point for almost all analytic work on truth in the post World War II period.

Tarski reached back for a simple and unproblematic definition of truth that echoes Plato's teaching in the *Theaetetus*: a true statement says what is as it is; a false statement says what is other than what is. "Theaetetus walks" is true if and only if Theaetetus walks. With formulas of that form, Tarski argues, problems with truth can be solved for all languages with a specified structure and without recourse to extra scientific entities. Tarski's primary interest was the formalized language of mathematics and logic where the use of the word "true" caused crippling paradoxes and antinomies. But he also suggested that a semantic truth theory might be extended to the sciences, and even to portions of natural language. Truth can be defined for any given language with a formalized structure by providing postulates that specify what it is that is designated by each name and what objects satisfy each predicate. Then, using standard logic, all other truths can be compiled. For Tarski, truth becomes "truth in a language," or simply what is true in that language. The key to the simplicity of the solution is the separation in Tarski's truth formulas between a metalanguage and an object language, a distinction that is marked by the name of the expression in quotes and the use of the expression without quotes. Paradoxes will occur in a language that is semantically "closed," that is in a language whose universe of discourse includes everything: things, predicates, and names of predicates. But when terms like "truth" are seen as terms in a metalanguage in which we talk about a language and not terms in one universal language, the paradoxes that result from self reference can be avoided. Nor is any mystifying reference to states of affairs or facts necessary.

The enthusiasm with which Tarski's theory of truth was received is illustrated in the paper that follows by Donald Davidson, which considerably extends the scope of a "semantic theory of truth." It follows from Tarski's view of truth, Davidson argues, that sharing a language with a specified structure means sharing a picture of the world that is true. If natural language can be shown to have such an embedded structure and that structure can be made clear with the use of Tarskian truth formulas, the way the world is and its basic ontology can be read off from those formulas. Once linguistic elements like demonstratives, tenses, adverbs, intensional contexts are translated into a logical idiom, the basic structure of reality comes clear.

In contemporary continental traditions of deconstruction and postmodernism, truth comes under attack in a different way, not because it causes logical anomalies but because it may carry with it unacceptable authoritarianism. Whether a theory of truth can be framed that does not involve intellectual domination is the subject of the last three readings in this section. Linda Martín Alcoff, drawing on Foucault's discourse theory and Gadamer's hermeneutics, proposes a revised coherence theory of truth. Here coherence is not consistency within a contained and formally structured language, but the coherence of scientific theories and their technological derivatives with a wide range of beliefs including political convictions and moral commitments. Coherence, Alcoff argues, can provide a theory of truth that does justice to the actual ways in which truths are discovered by beings who are always already involved in a world of activities, beliefs, and commitments. A coherence theory of truth does away with any lingering illusion that truth can be founded on a pure untainted empirical base, but does so without reversion to paralyzing skepticism.

David Theo Goldberg also questions the political implications of universal claims to truth. Using the example of racist language, he begins by pointing out the inadequacy of "totalized truth claims" as were prescribed for the sciences by Tarski. If "racist" is defined as the extension of a set – as specified results on attitude surveys, or as the presence of explicitly discriminatory legal language – then the deep grammar that continues to generate racist discourse and racist practices may be ignored along with experiences of exclusion, marginalization, unequal patterns of punishment that are the real substance of racism. For Goldberg, truth is not a monological set of consistent statements, but constellations of "truth claims" rooted in deep matrices of classification, values, metaphysical attitudes, and social relations. Truth is not a question of any superficial logical surface structure. It cannot be determined by fixing a reference, or finding a judgment to be a "tautology." Instead, reference and truth, as well as political and moral judgment, are in complex interactions which necessitate that truth be determined "pragmatically."

Finally, feminist philosopher Sandra Harding, drawing on historical studies of scientific research and on contemporary critical theories of science, questions the usefulness of truth. Is truth a useful ideal, or does it block the regional innovation and variety that make science flourish? Given a variety of natural habitats and human aims, can one truth or one metaphysics derived from that truth ever be desirable? This does not mean, Harding argues, that there should be no standards by which to decide whether some theories are less false than others, or that "innovative strategies" should not be used to harmonize and integrate various understandings of nature. For Harding, understanding the relative truth about a natural phenomenon cannot be divorced from the various interests that are taken in that phenomenon. To subordinate interests to those of one dominant group is to lose the advantage of cross-fertilization and adaptation between cultures, as has happened between the healing practices of traditional cultures and Western medicine.

25   The Semantic Theory of Truth

Alfred Tarski

This paper consists of two parts; the first has an expository character, and the second is rather polemical.

In the first part I want to summarize in an informal way the main results of my investigations concerning the definition of truth and the more general problem of the foundations of semantics. These results have been embodied in a work which appeared in print several years ago.[1] Although my investigations concern concepts dealt with in classical philosophy, they happen to be comparatively little known in philosophical circles, perhaps because of their strictly technical character. For this reason I hope I shall be excused for taking up the matter once again.[2]

Since my work was published, various objections, of unequal value, have been raised to my investigations; some of these appeared in print, and others were made in public and private discussions in which I took part.[3] In the second part of the paper I should like to express my views regarding these objections. I hope that the remarks which will be made in this context will not be considered as purely polemical in character, but will be found to contain some constructive contributions to the subject.

In the second part of the paper I have made extensive use of material graciously put at my disposal by Dr. Marja Kokoszyńska (University of Lwów). I am especially indebted and grateful to Professors Ernest Nagel (Columbia University) and David Rynin (University of California, Berkeley) for their help in preparing the final text and for various critical remarks.

Exposition

1. The main problem – a satisfactory definition of truth

Our discussion will be centered around the notion[4] of *truth*. The main problem is that of giving a *satisfactory definition* of this notion, i.e., a definition which is *materially adequate* and *formally correct*. But such a formulation of the problem, because of its generality, cannot be considered unequivocal, and requires some further comments.

In order to avoid any ambiguity, we must first specify the conditions under which the definition of truth will be considered adequate from the material point of view. The desired definition does not aim to specify the meaning of a

From "The Semantic Conception of Truth and the Foundations of Semantics." *Philosophy and Phenomenological Research*, 4 (1943–44), pp. 342–75. Copyright © Jan Tarski and Kristina Ehrenfehcht. By permission of the heirs of Alfred Tarski.

familiar word used to denote a novel notion; on the contrary, it aims to catch hold of the actual meaning of an old notion. We must then characterize this notion precisely enough to enable anyone to determine whether the definition actually fulfills its task.

Secondly, we must determine on what the formal correctness of the definition depends. Thus, we must specify the words or concepts which we wish to use in defining the notion of truth; and we must also give the formal rules to which the definition should conform. Speaking more generally, we must describe the formal structure of the language in which the definition will be given.

The discussion of these points will occupy a considerable portion of the first part of the paper.

2. *The extension of the term "true"*

We begin with some remarks regarding the extension of the concept of truth which we have in mind here.

The predicate "true" is sometimes used to refer to psychological phenomena such as judgments or beliefs, sometimes to certain physical objects, namely, linguistic expressions and specifically sentences, and sometimes to certain ideal entities called "propositions." By "sentence" we understand here what is usually meant in grammar by "declarative sentence"; as regards the term "proposition," its meaning is notoriously a subject of lengthy disputations by various philosophers and logicians, and it seems never to have been made quite clear and unambiguous. For several reasons it appears most convenient to *apply the term "true" to sentences*, and we shall follow this course.[5]

Consequently, we must always relate the notion of truth, like that of a sentence, to a specific language; for it is obvious that the same expression which is a true sentence in one language can be false or meaningless in another.

Of course, the fact that we are interested here primarily in the notion of truth for sentences does not exclude the possibility of a subsequent extension of this notion to other kinds of objects.

3. *The meaning of the term "true"*

Much more serious difficulties are connected with the problem of the meaning (or the intension) of the concept of truth.

The word "true," like other words from our everyday language, is certainly not unambiguous. And it does not seem to me that the philosophers who have discussed this concept have helped to diminish its ambiguity. In works and discussions of philosophers we meet many different conceptions of truth and falsity, and we must indicate which conception will be the basis of our discussion.

We should like our definition to do justice to the intuitions which adhere to the *classical Aristotelian conception of truth* – intuitions which find their expression in the well-known words of Aristotle's *Metaphysics*.

> To say of what is that it is not, or of what is not that it is, is false, while to say of what is that it is, or of what is not that it is not, is true.

If we wished to adapt ourselves to modern philosophical terminology, we could perhaps express this conception by means of the familiar formula:

> The truth of a sentence consists in its agreement with (or correspondence to) reality.

(For a theory of truth which is to be based upon the latter formulation the term "correspondence theory" has been suggested.)

If, on the other hand, we should decide to extend the popular usage of the term "designate" by applying it not only to names, but also to sentences, and if we agreed to speak of the designate of sentences as "states of affairs," we could possibly use for the same purpose the following phrase:

> A sentence is true if it designates an existing state of affairs.[6]

However, all these formulations can lead to various misunderstandings, for none of them is sufficiently precise and clear (though this applies much less to the original Aristotelian formulation than to either of the others); at any rate, none of them can be considered a satisfactory definition of truth. It is up to us to look for a more precise expression of our intuitions.

4. A criterion for the material adequacy of the definition[7]

Let us start with a concrete example. Consider the sentence "snow is white." We ask the question under what conditions this sentence is true or false. It seems clear that if we base ourselves on the classical conception of truth we shall say that the sentence is true if snow is white, and that it is false if snow is not white. Thus, if the definition of truth is to conform to our conception, it must imply the following equivalence:

The sentence "snow is white" is true if, and only if, snow is white.

Let me point out that the phrase "snow is white" occurs on the left side of this equivalence in quotation marks, and on the right without quotation-marks. On the right side we have the sentence itself, and on the left the name of the sentence. Employing the medieval logical terminology we could say that on the right side the words "snow is white" occur in *suppositio formalis*, and on the left in *suppositio materialis*. It is hardly necessary to explain why we must have the name of the sentence, and not the sentence itself, on the left side of the equivalence. For, in the first place, from the point of view of the grammar of our language, an expression of the form "X is true" will not become a meaningful sentence if we replace in it "X" by a sentence or by anything other than a name – since the subject of a sentence may be only a noun or an expression functioning like a noun. And, in the second place, the fundamental conventions regarding the use of any language require that in any utterance we make about an object it is the name of the object which must be employed, and not the object itself. In consequence, if we wish to say something about a sentence, for example that it is true, we must use the name of this sentence, and not the sentence itself.[8]

It may be added that enclosing a sentence in quotation marks is by no means the only way of forming its name. For instance, by assuming the usual order of letters in our alphabet, we can use the following expression as the name (the description) of the sentence "snow is white":

the sentence constituted by three words, the first of which consists of the 19th, 14th, 15th, and 23rd letters, the second of the 9th and 19th letters, and the third of the 23rd, 8th, 9th, 20th, and 5th letters of the English alphabet.

We shall now generalize the procedure which we have applied above. Let us consider an arbitrary sentence; we shall replace it by the letter 'p.' We form the name of this sentence and we replace it by another letter, say 'X.' We ask now what is the logical relation between the two sentences "X is true" and 'p.' It is clear that from the point of view of our basic conception of truth these sentences are equivalent. In other words, the following equivalence holds:

(T)   X is true if, and only if, p.

We shall call any such equivalence (with 'p' replaced by any sentence of the language to which the word true refers, and 'X' replaced by a name of this sentence) an "*equivalence of the form* (T)."

Now at last we are able to put into a precise form the conditions under which we will consider the usage and the definition of the term true as adequate from the material point of view: we wish to use the term "true" in such a way that all equivalences of the form (T) can be asserted, and *we shall call a definition of truth "adequate" if all these equivalences follow from it.*

It should be emphasized that neither the expression (T) itself (which is not a sentence, but only a schema of a sentence) nor any particular instance of the form (T) can be regarded as a definition of truth. We can only say that every equivalence of the form (T) obtained by replacing 'p' by a particular sentence, and 'X' by a name of this sentence, may be considered a partial definition of truth, which explains wherein the truth of this one individual sentence consists. The general definition has to be, in a certain sense, a logical conjunction of all these partial definitions.

(The last remark calls for some comments. A language may admit the construction of infinitely many sentences; and thus the number of partial definitions of truth referring to sentences of such a language will also be infinite. Hence to give our remark a precise sense we should have to explain what is meant by a "logical conjunction of infinitely many sentences"; but this would lead us too far into technical problems of modern logic.)

5. *Truth as a semantic concept*

I should like to propose the name "*the semantic conception of truth*" for the conception of truth which has just been discussed.

Semantics is a discipline which, speaking loosely, *deals with certain relations between expressions of a language and the objects* (or "states of affairs") "*referred to*" *by those expressions*. As typical examples of semantic concepts we may mention the concepts of *designation*, *satisfaction*, and *definition* as these occur in the following examples:

the expression the father of his country designates (denotes) George Washington;

snow satisfies the sentential function (the condition) "x is white";

the equation "2x = 1" defines (uniquely determines) the number 1/2.

While the words "designates;" "satisfies;" and "defines" express relations (between certain expressions and the objects "referred to" by these expressions), the word "true" is of a different logical nature: it expresses a property (or denotes a class) of certain expressions, viz., of sentences. However, it is easily seen that all the formulations which were given earlier and which aimed to explain the meaning of this word (cf. sections 3 and 4) referred not only to sentences themselves, but also to objects "talked about" by these sentences or possibly to "states of affairs" described by them. And, more-over, it turns out that the simplest and the most natural way of obtaining an exact definition of truth is one which involves the use of other semantic notions, e.g., the notion of satisfaction. It is for these reasons that we count the concept of truth which is discussed here among the concepts of semantics and the problem of defining truth proves to be closely related to the more general problem of setting up the foundations of theoretical semantics.

It is perhaps worthwhile saying that semantics as it is conceived in this paper (and in former papers of the author) is a sober and modest discipline which has no pretensions of being a universal patent-medicine for all the ills and diseases of mankind whether imaginary or real. You will not find in semantics any remedy for decayed teeth or illusions of grandeur or class conflicts. Nor is semantics a device for establishing that everyone except the speaker and his friends is speaking nonsense.

From antiquity to the present day the concepts of semantics have played an important role in the discussions of philosophers, logicians, and philologists. Nevertheless, these concepts have been treated for a long time with a certain amount of suspicion. From a historical standpoint, this suspicion is to be regarded as completely justified. For although the meaning of semantic concepts as they are used in everyday language seems to be rather clear and understandable, still all attempts to characterize this meaning in a general and exact way miscarried. And what is worse, various arguments in which these concepts were involved, and which seemed otherwise quite correct and based upon apparently obvious premises, led frequently to paradoxes and antinomies. It is sufficient to mention here the *antinomy of the liar*, Richard's *antinomy of definability* (by means of a finite number of words), and Grelling-Nelson's *antinomy of heterological* terms.[9]

I believe that the method which is outlined in this paper helps to overcome these difficult ties and assures the possibility of a consistent use of semantic concepts.

6. *Languages with a specified structure*

Because of the possible occurrence of antinomies, the problem of specifying the formal structure and the vocabulary of a language in which definitions of semantic concepts are to be given becomes especially acute; and we turn now to this problem.

There are certain general conditions under which the structure of a language is regarded as *exactly specified*. Thus, to specify the structure of a language, we must characterize unambiguously the class of those words and expressions which are to be considered *meaningful*. In particular, we must indicate all words which we decide to use without defining them, and which are called "*undefined* (or *primitive*) *terms*"; and we must give the so-called *rules of definition* for introducing new or *defined terms*. Furthermore, we must set up criteria for distinguishing within the class of expressions those which we call "*sentences*." Finally, we must formulate the conditions under which a sentence of the language can be *asserted*. In particular, we must indicate all *axioms* (or *primitive sentences*), i.e., those sentences which we decide to assert without proof; and we must give the so-called *rules of inference* (or *rules of proof*) by means of which we can deduce new asserted sentences from other sentences, which have been previously asserted. Axioms, as well as sentences deduced from them by means of rules of inference, are referred to as "*theorems*" or "*provable sentences*."

If in specifying the structure of a language we refer exclusively to the form of the expressions involved, the language is said to be *formalized*. In such a language theorems are the only sentences which can be asserted.

At the present time the only languages with a specified structure are the formalized languages of various systems of deductive logic, possibly enriched by the introduction of certain nonlogical terms. However, the field of application of these languages is rather comprehensive; we are able, theoretically, to develop in them various branches of science, for instance, mathematics and theoretical physics.

(On the other hand, we can imagine the construction of languages which have an exactly specified structure without being formalized. In such a language the assertability of sentences, for instance, may depend not always on their form, but sometimes on other, nonlinguistic factors. It would be interesting and important actually to construct a language of this type, and specifically one which would prove to be sufficient for the development of a comprehensive branch of empirical science; for this would justify the hope that languages with specified structure could finally replace everyday language in scientific discourse.)

The problem of the definition of truth obtains a precise meaning and can be solved in a rigorous way only for those languages whose structure has been exactly specified. For other languages – thus, for all natural, "spoken" languages – the meaning of the problem is more or less vague, and its solution can have only an approximate character. Roughly speaking, the approximation consists in replacing a natural language (or a portion of it in which we are interested) by one whose structure is exactly specified, and which diverges from the given language "as little as possible."

7. The antinomy of the liar

In order to discover some of the more specific conditions which must be satisfied by languages in which (or for which) the definition of truth is to be given, it will be advisable to begin with a discussion of that antinomy which directly involves the notion of truth, namely, the antinomy of the liar.

To obtain this antinomy in a perspicuous form,[10] consider the following sentence:

The sentence printed in this paper on p. 52, column B, ll. 28–29, is not true.

For brevity we shall replace the sentence just stated by the letter 's.'

According to our convention concerning the adequate usage of the term "true," we assert the following equivalence of the form (T):

(1)   's' is true if, and only if, the sentence printed in this paper on p. 52, column B, ll. 28–29 is not true.

On the other hand, keeping in mind the meaning of the symbol '*s.*' we establish empirically the following fact:

(2)   's' is identical with the sentence printed in this paper on p. 52, column B, ll. 28–29.

Now, by a familiar law from the theory of identity (Leibniz's law), it follows from (2) that we may replace in (1) the expression "the sentence printed in this paper on p. 52, column B. ll. 28–29" by the symbol " '*s.*' " We thus obtain what follows:

(3)   's' is true if, and only if, 's' is not true.

In this way we have arrived at an obvious contradiction.

In my judgment, it would be quite wrong and dangerous from the standpoint of scientific progress to depreciate the importance of this and other antinomies, and to treat them as jokes or sophistries. It is a fact that we are here in the presence of an absurdity, that we have been compelled to assert a false sentence [since (3), as an equivalence between two contradictory sentences, is necessarily false]. If we take our work seriously, we cannot be reconciled with this fact. We must discover its cause, that is to say, we must analyze premises upon which the antinomy is based; we must then reject at least one of these premises, and we must investigate the consequences which this has for the whole domain of our research.

It should be emphasized that antinomies have played a preeminent role in establishing the foundations of modern deductive sciences. And just as class-theoretical antinomies, and in particular Russell's antinomy (of the class of all classes that are not members of themselves), were the starting point for the successful attempts at a consistent formalisation of logic and mathematics, so the antinomy of the liar and other semantic antinomies give rise to the construction of theoretical semantics.

8. *The inconsistency of semantically closed language*

If we now analyze the assumptions which lead to the antinomy of the liar, we notice the following:

(I)   We have implicitly assumed that the language in which the antinomy is constructed contains, in addition to its expressions, also the names of these expressions, as well as semantic terms such as the term "*true*" referring to sentences of this language; we have also assumed that all sentences which determine the adequate usage of this term can be asserted in the language. A language with these properties will be called "*semantically closed.*"

(II)   We have assumed that in this language the ordinary laws of logic hold.

(III)   We have assumed that we can formulate and assert in our language an empirical premise such as the statement (2) which has occurred in our argument.

It turns out that the assumption (III) is not essential, for it is possible to reconstruct the antinomy of the liar without its help.[11] But the assumptions (I) and (II) prove essential. Since every language which satisfies both of these assumptions is inconsistent, we must reject at least one of them.

It would be superfluous to stress here the consequences of rejecting the assumption (II), that is, of changing our logic (supposing this were possible) even in its more elementary and fundamental parts. We thus consider only the possibility of rejecting the assumption (I). Accordingly, we decide *not to use any language which is semantically closed* in the sense given.

This restriction would of course be unacceptable for those who, for reasons which are not clear to me, believe that there is only one "genuine" language (or, at least, that all "genuine" languages are mutually translatable). However, this restriction does not affect the needs or interests of science in any essential way. The languages (either the formalized languages or – what is more frequently the case – the portions of everyday language) which are used in scientific discourse do not have to be semantically closed. This is obvious in case linguistic phenomena and, in particular, semantic notions do not enter in any way into the subject matter of a science; for in such a case the language of this science does not have to be provided with any semantic terms at all. However, we shall see in the next section how semantically closed languages can be dispensed with even in those scientific discussions in which semantic notions are essentially involved.

The problem arises as to the position of everyday language with regard to this point. At first blush it would seem that this language satisfies both assumptions (I) and (II), and that therefore it must be inconsistent. But actually the case is not so simple. Our everyday language is certainly not one with an exactly specified structure. We do not know precisely which expressions are sentences, and we know even to a smaller degree which sentences are to be taken as assertible. Thus the problem of consistency has no exact meaning with respect to this language. We may at best only risk the guess that a language whose structure has been exactly specified and which resembles our everyday language as closely as possible would be inconsistent.

9. Object language and metalanguage

Since we have agreed not to employ semantically closed languages, we have to use two different languages in discussing the problem of the definition of truth and, more generally, any problems in the field of semantics. The first of these languages is the language which is "talked about" and which is the subject matter of the whole discussion, the definition of truth which we are seeking applies to the sentences of this language. The second is the language in which we "talk about" the first language, and in terms of which we wish, in particular, to construct the definition of truth for the first language. We shall refer to the first language as "the object language," and to the second as "the metalanguage."

It should be noticed that these terms "object language" and "metalanguage" have only a relative sense. If, for instance, we become interested in the notion of truth applying to sentences, not of our original object language, but of its metalanguage, the latter becomes automatically the object language of our discussion; and in order to define truth for this language, we have to go to a new metalanguage – so to speak, to a metalanguage of a higher level. In this way we arrive at a whole hierarchy of languages.

The vocabulary of the metalanguage is to a large extent determined by previously stated conditions under which a definition of truth will be considered materially adequate. This definition, as we recall, has to imply all equivalences of the form (T):

(T)   X is true if, and only if, p.

The definition itself and all the equivalences implied by it are to be formulated in the metalanguage. On the other hand the symbol 'p' in (T) stands for an arbitrary sentence of our object language. Hence it follows that every sentence which occurs in the object language must also occur in the metalanguage; in other words, the metalanguage must contain the object language as a part. This is at any rate necessary for the proof of the adequacy of the definition – even though the definition itself can sometimes be formulated in a less comprehensive metalanguage which does not satisfy this requirement.

[The requirement in question can be somewhat modified, for it suffices to assume that the object-language can be translated into the metalanguage; this necessitates a certain change in the interpretation of the symbol 'p' in (T). In all that follows we shall ignore the possibility of this modification.]

Furthermore, the symbol 'X' in (T) represents the name of the sentence which 'p' stands for. We see therefore that the metalanguage must be rich enough to provide possibilities of constructing a name for every sentence of the object language.

In addition, the metalanguage must obviously contain terms of a general logical character, such as the expression "if, and only if."[12]

It is desirable for the metalanguage not to contain any undefined teens except such as are involved explicitly or implicitly in the remarks above, i.e.: terms of the object language; terms referring to the form of the expressions of the object language, and used in building names for these expressions; and terms of logic. In particular, we desire *semantic terms* (referring to the object language) *to be introduced into the metalanguage only by definition*. For, if this postulate is satisfied, the definition of truth, or of any other semantic concept, will fulfill what we intuitively expect from every definition; that is, it will explain the meaning of the term being defined in terms whose meaning appears to be completely clear and unequivocal. And, moreover, we have then a kind of guarantee that the use of semantic concepts will not involve us in any contradictions.

We have no further requirements as to the formal structure of the object language and the metalanguage; we assume that it is similar to that of other formalized languages known at the present time. In particular, we assume that the usual formal rules of definition are observed in the metalanguage.

10. Conditions for a positive solution of the main problem

Now, we have already a clear idea both of the conditions of material adequacy to which the definition of truth is subjected, and of the formal structure of the language in which this definition is to be constructed. Under these circumstances the problem of the definition of truth acquires the character of a definite problem of a purely deductive nature.

The solution of the problem, however, is by no means obvious, and I would not attempt to give it in detail without using the whole machinery of contemporary logic. Here I shall confine myself to a rough outline of the solution and to the discussion of certain points of a more general interest which are involved in it.

The solution turns out to be sometimes positive, sometimes negative. This depends upon some formal relations between the object language and its metalanguage, or, more specifically, upon the fact whether the metalanguage in its logical part is "*essentially richer*" than the object language or not. It is not easy to give a general and precise definition of this notion of "essential richness." If we restrict ourselves to languages based on the logical theory of types, the condition for the metalanguage to be "essentially richer" than the object language is that it contain variables of a higher logical type than those of the object language.

If the condition of "essential richness" is not satisfied, it can usually be shown that an interpretation of the metalanguage in the object language is possible; that is to say, with any given term of the metalanguage a well-determined term of the object language can be correlated in such a way that the assertible sentences of the one language turn out to be correlated with assertible sentences of the other. As a result of this interpretation, the hypothesis that a satisfactory definition of truth has been formulated in the metalanguage turns out to imply the possibility of reconstructing in that language the antinomy of the liar; and this in turn forces us to reject the hypothesis in question.

(The fact that the metalanguage, in its nonlogical part, is ordinarily more comprehensive than the object language does not affect the possibility of interpreting the former in the latter. For example, the names of expressions of the object language occur in the metalanguage, though for the most part they do not occur in the object language itself; but, nevertheless, it may be possible to interpret these names in terms of the object language.)

Thus we see that the condition of "essential richness" is necessary for the possibility of a satisfactory definition of truth in the metalanguage. If we want to develop the theory of truth in a metalanguage which does not satisfy this condition, we must give up the idea of defining truth with the exclusive help of those terms which were indicated above (in section 8). We have then to include the term "true," or some other semantic term, in the list of undefined terms of the metalanguage, and to express fundamental properties of the notion of truth in a series of axioms. There is nothing essentially wrong in such an axiomatic procedure and it may prove useful for various purposes.[13]

It turns out, however, that this procedure can be avoided. For *the condition of the "essential richness" of the metalanguage proves to be, not only necessary, but also sufficient for the construction of a satisfactory definition of truth*; i.e., if the metalanguage satisfies this condition, the notion of truth can be defined in it. We shall now indicate in general terms how this construction can be carried through.

11. The construction (in outline) of the definition[14]

A definition of truth can be obtained in a very simple way from that of another semantic notion, namely, of the notion of *satisfaction*.

Satisfaction is a relation between objects and certain expressions called "*sentential functions*." These are expressions like "*x* is white," "*x* is greater than *y*," etc. Their formal structure is analogous to that of sentences; however, they *may* contain the so-called free variables (like '*x*' and '*y*' in "*x* is greater than *y*"), which cannot occur in sentences.

In defining the notion of a sentential function in formalized languages, we usually apply what is called a "recursive procedure"; i.e., we first describe sentential functions of the simplest structure (which ordinarily presents no difficulty), and then we indicate the operations by means of which compound functions can be constructed from simpler ones. Such an operation may consist, for instance, in forming the logical disjunction or conjunction of two given functions, i.e., by combining them by the word "or" or "and." A sentence can now be defined simply as a sentential function which contains no free variables.

As regards the notion of satisfaction, we might try to define it by saying that given objects satisfy a given function if the latter becomes a true sentence when we replace in it free variables by names of given objects. In this sense, for example, snow satisfies the sentential function "x is white" since the sentence "snow is white" is true. However, apart from other difficulties, this method is not available to us, for we want to use the notion of satisfaction in defining truth.

To obtain a definition of satisfaction we have rather to apply again a recursive process cure. We indicate which objects satisfy the simplest sentential functions; and then we state the conditions under which given objects satisfy a compound function – assuming that we know which objects satisfy the simpler functions from which the compound one has been constructed. Thus, for instance, we say that given numbers satisfy the logical disjunction "x is greater than y or x is equal to y" if they satisfy at least one of the functions "x is greater than y" or "x is equal to y."

Once the general definition of satisfaction is obtained, we notice that it applies automatically also to those special sentential functions which contain no free variables, i.e., to sentences. It turns out that for a sentence only two cases are possible: a sentence is either satisfied by all objects, or by no objects. Hence we arrive at a definition of truth and falsehood simply by saying that *a sentence is true if it is satisfied by all objects, and false otherwise*.[15]

(It may seem strange that we have chosen a roundabout way of defining the truth of a sentence, instead of trying to apply, for instance, a direct recursive procedure. The reason is that compound sentences are constructed from simpler sentential functions, but not always from simpler sentences; hence no general recursive method is known which applies specifically to sentences.)

From this rough outline it is not clear where and how the assumption of the "essential richness" of the metalanguage is involved in the discussion; this becomes clear only when the construction is carried through in a detailed and formal way.[16]

[. . .]

17. Conformity of the semantic conception of truth with philosophical and common-sense usage

The question has been raised whether the semantic conception of truth can indeed be regarded as a precise form of the old, classical conception of this notion.

Various formulations of the classical conception were quoted in the early part of this paper (section 3). I must repeat that in my judgment none of them is quite precise and clear. Accordingly, the only sure way of settling the question would be to confront the authors of those statements with our new formulation, and to ask them whether it agrees with their intentions. Unfortunately, this method is impractical since they died quite some time ago.

As far as my own opinion is concerned, I do not have any doubts that our formulation does conform to the intuitive content of that of Aristotle. I am less certain regarding the later formulations of the classical conception, for they are very vague indeed.'[17]

Furthermore, some doubts have been expressed whether the semantic conception does reflect the notion of truth in its common-sense and everyday usage. I clearly realize (as I already indicated) that the common meaning of the word "true" – as that of any other word of everyday language – is to some extent vague, and that its usage more or less fluctuates. Hence the problem of assigning to this word a fixed and exact meaning is relatively unspecified, and every solution of this problem implies necessarily a certain deviation from the practice of everyday language.

In spite of all this, I happen to believe that the semantic conception does conform to a very considerable extent with the common-sense usage – although I readily admit I may be mistaken. What is more to the point, however, I believe that the issue raised can be settled scientifically, though of course not by a deductive procedure, but with the help of the statistical questionnaire method. As a matter of fact, such research has been carried on, and some of the results have been reported at congresses and in part published.[18]

I should like to emphasize that in my opinion such investigations must be conducted with the utmost care. Thus, if we ask a high-school boy, or even an adult intelligent man having no special philosophical training, whether he regards a sentence to be true if it agrees with reality, or if it designates an existing state of affairs, it may simply turn out that he does not understand the question; in consequence his response, whatever it may be, will be of no value for us. But his answer to the question whether he would admit that the sentence "it is snowing" could be true although it is not snowing, or could be false although it is snowing, would naturally be very significant for our problem.

Therefore, I was by no means surprised to learn (in a discussion devoted to these problems) that in a group of people who were questioned only 15% agreed that "true" means for them "agreeing with reality" while 90% agreed that a sentence such as "it is snowing" is true if and only if, it is snowing. Thus, a great majority of these people seemed to reject the classical conception of truth in its "philosophical" formulation while accepting the same conception when formulated in plain words (waiving the question whether the use of the phrase "the same conception" is here justified).

[...]

20. *Applicability of semantics to special empirical sciences*

We come to the last and perhaps the most important group of objections. Some strong doubts have been expressed whether semantic notions find or can find applications in various domains of intellectual activity. For the most part such doubts have concerned the applicability of semantics to the field of empirical science – either to special sciences or to the general methodology of this field; although similar skepticism has been expressed regarding possible applications of semantics to mathematical sciences and their methodology.

I believe that it is possible to allay these doubts to a certain extent, and that some optimism with respect to the potential value of semantics for various domains of thought is not without ground.

To justify this optimism, it suffices I think to stress two rather obvious points. First, the development of a theory which formulates a precise definition of a notion and establishes its general properties provides *eo ipso* a firmer basis for all discussions in which this notion is involved; and, therefore, it cannot be irrelevant for anyone who uses this notion, and desires to do so in a conscious and consistent way. Secondly, semantic notions are actually involved in various branches of science, and in particular of empirical science.

The fact that in empirical research we are concerned only with natural languages and that theoretical semantics applies to these languages only with certain approximation, does not affect the problem essentially. However it has undoubtedly this effect that progress in semantics will have but a delayed and somewhat limited influence in this field. The situation with which we are confronted here does not differ essentially from that which arises when we apply laws of logic to arguments in everyday life – or, generally, when we attempt to apply a theoretical science to empirical problems.

Semantic notions are undoubtedly involved, to a larger or smaller degree, in psychology, sociology, and in practically all the humanities. Thus, a psychologist defines the so-called intelligence quotient in terms of the numbers of *true* (right) and *false* (wrong) answers given by a person to certain questions; for a historian of culture the range of objects for which a human race in successive stages of its development possesses adequate *designations* may be a topic of great significance; a student of literature may be strongly interested in the problem whether a given author always uses two given words with the same *meaning*. Examples of this kind can be multiplied indefinitely.

The most natural and promising domain for the applications of theoretical semantics is clearly linguistics – the empirical study of natural languages. Certain parts of this science are even referred to as "semantics," sometimes with an additional qualification. Thus, this name is occasionally given to that portion of grammar which attempts to classify all words of a language into parts of speech, according to what the words mean or designate. The study of the evolution of meanings in the historical development of a language is sometimes called historical semantics. In general, the totality of investigations on semantic relations which occur in a natural language is referred to as descriptive semantics. The relation between theoretical and descriptive semantics is analogous to that between pure and applied mathematics, or perhaps to that between theoretical and empirical physics; the role of formalized languages in semantics can be roughly compared to that of isolated systems in physics.

It is perhaps unnecessary to say that semantics cannot find any direct applications in natural sciences such as physics, biology, etc.; for in none of these sciences are we concerned with linguistic phenomena, and even less with semantic relations between linguistic expressions and objects to which these expressions refer. We shall see, however, in the next section that semantics may have a kind of indirect influence even on those sciences in which semantic notions are not directly involved.

21. *Applicability of semantics to the methodology of empirical science*

Besides linguistics, another important domain for possible applications of semantics is the methodology of science; this term is used here in a broad sense so as to embrace the theory of science in general. Independent of whether a science is conceived merely as a system of statements or as a totality of certain statements and human activities, the study of scientific language constitutes an essential part of the methodological discussion of a science. And it seems to me clear that any tendency to eliminate semantic notions (like those of truth and designation) from this discussion would make it fragmentary and inadequate.[19] Moreover, there is no reason for such a tendency today, once the main difficulties in using semantic terms have been overcome. The semantics of scientific language should be simply included as a part in the methodology of science.

I am by no means inclined to charge methodology and, in particular, semantics – whether theoretical or descriptive – with the task of clarifying the meanings of all scientific terms. This task is left to those sciences in which the terms are used, and is actually fulfilled by them (in the same way in which, e.g., the task of clarifying the meaning of the term "*true*" is left to, and fulfilled by, semantics). There may be, however, certain special problems of this sort in which a methodological approach is desirable or indeed necessary (perhaps, the problem of the notion of causality is a good example here); and in a methodological discussion of such problems semantic notions may play an essential role. Thus, semantics may have some bearing on any science whatsoever.

The question arises whether semantics can be helpful in solving general and, so to speak classical problems of methodology. I should like to discuss here with some detail a special though very important aspect of this question.

One of the main problems of the methodology of empirical science consists in establishing conditions under which an empirical theory or hypothesis should be regarded as acceptable. This notion of acceptability must be relativized to a given stage of the development of a science (or to a given amount of presupposed knowledge). In other words we may consider it as provided with a time coefficient; for a theory which is acceptable today may become untenable tomorrow as a result of new scientific discoveries.

It seems a priori very plausible that the acceptability of a theory somehow depends on the truth of its sentences, and that consequently a methodologist in his (so far rather unsuccessful) attempts at making the notion of acceptability precise, can expect some help from the semantic theory of truth. Hence we ask the question: Are there any postulates which can be reasonably imposed on acceptable theories and which involve the notion of truth? And, in particular, we ask whether the following postulate is a reasonable one:

An acceptable theory cannot contain (or imply) any false sentences.

The answer to the last question is clearly negative. For, first of all, we are practically sure, on the basis of our historical experience, that every empirical theory which is accepted today will sooner or later be rejected and replaced by another theory. It is also very probable that the new theory will be incompatible with the old one; i.e., will imply a sentence which is contradictory to one of the sentences contained in the old theory. Hence, at least one of the two theories must include false sentences, in spite of the fact that each of them is accepted at a certain time. Secondly, the postulate in question could hardly ever be satisfied in practice; for we do not know, and are very unlikely to find, any criteria of truth which enable us to show that no sentence of an empirical theory is false.

The postulate in question could be at most regarded as the expression of an ideal limit for successively more adequate theories in a given field of research; but this hardly can be given any precise meaning.

Nevertheless, it seems to me that there is an important postulate which can be reasonably imposed on acceptable empirical theories and which involves the notion of truth. It is closely related to the one just discussed, but is essentially weaker. Remembering that the notion of acceptability is provided with a time coefficient, we can give this postulate the following form:

As soon as we succeed in showing that an empirical theory contains (or implies) false sentences, it cannot be any longer considered acceptable.

In support of this postulate, I should like to make the following remarks.

I believe everybody agrees that one of the reasons which may compel us to reject an empirical theory is the proof of its inconsistency: a theory becomes untenable if we succeed in deriving from it two contradictory sentences. Now we can ask what are the usual motives for rejecting a theory on such grounds. Persons who are acquainted with modern logic are inclined to answer this question in the following way: A well-known logical law shows that a theory which enables us to derive two contradictory sentences enables us also to derive every sentence; therefore, such a theory is trivial and deprived of any scientific interest.

I have some doubts whether this answer contains an adequate analysis of the situation. I think that people who do not know modern logic are as little inclined to accept an inconsistent theory as those who are thoroughly familiar with it; and probably this applies even to those who regard (as some still do) the logical law on which the argument is based as a highly controversial issue, and almost as a paradox. I do not think that our attitude toward an inconsistent theory would change even if we decided for some reasons to weaken our system of logic so as to deprive ourselves of the possibility of deriving every sentence from any two contradictory sentences.

It seems to me that the real reason of our attitude is a different one: We know (if only intuitively) that an inconsistent theory must contain false sentences; and we are not inclined to regard as acceptable any theory which has been shown to contain such sentences.

There are various methods of showing that a given theory includes false sentences. Some of them are based upon purely logical properties of the theory involved; the method just discussed (i.e., the proof of inconsistency) is not the sole method of this type, but is the simplest one, and the one which is most frequently applied in practice. With the help of certain assumptions regarding the truth of empirical sentences, we can obtain methods to the same effect which are no longer of a purely logical nature. If we decide to accept the general postulate suggested above, then a successful application of any such method will make the theory untenable.

22. *Applications of semantics to deductive science*

As regards the applicability of semantics to mathematical sciences and their methodology, i.e., to metamathematics, we are in a much more favorable position than in the case of empirical sciences. For, instead of advancing reasons which justify some hopes for the future (and thus making a kind of pro-semantics propaganda), we are able to point out concrete results already achieved.

Doubts continue to be expressed whether the notion of a true sentence – as distinct from that of a provable sentence – can have any significance for mathematical disciplines and play any part in a methodological discussion of mathematics. It seems to me, however, that just this notion of a true sentence constitutes a most valuable contribution to meta-mathematics by semantics. We already possess a series of interesting metamathematical results gained with the help of the theory of truth. These results concern the mutual relations between the notion of truth and that of provability; establish new properties of the latter notion (which, as well known, is one of the basic notions of metamathematics); and throw some light on the fundamental problems of consistency and completeness. . . .

Furthermore, by applying the method of semantics we can adequately define several important metamathematical notions which have been used so far only in an intuitive way – such as, e.g., the notion of definability or that of a model of an axiom system; and thus we can undertake a systematic study of these notions. In particular the investigations on definability have already brought some interesting results, and promise even more in the future.

We have discussed the applications of semantics only to metamathematics, and not to mathematics proper. However, this distinction between mathematics and metamathematics is rather unimportant. For metamathematics is itself a deductive discipline and hence, from a certain point of view, a part of mathematics; and it is well known that – due to the formal character of deductive method – the results obtained in one deductive discipline can be automatically extended to any other discipline in which the given one finds an interpretation. Thus, for example, all metamathematical results can be interpreted as results of number theory. Also from a practical point of view there is no clearcut line between metamathematics and mathematics proper; for instance, the investigations on definability could be included in either of these domains.

23. Final remarks

I should like to conclude this discussion with some general and rather loose remarks concerning the whole question of the evaluation of scientific achievements in terms of their applicability. I must confess I have various doubts in this connection.

Being a mathematician (as well as a logician, and perhaps a philosopher of a sort), I have had the opportunity to attend many discussions between specialists in mathematics, where the problem of applications is especially acute, and I have noticed on several occasions the following phenomenon: If a mathematician wishes to disparage the work of one of his colleagues, say A, the most effective method he finds for doing this is to ask where the results can be applied. The hard-pressed man, with his back against the wall, finally unearths the researches of another mathematician B as the locus of the application of his own results. If next B is plagued with a similar question he will refer to another mathematician C. After a few steps of this kind we find ourselves referred back to the researches of A, and in this way the chain closes.

Speaking more seriously, I do not wish to deny that the value of a man's work may be increased by its implications for the research of others and for practice. But I believe, nevertheless, that it is inimical to the progress of science to measure the importance of any research exclusively or chiefly in terms of its usefulness and applicability. We know from the history of science that many important results and discoveries have had to wait centuries before they were applied in any field. And, in my opinion, there are also other important factors which cannot be disregarded in determining the value of a scientific work. It seems to me that there is a special domain of very profound and strong human needs related to scientific research, which are similar in many ways to aesthetic and perhaps religious needs. And it also seems to me that the satisfaction of these needs should be considered an important task of research. Hence, I believe; the question of the value of any research cannot be adequately answered without taking into account the intellectual satisfaction which the results of that research bring to those who understand it and care for it. It may be unpopular and out-of-date to say – but I do not think that a scientific result which gives us a better understanding of the world and makes it more harmonious in our eyes should be held in lower esteem than, say, an invention which reduces the cost of paving roads, or improves household plumbing.

It is clear that the remarks just made become pointless if the word "application" is used in a very wide and liberal sense. It is perhaps not less obvious that nothing follows from these general remarks concerning the specific topics which have been discussed in this paper; and I really do not know whether research in semantics stands to gain or lose by introducing the standard of value I have suggested.

Notes

1 Compare Tarski [2] (see Bibliography following Notes). This work may be consulted for a more detailed and formal presentation of the subject of the paper, especially of the material included in sections 6 and 9–13. It contains also references to my earlier publications on the problems of semantics (a communication in Polish, 1930; the article Tarski [1] in French, 1931; a communication in German, 1932; and a book in Polish, 1933). The expository part of the present paper is related in its character to Tarski [3]. My investigations on the notion of truth and on theoretical semantics have been reviewed or discussed in Hofstadter [1], Juhos [1], Kokoszyńska [1] and [2], Kotarbiński [2], Scholz [1], Weinberg [1], et al.

2 It may be hoped that the interest in theoretical semantics will now increase, as a result of the recent publication of the important work of Carnap [2].

3 This applies, in particular, to public discussions during the I. International Congress for the Unity of Science (Paris, 1935) and the Conference of International Congresses for the Unity of Science (Paris, 1937); cf., e.g., Neurath [1] and Gonseth [1].

4 The words "notion" and "concept" are used in this paper with all of the vagueness and ambiguity with which they occur in philosophical literature. Thus, sometimes they refer simply to a term, sometimes to what is meant by a term, and in other cases to what is denoted by a term. Sometimes it is irrelevant which of these interpretations is meant; and in certain cases perhaps none of them applies adequately. While on principle I share the tendency to avoid these words in any exact discussion, I did not consider it necessary to do so in this informal presentation.

5 For our present purposes it is somewhat more convenient to understand by "expressions," "sentences," etc., not individual inscriptions, but classes of inscriptions of similar form (thus, not individual physical things, but classes of such things).

6 For the Aristotelian formulation see Aristotle [1], y, 7, 27. The other two formulations are very common in the literature, but I do not know with whom they originate. A critical discussion of various conceptions of truth can be found, e.g., in Kotarbiński [1] (so far available only in Polish), pp. 123ff., and Russell [1], pp. 362ff.

7 For most of the remarks contained in sections 4 and 8, I am indebted to the late S. Leśniewski who developed them in his unpublished lectures in the University of Warsaw (in 1919 and later). However, Leśniewski did not anticipate the possibility of a rigorous development of the theory of truth, and still less of a definition of this notion; hence, while indicating equivalences of the form (T) as premises in the antinomy of the liar, he did not conceive them as any sufficient conditions for an adequate usage (or definition) of the notion of truth. Also the remarks in section 8 regarding the occurrence of an empirical premise in the antinomy of the liar, and the possibility of eliminating this premise, do not originate with him.

8 In connection with various logical and methodological problems invoked in this paper the reader may consult Tarski [6].

9 The antinomy of the liar (ascribed to Eubulides or Epimenides) is discussed here in sections 7 and 8. For the antinomy of definability (due to J. Richard) see, e.g., Hilbert-Bernays [1], vol. 2, pp. 263ff., for the antimony of heterological terms see Grelling-Nelson [1], p. 307.

10 Due to Professor J. Lukasiewicz (University of Warsaw).

11 This can roughly be done in the following way. Let S be any sentence beginning with the words "Every sentence." We correlate with S a new sentence S^* by sub-

jecting S to the following two modifications we replace in S the first word, "Every," by "The"; and we insert after the second word, "sentence," the whole sentence S enclosed in quotation marks. Let us agree to call the sentence S "(self-)applicable" or "non-(self-)applicable" dependent on whether the correlated sentence S* is true or false. Now consider the following sentence:

Every sentence is nonapplicable.

It can easily be shown that the sentence just stated must be both applicable and nonapplicable; hence a contradiction. It may not be quite clear in what sense this formulation of the antinomy does not involve an empirical premiss; however, I shall not elaborate on this point.

12 The terms "logic" and "logical" are used in this paper in a broad senses which has become almost traditional in the last decades; logic is assumed here to comprehend the whole theory of classes and relations (i.e., the mathematical theory of sets). For many different reasons I am personally inclined to use the term "logic" in a much narrower sensed so as to apply it only to what is sometimes called "elementary logic," i.e., to the sentential calculus and the (restricted) predicate calculus.

13 Cf. here, however, Tarski [3], pp. 5f.

14 The method of construction we are going to outline can be applied – with appropriate changes – to all formalized languages that are known at the present time; although it does not follow that a language could not be constructed to which this method would not apply.

15 In carrying through this idea a certain technical difficulty arises. A sentential function may contain an arbitrary number of free variables; and the logical nature of the notion of satisfaction varies with this number. Thus, the notion in question when applied to functions with one variable is a binary relation between these functions and single objects; when applied to functions with two variables it becomes a ternary relation between functions and couples of objects; and so on. Hence, strictly speaking, we are confronted, not with one notion of satisfaction, but with infinitely many notions; and it turns out that these notions cannot he defined independently of each other, but must all be introduced simultaneously.

To overcome this difficulty, we employ the mathematical notion of an infinite sequence (or, possibly, of a finite sequence with an arbitrary number of terms). We agree to regard satisfaction, not as a many-termed relation between sentential functions and an indefinite number of objects, but as a binary relation between functions and sequences of objects. Under this assumption the formulation of a general and precise definition of satisfaction no longer presents any difficulty; and a true sentence can now be defined as one which is satisfied by every sequence.

16 To define recursively the notion of satisfaction, we have to apply a certain form of recursive definition which is not admitted in the object-language. Hence the "essential richness" of the metalanguage may simply consist in admitting this type of definition. On the other hand, a general method is known which makes it possible to eliminate all recursive definitions and to replace them by normal, explicit ones. If we try to apply this method to the definition of satisfaction, we see that we have either to introduce into the metalanguage variables of a higher logical type than those which occur in the object language; or else to assume axiomatically in the metalanguage the existence of classes that are more comprehensive than all those whose existence can be established in the object-language. See here Tarski [2], pp. 393ff., and Tarski [5], p. 110.

17 Most authors who have discussed my work on the notion of truth are of the opinion that my definition does conform with the classical conception of this notion; see, e.g., Kotarbiński [2] and Scholz [1].

18 Cf. Ness [1]. Unfortunately, the results of that part of Ness' research which is especially relevant for our problem are not discussed in his book: compare p. 148, footnote 1.

19 Such a tendency was evident in earlier works of Carnap (see, e.g., Carnap [1], especially part V) and in writings of other members of Vienna Circle. Cf. Kokoszyńska [1] and Weinberg [1].

Bibliography

Aristotle [1]. *Metaphysica*. (*Works*, vol. VIII.) English translation by W. D. Ross. (Oxford: 1908).

Carnap, R. [1]. *Logical Syntax of Language*. (London and New York: 1937).

—— [2]. *Introduction to Semantics*. (Cambridge: 1942).

Gödel, K. [1]. "Über formal unentscheidbare Sätze der *Principia Mathematica* und verwandter Systeme, I." *Monatshefte für Mathematik und Physik*, XXXVIII (1931), pp. 173–98.

—— [2]. "Über die Länge von Beweisen." *Ergebnisse eines mathematischen Kolloquiums*, vol. VII (1936), pp. 23–4.

Gonseth, F. [1]. "Le Congrès Descartes. Questions de Philosophie scientifique." *Revue thomiste*, vol. XLIV (1938), pp. 183–93.

Grelling, K., and Nelson, L. [1]. "Bemerkungen zu den Paradoxien von Russell und Burali-Forti." *Abhandlungen der Fries'schen Schule*, vol. II (new series), (1908), pp. 301–34.

Hilbert, D., and Bernays, P. [1]. *Grundlagen der Mathematik*. 2 vols. (Berlin: 1934–1939).

Hofstadter, A. [1]. "On Semantic Problems." *The Journal of Philosophy*, vol. XXXV (1938), pp. 225–32.

Juhos, B. von. [1]. "The Truth of Empirical Statements." *Analysis*, vol. IV (1937), pp. 65–70.

Kokoszyńska, M. [1]. "Über den absoluten Wahrheitsbegriff und einige andere semantische Begriffe." *Erkenntnis*, vol. VI (1936), pp. 143–65.

—— [2]. "Syntax, Semantik und Wissenschaftslogik." *Actes du Congrès International de Philosophie Scientifique*, vol. III (Paris: 1936), pp. 9–14.

Kotarbiński, T. [1]. *Elementy teorji poznania, lokiki formalnej i metodologji nauk. (Elements of Epistemology, Formal Logic, and the Methodology of Sciences*, in Polish.) (Lwów: 1929).

—— [2]. "W sprawie pojęcia prawdy." ("*Concerning the Concept of Truth*," in Polish.) *Przeglgd filozoficzny*, vol. XXXVII, pp. 85–91.

Lindenbaum, A., and Tarski, A. [1]. "Über die Beschränktheit der Ausdrucksmittel deduktiver Theorien." *Ergebnisse eines mathematischen Kolloquiums*, vol. VII (1936), pp. 15–23.

Nagel, E. [1]. Review of Hofstadter [1]. *The Journal of Symbolic Logic*, vol. III (1938), p. 90.

—— [2]. Review of Carnap [2]. *The Journal of Philosophy*, vol. XXXIX (1942), pp. 468–73.

Ness, A. [1]. " 'Truth' As Conceived by Those Who Are Not Professional Philosophers." *Skrifter utgitt av Det Norske Videnskaps-Akademi i Oslo, II. Hist.-Filos. Klasse*, vol. IV (Oslo: 1938).

Neurath, O. [1]. "Erster Internationaler Kongress für Einheit der Wissenschaft in Paris 1935." *Erkenntnis*, vol. V (1935), pp. 377–406.

Russell, B. [1]. *An Inquiry Into Meaning and Truth* (New York: 1940).

Scholz, H. [1]. Review of *Studia philosophica*, vol. I. *Deutsche Literaturzeitung*, vol. LVIII (1937), pp. 1914–17.

Tarski, A. [1]. "Sur les ensembles définissables de nombres réels. I." *Fundamenta methematicae*, vol. XVII (1931), pp. 210–39.

—— [2]. "Der Wahrheitsbegriff in den formalisierten Sprachen." (German translation of a book in Polish, 1933.) *Studia philosophica*, vol. I (1935), pp. 261–405.

—— [3]. "Grundlegung der wissenschaftlichen Semantik." *Actes du Congrès International de Philosophie Scientifique*, vol. III (Paris: 1936), pp. 1–8.

—— [4]. "Über den begriff der logischen Folgerung." *Actes du Congrès International de Philosophie Scientifique*, vol. VII (Paris: 1937), pp. 1–11.

—— [5]. "On Undecidable Statements in Enlarged Systems of Logic and the Concept of Truth." *The Journal of Symbolic Logic*, vol. IV (1939), pp. 105–12.

—— [6]. *Introduction to Logic.* (New York: 1941).

Weinberg, J. [1]. Review of *Studia philosophica*, vol. I. *The Philosophical Review*, vol. XLVII, pp. 70–7.

26   The Method of Truth in Metaphysics

Donald Davidson

In sharing a language, in whatever sense this is required for communication, we share a picture of the world that must, in its large features, be true. It follows that in making manifest the large features of our language, we make manifest the large features of reality. One way of pursuing metaphysics is therefore to study the general structure of our language. This is not, of course, the sole true method of metaphysics; there is no such. But it is one method, and it has been practised by philosophers as widely separated by time or doctrine as Plato, Aristotle, Hume, Kant, Russell, Frege, Wittgenstein, Carnap, Quine and Strawson. These philosophers have not, it goes without saying, agreed on what the large features of language are or on how they may best be studied and described; the metaphysical conclusions have in consequence been various.

The method I will describe and recommend is not new; every important feature of the method can be found in one philosopher or another, and the leading idea is implicit in much of the best work in philosophy of language.

From *Midwest Studies in Philosophy*, vol. 2, ed. P. A. French, T. E. Kehling Jr., H. K. Wettstein. Minneapolis, Minn.: University of Minnesota Press, 1977, pp. 199–214. Copyright © 1977 by the University of Minnesota Press. By permission of the publisher and author.

What is new is the explicit formulation of the approach, and the argument for its philosophical importance. I begin with the argument; then comes a description of the method; finally, some applications are sketched.

I

Why must our language – any language – incorporate or depend upon a largely correct, shared, view of how things are? First consider why those who can understand one another's speech must share a view of the world, whether or not that view is correct. The reason is that we damage the intelligibility of our readings of the utterances of others when our method of reading puts others into what we take to be broad error. We can make sense of differences all right, but only against a background of shared belief. What is shared does not in general call for comment; it is too dull, trite, or familiar to stand notice. But without a vast common ground, there is no place for disputants to have their quarrel. Of course, we can no more agree than dis-agree with someone else without much mutuality; but perhaps this is obvious.

Beliefs are identified and described only within a dense pattern of beliefs. I can believe a cloud is passing before the sun, but only because I believe there is a sun, that clouds are made of water vapour, that water can exist in liquid or gaseous form; and so on without end. No particular list of further beliefs is required to give substance to my belief that a cloud is passing before the sun; but some appropriate set of related beliefs must be there. If I suppose that you believe a cloud is passing before the sun, I suppose you have the right sort of pattern of beliefs to support that one belief, and these beliefs I assume you have must, to do their supporting work, be enough like my beliefs to justify the description of your belief as a belief that a cloud is passing before the sun. If I am right in attributing the belief to you, then you must have a pattern of beliefs much like mine. No wonder, then, I can interpret your words correctly only by interpreting so as to put us largely in agreement.

It may seem that the argument so far shows only that good interpretation breeds concurrence, while leaving quite open the question whether what is agreed upon is true. And certainly agreement, no matter how widespread, does not guarantee truth. This observation misses the point of the argument, however. The basic claim is that much community of belief is needed to provide a basis for communication or understanding; the extended claim should then be that objective error can occur only in a setting of largely true belief. Agreement does not make for truth, but much of what is agreed must be true if some of what is agreed is false.

Just as too much attributed error risks depriving the subject of his subject matter, so too much actual error robs a person of things to go wrong about. When we want to interpret, we work on one or another assumption about the general pattern of agreement. We suppose that much of what we take to be common is true but we cannot, of course, assume we know where the truth lies. We cannot interpret on the basis of known truths, not because we know none, but because we do not always know which they are. We do not need to be omniscient to interpret, but there is nothing absurd in the idea of a omniscient interpreter; he attributes beliefs to others, and interprets their speech on the basis of his own beliefs, just as the rest of us do. Since he does this as the rest of us do, he perforce finds as much agreement as is needed to make sense of his attributions and interpretations; and in this case, of course, what is agreed is by hypothesis true. But now it is plain why massive error about the world is simply unintelligible, for to suppose it intelligible is to suppose there could be an interpreter (the omniscient one) who correctly interpreted someone else as being massively mistaken, and this we have shown to be impossible.

II

Successful communication proves the existence of a shared, and largely true, view of the world. But what led us to demand the common view was the recognition that sentences held true – the linguistic representatives of belief – determine the meanings of the words they contain. Thus the common view shapes the shared language. This is why it is plausible to hold that by studying the most general aspects of language we will be studying the most general aspects of reality. It remains to say how these aspects my be identified and described.

Language is an instrument of communication because of its semantic dimension, the potentiality for truth or falsehood of its sentences, or better, of its utterances and inscriptions. The study of what sentences are true is in general the work of the various sciences; but the study of truth conditions is the province of semantics. What we must attend to in language, if we want to bring into relief general features of the world, is what it is in general for a sentence in the language to be true. The suggestion is that if the truth conditions of sentences are placed in the context of a comprehensive theory, the linguistic structure that emerges will reflect large features of reality.

The aim is a theory of truth for a reasonably powerful and significant part of a natural language. The scope of the theory – how much of the language is captured by the theory, and how convincingly – will be one factor on which the interest of any metaphysical results depends. The theory must show us how we can view each of a potential infinity of sentences as composed from a finite stock of semantically significant atoms (roughly, words) by means of a finite number of applications of a finite number of rules of composition. It must then give the truth conditions of each sentence (relative to the circumstances of its utterance) on the basis of its composition. The theory may thus be said to explain the conditions of truth of an utterance of a sentence on the basis of the roles of the words in the sentence.

Much here is owed to Frege. Frege saw the importance of giving an account of how the truth of a sentence depends on the semantic features of its parts, and he suggested how such an account could be given for impressive stretches of natural language. His method was one now familiar: he introduced a standardized notation whose syntax directly reflected the intended interpretation, and then urged that the new notation, as interpreted, had the same expressive power as important parts of natural language. Or rather, not quite the same expressive power, since Frege believed natural language was defective in some respects, and he regarded his new language as an improvement.

Frege was concerned with the semantic structure of sentences, and with semantic relations between sentences, in so far as these generated entailments. But he cannot be said to have conceived the idea of a comprehensive formal theory of truth for a language as a whole. One consequence was a lack of interest in the semantic paradoxes. Another was an apparent willingness to accept an infinity of meanings (senses) and referents for every denoting phrase in the language.

Because Frege took the application of function to argument to be the sole mode of semantic combination, he was bound to treat sentences as a kind of name – the name of a truth value. Seen simply as an artful dodge on the way to characterizing the truth conditions of sentences, this device of Frege's is unexceptionable. But since sentences do not operate in language the way names do, Frege's approach undermines confidence that the ontology he needs to work his semantics has any direct connection with the ontology implicit in natural language. It is not clear, then, what one can learn about metaphysics from Frege's language. It is not clear, then, what one can learn about metaphysics from Frege's method. (I certainly do not mean by this that we can't learn about metaphysics from Frege's work; but to see how, arguments different from mine must be marshalled.)

Quine provided an essential ingredient for the project at hand by showing how a holistic approach to the problem of understanding a language supplies the needed empirical foundation. If metaphysical conclusions are to be drawn from a theory of truth in the way that I propose, the approach to language must be holistic. Quine himself does not see holism as having such direct metaphysical significance, however, and for a number of reasons. First, Quine has not made the theory of truth central either as a key to the ontology of a language, or as a test of logical form. Second, like Frege, he views a satisfactorily regimented language as an improvement on natural language rather than as part of a theory about it. In one important respect, Quine seems even to go beyond Frege, for where Frege thinks his notation makes for better language, Quine thinks it also makes for better science. As a consequence, Quine ties his metaphysics to his canonical notation rather than to natural language; as he puts it, 'The quest of a simplest, clearest overall pattern of canonical notation is not to be distinguished from a quest of ultimate categories, a limning of the most general traits of reality.'[1]

The formal languages towards which I gravitate – first-order languages with standard logic – are those preferred by Quine, But our reasons for this choice diverge somewhat. Such languages please Quine because their logic is simple, and the scientifically respectable parts of natural language can be translated into them; and with this I agree. But since I am not interested in improving on natural language, but in understanding it, I view formal languages or canonical notations as devices for exploring the structure of natural language. We know how to give a theory of truth for the formal language; so if we also knew how to transform the sentences of a natural language systematically into sentences of the formal language, we would have a theory of truth for the natural language. From this point of view, standard formal languages are intermediate devices to assist us in treating natural languages as more complex formal languages.

Tarski's work on truth definitions for formalized languages serves as inspiration for the kind of theory of truth that is wanted for natural languages.[2] The method works by enumerating the semantic properties of the items in a finite vocabulary, and on this basis recursively characterizes truth for each of the infinity of sentences. Truth is reached from the basis by the intervention of a subtle and powerful concept (satisfaction) which relates both sentences and non-sentential expressions to objects in the world. An important feature of Tarski's approach is that a characterization of a truth predicate 'x is true in L', is accepted only if it entails, for each sentence of the language L, a theorem of the form 'x is true in L if and only if . . .' with 'x' replaced by a description of the sentence and the dots replaced by a translation of the sentence into the language of the theory.

It is evident that these theorems, which we may call T-sentences, require a predicate that holds of just the true sentences of L. It is also plain, from the fact that the truth conditions for a sentence translate that sentence (i.e., what appears to the right of the 'if and only if' in a T-sentence translates the sentence described on the left), that the theory shows how to characterize truth for any given sentence without appeal to conceptual resources not available in that sentence.

These remarks are only roughly correct. A theory of truth for a natural language must relativize the truth of a sentence to the circumstances of utterance, and when this is done the truth conditions given by a T-sentence will no longer translate the described sentence, nor will it be possible to avoid using concepts that are, perhaps, semantical, in giving the truth conditions of sentences with indexical elements. More important, the notion of translation, which can be made precise for artificial languages on which interpretations are imposed by fiat, has no precise or even clear application to natural languages.

For these, and other reasons, it is important to stress that a theory of truth for a natural language (as I conceive it) differs widely in both aim and interest from Tarski's truth definitions. Sharpness of application is lost, and with it most of what concerns mathematicians and logicians: consequences for consistency, for example. Tarski could take translation as syntactically specified, and go on to define truth. But in application to a natural language it makes more sense to assume a partial understanding of truth, and use the theory to throw light on meaning, interpretation, and translation.[3] Satisfaction of Tarski's Convention T remains a desideratum of a theory, but is no longer available as a formal test.

What a theory of truth does for a natural language is reveal structure. In treating each sentence as composed in accountable ways out of a finite number of truth-relevant words, it articulates this structure. When we study terms and sentences directly, not in the light of comprehensive theory, we must bring metaphysics to language; we assign roles to words and sentences in accord with the categories we independently posit on epistemological or metaphysical grounds. Operating in this way, philosophers ponder such questions as whether there must be entities, perhaps universals, that correspond to predicates, or non-existent entities to correspond to non-denoting names or descriptions; or they argue that sentences do, or do not, correspond to facts or propositions.

A different light is shed on these matters when we look for a comprehensive theory of truth, for such a theory makes its own unavoidable demands.

III

Now let us consider some applications. We noticed that the requirement that the truth conditions of a sentence be given using only the conceptual resources of that sentence is not entirely clear where it seems that it can be met, nor everywhere applicable. The cases that invite exception are sentences that involve demonstratives, and here the cure of the difficulty is relatively simple.[4] These cases aside, the requirement, for all its obscurity, has, I think, important implications.

Suppose we were to admit a rule like this as part of a theory of truth: 'A sentence consisting of a singular term followed by a one-place predicate is true if and only if the object named by the singular term belongs to the class determined by the predicate.'[5] This rule offends the requirement, for if the rule were admitted, the T-sentence for 'Socrates is wise' would be ' "Socrates is wise" is true if and only if the object named by "Socrates" belongs to the class determined by the predicate "is wise",' and here the statement of truth conditions involves two semantic concepts (naming and determining a class) not plausibly among the conceptual resources of 'Socrates is wise'.

It would be easy to get from the tendentious T-sentence just mentioned to the non-committal and admissible ' "Socrates is wise" is true if and only if Socrates is wise' if the theory also contained as postulates statements that the object named by 'Socrates' is Socrates and that x belongs to the class determined by the predicate 'is wise' if and only if x is wise. If enough such postulates are available to care for all proper names and primitive predicates, the results are clear. First, T-sentences free from unwanted semantic terms would be available for all the sentences involved; and the extra semantic terms would be unnecessary. For there would have to be a postulate for each name and predicate, and this there could be only if the list of names and primitive predicates were finite. But if the list were finite, there would be only a finite number of sentences consisting of a name and a one-place predicate, and nothing would stand in the way of giving the truth conditions for all such sentences straight off – the T-sentences themselves could serve as the axioms.

The example illustrates how keeping the vocabulary finite may allow the elimination of semantic concepts; it also shows how the demand for a satisfactory theory has ontological consequences. Here, the call for entities to correspond to predicates disappears when the theory is made to produce T-sentences without excess semantic baggage. Indeed in the case at hand the theory does not need to put expressions and objects into explicit correspondence at all, and so no ontology is involved; but this is because the supply of sentences whose truth conditions are to be given is finite.

Not that an infinity of sentences necessarily demands ontology. Given the finite supply of sentences with unstructured predicates that we have been imagining, it is easy to go on to infinity, by adding one or more iterable devices for constructing sentences from sentences, like negation, conjunction, or alternation. If ontology was not required to give the truth conditions for the simplest sentences, these devices will not call for more.

In general, however, semantically relevant structure is apt to demand ontology. Consider, for example, the view that quotations are to be treated as semantic atoms, on a par with proper names in lacking significant structure. Tarski says of this way of viewing quotation that it 'seems to be the most natural one and completely in accordance with the customary way of using quotation marks'.[6] He gives a model argument to show that quotation marks cannot be treated as an ordinary functional expression since a quotation does not name any entity that is a function of anything named by what the quotation marks enclose. About this Tarski is certainly right, but the moral of the lesson cannot be that quotations are like proper names – not, anyway, if a Tarski-style theory of truth can be given for a language containing quotation. For clearly there are infinitely many quotations.

One idea for a possible solution can be extracted from Quine's remark that quotations may be replaced by spelling (much the same is said by Tarski). Spelling does have structure. It is a way of giving a semantically articulate description of an expression by the use of a finite number of expressions: the concatenation sign, with associated parentheses, and (proper) names of the letters. Following this line, we should think of a quotation like '"cat"' as having a form more clearly given by '"c"⌒"a"⌒"t"', or, better still, by '(see⌒eh)⌒tee'. This idea works, at least up to a point. But note the consequences. We no longer view the quotation '"cat"' as unstructured; rather we are treating it as an abbreviation of a sort for a complex description. Not, however, as an arbitrary abbreviation to be specified for the case at hand, but as a *style* of abbreviation that can be expanded mechanically into a description that shows structure more plainly. Indeed, talk of abbreviation is misleading; we may as well say this theory treats quotations as complex descriptions.

Another consequence is that in giving structure to quotations we have had to recognize in quotations repeatable and independent 'words': names of the individual letters, and the concatenation sign. These 'words' are, of course, finite in number – that was required – but they also reveal an ontological fact not apparent when quotations were viewed as unstructured names, a commitment to letters. We get a manageable theory when we explain molecules as made from atoms of a finite number of kinds; but we also get atoms.

A more stirring example of how postulating needed structure in language can bring ontology in its wake is provided by Frege's semantics for the oblique contexts created by sentences about propositional attitudes. In Frege's view, a sentence like 'Daniel believes that there is a lion in the den' is dominated by the two-place predicate 'believes' whose first place is filled by the singular term 'Daniel' and whose second place is filled by a singular term that names a proposition or 'sense'. Taking this line not only requires us to treat sentences as singular terms, but to find entities for them to name. And more is to come. For clearly an infinite number of sentences may occupy the spot after 'Daniel believes that . . .'. So if we are to provide a truth definition, we must discover semantic structure in these singular terms: it must be shown how they can be treated as descriptions of propositions. To avoid the absurdities that would ensue if the singular terms in a sentence had their usual reference, Frege takes them as referring instead to intensional entities. Analogous changes must come over the semantic features of predicates, quantifiers, and sentential connectives. So far, a theory of truth of the sort we have been looking for can handle the situation, but only by treating each work of the language as ambiguous, having one interpretation in ordinary contexts and another after 'believes that' and similar verbs. What is to the eye one word must, from the vantage point of this theory, be treated as two. Frege appreciated this, and held the ambiguity against natural language; Church, in the artificial languages of 'A Formulation of the Logic of Sense and Denotation', eliminated the ambiguity by introducing distinct expressions, differing in subscript.[7]

Frege suggested that with each addition of a verb of propositional attitude before a referring expression that expression comes to refer to an entity of a higher semantical level. Thus every word and sentence is infinitely many-ways ambiguous; on Church's theory there will be an infinite basic vocabulary. In neither case is it possible to provide a theory of truth of the kind we want.

Frege was clear on the need, if we are to have a systematic theory, to view the truth value of each sentence as a function of the semantic roles of its parts or aspects, far clearer that anyone who went before, and clearer than most who followed. What Frege did not appreciate as this last example brings out, was the additional restraints, in particular to a finite vocabulary, that flow from the demand for a comprehensive theory of truth. Frege brought semantics to a point where the demand was intelligible and even, perhaps, satisfiable; but it did not occur to him to formulate the demand.

Let us take a closer look at the bootstrap operation that enables us to bring latent structure to light by characterizing a truth predicate. Early steps may be illustrated by as simple a sentence as 'Jack and Jill went up the hill' – under what conditions is this sentence true? The challenge lies in the presence in the sentence of an iterative device – conjunction. Clearly we can go on adding phrases like 'and Mary' after the word 'Jill' *ad libitum*. So any statement of truth conditions for this sentence must bear in mind the infinity of sentences, generated by the same device, that lie waiting for treatment. What is called for is a recursive clause in the truth theory that can be called into play as often as needed. The trick, as we all know, is to define truth for a basic, and finite, stock of simplest sentences, such as 'Jack went up the hill' and 'Jill went up the hill', and then make the truth conditions of 'Jack and Jill went up the hill' depend on the truth conditions of the two simple sentences. So we get:.

'Jack and Jill went up the hill' is true if and only if Jack went up the hill and Jill went up the hill.

as a consequence of a theory of truth. On the left, a sentence of the vernacular, its structure transparent or not, is described; on the right of the 'if and only if' a sentence of that same vernacular, but a part of the vernacular chosen for its ability to make explicit, through repeated applications of the same simple devices, the underlying semantic structure. If a theory of truth yields such a purified sentence for every sentence in the language, the portion of the total language used on the right may be considered a canonical notation. Indeed, with symbols substituted for some words, and grouping made plain by parentheses or some equivalent device, the part of the language used in stating truth conditions for all sentences may become indistinguishable from what is often called a formalized or artificial language. It would be a mistake, however, to suppose that it is essential to find such a canonical subdivision of the language. Since 'and' may be written between sentences in English, we take the easy route of transforming 'Jack and Jill went up the hill' into 'Jack went up the hill and Jill went up the hill' and then giving the truth conditions of the latter in accord with a rule that says a conjunction of sentences is true if and only if each conjunct is. But suppose 'and' never stood between sentences; its role as sentential connective would still be recognized by a rule saying that a sentence composed of a conjunctive subject ('Jack and Jill') and a predicate ('went up the hill') is true if and only if the sentence composed of the first conjoined subject and the predicate, and the sentence composed of the second conjoined subject and the predicate are true. The rule required is less perspicuous, and needs to be supplemented with others, to do the work of the simple original rule. But the point remains: canonical notation is a convenience we can get along without if need be. It is good, but not necessary, to bring logical form to the surface.

Similarly, it would greatly ease the treatment of negation if we could plausibly transform all sentences containing negation into sentences, recognizably the same in truth value, in which the negating phrase always governs a sentence (as with, 'it is not the case that'). But if this were not possible, negation would still be a sentential connective if the truth condition of a sentence like 'Coal is not white' were given by adverting to the truth condition of 'Coal is white.' ('Coal is not white' is true if and only if 'Coal is white' is not true.)

The issue of ontology is forced into the open only were the theory finds quantificational structure, and that is where the theory best accounts for the pattern of truth dependencies by systematically relating expressions to objects. It is striking how firmly the demand for theory puts to rest one ancient source of aporia: the question how to demonstrate the asymmetry, if any of subject and predicate. As long as our attention is focused on single, simple sentences, we may wonder why an explanation of truth should involve predicates in ontology any less than singular terms. The class of wise objects (or the property of wisdom) offers itself as what might correspond to the predicate 'wise' in 'Socrates is wise' in much the same way Socrates corresponds to 'Socrates'. As pointed out above, no finite number of such sentences requires a theory of truth to bring ontology into the picture. When we get to mixed quantification and predicates of any degree of complexity, however, the picture changes. With complex quantificational structure, the theory will match up expressions with objects. But there is no need, as long as the underlying logic is assumed to be first order, to introduce entities to correspond to predicates. Recognition of this fact will not, of course, settle the question whether there are such things as universals or classes. But it does demonstrate that there is a difference between singular term and predicate; for large stretches of language, anyway, variables, quantifiers, and singular terms must be construed as referential in function; not so for predicates.

It is not always evident what the quantificational structure of a sentence in natural language is; what appear to be singular terms sometimes melt into something less ontic in implication when their logical relations with other sentences are studied, while the requirements of theory may suggest that a sentence plays a role which can be explained only by treating it as having a quantificational structure not apparent on the surface. Here is a familiar illustration.

What is the ontology of a sentence like:

'Jack fell down before Jack broke his crown'?

Jack and his crown seem to be the only candidates for entities that must exist if this sentence is to be true. And if, in place of 'before', we had 'and', this answer might satisfy us for the reason already explored: namely, that we can state, in a way that will work for endless similar cases, the truth conditions of the whole sentence 'Jack fell down *and* Jack broke his crown' on the basis just of the truth of the component sentences, and we can hope to give the truth conditions for the components without more ontology than Jack and his crown. But 'Jack fell down before Jack broke his crown' does not yield to this treatment, because 'before' cannot be viewed as a truth-functional semantic connective: to see this, reflect that for the sentence to be true, both component sentences must be true, but this is not sufficient for its truth, since interchanging the components will make it false.

Frege showed us how to cope with the case: we can formulate the truth conditions for the sentence 'Jack fell down before Jack broke his crown' as follows: it is true if and only if there exists a time t and there exists a time t' such that Jack fell down at t, Jack broke his crown at t', and t is before t'. So apparently we are committed to the existence of times if we accept any such sentence as true. And thinking of the holistic character of a truth definition, the discovery of hidden ontology in sentences containing 'before' must carry over to other sentences: thus, 'Jack fell down' is true if and only if there exists a time t such Jack fell down at t.

Now for a more disturbing example. Consider first 'Jack's fall caused the breaking of his crown.' Here it is natural to take 'Jack's fall' and 'the breaking of his crown' as singular terms describing events, and 'caused' as a two-place, or relational, predicate. But then, what is the semantic relation between such general terms as 'fall' in 'Jack's fall' or 'the fall of Jack' and such verbs as 'fell' in 'Jack fell'? For that matter, how does 'Jack's fall caused the breaking of his crown' differ, in its truth conditions, from 'Jack fell, which caused it to be the case that Jack broke his crown', where the phrase 'which caused it to be the case that' is, on the face of it, a sentential connective?

The correct theory of 'caused'. as I have argued at more length elsewhere, is parallel to Frege's theory for 'before'.[8] I suggest that 'Jack fell down, which caused a breaking of his crown' is true if and only if there exists events e and f such that e is a fall Jack took, f is a breaking his crown suffered, and e caused f. According to this proposal, the predicate 'is a fall', true of events, becomes primary, and contexts containing the verb are derived. Thus 'Jack fell' is true if and only if there is a fall such that Jack took it, 'Jack took a walk' is true if and only if there is a walk that he took, and so on. On this analysis, a noun phrase like 'Jack's fall' becomes a genuine description, and what it describes is the one fall that Jack took.

One consideration that may help reconcile us to an ontology of particular events is that we may then dispense with the abstract ontology of times we just now tentatively accepted, for events are as plausibly the relata of the before-relation as times. Another consideration is that by recognizing our commitment to an ontology of events we can see our way to a viable semantics of adverbs and adverbial modification. Without events, there is the problem of explaining the logical relations between sentences like 'Jones nicked his cheek while shaving with a razor in the bathroom on Saturday', and 'Jones nicked his cheek in the bathroom', and 'Jones nicked his cheek'. It seems that some iterative device is at work; yet what, from a semantic point of view, can the device be? The books on logic do not say: they analyse these sentences to require relations with varying numbers of places depending on the number of adverbial modifications, but this leads to the unacceptable conclusion that there is an infinite basic vocabulary, and it fails to explain the obvious inferences. By interpreting these sentences as being about events, we can solve the problems. Then we can say that 'Jones nicked his cheek in the bathroom on Saturday' is true if and only if there exists an event that is a nicking of his cheek by Jones, *and* that event took place in the bathroom, *and* it took place on Saturday. The iterative device is now obvious: it is the familiar collaboration of conjunction and quantification that enables us to deal with 'Someone fell down and broke his crown'.

This device works, but as we have seen, it takes an ontology to make it work: an ontology including people for 'Someone fell down and broke his crown', an ontology of events (in addition) for 'Jones nicked his cheek in the bathroom on Saturday'. It is mildly ironic that in recent philosophy it has become a popular maneuver to try to *avoid* ontological problems by treating certain phrases as adverbial. One such suggestion is that we can abjure sense-data if we render a sentence like 'The mountain appears blue to Smith' as 'The mountain appears bluely to Smith'. Another similar idea is that we can do without an ontology of intensional objects by thinking of sentences about propositional attitudes as essentially adverbial: 'Galileo said that the earth moves' would then come out, 'Galileo spoke in a-that-the-earth-moves-fashion'. There is little chance, I think, that such adverbial clauses can be given a systematic semantical analysis without ontological entanglements.

There is a further, rather different, way in which a theory of truth may have metaphysical repercussions. In adjusting to the presence of demonstratives, and of the demonstrative elements like tense, in a natural language, a theory of truth must treat truth as an attribute of utterances that depends (perhaps among other things) on the sentence uttered, the speaker, and the time. Alternatively, it may be possible to treat truth as a relation between speakers, sentences and times. Thus an utterance of 'I am five feet tall' is true if spoken at some times in the lives of most people, and true if spoken at any time during a considerable span in the lives of a few. 'Your slip is showing' may be true when uttered by a speaker at a time when he faces west, though it might not have been true if he had faced north; and 'Hillary climbed Everest' was for a long time false, and is now forever true. Sentences without demonstrative elements cannot do the work of sentences with demonstrative elements, but if we are to have a theory of truth, we must be able to state, without the use of demonstratives, a rule that explains under what conditions sentences with demonstratives are true. Such rules will give the truth condition of sentences like 'Hillary climbed Everest' only by quantifying over utterances, speakers, and times, or, perhaps, events.

If explicit appeal must be made to speakers and their circumstances in giving a theory of truth, then on the assumption that the general features of language reflect objective features of the world, we must conclude that an intelligible metaphysics will assign a central place to the idea of people (= speakers) with a location in public space and time.

It should be clear that 'the method of truth' in metaphysics does not eliminate recourse to more standard, often essentially non-linguistic, arguments or decisions. What it is possible to do in a theory of truth, for example, depends to a large extent on the logical resources the theory itself deploys, and the theory cannot decide this for us. Nor, as we have seen, does the method suggest what truths, beyond those it counts as logical, we must accept as a condition of mutual understanding. What a theory of truth does is describe the pattern truth must make among the sentences, without telling us where the pattern falls. So, for example, I argue that a very large number of our ordinary claims about the world cannot be true unless there are events. But a theory of truth, even if it took the form I propose, would not specify which events exist, or even that any do. However, if I am right about the logical form of sentences concerning change, then unless there are events, there are no true sentences of very common kinds about change. And if there are no true sentences about change, there are no true sentences about objects that change. A metaphysician who is willing to suppose no sentences like 'Vesuvius erupted in March 1944' or 'Caesar crossed the Rubicon' are true will not be forced by a theory of truth to admit the existence of events or even, perhaps, of people or mountains. But if he accepts that many such sentences are true (whichever they may be), then it is obvious that he must accept the existence of people and volcanoes; and, if I am right, the existence of events like eruptions and crossings.

The merit of the method of truth is not that it settles such matters once and for all, or even that it settles them without further metaphysical reflection. But the method does serve to sharpen our sense of viable alternatives, and gives a comprehensive idea of the consequences of a decision. Metaphysics has generality as an aim; the method of truth expresses that demand by requiring a theory that touches all the bases. Thus the problems of metaphysics, while neither solved nor replaced, come to be seen as the problems of all good theory building. We want a theory that is simple and clear, with a logical apparatus that is understood and justified, and that accounts for the facts about how our language works. What those facts are may remain somewhat in dispute, as will certainly the wisdom of various trade-offs as between simplicity and clarity. These questions will be, I do not doubt, the old questions of metaphysics in new dress. But the new dress is in many ways an attractive one.

Notes

1 W. V. O. Quine, *Word and Object* (Cambridge, Mass.: MIT Press, 1900), p. 161.
2 A. Tarski, 'The Concept of Truth in Formalized Languages', in *Logic, Semantics, Metamathematics* (Oxford: Clarendon Press, 1956).
3 See Essays 9 and 10 in *Inquiries into Truth and Interpretation* (Oxford: Clarendon Press, 1984).
4 See S. Weinstein, 'Truth and Demonstratives', *Noûs*, 8 (1974), pp. 179–84.
5 Compare R. Carnap, *Meaning and Necessity* (Chicago: University of Chicago Press, 1947), p. 5.
6 A. Tarski, 'The Concept of Truth in Formalized Languages', p. 160.
7 A. Church, 'A Formulation of the Logic of Sense and Denotation', in *Structure, Method and Meaning*, ed. P. Henle, H. M. Kallen and S. K. Langer (New York: Liberal Arts Press, 1951).
8 See Essay 7 in D. Davidson, *Essays on Actions and Events* (Oxford: Oxford University Press, 1980).

---

27   Truth as Coherence

Linda Martín Alcoff

In the real world, knowledge always involves a political dimension. But this does not mean we need to give up realism or the possibility of truth. Coherence

Reprinted with minor revisions from *Real Knowing: New Versions of the Coherence Theory*. Ithaca, NY: Cornell University Press, 1996, pp. 5–13. Copyright © 1996 by Cornell University. By permission of the publisher.

theories of knowledge and truth have the potential to explain how realism can coexist with a political self-consciousness about human claims to know.

A typical formulation of coherentism goes as follows: "a belief is justified to the extent to which the belief-set of which it is a member is coherent."[1] What it means for a set of beliefs to be coherent is more variously defined. Some minimalist formulations of coherence require only simple consistency, while other, stronger versions require mutual entailment. The problem with the latter requirement is that it renders most actual belief sets incoherent and therefore unjustified, while the problem with the former is that it would force us into the position of accepting a huge number of questionable or even fictional systems as justified beliefs if only they have internal consistency. A middle position which avoids these problems requires that the elements in a belief set be mutually explanatory. This involves symmetrical relations of support rather than the relations of logical dependence implied in the concept of mutual entailment. Explanatory support can be offered in a number of ways, by inference, correlation, analogy, or even similarity.

If a coherence theory of truth is adopted along with a coherence theory of justification, then it is held that "a proposition is true iff it is a member of a coherent set."[2] It is this more robust form of coherentism which offers the possibility for reconceptualizing truth. Robust coherentism has the neo-Hegelian aspiration to locate knowledge in such a way that the binary between nature and human construction is transcended. Knowledge has most often been defined as a kind of affinity between two essentially dissimilar entities: a linguistic item and a bit of nature or a phenomenological experience, a mental entity and a corporeal one, a systematized set of propositions and a Ding-an-sich. Truth has been located at the intersection, as a bridge spanning the chasm between two "worlds" or as piercing an obstructive "veil." Coherentist epistemology, at least in its more robust manifestations, represents an attempt to reconfigure and transform – not merely rearrange – the basic building blocks of truth: knowledge, reality, social practice. If this project is a viable one, it holds out the promise of avoiding the problems of both foundationalist philosophies and epistemologically nihilist ones.

Foundationalist epistemologies which identify knowledge in terms of its relationship to a mind-independent reality have become increasingly difficult to maintain. One of the principal reasons for this is the changing conception of the sciences since the nineteenth century. Science, and particularly natural science, has served as the paradigm of justified belief in the West since Bacon. The cause of its valued status arguably had more to do with the role science could play in the societies of burgeoning commodity capitalism and colonialism than with Bacon's formulation of the scientific method, and on this view, his contribution was to provide an ideological articulation for the latest form of epistemological authoritarianism. Nonetheless, scientific beliefs have seemed to instantiate a level of objectivity elusive for other fields of inquiry. Bacon's formulation ensured this identification between science and objectivity by claiming that it is nature herself (this is Bacon's gendering, not mine) that determines which theories shall be confirmed, which knowledge claims accepted and which rejected, rather than the desire of some experimental scientist or the consensus of judgment among communities of scientists.

But as science has become more and more removed from common sense beliefs and observable experience, or, to use Quine's terminology, as the (recognized) disparity between our meager input and our torrential output expanded, this assumption of the determining role of nature has become increasingly implausible. The past hundred years have witnessed a growing amount of evidence and suspicion against this belief. Since Popper it has become widely accepted, for example, that it is impossible to actually *confirm* theoretical claims in science. This is not to say that there is no reason to continue to accept science's claims, but that we need to reconsider what their acceptability *means*. There is no available method by which we can isolate singular scientific claims for epistemic evaluation. Nor have we been able to rid science of its reliance on and use of irreducible metaphysical assumptions. The project of finding a justification for our reliance on induction has failed, at least thus far. We have failed to explicate methodically the rules for induction or the most reliable processes for the discovery of hypotheses. For the most widely used and confirmed theory of the twentieth century – quantum mechanics – we have failed to translate its implications into a coherent ontology. And ironically, despite obvious advances in technological production, many philosophers concur that we have no way to prove that, at least in traditional realist terms, the knowledge we have about nature has actually progressed.

For many of us, the implications to be drawn from these failures, and from the growing sense that we cannot completely erase the effects of the knower on the known, is that we need to redefine and rethink what claims "to know," in science as well as elsewhere, actually mean. Analytic philosophers are overly fond of using such examples as whether "it is raining" to support correspondence theories of truth, but relatively few truth claims (and certainly none of the interesting and complicated ones) permit such easy characterizations. When any of the sciences are used as the paradigm of knowledge rather than immediate sensory experience, it quickly becomes apparent that our assumptions about truth as correspondence to the intrinsic features of a mind-independent reality and our notion of reason as a transhistorical and rule-governed methodology are dubitable and inadequate, if not laughably simplistic.

Responses to this predicament by analytic epistemologists can probably be grouped into three categories. First, W. V. O. Quine initiated the development of a naturalistic approach that uses coherence to the scientific web of belief as the principal criterion of truth. This means that we can simply take what science believes as largely true without having to establish science's privileged access to a transcendental reality. However, for Quine, the criterion of coherence in science operates outside of history, culture, or political influence. A second response, developed in the work of Roderick Chisholm, bases human knowledge on a foundation of incorrigible, or indubitable, phenomenological states, such as simple perceptual states. The problem here is how to justify the entire complex of scientific beliefs as well as other apparently well justified human beliefs based only on the foundation of these thin, subjective experiences. A third major response has been to reduce the question of truth to the question of language, and thus to deny that truth is a *metaphysical* issue. Paradoxically, both Tarski and Rorty would fit here. This third response is only viable if we can be persuaded that truth has nothing to do with our relation to the world, and has only to do with semantic rules. I see this as a kind of avoidance strategy, based on the desire to avoid any messy metaphysical problems that are not susceptible to technical resolution.

I find it fascinating that continental philosophy has largely turned away from theories of truth as well. The reasons given for this include the new skepticism toward a naive scientific realism sketched above but also include claims about the ultimately undecidable status of meaning. If meaning is based not on identity (as it would be if it were determined by reference, for example) but rather on difference, then meaning can have no intrinsic content which remains stable outside the constantly shifting terms within multiple contexts which determine it. Unlike sameness or identity, which could offer a determinate meaning, difference always involves an open relation ("difference from X" where X is an undefined variable) and therefore it is never fixed or finally decided. Since truth depends on meaning, the undecidability of meaning is taken by many theorists in this tradition to entail that claims to truth (which necessarily would presume to fix or stabilize meaning) are always the result of a kind of fudging.

The continental turn away from ontology and truth has also been motivated by an acknowledgment of the constitutive influence of what is called the "other" of reason: most notably, desire and power. Claims to truth close down discussion and debate by claiming a relationship to a realm which is constant and fixed and therefore beyond challenge or debate. For Lyotard, if we continue to deny that such a strategy has anything to do with power, we will be vulnerable to a kind of epistemic "terrorism."[3] If truth exists, it exists in the realm of the ineffable; within language, there is only heteroglossia. We should strive not for coherence or consensus but for an open system like science in which the only constant value is the ability to generate new and different rules. Thus, on the one side we have analytic approaches which continue to be rooted in ahistorical pretensions, and on the other we have continental approaches that embrace an apparent skepticism toward the possibility of any truth at all. Both orientations divert us from the work of reconceptualizing truth with a newly awakened recognition of the complexities involved.

I believe that a revised coherentist approach can show us how philosophy can survive its newly awakened political self-consciousness without lapsing into skepticism. Why coherence in particular? A coherentist account of knowledge has the potential to overcome important hurdles that previous epistemologies – primarily foundationalist ones – are inherently incapable of overcoming.

1.   First, coherentism can provide a more realistic and feasible account of the way in which beliefs are justified than accounts which would require an uninterpreted, pre-theoretical, self-presenting experiential state or mode of cognition. Coherentism traditionally holds that beliefs are justified by other beliefs, which means that a correspondence relation between beliefs and an extra-

discursive, transparent reality is not required for knowledge. The experience and empirical evidence that play a determining role in the confirmation of many beliefs can be acknowledged as themselves the product (at least in part) of interpretation and theoretical commitments. This follows because on a coherentist view experience and evidence are recognized as beliefs, not self-presenting phenomenological states whose meaning is transparent. Coherentism also takes account of the actual mechanisms most often used to judge new contenders for belief: their plausibility in light of the beliefs one already holds, and the tendency we all have to conserve beliefs. Coherentism thus posits a picture of belief formation which does not require the knower to be able to suspend all of her or his beliefs, nor does it require a pristine mind confronting a transparent reality, what Dewey called the "spectator theory of knowledge" and Adorno named "peephole metaphysics." In contrast to this view, the initial position coherentism starts with is a knower that always already has a great many beliefs, and thus a knower that is always already "in the world," and coherentism further recognizes that these prior beliefs interpret and inform every experience the knower has. Connected to this, it is easier for coherentism to shift from an individualist account of knowing to a collectivist account, a shift which is long overdue in Western epistemologies, because coherentism posits the knower as always already committed to a variety of beliefs based on the testimony of others. And this suggests that for coherentism the interpersonal and cooperative nature of belief-justification will more readily be included as part of the central issues for an epistemology to address, rather than being thought of as side issues or even irrelevant considerations. (Of course, it is true that Anglo-American coherentisms have by and large failed to address this issue. But I am arguing here for the *potential* of coherentist epistemologies, a potential which is developed by theorists such as Gadamer, Foucault, Davidson and Putnam.[4])

2.   A second advantage is that coherentism can provide a way to show how and why apparently disparate elements are and even should be involved in theory-choice and belief-justification. Political considerations, moral commitments, even metaphysical beliefs, have not been considered germane to the justification of beliefs which claim referentiality or truth, much less such elements as are included in the "other" of reason – desire and power. To admit the ineliminable influence of such elements would seem to spell the demise of any hope for knowledge. But this is only because traditionally dominant accounts of justification have presented, as Peirce said long ago, a linear, single-line, inferential model of knowledge in which politics, values, and desire could only be seen as obstacles at worst, irrelevant at best.[5] Coherentist models that understand the process of justification as involving, not a single linear chain of inference, but a complicated, heterogeneous web of belief, make it much easier to see how different kinds of elements can be not only involved in justification but justification-conferring. On a linear model, the claim that authoritarianism is involved in the justification of "master molecule" theories will seem highly implausible; the two ideas may appear metaphorically similar but it will be difficult to show how a biological theory could reasonably follow from a political premise which operates in a different plane of discourse. On a coherentist model, however, the

metaphorical similarity between political authoritarianism and master molecule theories can be seen to offer mutual support, and thus the relevance of various political assumptions to theory-choice in the sciences can be more easily explained, and explained in a way that does not attribute intentional bias to most scientists (or, for that matter, philosophers). Where coherence is taken to be the principal criterion for knowledge, and where the entire web is involved in the process (though different parts of the web are involved to different degrees), it becomes much easier to account for the inclusion of politics in science, ethics in epistemology, and desire in philosophy.[6]

3. The third advantage coherentist accounts can claim accrues only to what I have called more robust accounts, that is, when coherence is taken to involve in some manner the definition of truth rather than (as Laurence Bonjour argues, for example) simply the means by which one can achieve truth in the sense of correspondence.

Coherence epistemology is frequently cited as the principal contender against and ultimate contrast with a foundationalist view.[7] I believe that this opposition is based primarily on the fact that coherentism offers an immanent account of knowledge against foundationalism's transcendental account. That is, for coherentism, knowledge is ultimately a product of phenomena which are immanent to human belief systems and practices, social organizations, and lived reality, whereas for foundationalism if a belief is to count as knowledge it must ultimately be able to establish some link to transcendent phenomena or something which is entirely extrinsic to human existence (i.e. the way the world would be if we had never existed). Where foundationalism ties justification to an external realm beyond beliefs and belief sets, and understands truth as a relationship of a certain sort with this external realm, coherentism holds to an understanding of knowledge as immanent. Justification is an immanent feature of beliefs in that it refers to their interrelationships and, if truth is defined as what coheres, truth is also emergent from immanent relationships rather than relationships with an external or transcendental realm.

This immanent account is advantageous principally because it does not require us to first posit and then find access to a realm defined as beyond all human interpretation and knowledge. Nor does it necessitate establishing a "god's eye view" which can step outside of language, and of all belief systems and interpretive modes, to check on the correspondence between human claims and an extra-human reality. This is not because coherentism posits an idealism in a Berkeleyan sense in which reality is conceived to be causally determined by "mind" or to simply consist in mental properties but because, at least as I tell the story, coherentism starts from a Hegelian phenomenological ontology which sets up no absolute separation between human beings and the world, but sees us as always already in the world, engaged in practical activities, encumbered with myriad beliefs and commitments, and constitutively linked in various complex ways to that about which we are seeking to know. This is a more metaphysically adequate descriptive starting point from which to think about knowledge and it has the added bonus of making the problem of skepticism vanish from the frame. It has the further advantage of making it possible to account for the historical and social embeddedness of all truth claims without lapsing into epistemological nihilism.

Notes

1 Jonathan Dancy, *Introduction to Contemporary Epistemology* (Oxford: Blackwell, 1985), p. 116.
2 Dancy, p.112.
3 Jean-François Lyotard, *The Postmodern Condition*, trans. Geoff Bennington and Brian Massumi (Minneapolis, MN: University of Minnesota Press, 1984), p. 66.
4 I discuss these in detail in *Real Knowing: New Versions of the Coherence Theory* (Ithaca, NY: Cornell University Press, 1996).
5 Charles Sanders Peirce, *Collected Papers*, 5.265. Quoted in Richard Bernstein, *The New Constellation* (Cambridge, MA: MIT Press, 1992), p. 327.
6 Cf. Linda Alcoff, "Justifying Feminist Social Science," *Hypatia* 2 (Fall 1987), 107–27; and Lynn Hankinson Nelson, *Who Knows: From Quine to a Feminist Empiricism* (Philadelphia, PA: Temple University Press, 1990).
7 A recent, intriguing exception to this is Michael Williams, who has recently argued that coherentism is a form of foundationalism. See his *Unnatural Doubts: Epistemological Realism and the Basis of Scepticism* (Cambridge, MA: Blackwell, 1991).

---

28   Truth, Reference and the Pragmatics of (Racial) Meaning

David Theo Goldberg

The political perspectives, views, or theories that unambiguously and self-confidently proclaim the end of racism restrict the range of pertinent expressions to a shrunken totalization of an uncontested Truth. That Judge David Souter can proclaim *unchallenged* during the Senate Judiciary Committee hearings to confirm him as a justice of the U.S. Supreme Court that there is 'no racism in New Hampshire'; that the director of the British Information Service in the United States can respond in 1978 to the controversy surrounding the film *Blacks Britannica* that 'racism is not a significant factor in British life and politics'; that Thomas Sowell can imply in 1984 that institutional discrimination is no more[1] can only be grounded in the totalized closure of the Truth claims themselves. They are grounded, that is, in the exclusions marked by totalized criteria (lack of

Edited version of material from *Racist Culture: Philosophy and the Politics of Meaning*. Oxford: Blackwell, 1993. By permission of the publisher and author.

intentionality or institutional rules), or in the exclusive totalization of formal methods by which claims to racial Truth can be established (social science surveys and attitude studies of personal prejudice, or legally sanctioned reports of discriminatory institutional rules). The denials and delimitations accordingly entailed erase the exclusionary experiences of racialized subjectivities, the effects of racist patterns of discipline and deprivation, and the marginalizations and periphrases insinuated into the racial ambiguities of social practices. Totalized racial Truth excises differentiated experience, extends the silences of those racially othered, wipes away as it claims to clean up the historical subjectivities and subjections of racialized Others, of othering, of otherness itself.

[. . .]

In racial discourse, as in assertive discourses generally, what is generally circulated and exchanged is not simply Truth but truth-claims or representations. These representations draw their efficacy from traditions, conventions, institutions, and tacit modes of mutual comprehension. Two sorts of basic question arise here: The first concerns the objects to which the discursive representations refer and the styles of reference to be found in the figures of speech and metaphors as well as in the categories and expressions of the discursive field. The second involves a more abstract concern, for in the relations between the expressions lies a *grammar*, and underlying the categories representing the objects is a *preconceptual plane* or set of *primitive terms*. Analysis of the structures of a discourse like the racial must seek to uncover this grammar and its preconceptual primitives.

The close relation between the two sorts of questions is revealed in posing two related puzzles: whether a unified grammar of (in this case racialized) discourse can be identified, and how this grammar orders discursive (here racist) expression. If a unifying grammar cannot be specified, if the unity of (racialized) discourse seems chimerical more than simply its existence is thrown in doubt. Skeptics may gather strength in claiming that the public expression of the discourse in question (racism) has been much less pronounced than its critics charge. Indeed, something like this skeptical claim regarding racist expression has been circulated recently in popular media by Dinesh D'Souza.[2] As the extremity of D'Souza's claims illustrate, the implications for public policy and for moral judgments of individual behavior are considerable.

. . . The metaphors of racialized discourse, and more particularly of racist expression, are not reducible to a single form: 'Nigger dogs' or 'Blacks (or Red Indians) are savages' differ in form, substance, and probably in the specificity of their purposes from 'the Jewish conspiracy' or Houston Stewart Chamberlain's 'Aryan race-soul' but also from 'Sambo, the typical plantation slave [as] docile but irresponsible, loyal but lazy, humble but . . . lying and stealing.' It is not simply that color racism and anti-Semitism differ in virtue of the fact that blacks are referred to as animals and Jews only in the context of some abstruse mythology. Jews are often described in terms of animal imagery; and a color racism relying upon character-trait stereotyping need have no recourse to animal metaphors.

It is equally misleading to consider the discursive unity of racist expression and racialized discourse a function either of a prevailing corpus of norms or of a prevailing style. Such norms are supposed to be established in terms of a series of descriptive statements about others that delimit the way we perceive them. Style, in turn, is the dominant mode of discursive expression. Prevailing norms and style are inadequate to the task of unifying racist expression and by extension, racialized discourse. The underlying point here is that racialized discourse does not consist simply in descriptive representations of others. It includes a set of hypothetical premises about human kinds (e.g., the 'great chain of being,' classificatory hierarchies, etc.) and about the differences between them (both mental and physical). It involves a class of ethical choices (e.g., domination and subjugation, entitlement and restriction, disrespect and abuse). And it incorporates a set of institutional regulations, directions, and pedagogic models (e.g., *apartheid*, separate development, educational institutions, choice of educational and bureaucratic language, and so on). [See Foucault, this volume.] Norms or prescriptions for behavior are contextually circumscribed by specific hypotheses, ethical choices, regulations, and models. Yet no unidirectional norms are basic to racialized discourse: a decision that one race is intellectually inferior to another may be taken as grounds for a norm of exclusion from educational institutions or of the concentration of special resources.

Similarly, the mode of racist expression – its style – may be interpreted variously as aversive, academic or scientific, legalistic, bureaucratic, economic, cultural linguistic, religious, mythical or ideological. Racialized descriptions, hypotheses, choices, and modes and rules of discourse have altered over time. This precludes the possibility of establishing a singular transhistorical stylistic or normative pattern.

A complementary criticism can be launched against attempts to establish discursive unity on the basis of common objects referred to, or common themes developed and spoken about in the discourse of and concerning race. Anti-Semitic statements pick out objects different from those racist statements that objectify black persons. The theme of an anti-Semitic slur (e.g., 'Communist conspirators!' or 'Red kikes' as grounds for excluding Jews from trade unions or political office) differs largely from that of black ones ('Dumb nigger!' as the ground for restricting blacks to manual labor or slavery). Various objects are named, described, analyzed, and judged – in a word, emerge – *in* the discourse; just as themes are chosen, delineated, and developed *in* speaking. Determined by the discursive field, these objects and themes cannot be all that differentiates the discourse of race from other discourses.

Themes and objects emerge only *in* discourse, delineated by the set of norms, principles, hypotheses, and choices, and articulated in figures of speech and styles. The grammar of racialized discourse assumes coherence and uniqueness only when compared from the vantage point of the discourse as a whole with other discursive fields like those of nation or class or gender. If discursive unity is to be achieved, it can only be a product of those underlying factors which directly generate the discursive field. Foucault calls this set of factors the *preconceptual* level. These factors may be likened to 'primitive terms' in an artificial language. Grammatical changes in descriptions, hypotheses, rules, models, norms, and styles are reflected in transformations in the preconceptual grounds of racialized discourse. Accordingly, the structural unity of the discourse must be sought in a transformational schema of its preconceptual set and in the implicative 'interplay between their location, arrangement and displacement.'[3]

The preconceptual set for racialized discourse consists of those factors both reflective and constitutive of power, including dominant values, that directly enable the expression of racialized discourse. These conceptual primitives are not abstract a priori essences; they do not constitute an ideal foundation of the racialized discursive formation. Nor are they to be confused with the actual, explicit concepts and terms by which racialized discourse is usually expressed. The primitive terms are manifestations of power relations vested in and between historically located subjects, and they are effects of a determinate social history. These factors of power effect 'implicatures' that circumscribe the transformations, inferences, and references for the field of discourse. They generate the concepts and categories in terms of which racism is actually expressed and comprehended. Thus, these preconceptual factors define in a general way the expression of those agents, and only those, who speak and act in terms of racialized discourse and racist expression.

It follows that the unity of racialized discourse is not given in any purportedly ahistorical durability of race or racism. The discourse of race transforms – arises, alters, and perhaps will eventually disintegrate – both with actual social conditions and with conceptual reformulations, with implicative redirection. The overall coherence of racialized expression and the racist project, rather, turns on the preconceptual elements structuring dispositions and the drawing of implications. These elements include classification, order, value, and hierarchy; differentiation and identity, discrimination and identification; exclusion, domination, subjection, and subjugation; as well as entitlement and restriction.

The relations of power expressed in terms of and by these conceptual primitives inscribe social conditions of racialized violation and violence. In turn, the preconceptual elements or primitives of racialized discourse and of the conditions, implications, and practices that they inform are embedded in social discourses central to and legitimized by practices and relations constitutive of modernity. Normalization of racialized expression and racist exclusion turns on the embedding of their conditions of possibility deep in modernity's formative sociodiscursive structures and scientific vision. It is from this broad social context that such primitives are to be derived.

Classification is basically the scientific extension of the epistemological drive to place phenomena under categories. The impulse to classify data goes back at least to Aristotle. However, it is only with the '*esprits simplistes*' of the seventeenth century and the Enlightenment that classification is established as a fundament of scientific methodology. With its catalogues, indices, and inventories, classification establishes an ordering of data; it thereby systemizes observation. But it also claims to reflect the natural order of things. This ordering of representations accordingly always presupposes value: Nature ought to be as it is; it cannot be otherwise. So the seemingly naked body of pure facts is veiled in value.

In the eighteenth century, the data that lent themselves most readily to systematic seeing, to representations by rules, were those of biology and of natural history. Extended to human affairs, the pervasive spirit of simplicity sought to reproduce for social relations the sort of simple order thought to inhere in nature. Hence the application of categories of speciation (e.g., racial classification) to human groupings on the basis of natural characteristics. Unsurprisingly, a major assumption underlying anthropological classification at the time turns out to be that identification of races in terms of their differentia is adequate to establish the laws of behavior for their members.

So classification is central to scientific methodology, and scientific method has long been taken as the ideal model of rationality. The capacity for rationality, in turn, was considered the mark of humanity. It seemed obviously to follow that the anthropological ordering into a system of races in terms of rational capacity would establish a *hierarchy* of humankind. The race represented by the classifiers was assumed as a matter of course to stand at the hierarchical apex. Racial ordering accordingly implied a racial hierarchy and a behavioral expectation. The rational hierarchy was thought to be revealed through its physical, its natural, correlates: skin color, head shape, body size, smell hair texture, and the like. This engendered a metaphysical pathos, an aesthetic empathy or aversion. Because so 'obviously' natural, this pathos was assumed unquestioningly to be rational.[4]

Thus, racial classification – the ordering of human groups on the basis of putatively natural (inherited or environmental) differences – implied a hierarchy of races. The derivation of hierarchy from classification rested upon the long-standing assumption that the universe is perfectly intelligible to reason and on the *principle of gradation* inherent in this. Formulated initially as Aristotle's 'hierarchy of being,' this principle was adopted later as a fundament of Christian thought. It evolved systematically 'from a less to a greater degree of fullness and excellence.'[5] The neutrality and objectifying distantiation of the rational scientist created the theoretical space for a view to develop of subjectless bodies. Once objectified, these bodies could be analyzed, categorized, classified, and ordered with the cold gaze of scientific distance.

[. . .]

I have argued that the conditions of racialized discourse and the variety of racist exclusions prompted in specific contexts are deeply embedded in the shifting space-time conjunctures of modern and contemporary socio-intellectual history. Race has fashioned and continues to mold personal and social identity, the bounds of who one is and can be, of where one chooses to be or is placed, what social and private spaces one can and dare not enter or penetrate. Race categorically and materially inscribes and circumscribes the experiences of space and time, of geography and history, just as race itself acquires its specificity in terms of space-time correlates. Changing one's place in the world will in this sense likely change one's world. Nevertheless, the history of racialized expression has served to fix social subjects in place and time, no matter their spatial location, to delimit privilege and possibilities, to open opportunities to some while excluding the range of racialized Others. And in so fixing, these imposed and imagined histories freeze not only the racial Other but also those so privileged into given identities, perspectives, and dispositions.

Some philosophers have argued that assertions involving racist terms like 'nigger' or 'kike' are neither true nor false because there are no such things as niggers or kikes in the world. There is nothing on this view to which such racist terms refer.[6] Now it is indeed true that there are literally no such entities in the world as 'niggers' and 'kikes' though this doesn't preclude the terms from referring. They refer in terms of the thick contextualization of the fabric of racialized discourse I have laid out above. Indeed the fact of their reference causes pain and suffering which no amount of philosophical denial serves to mitigate. The terms refer respectively to black and Jewish people, expressing of course pernicious judgments about them. As Kriste Taylor argues, terms like 'nigger' and 'kike' would fail to refer only if there were some 'linguistic rule' or 'linguistic convention' which prevented these kinds of expression from 'securing reference.' There is no formulated linguistic rule which prohibits reference from being secured by such terms. And were some such rule readily available, there would be no principled, context independent way of judging whether the use of a particular term transgresses the rule at issue.[7] How in any but context-bound pragmatic ways would one distinguish between the referentiality *and* admissibility of claims like 'Nigger, do as I command!' issued by a white person in Jim Crow Georgia, and 'Nigger, please!' addressed ironically or castigatingly by one black person to another; between 'Don't act like a nigger' expressed by a white school teacher to a student, white or black, and 'Never use the word "nigger"' addressed by a mother (white or black) to her child (black or white)?

The truth of a claim – at the extreme, a tautological and necessary truth like 'Jews are Jews' – may bear value judgments beyond mere reference. The truth of the claim alone, and the validity of the inference involving the claim, cannot alone preclude their being racist, given the 'appropriate' context. It is the use of expressions to make claims in established contexts, and the manner in which claims are made, which determine that expressions and claims are racist. There are indeed strong ethical considerations not to refer to black and Jewish people as niggers and kikes respectively. But ethical considerations only exhort that black and Jewish people ought not to be referred to thus. They cannot determine that these groups are not so referenced. Many, all too many, do refer by the use of such terms, and reference is secured – in the cases at hand, to black and Jewish people respectively. This does not entail the existence of niggers and kikes but of black and Jewish people who by such reference are being judged perniciously. So such reference terms, besides referring, also make pernicious judgments. In condemning such usage it is not just the reference nor just the judgment that is the object of the objection, but the reference in order to make the judgment, the relation between reference and judgment. No traditional theory of truth and reference other than a pragmatic one can sustain the line of

argument I am suggesting that runs together contextually truth, reference, political and moral judgment. And yet such socially contextualized judgments
seem to require just such complexity.

These considerations underline an interesting feature of the relations between
linguistic practices and moral proscriptions. Once acknowledged, ethical and
political considerations may alter the way others are spoken about and referred
to. They may change the conventions for referring. Witness, for example, the
shifts from 'non-European' to 'Negro', from 'black' to 'African-American.'
Changes in the modes of referring to, speaking about, representing and acting
towards others are likely to follow from altering prevailing social relations even
as they promote such changes. It is very difficult to change the ways others are
spoken of absent wider social changes. Political and ethical analysis and con-
demnation must be aimed primarily at the context of use and expression, at the
conditions which render warrantable or acceptable the use of such terms. Of
course, improving the way racial others are referred to and spoken about enables or circumscribes general social relations. Success in excising racist
expressions from ways we speak – from both what is said and how it is expressed – depends ultimately upon wider social commitments of which theories of truth and reference play a part but not from which they stand apart.

If one is to be committed to a theory of truth and reference that proscribes
the use of such terms it would have to be one that builds in ethical and political
judgments about the use – about resisting the use – of such terms, and such a
theory would necessarily be pragmatic. For a pragmatic theory of truth and
reference acknowledges that any theory – and so any theory of truth and reference – is built upon the basis of at least implicit value assumptions. A pragmatic
theory is committed to explicating those assumptions, and a progressive pragmatic theory to making assumptions that resist judgments sustaining the variety
of racist exclusions.[8]

What is necessary in facing down racism then is a firm commitment to the
practical reasoning, the intersections of theory with practices, required by
antiracism. The concern is to end racist exclusions and the conditions that given
rise to and sustain such exclusions, however and whenever they manifest. This
may sometimes call for recognizing nonexclusionary racial distinctions as a (potential) site of resistance or (self-) affirmation, while in other contexts it may also
necessitate resisting the imposition of racial categories, of racializing. For the
liberal, the standard of nondiscrimination necessarily entails a commitment to
nonracialism, to ignoring race. Antiracisms, on the other hand, recognize the
possibilities of multiple manifestations of racist exclusions, of exclusionary
resurgences and redefinitions, of newly emergent racisms or expressive recur-
rences, of different discursive impositions or terminological transformations. It is
in this sense that antiracists must repeatedly recommit themselves to root out the
weeds of racist cultures, though not necessarily the culture of race, wherever they
may sprout.

True representations are those the circumstances most likely bear out. Truth
is context-bound, reference more or less specific.[9] In this sense, both truth and
reference are always more or less contestable. A pragmatic theory of truth and

knowledge accordingly entails – somewhat ironically because this too is a generalization subject to conditions of warrantability – that there is no transcendental proof or grounds, no universal foundation, and so no warrantable (that is, no non-revisable) universality for *any* representation, for any truth- or knowledge-claims.[10]

Notes

1   T. Sowell, *Civil Rights: Rhetoric or Reality?* (New York: Basic Books, 1984), p. 116.
2   Dinesh D'Souza, *The End of Racism* (New York: The Free Press, 1995).
3   M. Foucault, *The Archeology of Knowledge*, trans. A. Sheridan-Smith (London: Tavistock, 1972), p. 60.
4   The assumptions and reasoning are uniform, whether those of Kant's hardhearted rationalism or of Buffon's and Lamarck's environmentalism. Though author of the principle that 'all men are (created) equal,' Jefferson believed that nature condemned the 'Negro' to inferiority on the scale of being: 'Blacks, whether originally a distinct race or made distinct by time and circumstance, are inferior to the whites in the endowment both of body and mind.' Thomas Jefferson, *Notes on the State of Virginia* (Chapel Hill: University of North Carolina Press, 1954), p. 143. These premises run clear through Darwinism, eugenicism, and the IQ movement.
5   A. Lovejoy, *The Great Chain of Being* (New York: Harper Torchbooks, 1960).
6   Cf. Patrick Grim, 'A Note on the Ethics of Theories of Truth,' in *Sexist Language*, ed. Mary Vetterling-Braggin (New Jersey: Rowman and Allanheld, 1981), pp. 290–3.
7   K. Taylor, 'Reference and Truth: The Case of Sexist and Racist Utterances,' in *Sexist Language*, op. cit., pp. 313–15.
8   For a more naive set of arguments concerning theories of reference, see my 'A Grim Dilemma of Racist Referring Expressions,' *Metaphilosophy* 17, 4 (October 1986), pp. 224–9.
9   Even necessary truths – tautologies, definitions, identity claims – acquire their truthfulness contextually, that is, by narrowing the context of applicability, by specifying the boundary conditions of the terms of the claim.
10 For a fuller discussion in the context of multiculturalism, see my 'Multicultural Conditions,' in *Multiculturalism: A Critical Reader*, ed. David Theo Goldberg (Oxford: Blackwell, 1994), pp. 1–44.

29   Are Truth Claims in Science Dysfunctional?

Sandra Harding

Problems with the Truth Ideal

Do we need truth claims? Should we want them? No doubt there are contexts in which they have valuable functions. However, the argument here is that in the case of the sciences, their costs appear to outweigh their benefits. While some conventional philosophies of science, famous scientists' recollections, and popular thought all have assumed truth claims to be a valuable goal for the sciences even if in practice unattainable, a critical evaluation of this assumption has emerged from three schools of science studies developed since World War II: Euro-American studies in the philosophy, history, sociology, and ethnography of science, feminist science studies, and postcolonial science studies. From the perspectives of central themes in these accounts, the ideal of truth obstructs the production of knowledge. Moreover, claims to truth support anti-democratic tendencies in science and society because a democratic social order in a multicultural world cannot provide the necessary conditions for agreement.

It should be noted immediately that almost all writers in all of these schools of science studies hold that it is possible and desirable to avoid adopting an epistemological relativism that forecloses the possibility of rationally sorting beliefs. Giving up the truth ideal does not force one to an epistemologically damaging relativism. Obviously these are complex and contentious matters. The evidence for such claims depends on detailed philosophic, historical and cross-cultural studies of scientific traditions, as well as from political philosophy. To make such claims fully plausible would require far more empirical detail and theoretical analysis than can be provided here. Nevertheless, it is possible to outline the arguments in a way that makes apparent the usefulness of further pursuit of these issues.

Earlier Skeptical Accounts: Duhem, Quine, Kuhn and Feyerabend

Let us begin with arguments from Euro-American studies of modern sciences and technologies. One immediately notes that skepticism about the truth ideal is by no means new, that it can be found, among other places, in the work of philosophers and historians regarded as mainstream and perhaps even old-fashioned. Back in the 1950s philosopher W. V. O. Quine argued that analytic

Written for this volume. By permission of the author.

and synthetic claims were not as independent of each other as had been supposed. Scientific hypotheses cannot meet the tribunal of experience one by one, but only as parts of networks of largely unarticulated everyday and scientific assumptions about the reliability of experimental instruments, particular observers' sight and hearing, principles of optics, assessments of prevailing atmospheric conditions, expectations about possibilities of divine intervention, and a huge number of other matters – including even the laws of logic (Quine 1953). Scientific and everyday thought form a seamless web of belief. In each scientific experiment, though scientists focus on only one or a few hypotheses, in effect the entire network is tested all at once.

In his development of such insights, Quine was pursuing Pierre Duhem's arguments from early in the century against the possibility of a crucial experiment that could simultaneously confirm one hypothesis while disconfirming all others. Duhem argued that because of the role that background beliefs played in testing procedures and the necessity of holding even well-confirmed hypotheses open to the collection of possibly disconfirming further evidence, no hypothesis could be conclusively confirmed or proven true (Duhem 1906/ 1954).

Karl Popper subsequently argued that hypotheses could be conclusively disconfirmed; the best strategy for scientists was to think up the most severe tests for hypotheses, ones that only the strongest hypotheses could survive. For Popper, inductivism could not explain modern science's successes; but deductivism – "conjectures and refutations" as the title of one of his books put the matter – could. He also argued that it was a sign of a dogmatic attitude to think that one's beliefs were true and thus irrefutable; religion, Marxism and psychoanalysis were his examples of belief systems lacking the possibility of empirical falsification. Scientific beliefs could be contrasted in that scientists always insisted on holding beliefs open to the risks of possible future falsification (Popper 1972).

Quine went further to argue that useful as severe tests were for advancing the growth of knowledge, deductivism could never produce absolute disconfirmations of any single hypothesis by itself. Nature's "nay," as he put the point, always left scientists free to attribute the apparent mismatch between scientific statement and nature's order to any of innumerable background assumptions or even to the empirical observations no less than to the articulated hypothesis on which attention had been focussed. Some background beliefs would always appear more reasonably doubtful than others. However, when all such reasonable doubts failed to turn up a culprit, yet other background beliefs, initially beyond suspicion, would be examined for the possibility of revision. To put the point another way, empirical observations, theoretical hypothesis and background beliefs could not gain the independence from each other that the conventional "logics of justification" required. In principle, Quine famously proposed, a scientific community could reasonably decide to revise even the laws of logic in order to save a favored hypothesis. The laws of logic, too, have their final justification in their usefulness for helping us make sense of the world around us.[1] Although "true" could not in principle be ascribed in an absolute way to any claims made by sciences, "less false than other claims tested" was a reasonable and useful goal for scientific methods.

Subsequent analyses of scientists' actual reasoning and social histories of science produced in the post-War period uncovered just such *ad hoc* assignments of error. Philosopher Paul Feyerabend polemically proposed that the history of science revealed that apparently "anything goes" in scientists' struggles to bring their observations and hypotheses into alignment with each other (Feyerabend 1975). Thomas S. Kuhn's studies of the history of science showed how the earlier linear model of the growth of scientific knowledge, whether inductively or deductively modeled, failed to capture the importance of conceptual shifts that left succeeding scientific theories if not completely incommensurable with each other, then at least not completely commensurable with each other in the way that the truth ideal required. Kuhn captured the difficulty with retaining either the truth ideal or an absolute falsity ideal in his observation that perhaps it would be better to say that science in general progresses away from falsity rather than that it progresses toward truth (Kuhn 1962/1970). Kuhn also understood that such a position did not force one to a damaging relativism, for his historical account showed that scientific claims could reasonably, if only provisionally, be regarded as "less false" than those (and only those) against which they had been tested.

Recent Analyses

Since the 1960s, historians' arguments (including those of influential historians of philosophy) have continued to show that there is no evidence that either absolute truth or absolute falsity can ever be achieved in the sciences and lots of evidence that they cannot.

One problem is that the very elements of sciences and their practices responsible for historical, cultural specificity – "localness" – are also sometimes responsible for successes. There is no aspect of science that can be immunized from the social and cultural conditions of its time and place – not its choices of problems, concepts, models of nature, research designs, techniques, instrumentation, collection and interpretation of data, ways in which scientists communicate with each other or other norms of scientific communities; not its representations of results of research (mathematical or not), let alone patterns of dissemination, meanings, applications, technologies, or other consequences. Moreover, every element of scientific work contributes to the standards for scientific inquiry, and thus has epistemological consequences. Thus culturally local resources do not just influence sciences; they constitute – bring into visibility and articulation – its technical, cognitive core. So if "true" scientific claims are taken to mean trans-cultural ones, there are no such claims in principle – not just in practice – in the sciences.

Moreover, these studies bring out another problem with the truth ideal. The prevailing conception of truth in the natural sciences has been a correspondence theory of truth: true scientific claims correspond to or are congruent with nature's order. This particular theory or hypothesis cannot fully be understood in isolation from the rest of the epistemological model of which it is a constituent part. It is linked to a network of assumptions about the natural order, science, ideal standards of knowledge, the social order, and relations between such elements, a meta web-of-belief that has developed and changed over time no less than scientific beliefs themselves.

The "unity-of-science" project has been one such constellation of assumptions within which the truth ideal has played a central role. This project flourished in the first half of this century, but has been abandoned since World War II by much of the philosophical and historical tradition that developed it – in no small part due to the work of Quine, Feyerabend, Kuhn, and others writing a generation and more ago. Nevertheless, its assumptions still shape leading epistemologies in the social sciences, some scientists' (mainly physicists') conception of their mission, and popular thinking about the sciences.

The unity-of-science thesis overtly makes three claims: there exists just one unified world, one and only one possible true account of that world ("one truth"), and one unique science that can piece together the one account that will accurately reflect the one truth about that one world. The viability of this still popular home for the truth ideal depends upon it, first, making sense and, second, being a resource for the growth of knowledge. Is it still useful to the growth of knowledge to assume that there is "one world" and one and only one science that could represent the unique correspondence or congruence relations between our claims about nature's order and nature's order itself? All three of these assumptions about the world, its true order, and science now appear to be either implausible or else no longer clearly and uncontroversially meaningful, and each seems to obstruct the growth of scientific knowledge.[2]

Ian Hacking points out that the concept of one science has for different thinkers emphasized or sometimes blended two distinct ideas: singleness and integrated harmony. Singleness and integrated harmony have been weighted in different proportions in defenses of diverse kinds of metaphysical unity, methodological unity, and logical or "styles of reasoning" unities. Surveying diverse arguments for just metaphysical and methodological unities, Hacking identifies a metaphysical sentiment, three metaphysical theses, three practical precepts, and two logical maxims, each of which weights differently unity as singleness and as harmony. Moreover, there evidently are as many styles of scientific reasoning as there are of effective human reasoning more generally. As Hacking points out, Crombie (1994) identifies six important ones, each of which brings its own standards of adequacy (Hacking 1996).

Indeed, it is now widely recognized that science cannot plausibly be understood as one single kind of thing at all. "There is no set of features peculiar to all the sciences, and possessed only by sciences. There is no necessary and sufficient condition for being a science" (Hacking 1996, 68). In the face of such disunity, many different kinds of techniques serve as "unifiers," as Hacking refers to them. Mathematics is the earliest recognized to have such a function. However, it turns out that there is no "one thing" that is mathematics since it, like the sciences to which it gives an appearance of unity, is a diverse collection of principles and practices, as historians of mathematics point out (Bloor 1977, Kline 1980, Restivo 1992). Numerous other such collections of unifiers are to be found among scientific instruments, techniques, attitudes . . . all those inventive strategies that occur in the "trading zones" within which scientists work to communicate across the diverse cultural and natural conditions that separate them (Pickering 1991). Thus the appearance of "one truth" to which all of the sciences contribute their pieces is created through innovative strategies that enable scientists to integrate more or less harmoniously their diverse understandings of nature's order(s) while still showing nature's role in generating the results of their research. Such accounts show scientific work to be much more difficult and creative than simplistic accounts of truth claims would indicate.

Postcolonial and feminist accounts have also contributed to the understanding of the necessary "localness" of truth claims. Postcolonial, anti-Eurocentric cross-cultural studies of other cultures' scientific and technological traditions emphasize the scientific value of the local resources that local cultures bring to their studies of nature's order. So-called high cultures such as those of China or India developed mathematical, scientific, and technological under-standings that enabled them to flourish, many elements of which were later adopted into modern Western science, and elements continue to arrive and be adopted after centuries of indifference to or rejection of them. Moreover, even purportedly underdeveloped, so-called simple societies understand aspects of their natural environments that enable them to farm effectively in fragile environments, prevent and cure diseases with local techniques and pharmacologies, and otherwise live well in their parts of nature's heterogeneous order. Of course such observations should not be taken to imply that all belief identifiable as local is preferable to belief claimed to be universally valid; obviously many local beliefs lead their holders to nasty, brutish, and short lives. This is the case for some of the assumptions and beliefs of modern science as well as those of other cultures' knowledge systems. Modern scientific belief systems have contained systematic ignorance about causes and processes of environmental destruction, infectious disease, human nutrition, women's physiology, and the physical features of non-white races, as well as about the effects of smoking, radiation, and other such aspects of nature's order. Politics as well as science – or, rather, scientific inquiry constituted and maintained by political action – have been required to make space for the growth of knowledge on such topics. The low visibility of other cultures' scientific and technological achievements to modern Western eyes has been due primarily to Eurocentric rhetorical and political practices, including the invention of "underdevelopment" by Northern nations and the international agencies in which their voices are predominant. (Cf., e.g., Goonatilake 1984, Hess 1995, Petitjean et al. 1992.)

Feminists have similarly charted distinctive patterns of systematic knowledge and ignorance in modern sciences that mark the latter as androcentric. Insofar as women and men have been assigned, by nature or by social relations, distinctive activities, they will have distinctive interactions with their natural and social environments, and develop distinctive patterns of knowledge (and ignorance). Indeed in many or, perhaps, most societies women are assigned distinctive activities in households, other workplaces, and in community life. Thus women everywhere tend to have more knowledge, for example, about the bodies of infants, children, the elderly and sick, and in many parts of the world about agriculture, silviculture, and animal husbandry. (Cf., e.g., Harcourt 1994, Harding 1997, 1998.)

These three schools of post World War II science and technology studies all indicate that the constellation of human systems of knowledge about nature's order as well as modern science in particular are multicultural. There are many culturally distinctive local sciences that enable believers to succeed at a goodly number of projects while failing at others, projects that are always to some degree incompatible with other cultures' knowledge systems. We can summarize why this necessarily occurs by noting four features of all knowledge systems. First, they are developed for some set of human interactions in different locations in nature's order – for deserts, or rain forests, fertile plains or rocky islands, for environments shared with mosquitoes or AIDS viruses, for surviving from Genoa to the Caribbean, or from Cape Kennedy to the moon. And these environments historically change through natural and social processes, offering ever new challenges to local knowledge systems.

Second, even in "the same" environment, different cultures have different interests in the world around them. Living on the shores of the Atlantic, one culture will be interested in fishing, another using the sea as a coastal trade route, a third to retrieving oil and gas under the ocean floor, a fourth in using the sea as a garbage dump, a fifth in using it as a military route for submarines and torpedoes, yet another in desalinizing its waters, and so forth. They will develop different patterns of systematic knowledge and systematic ignorance about oceans. Third, they will have available to them different discursive traditions with different resources of metaphors, models, analogies, and narratives to be used to identify and explain features of the world around them. Fourth, each culture will have distinctive ways of producing knowledge enabling it to detect some of nature's regularities while obscuring others. How the production of knowledge is organized is related to how cultures organize the rest of their activities – work, social relations, domestic life, etc. How we interact with nature both enables and limits what we can know about it (Harding 1998).

Thus scientific and technological knowledge systems will always be local. Moreover, while there can be and often is a great deal of overlap between different cultures' patterns of knowledge about "the same" phenomenon, these different patterns of knowledge cannot fit together like pieces of a jig-saw puzzle as stronger forms of the unity-of-science thesis assumed, since some of these local patterns preclude others, as indicated above. Even in the history of Western science one can reflect on the usefulness of various representations of nature as an organism, as a mechanism such as a clock, as a more complex mechanism such as a computer, or as a lifeboat or a spaceship. Each of these has played an important role in directing scientists to new knowledge and guiding them in revising their assumptions when observations have failed to support hypotheses. Conceiving of nature in any one way precludes whole other ways of understanding it and of grasping "facts" to which other conceptions direct our attention. And these different discourses about nature's order are incompatible with each other in significant respects – just as are, for example, discipline-specific approaches such as environmental vs. biomedical conceptions of "the causes of cancer." From the perspective of these kinds of reflections the goal of only one true account of the natural world seems far too little to ask.

One Knower?

The unity-of-science thesis and its claim that there is just one science that can discover the one truth about nature also assumes that there is a distinctive universal human "class" – some distinctive group of humans – to whom the unique truth about the world could become evident. However, as feminists and postcolonial thinkers have pointed out, this is no longer a plausible assumption for most of the world's peoples. This assumption has remained unarticulated and perhaps even unidentified by unity-of-science defenders as well as by most of their critics. Who could such a group be? And how could any group democratically achieve recognition as such by other than its own members?

For early modern scientists and philosophers, members of the new educated classes whose minds were trained to reflect the order of nature that God's mind had created, were an elect group. God's mind, human minds, and nature's order were assumed to be congruent with each other. Scientists and the educated classes that could see the truth and importance of scientific accounts represented the ideally human, the universal class that could learn to detect the one possible true account of nature's order. Such assumptions still shape the contemporary liberal belief that anyone can gain the one true scientific account of nature if one learns the right concepts, reads the right books, or gets some other kind of standard education to qualify as the ideal knower. For nineteenth and twentieth century Marxists, it was the proletariat that represented the universal class. This class alone, since it was their labor that transformed nature into necessities for everyday human life to exist, had the potential to understand natural and social orders that had been obscured by hegemonic bourgeois ideology, and thus to become the unique representative of distinctively human knowers. This class alone had the potential to detect the real relations of nature and social life beneath the distorted appearances produced by class society. Some forms of feminism have flirted with a similar kind of transvaluation of genders which considers the possibility that women are the uniquely human gender. If it made sense in sexist society to imagine men as the model of the uniquely human, then perhaps it was reasonable to consider how women's characteristics – their claimed altruism, peace-loving, sensitivity to others' needs, or some other putative virtue – were uniquely valuable models of the human, capable of producing less distorted understandings of natural and social orders. Similarly some African Americans have claimed that the suffering, compassion, or some other characteristic of African Americans under the horrible conditions of colonialism, slavery, and their aftermaths uniquely equips them to understand natural and social orders in distinctive ways.

There are important insights behind such claims.[3] In the contemporary world of multicultural, global and (more complex and diverse) feminist politics and social theories, however, faith has declined in the possibility and desirability of such a universal class – whether Enlightenment, proletarian, womanly, or culturally distinctive. In the various worlds in which we all live how could such a distinctively human, universal class be identified? Which group could democratically gain assent from others uniquely to represent universal human interests, discursive resources, or ways of producing knowledge? In contemporary life, many kinds of important differences between humans – social, economic, political, and psychic—are recognized as resources both for producing effective knowledge about nature's order and for advancing democratic social relations.[4]

Dysfunctional Truth

This brief account has identified a number of arguments against the functionality of the truth ideal that have appeared in three schools of science and technology studies developed since World War II. My argument is not that there are no good uses for truth ideals in contemporary social relations, for others may be able to show their importance. Rather, the argument here is that main tendencies in several recent generations of philosophy and history of science, including feminist and postcolonial studies during this same period, fail to support the assumption that the growth of knowledge is advanced by claims to the possibility or even desirability of holding that sciences' research results could be uniquely true. Moreover, in light of the importance of cultural elements to the growth of scientific knowledge, the truth ideal appears to work against the nourishment of democratic social relations. In turn, the reduction of democratic social relations destroys resources that the most politically and economically vulnerable cultures have developed to aid them in understanding and surviving natural and social relations – resources that have also sometimes advanced modern Western knowledge. So the truth-ideal's anti-democratic and anti-scientific tendencies support each other.

The fact that these analyses have developed during this particular historical period is significant, for while the Cold War that followed World War II brought an immense increase in Western governments' investment in scientific and technological research projects that were thought to advance Western military interests, the end of World War II also marked the beginnings of a rising chorus of complaints about the costs of modern sciences and their ideals of truth, objectivity, and rationality for politically vulnerable groups and for democratic social relations. This second theme of the last half-century's scholarly science studies and public discourses enables us to see that the cultural resources sciences use are toolboxes as well as prisonhouses for the growth of knowledge, enabling the production of patterns both of systematic knowledge and of systematic ignorance. Each historical and cultural moment will bring its own fresh possibilities for understanding yet other aspects of nature's order, though the partially useful urge to integrate disparate patterns of knowledge will always also result in the loss as well as the expansion of knowledge. The kinds of cognitive diversity generated by culturally local knowledge projects is a great resource of our species, and the truth ideal shrinks rather than expands our appreciation for such resources.

What can be substituted for truth? Evidently only something much less inspiring and impressive to aspiring young scientists and to those groups to whom have been distributed a disproportionate share of the benefits of science. However, perhaps we can find a more widely beneficial substitute. We can aim for the provisionally least false of all and only those hypotheses already tested. In the real world of daily interactions in natural and social environments, we can think of knowledge seeking as pursuing effective strategies for achieving local goals, whether these be getting to the moon, reducing malaria and contagious viruses such as AIDS, or farming fragile environments. Such a formulation has the benefit of directing our attention to the importance of public discussion of the relative desirability of competing local goals. In such discussions, establishing the absolute truth of claims would be less important than establishing the wisdom of chosen interventions in natural and social orders and their effectiveness in producing improved natural and social conditions.[5]

Notes

1 See Kline's (1980) similar arguments about mathematical principles and Restivo's (1992) development of a sociology of mathematical concepts, principles, and claims.
2 We shall not here pursue important arguments against the first of these assumptions about the unity of nature that have emerged from within the natural sciences themselves as well as from philosophy.
3 Such insights are the beginning of the development of standpoint epistemologies – only the beginning, not the end, since these insights express "identity epistemologies" while standpoint epistemologies center not socially unmediated experience but distinctive kinds of critically and dialogically achieved discourses as generators of knowledge.
4 Thanks to Val Plumwood for pointing out to me this fourth assumption in the unity-of-science thesis.
5 Thanks to Susan Castro and Andrea Nye for useful comments on an earlier draft.

References

Bloor, David. 1977. *Knowledge and Social Imagery*. London: Routledge and Kegan Paul.

Crombie, A. C. 1994. *Styles of Scientific Thinking in the European Tradition*. London: Duckworth.

Duhem, Pierre. 1906/1954. *The Aim and Structure of Physical Theory*, trans. P. P. Weiner. Princeton, NJ: Princeton University Press.

Feyerabend, Paul K. 1975. *Against Method*. London: New Left Books.

Goonatilake, Susantha. 1984. *Aborted Discovery: Science and Creativity in the Third World*. London: Zed Press.

Hacking, Ian. 1996. "The Disunities of the Sciences," in *The Disunity of Science*, ed. Peter Galison and David J. Stump. Stanford, CA: Stanford University Press.

Harcourt, Wendy, ed. 1994. *Feminist Perspectives on Sustainable Development*. London: Zed Press.

Harding, Sandra, ed. 1976. *Can Theories Be Refuted? Essays on the Duhem-Quine Thesis*. Dordrecht: Reidel/Kluwer.

——. 1992. "Rethinking Standpoint Epistemologies," in *Feminist Epistemologies*, ed. Linda Alcoff and Elizabeth Potter. New York: Routledge.

——. 1997. "Are There Women's Standpoints on Nature?," *Osiris* 12, 1–15.

——. 1998. *Is Science Multicultural? Postcolonialism, Feminism and Epistemology*. Bloomington, IN: Indiana University Press.

Hess, David. 1995. *Science and Technology in a Multicultural World: The Cultural Politics of Facts and Artifacts*. New York: Columbia University Press.

Kline, Morris. 1980. *Mathematics: The Loss of Certainty*. New York: Oxford University Press.

Kuhn, Thomas S. 1962/1970. *The Structure of Scientific Revolutions*, 2nd edn. Chicago: University of Chicago Press.

Petitjean, Patrick, et al., eds. 1992. *Science and Empires: Historical Studies About Scientific Development and European Expansion*. Dordrecht: Kluwer.

Pickering, Andrew. 1991. "Objectivity and the Mangle of Practice," in *Deconstructing and Reconstructing Objectivity*. Special issue, *Annals of Scholarship* 8, 409–25.

Popper, Karl. 1972. *Conjectures and Refutations*, 4th edn. rev. London: Routledge and Kegan Paul.

Quine, W. V. O. 1953. "Two Dogmas of Empiricism," in *From a Logical Point of View*. Cambridge, MA: Harvard University Press.

Restivo, Sal. 1992. *Mathematics in Society and History: Sociological Inquiries*. Dordrecht: Kluwer.

PART SIX

OTHER MINDS AND FOREIGN TONGUES:
HOW IS IT POSSIBLE TO UNDERSTAND WHAT SOMEONE ELSE SAYS?

Introduction

Understanding the members of one's own family can be taxing. Understanding across differences of class, race, gender, religion can seem all but impossible. Perhaps the most extreme test of understanding is the project the philosopher W. V. O. Quine calls "radical translation": the attempt to comprehend an unknown language that has no common roots in any language known to the translator. The first reading in this section looks to an anthropologist, Bronislaw Malinowski, for a field linguist's account of this difficult task. Malinowski was both a practical linguist with a prodigious facility for learning languages and a linguistic theorist with distinctive views on how unknown languages can be translated. The excerpt reprinted here is from the introduction to his exhaustive description of the rich and complex linguistic forms used by Trobriand Islanders related to gardening.

The task of the anthropological linguist, as Malinowski describes it, is not to show the deficiencies of "primitive" languages or to locate any primal origin of language, but to understand native speakers in their own terms. To this end, he argues, there can be no "translation manual" that finds exact equivalences between native words and English words anymore than there could be such a definitive manual for translating between European languages. Instead, the meanings of words must be understood and described within "contexts of cultural reality" often radically different from one's home language. Practical and ritual activities, facial expressions and gestures, story-telling and conversation, social interactions and ceremonial interchanges, all contribute to the social contexts in which words must be understood. Only after a long process of assigning a rough approximation of meaning, a dawning intuition of the role words play in sentences, an appreciation of the use of words to coordinate activities and advance teaching methods, and a grasp of the force of words when used ritually – only after all this and more can the linguist begin to interpret what is meant by expressions in an unknown language.

Quine's philosophical account of radical translation is very different. Malinowski insisted that, unlike administrators, missionaries, and tourists whose goal is to make what English speakers say intelligible to native speakers, the field linguist's proper aim is to make native speakers intelligible to non-natives. Quine reidentifies understanding an unknown language – or "Jungle", as he generically labels such languages – as the compilation of a "translation manual" which serves as "an aid to negotiation," ensures "smoothness of conversation," and predicts native behavior. Any other aim, he argues, must be illusory. Persons are "organisms" on whose "nerve nets" "stimulations" impinge. The mark of human intelligence and the function of language is the constructing of theories that allow the successful prediction of future stimulations. All an interpreter can do, therefore, is to attempt to match up native verbal responses to stimuli with his own verbal responses to the same stimuli. Whether a native speaker feels or sees as the linguist does is irrelevant to the task of translation. From these premises, Quine draws the conclusions for which he is famous. Translation is indeterminate: there might always be alternative translation manuals that account for observed responses but that map native sentences onto English sentences differently. Ontology, or the objects to which the native refers, is also indeterminate: all that can be compiled are the native's assent or dissent to sentences in the presence of a "stimulus"; what the natives take that stimulus to be cannot be determined. Furthermore, Quine argues, indeterminacy applies equally to understanding of another speaker in one's home language. All we can ever do in learning a language, or in understanding another person, is to match up another's verbal responses with our own.

A very different account of translation comes from another linguistic anthropologist, Benjamin Whorf. Embedded in the grammar and lexicon of the language of the American Hopi people, Whorf argues, is an ontology and a metaphysics radically different from those found in European languages. Although a degree of smoothness of conversation and some success at negotiation might be accomplished in a correlation of native and English sentences that roughly accounts for behavior, when a linguist "imposes his own ontology and linguistic patterns on the native," he fails to understand the Hopi speaker. Hopi grammar, with no verb tenses as we know them and with no reference to kinetic rather than dynamic motion, is not an alternative way to express Western Newtonian time and space. It is an alternative way of understanding the basic elements of reality. Although pragmatically equivalent English expressions can be "recast" in Hopi terms, this should not be confused with understanding. The Hopi view of the world, although properly expressible only in Hopi, must be evoked by concepts "worked up into relative consonance with the system underlying the Hopi view of the universe." On Whorf's view of understanding, it is not native expressions that are mapped approximately onto the usage of a home language, but the concepts of the home language that are reshaped to communicate a different and alien view of the world.

That such a difference in conceptual scheme is possible is denied by Donald Davidson in his paper, "On the Very Idea of a Conceptual Scheme." Intelligible differences between languages, Davidson argues, can always be explained in some common language, just as Whorf was able to describe the Hopi conceptual scheme in English. If a language is not translatable into English or some known language then it is not a language at all.

Evident in Davidson's paper is the concern behind many analytic discussions of translation. The major interest of Davidson and Quine is not in understanding native peoples, but in the challenge posed by critical science studies, as were discussed in the essay by Sandra Harding in part V. Are "conceptual schemes" in science commensurable? Can we flatly say that the alchemists were wrong? Can we say definitively that the earth is not at the center of the universe as Ptolemy claimed? The suggestion that scientific truth is relative to a conceptual scheme is the target of both Davidson and Quine. At the same time they profit from a scenario taken from anthropology. Just as the Western historian approaches the peculiarities of alchemy or Ptolemaic astronomy, so does a field linguist approach the "jungle" language of a native people. In both cases, argues Davidson, there is no way to make sense of the idea that there might be incommensurable conceptual schemes, or that other people or other sciences might have different valid ways of seeing and representing reality. Malinowski and Whorf have simply not understood what they were doing.

Adopting Quine's account of the field linguist's methods, and adding on Tarski's semantic theory of truth, Davidson argues that identifying patterns of true and false sentences and "translating" those mappings onto a home language is the only way to gain a footing in an unknown language. There is no reality for reference point apart from identified objects, there is no experience that is not already separated into objects and events. All we can do is assume "charitably" that the native believes as we do and then attempt in our mapping to make him seem rational, maximizing agreement as much as is possible. In neither case does it make sense to speak of indeterminacy or relativity.

The readings from Gloria Anzaldúa and Wole Soyinka widen the discussion. Here the problem of understanding is not to understand a hitherto unknown people or to restore truth to science; it is the more immediate problem of negotiating social and political conflict between speakers of different languages. These articles reflect neither the "holistic" world of Western science nor a dualistic split between native subject and Western anthropologist, but the current babel of tongues in a multicultural global environment. In that environment, there is no simple division between jungle natives and Western observers. The language one speaks and how one speaks it are one facet of contested racial, economic, and social identity. Languages are not parceled out in rationally consistent conceptual schemes; they overlap, interact, fuse, form, and are deformed. Anzaldúa describes complex relations between Castilian Spanish, Chicano Spanish, broken English, Chicano English. These relations reflect shades of linguistic meaning rooted in historical conflict and in oppressive social relations, communicated in accent, intonation, gesture, as well as in semantic content. If language ratifies and expresses social hierarchies, in Anzaldúa's view it also provides a medium for liberation as new meanings are created at points of language conflict. Here Whorf's incommensurability becomes the occasion for creativity and protest, as new hybrid concepts emerge from clashes between dissonant and incommensurable tongues.

Wole Soyinka, the Nigerian writer and theorist, strikes a different note. Here again the context is language conflict. In Africa, where language divides tribal groups, language differences can ratify tribal conflict and foment hostility. Although Soyinka defends the conservation of all language cultures, he also calls for a national and even continental linguistic strategy for Africa, a "lingua franca" that can provide a basis for understanding and unity between diverse peoples.

30   The Translation of Untranslatable Words

Bronislaw Malinowski

It might seem that the simplest task in any linguistic enquiry would be the translation of individual terms. In reality the problem of defining the meaning of a single word and of proceeding correctly in the translating of terms is as difficult as any which will face us. It is, moreover, in methodological order not the first to be tackled. It will be obvious to anyone who has so far followed my argument that isolated words are in fact only linguistic figments, the products of an advanced linguistic analysis. The sentence is at times a self-contained linguistic unit, but not even a sentence can be regarded as a full linguistic datum. To us, the real linguistic fact is the full utterance within its context of situation.

But still, as in all work of analysis, it does not matter very much where we begin. Since in the translation of texts we have to proceed by giving a word for word rendering, let us discuss this first. It will soon enough lead us into the apparently more complicated, but in reality more elementary, question of how to treat native texts and contexts.

Let me start with the apparently paradoxical and yet perfectly plain and absolutely true proposition that the words of one language are never translatable into another. This holds of two civilised languages as well as of a 'native' and a 'civilised' one, though the greater the difference between two cultures the greater the difficulty of finding equivalents.

Turning for a moment to more familiar European languages – anyone who has faced the difficulties of translating a novel or scientific book from Russian or Polish into English, or vice versa, will know that strict verbal equivalents are never to be found. Translation must always be the re-creation of the original into something profoundly different. On the other hand, it is never a substitution of word for word but invariably the translation of whole contexts.

It would be easy to skim the surface of any language for completely untranslatable terms. Such German words as *Sehnsucht*, or *Sauerkraut*, *Weltschmerz* or *Schlachtfest*, *Blutwurst* or *Grobheit*, *Gemüt* or *Gemeinheit* are not to be equated to any word in English, or, for that matter, in any other European language. Such English words as 'sport', 'gentleman', 'fair-play', 'kindness', 'quaint', 'forlorn' – to mention only a few from a legion – are never translated in a foreign tongue; they are simply reproduced. International currency has been achieved by many Italian words: *bel canto, basta, maccaroni, diva, salami*, as well as terms from music and painting. If we were to enquire why these, with certain French words referring to technicalities of love-making such as

From *The Language of Magic and Gardening*. Bloomington, IN: Indiana University Press, 1965, pp. 11–15, 21–2. First published 1935.

liaison, *maîtresse*, *au mieux*, *complaisance*; or to culinary compositions and details of menu; to fashion or to niceties of literary craft, such as *belles-lettres*, *mot juste*, *connaisseur* are untranslatable – the answer would be easy. In each culture certain aspects are more openly, minutely or pedantically cultivated: sport in England, good cooking and lovemaking in France; sentimentality and metaphysical profundities in Germany; music, noodles and painting in Italy.

Words referring to moral or personal values change their meaning deeply even if the form is similar: compare French *honneur*, Spanish *honra*, English 'honour', and German *Ehre*; or 'faith', *foi*, *Glaube*, and *fe*; or *patrie*, *Vaterland*, 'home', and *la peninsula*. English changes east of Suez; it becomes a different language in India, Malaya and South Africa. The question whether American is English is very fruitful from the present point of view: you cannot swear in English in the U.S.A. and vice versa. You cannot order your food in an 'eat-house' nor 'get outside your drinks' by the same verbal symbols in a 'saloon' as in a 'pub'; while Prohibition has introduced words corresponding to the change of institutions and values surrounding drink. In brief, every language has words which are not translatable, because they fit into its culture and into that only; into the physical setting, the institutions, the material apparatus and the manners and values of a people.

With all this, it might appear that such words, however frequent, are but freaks or peculiarities. Surely, it will be contended, numerals, parts of the body, terms of relationship, conjunctions, adverbs, prepositions, words as ordinary as bread and butter, milk and meat, are simply, plainly, adequately and completely translated between any two languages of the Western cultures. A brief consideration convinces us that this is not so. Were we to aim merely at achieving some approximate indication of correspondence between two words, sufficient to order a meal, to bargain over the price of an umbrella or ask our way in the street, then even the linguistic instruction supplied on a few pages of our Baedecker, certainly a cheap pocket dictionary or an Ollendorf, will give adequate translations. But if in our scientific analysis we define words as devices used in a number of verbal and situational contexts, then translation must be defined as the supplying of equivalent devices and rules. This makes our point clearer: there is no simple equivalence between two languages ever to be found which could be used right through, replacing the German word by the English, or vice versa.

Let us take the simplest example, the numeral 'one', *un*, *ein*. They correspond closely in counting. But *un homme*, *ein Mann* is not 'one man' but 'a man'. 'One man one vote' could not be translated by *un homme un vote*, nor is *ein Mann ein Wort* translatable into 'one man one word'. Nor is *c'est un homme honnête* equivalent to 'this is one honest man'. As soon as we come to derived uses, to subsidiary meanings, to idiomatic handling of words, the equivalence breaks down. Translation as an act of putting 'one'=*un* appears to us at once as a matter of rough, preliminary, makeshift arrangement which has to be supplemented by a long series of additional data.

Or take the parts of the human body: we have at once to face up to the fact that the conventional restrictions, euphemisms, and twists obfuscate the meaning in English to a much larger degree than in French or in German. For instance 'belly' is not equivalent to *Bauch* or *ventre*; 'stomach' reaches almost to the knees, legs are curtailed in their upper reaches. Such words as 'breast', *gorge, sein, Brust, Busen* become untranslatable. And in English again the word 'navel', associated in a daring anatomical metaphor with an orange, shocks many a continental damsel who thinks herself absolutely protected by English prudery on this side of the Channel. 'Eye', 'hand', 'food, and 'arm', 'mouth' and 'ears' seem so well defined and precise that here a simple = might be enough. But even here some European languages, for instance Slavonic, use the term 'hand' often to embrace the 'arm', as in Polish and Russian, where instead of having 'feet' and 'legs' we have only lower extremities. Moreover, in every European language the derived and metaphorical and idiomatic uses of 'eye', 'hand' and 'foot' are so little co-ordinated that they cannot be equated. 'My two legs' could not be set = *meine zwei Beine*; it would have to be *meine beiden Beine*. We neither eat nor sleep linguistically in the same manner: while the Englishman 'sleeps with', the Frenchman *couche avec*. As to eating, a Frenchman's *bien manger* becomes in German *gut speisen*, while the Englishman 'dines well'. As regards adverbs and conjunctions, no one brought up in a continental language will ever live down the absence of *déjà, schon, già* or *ya*. Such German adverbs or particles as *doch, nanu, also*, the French *mais non, mais oui* – not equivalent to the German *aber nein, aber ja* – can neither be equated nor reproduced in English.

We have now whittled down our paradox to the platitude that words from one language are never translatable into another; that is, we cannot equate one word to another. If by translation we mean the supplying of the full range of equivalent devices, metaphorical extensions and idiomatic sayings – such a process is of course possible. But even then it must be remembered that something more than mere juggling with words and expressions is needed. When we pass even from one European country to another we find that cultural arrangements, institutions, interests and systems of values change greatly. Translation in the correct sense must refer therefore not merely to different linguistic uses but often to the different cultural realities behind the words. All the new systems of teaching modern languages – whether it be Toussain-Langenscheidt, Pelman or Berlitz – have in practice fully adopted this contextual theory of language and realised the untranslatability of words. In the case of words which have to be international, e.g. scientific terms, congresses have to deal with their unification; and it can only be achieved because the apparatus of science is uniform, because such arrangements as the metric system have been widely adopted and because the institutional side of scientific training, laboratory organisation and academic life is sufficiently similar.

In diplomatic documents and international treaties, which must not contain any linguistic ambiguity, we are again faced with the difficulty of finding a safe and unequivocal common denominator to untranslatable words. Whether this is mainly due to the fact that diplomatic language is used to conceal thought – according to the definition of one of the most famous diplomats of history – or whether it honestly attempts to serve its purpose, need not be discussed here.

The translatability of words or texts between two languages is not a matter of mere readjustment of verbal symbols. It must always be based on a unification of cultural context. Even when two cultures have much in common, real understanding and the establishment of a community of linguistic implements is always a matter of difficult, laborious and delicate readjustment.

When two cultures differ as deeply as that of the Trobrianders and the English; when the beliefs, scientific views, social organisation, morality and material outfit are completely different, most of the words in one language cannot be even remotely paralleled in the other.

Let us turn at once to our own special case, that of Trobriand agricultural terminology. The simplest word to be considered is 'garden'. But obviously the English term may suggest anything from a suburban plot to a park, from an allotment to a market-garden, and in none of these senses, nor yet in any of the metaphorical extensions to which this word is liable, could it be translated into Trobriand. So that at once we are faced with a serious 'gap' in the vocabulary of our Melanesian friends. For they really have no word corresponding to our general term 'garden'.

Instead they have a series of words: *bagula, buyagu, tapopu, kaymata, kaymugwa, baleko,* each of which describes a certain type or kind, aspect or phase of 'garden'. But to 'translate' any of these native terms by equating it to an English word would not merely be wrong, but impossible; or rather it would be impossible to find an English word exactly corresponding to any one of the native ones. Furthermore, to label the native term by even a combination of English words is at least misleading.

[. . .]

We can now lay down a number of points, some theoretical and some practical, which it will be necessary to bear in mind throughout the following analysis:–

1.   The mere lexical equation of an English and a native word is necessary for practical convenience but theoretically inadequate. For practical convenience it is necessary because if we used a native term wherever possible an ethnographic book would become an unreadable jumble of native and English, of native technical expressions and sociological concepts sticking out of the grammatical framework of the English language.

2.   At times it becomes necessary to use an English term with Trobriand implications, that is, a word from our own language in a native sense. For an ethnographic description must not merely reproduce the native outlook, still less confine itself to the native linguistic compass, but must operate with general sociological concepts.

3.   The correct translation of each native term, besides its rough and ready labelling, is indispensable. This is achieved by reference to ethnographic descriptions and by the placing of the word in its context of culture, in the context of cognate words and opposites and in the context of appropriate utterances.

4. The various meanings of a homonym must be kept apart. We have to consider the use of the same sound with several distinct meanings, not as a linguistic vagueness or lumping together or confusion, but as what it really is – a series of distinct uses.

All these considerations simply mean that language is a part, and an essential part at that, of other cultural realities. The language of agriculture enters deeply into the Trobrianders' gardening activities. Unless we know how they make their gardens we can give no sense to their terms, nor meaning to their magical formulae, nor yet develop any interest in their gardening phraseology. Without this cultural foundation linguistics must remain always a house of cards. Equally true is it that without the language the knowledge of any aspect of culture is incomplete.

This is really tantamount to saving, as we did above, that language is a cultural force in its own right. It enters into manual and bodily activities and plays a significant part in them, a part *sui generis* which cannot be replaced, even as it does not replace anything else.

What this part is, however, and in what consists the placing of a word against the context of culture, we still have not defined with any precision. It is obvious that words do not live as labels attached to pieces of cultural reality. Our Trobriand garden is not a sort of botanical show with tags tied on to every bush, implement or activity. It will be our business to reconstruct what speech achieves in a primitive culture, or, for that matter, in a highly developed one.

But first it is necessary to realise that words do not exist in isolation. The figment of a dictionary is as dangerous theoretically as it is useful practically. Words are always used in utterances, and though a significant utterance may sometimes shrink to a single word, this is a limiting case. A one-word sentence, such as a command, 'come', 'go', 'rise', a 'yes' or a 'no', may under exceptional circumstances be significant through its context of situation only. Usually a one-word sentence will have to be explained by connecting it with utterances which preceded it or which follow. To start with single words – even if such words might occasionally be uttered in isolation – is the wrong procedure: But this I do not need to elaborate; for it is now a commonplace of linguistics that the lowest unit of language is the sentence, not the word. Our task is rather to show that even the sentence is not a self-contained, self-sufficient unit of speech. Exactly as a single word is – save in exceptional circumstances – meaningless, and receives its significance only through the context of other words, so a sentence usually appears in the context of other sentences and has meaning only as a part of a larger significant whole. I think that it is very profitable in linguistics to widen the concept of context so that it embraces not only spoken words but facial expression, gesture, bodily activities, the whole group of people present during an exchange of utterances and the part of the environment on which these people are engaged.

I have spoken several times of the *context of cultural reality.* By that I mean the material equipment, the activities, interests, moral and aesthetic values with which the words are correlated. I shall now try to show that this context of cultural reality is strictly analogous to the context of speech. Words do not live in a sort of super-dictionary, nor in the ethnographer's notebook. They are used in free speech, they are linked into utterances and these utterances are linked up with the other human activities and the social and material environment. The whole manner which I have adopted for the presentation of my linguistic and ethnographic material brings the concept of context to the fore. Not only have I tried in the definition of technical terms to show how these terms form groups of kindred entities, not only have I tried, by placing the linguistic account against an outline of real activities, to give them life and body; but the division of the linguistic material under headings which closely correspond to the chapters of the descriptive account keeps every word, every phrase and every text within its proper context of culture.

31   Indeterminacy of Translation

W. V. O. Quine

14. The Field Linguist's Entering Wedge

Philosophers in ancient India disputed over whether sentences or words were the primary vehicles of meaning. The argument in favor of words is that they are limited in number and can be learned once for all. Sentences are unlimited in number; we can fully master them only by learning how to construct them as needed from words learned in advance. Despite this situation, however, words can still be said to owe their meaning to their roles in sentences. We learn short sentences as wholes, we learn their component words from their use in those sentences, and we build further sentences from words thus learned.

The quest for a clear and substantial notion of meanings then should begin with an examination of sentences. The meaning of a sentence of one language is what it shares with its translations in another language so I propounded my thought experiment of radical translation. It led to a negative conclusion, a thesis of indeterminacy of translation.

Critics have said that the thesis is a consequence of my behaviorism. Some have said that it is a *reductio ad absurdum* of my behaviorism. I disagree with this second point but I agree with the first. I hold further that the behaviorist approach is mandatory. In psychology one may or may not be a behaviorist but in linguistics one has no choice. Each of us learns his language by observing other people's verbal behavior and having his own faltering verbal behavior observed and reinforced or corrected by others. We depend strictly on overt

From *The Pursuit of Truth*. Cambridge, MA: Harvard University Press, 1990, pp. 37–49. Copyright © 1990 by the President and Fellows of Harvard College. By permission of the publisher.

behavior in observable situations. As long as our command of our language fits all external checkpoints where our utterance or our reaction to someone's utterance can be appraised in the light of some shared situation, so long all is well. Our mental life between checkpoints is indifferent to our rating as a master of the language. There is nothing in linguistic meaning beyond what is to be gleaned from overt behavior in observable circumstances.

In my thought experiment the source language, as the jargon has it, is Jungle; the "target language" is English. Jungle is inaccessible through any known languages as way stations, so our only data are native utterances and their concurrent observable circumstances. It is a meager basis, but the native speaker himself has had no other.

Our linguist would construct his manual of translation by conjectural extrapolation of such data but the confirmations would be sparse. Usually the concurrent publicly observable situation does not enable us to predict what a speaker even of our own language will say, for utterances commonly bear little relevance to the circumstances outwardly observable at the time; there are ongoing projects and unshared past experiences. It is only thus, indeed, that language serves any useful communicative purpose; predicted utterances convey no news.

There are sentences, however, that do hinge pretty strictly on the concurrent publicly observable situation, namely the observation sentences. We saw these in Chapter I as the primary register of evidence about the external world, and also as the child's entering wedge into cognitive language. They are likewise the field linguist's entering wedge into the jungle language. Other utterances – greetings, commands, questions – will figure among the early acquisitions too, but the first declarative sentences to be mastered are bound to be observation sentences and usually one word long. The linguist tentatively associates a native's utterance with the observed concurrent situation hoping that it might be simply an observation sentence linked to that situation. To check this he takes the initiative, when the situation recurs and volunteers the sentence himself for the native's assent or dissent

This expedient of query and assent or dissent embodies, in miniature, the advantage of an experimental science such as physics over a purely observational science such as astronomy. To apply it the linguist must be able to recognize, if only conjecturally, the signs of assent and dissent in Jungle society. If he is wrong in guessing those signs, his further research will languish and he will try again. But there is a good deal to go on in identifying those signs. For one thing, a speaker will assent to an utterance in any circumstance in which he would volunteer it.

What the native's observation sentence and the linguist's translation have in common, by this account, is the concurrent observable situation to which they are linked. But the notion of a situation has seemed too vague to rest with. In earlier writings I have accordingly represented the linguist as trying to match observation sentences of the jungle language with observation sentences of his own that have the same stimulus meanings. That is to say, assent to the two sentences should be prompted by the sense stimulations; likewise dissent.

15. Stimulation Again

It would seem then that this matching of observation sentences hinges on sameness of stimulation of both parties the linguist and the informant. But an event of stimulation, as I use the term, is the activation of some subset of the subject's sensory receptors. Since the linguist and his informant share no receptors, how can they be said to share a stimulation? We might say rather that they undergo *similar* stimulation, but that would assume still an approximate homology of nerve endings from one individual to another. Surely such anatomical minutiae ought not to matter here.

I was expressing this discomfort as early as 1965.[1] By 1981 it prompted me to readjust my definition of observation sentence. In my original definition I had appealed to sameness of stimulus meaning between speakers,[2] but in 1981 I defined it rather for the single speaker by the following condition:

> If querying the sentence elicits assent from the given speaker on one occasion, it will elicit assent likewise on any other occasion when the same total set of receptors is triggered; and similarly for dissent.[3]

Then I accounted a sentence observational for a whole community when it was observational for each member. In this way the question of intersubjective sameness of stimulation could be bypassed in studies of scientific method, I felt, and deferred to studies of translation. There it continued to rankle.

The question was much discussed in the course of a closed conference with Davidson, Dreben, and Føllesdal at Stanford in 1986.[4] Two years later at the St Louis conference on my philosophy,[5] Lars Bergström observed that even my bypassing of the question within studies of scientific method was unsuccessful, since a sentence could be observational for each of various speakers without their being disposed to assent to it in the same situations. It is odd that I overlooked this, for already in a lecture of 1974 I had remarked in effect that the fisherman's sentence "I just felt a nibble" qualifies as observational for all individuals and not for the group.[6]

At the Stanford conference Davidson proposed providing for intersubjective likeness of stimulation by locating the stimulus not at the bodily surface but farther out, in the nearest shared cause of the pertinent behavior of the two subjects. Failing a rabbit or other body to the purpose, perhaps the stimulus would be a shared situation, if ontological sense can be made of situations. But I remain unswerved in locating stimulation at the neural input, for my interest is epistemological, however naturalized. I am interested in the flow of evidence from the triggering of the senses to the pronouncements of science. My naturalism does allow *me* free reference to nerve endings, rabbits, and other physical objects, but my epistemology permits the subject no such starting point. *His* reification of rabbits and the like is for me part of the plot, not to be passed over as part of the setting.

16. To Each His Own

The view that I have come to regarding intersubjective likeness of stimulation, is rather that we can simply do without it. The observation sentence "Rabbit" has its stimulus meaning for the linguist and "Gavagai" has its stimulus meaning for the native. The linguist observes natives assenting to "Gavagai" when he, in their position, would have assented to "Rabbit." So he tries assigning *his* stimulus meaning of "Rabbit" to "Gavagai" and bandying "Gavagai" on subsequent occasions for his informant's approval. Encouraged, he tentatively adopts "Rabbit" as translation.

Empathy dominates the learning of language, both by child and by field linguist. In the child's case it is the parent's empathy. The parent assesses the appropriateness of the child's observation sentence by noting the child's orientation and how the scene would look from there. In the field linguist's case it is empathy on his own part when he makes his first conjecture about "Gavagai" on the strength of the native's utterance and orientation, and again when he queries "Gavagai" for the native's assent in a promising subsequent situation. We all have an uncanny knack for empathizing another's perceptual situation, however ignorant of the physiological or optical mechanism of his perception. The knack is comparable, almost, to our ability to recognize faces while unable to sketch or describe them.

Empathy guides the linguist still as he rises above observation sentences through his analytical hypotheses though there he is trying to project into the native's associations and grammatical trends rather than his perceptions. And much the same must be true of the growing child.

As for the lacuna that Bergström noted, my definition of observation sentence reflects the correction in a rough and ready form. More fully: I retain my 1981 definition of observation sentence for the single speaker, and then account a sentence observational for a group if it is observational for each member *and* if each would agree in assenting to it, or dissenting, on witnessing the occasion of utterance. We judge what counts as witnessing the occasion, as in the translation case, by projecting ourselves into the witness's position.

A pioneer manual of translation has its utility as an aid to negotiation with the native community. Success in communication is judged by smoothness of conversation, by frequent predictability of verbal and nonverbal reactions, and by coherence and plausibility of native testimony. It is a matter of better and worse manuals rather than flatly right and wrong ones. Observation sentences continue to be the entering wedge for child and field linguist, and they continue to command the firmest agreement between rival manuals of translation; but their distinctive factuality is blurred now by the disavowel of shared stimulus meaning. What is utterly factual is just the fluency of conversation and the effectiveness of negotiation that one or another manual of translation serves to induce.

In *Word and Object* (p. 8) I pointed out that communication presupposes no similarity in nerve nets. Such was my parable of the trimmed bushes, alike in outward form but wildly unlike in their inward twigs and branches. The outward uniformity is imposed by society, in inculcating language and pressing for smooth communication. In a computer figure, we are dissimilar machines similarly programmed. Performance is mandated, implement it how one may. Such is the privacy of the nerve net. Dreben has likened it to the traditional privacy of other minds. Now in my new move I give the subject yet wider berth, allowing him the privacy even of his sensory receptors.

Unlike Davidson, I still locate the stimulations at the subject's surface and private stimulus meaning with them. But they may be as idiosyncratic, for all I care, as the subject's internal wiring itself. What floats in the open air is our common language which each of us is free to internalize in his peculiar neural way. Language is where intersubjectivity sets in. Communication is well named.

Stimulus synonymy, unlike stimulus meaning, can still be defined intersubjectively over the community. Sentences are stimulus-synonymous for the individual if they have the same stimulus meaning for him, and stimulus-synonymous for the community if stimulus-synonymous for each member. But this does not work between languages.

17. Translation Resumed

Our linguist then goes on tentatively identifying and translating observation sentences. Some of them are perhaps compounded of others of them, in ways hinting of our logical particles "and," "or," "but," "not." By collating the situations that command the natives assent to the compounds with the situations that command assent to the components and similarly for dissent the linguist gets a plausible line on such connectives.

Unlike observation sentences, most utterances resist correlation with concurrent stimulations. Taking the initiative, the linguist may volunteer and query such a sentence for assent or dissent in various situations, but no correlation with concurrent stimulation is forthcoming. What next?

He can keep a record of these unconstrued sentences and dissect them. Some of the segments will have occurred also in the already construed observation sentences. He will treat them as words and try pairing them off with English expressions in ways suggested by those observation sentences. Such are what I have called analytical hypotheses. There is guesswork here, and more extravagant guesswork to follow. The linguist will turn to the unconstrued, nonobservational sentences in which these same words occurred, and he will project conjectural interpretations of some of those sentences on the strength of these sporadic fragments. He will accumulate a tentative Jungle vocabulary, with English translations, and a tentative apparatus of grammatical constructions. Recursion then sets in determining tentative translations of a potential infinity of sentences. Our linguist keeps testing his system for its efficacy in dealing with natives, and he goes on tinkering with it and guessing again. The routine of query and assent that had been his standby in construing observation sentences continues to be invaluable at these higher and more conjectural levels.

Clearly the task is formidable and the freedom for conjecture is enormous. Linguists can usually avoid radical translation by finding someone who can interpret the language, however haltingly, into a somewhat familiar one. But it is only radical translation that exposes the poverty of ultimate data for the identification of meanings.

Let us consider, then, what constraints our radical translator can bring to bear to help guide his conjectures. Continuity is helpful: successive utterances may be expected to have some bearing on one another. When several such have been tentatively interpreted, moreover, their interrelation itself may suggest the translation of a linking word that will be helpful in spotting similar connections elsewhere.

The translator will depend early and late on psychological conjectures as to what the native is likely to believe. This policy already governed his translations of observation sentences. It will continue to operate beyond the observational level, deterring him from translating a native assertion into too glaring a falsehood. He will favor translations that ascribe beliefs to the native that stand to reason or are consonant with the native's observed way of life. But he will not cultivate these values at the cost of unduly complicating the structure to be imparted to the native's grammar and semantics, for this again would be bad psychology; the language must have been simple enough for acquisition by the natives, whose minds, failing evidence to the contrary, are presumed to be pretty much like our own. Practical psychology is what sustains our radical translator all along the way, and the method of his psychology is empathy: he imagines himself in the native's situation as best he can.

Our radical translator would put his developing manual of translation continually to use, and go on revising it in the light of his successes and failures of communication. The successes consist – to repeat – in successful negotiation and smooth conversation. Reactions of astonishment or bewilderment on a native's part, or seemingly irrelevant responses, tend to suggest that the manual has gone wrong.

We readily imagine the translator's ups and downs. Perhaps he has tentatively translated two native sentences into English ones that are akin to each other in some semantic way, and he finds this same kinship reflected in a native's use of the two native sentences. This encourages him in his pair of tentative translations. So he goes on blithely supposing that he is communicating, only to be caught up short. This may persuade him that his pair of translations was wrong after all. He wonders how far back, in the smooth-flowing antecedent conversation, he got off the beam.

18. Indeterminacy of Translation

Considerations of the sort we have been surveying are all that the radical translator has to go on This is not because the meanings of sentences are elusive or inscrutable; it is because there is nothing to them, beyond what these fumbling procedures can come up with. Nor is there hope even of codifying these procedures and then *defining* what counts as translation by citing the procedures; for the procedures involve weighing incommensurable values. How much grotesqueness may we allow to the native's beliefs, for instance, in order to avoid how much grotesqueness in his grammar or semantics?

These reflections leave us little reason to expect that two radical translators, working independently on Jungle, would come out with interchangeable manuals. Their manuals might be indistinguishable in terms of any native behavior that they give reason to expect, and yet each manual might prescribe some translations that the other translator would reject. Such is the thesis of indeterminacy of translation.

A manual of Jungle-to-English translation constitutes a recursive, or inductive, definition of a *translation relation* together with a claim that it correlates sentences compatibly with the behavior of all concerned. The thesis of indeterminacy of translation is that these claims on the part of two manuals might both be true and yet the two translation relations might not be usable in alternation, from sentence to sentence, without issuing in incoherent sequences. Or, to put it another way, the English sentences prescribed as translation of a given Jungle sentence by two rival manuals might not be interchangeable in English contexts.

The use of one or the other manual might indeed cause differences in speech afterward, as remarked by Robert Kirk in connection with the idioms of propositional attitude; but the two would do equal justice to the status quo.

I have directed my indeterminacy thesis on a radically exotic language for the sake of plausibility, but in principle it applies even to the home language. For given the rival manuals of translation between Jungle and English, we can translate English perversely into English by translating it into Jungle by one manual and then back by the other.

The indeterminacy of translation is unlikely to obtrude in practice, even in radical translation. There is good reason why it should not. The linguist assumes that the native's attitudes and ways of thinking are like his own, up to the point where there is contrary evidence. He accordingly imposes his own ontology and linguistic patterns on the native wherever compatible with the native's speech and other behavior, unless a contrary course offers striking simplifications. We could not wish otherwise. What the indeterminacy thesis is meant to bring out is that the radical translator is bound to impose about as much as he discovers.

Notes

1 E.g. in a lecture "Propositional Objects," published in *Ontological Relativity and Other Essays* (New York: Columbia University Press, 1969).
2 Thus *Word and Object* (Cambridge, MA: MIT Press, 1960), p. 43.
3 *Theories and Things* (Cambridge: MA: Harvard University Press, 1981), p. 25.
4 July 14–17, supported by Stanford's Center for the Study of Language and Information.
5 "Perspectives on Quine," Washington University, April 9–13, 1988.

6   "The Nature of Natural Knowledge," in J. Guttenberg (ed.), *Mind and Language* (Oxford: Clarendon Press, 1975), p. 72.

32   An American Indian Model of the Universe

Benjamin Lee Whorf

I find it gratuitous to assume that a Hopi who knows only the Hopi language and the cultural ideas of his own society has the same notions, often supposed to be intuitions, of time and space that we have, and that are generally assumed to be universal. In particular, he has no general notion or intuition of *time* as a smooth flowing continuum in which everything in the universe proceeds at an equal rate, out of a future, through a present, into a past; or, in which, to reverse the picture, the observer is being carried in the stream of duration continuously away from a past and into a future.

After long and careful study and analysis, the Hopi language is seen to contain no words, grammatical forms, constructions or expressions that refer directly to what we call "time," or to past, present, or future, or to enduring or lasting, or to motion as kinematic rather than dynamic (i.e. as a continuous translation in space and time rather than as an exhibition of dynamic effort in a certain process), or that even refer to space in such a way as to exclude that element of extension or existence that we call time, and so by implication leave a residue that could be referred to as time. Hence, the Hopi language contains no reference to "time," either explicit or implicit.

At the same time, the Hopi language is capable of accounting for and describing correctly, in a pragmatic or operational sense, all observable phenomena of the universe. Hence, I find it gratuitous to assume that Hopi thinking contains any such notion as the supposed intuitively felt flowing of time, or that the intuition of a Hopi gives him this as one of its data. Just as it is possible to have any number of geometries other than the Euclidean which give an equally perfect account of space configurations, so it is possible to have descriptions of the universe, all equally valid, that do not contain our familiar contrasts of time and space. The relativity viewpoint of modern physics is one such view, conceived in mathematical terms, and the Hopi Weltanschauung is another and quite different one, nonmathematical and linguistic.

Thus, the Hopi language and culture conceals a *metaphysics*, such as our so-called naïve view of space and time does, or as the relativity theory does; yet it is

From *Language, Thought, and Reality*, ed. John M. Carrol. Cambridge, MA: MIT Press, 1956, pp. 57–64. Copyright © 1956 by the Massachusetts Institute of Technology. By permission of the publisher.

a different metaphysics from either. In order to describe the structure of the universe according to the Hopi, it is necessary to attempt – insofar as it is possible – to make explicit this metaphysics, properly describable only in the Hopi language, by means of an approximation expressed in our own language, somewhat inadequately it is true, yet by availing ourselves of such concepts as we have worked up into relative consonance with the system underlying the Hopi view of the universe.

In this Hopi view, time disappears and space is altered, so that it is no longer the homogeneous and instantaneous tuneless space of our supposed intuition or of classical Newtonian mechanics. At the same time, new concepts and abstractions flow into the picture, taking up the task of describing the universe without reference to such time or space – abstractions for which our language lacks adequate terms. These abstractions, by approximations of which we attempt to reconstruct for ourselves the metaphysics of the Hopi, will undoubtedly appear to us as psychological or even mystical in character. They are ideas which we are accustomed to consider as part and parcel either of so-called animistic or vitalistic beliefs, or of those transcendental unifications of experience and intuitions of things unseen that are felt by the consciousness of the mystic, or which are given cult in mystical and (or) so-called occult systems of thought. These abstractions are definitely given either explicitly in words – psychological or metaphysical terms – in the Hopi language, or, even more, are implicit in the very structure and grammar of that language, as well as being observable in Hopi culture and behavior. They are not, so far as I can consciously avoid it, projections of other systems upon the Hopi language and culture made by me in my attempt at an objective analysis. Yet, if *mystical* be perchance a term of abuse in the eyes of a modern Western scientist, it must be emphasised that these underlying abstractions and postulates of the Hopian metaphysics are, from a detached viewpoint, equally (or to the Hopi, more) justified pragmatically and experientially, as compared to the flowing time and static space of our own metaphysics, which are *au fond* equally mystical. The Hopi postulates equally account for all phenomena and their interrelations, and lend themselves even better to the integration of Hopi culture in all its phases.

The metaphysics underlying our own language, thinking, and modern culture (I speak not of the recent and quite different relativity metaphysics of modern science) imposes upon the universe two grand *cosmic forms*, space and time; static three-dimensional infinite space, and kinetic one-dimensional uniformly and perpetually flowing time – two utterly separate and unconnected aspects of reality (according to this familiar way of thinking). The flowing realm of time is, in turn, the subject of a threefold division: past, present, and future.

The Hopi metaphysics also has its cosmic forms comparable to these in scale and scope. What are they? It imposes upon the universe two grand cosmic forms, which as a first approximation in terminology we may call *manifested* and *manifesting* (or, *unmanifest*) or, again, *objective* and *subjective*. The objective or manifested comprises all that is or has been accessible to the senses, the historical physical universe, in fact, with no attempt to distinguish between present and past but excluding everything that we call future. The subjective or manifesting comprises all that we call future, *but not merely this*, it includes equally and indistinguishably all that we call mental – everything that appears or exists in the mind, or, as the Hopi would prefer to say, in the *heart*, not only the heart of man, but the heart of animals, plants, and things, and behind and within all the forms and appearances of nature in the heart of nature, and by an implication and extension which has been felt by more than one anthropologist, yet would hardly ever be spoken of by a Hopi himself, so charged is the idea with religious and magical awesomeness, in the very heart of the Cosmos, itself. The subjective reality (subjective from our viewpoint, but intensely real and quivering with life, power, and potency to the Hopi) embraces not only our *future*, much of which the Hopi regards as more or less predestined in essence, if not in exact form, but also all mentality, intellection, and emotion, the essence and typical form of which is the striving of purposeful desire, intelligent in character, toward manifestation – a manifestation which is much resisted and delayed, but in some form or other is inevitable. It is the realm of expectancy, of desire and purpose, of vitalizing life, of efficient causes, of thought thinking itself out from an inner realm (the Hopian *heart*) into manifestation. It is in a dynamic state, yet not a state of motion – it is not advancing toward us out of a future, but *already with us* in vital and mental form, and its dynamism is at work in the field of eventuating or manifesting, i.e. evolving without motion from the subjective by degrees to a result which is the objective. In translating into English, the Hopi will say that these entities in process of causation "will come" or that they – the Hopi – "will come to" them, but, in their own language, there are no verbs corresponding to our "come" and "go" that mean simple and abstract motion, our purely kinematic concept. The words in this case translated "come" refer to the process of eventuating without calling it motion – they are "eventuates to here" (*pew'i*) or "eventuates from it" (*angqö*) or "arrived" (*pitu*, pl. *öki*) which refers only to the terminal manifestation, the actual arrival at a given point, not to any motion preceding it.

This realm of the subjective or of the process of manifestation, as distinguished from the objective, the result of this universal process, includes also – on its border but still pertaining to its own realm – an aspect of existence that we include in our present time. It is that which is beginning to emerge into manifestation; that is, something which is beginning to be done, like going to sleep or starting to write, but is not yet in full operation. This can be and usually is referred to by the same verb form (the *expective* form in my terminology of Hopi grammar) that refers to our future, or to wishing, wanting, intending, etc. Thus, this nearer edge of the subjective cuts across and includes a part of our present time, viz. the moment of inception, but most of our present belongs in the Hopi scheme to the objective realm and so is indistinguishable from our past. There is also a verb form, the *inceptive* which refers to this *edge* of emergent manifestation in the reverse way – as belonging to the objective, as the edge at which objectivity is attained; this is used to indicate beginning or starting, and in most cases there is no difference apparent in the translation from the similar use of the expective. But, at certain crucial points, significant and fundamental differences appear. The inceptive, referring to the objective and result side, and not like the expective to the subjective and causal side, implies the ending of the work of causation in the same breath that it states the beginning of manifestation. If the verb has a suffix which answers somewhat to our passive, but really means that causation impinges upon a subject to effect a certain result – i.e. "the food is being eaten," then addition of the *inceptive* suffix in such a way as to refer to the basic action produces a meaning of causal cessation. The basic action is in the inceptive state; hence whatever causation is behind it is ceasing; the causation explicitly referred to by the causal suffix is hence such as *we* would call past time, and the verb includes this and the incepting and the decausating of the final state (a state of partial or total eatenness) in one statement. The translation is "it stops getting eaten." Without knowing the underlying Hopian metaphysics, it would be impossible to understand how the same suffix may denote starting or stopping.

If we were to approximate our metaphysical terminology more closely to Hopian terms, we should probably speak of the subjective realm as the realm of *hope* or *hoping*. Every language contains terms that have come to attain cosmic scope of reference, that crystallize in themselves the basic postulates of an unformulated philosophy, in which is couched the thought of a people, a culture, a civilization, even of an era. Such are our words "reality, substance, matter, cause," and as we have seen "space, time, past, present, future." Such a term in Hopi is the word most often translated "hope" – *tunátya* – "it is in the action of hoping, it hopes, it is hoped for, it thinks or is thought of with hope," etc. Most metaphysical words in Hopi are verbs, not nouns as in European languages. The verb *tunátya* contains in its idea of hope something of our words "thought," "desire," and "cause," which sometimes must be used to translate it. The word is really a term which crystallizes the Hopi philosophy of the universe in respect to its grand dualism of objective and subjective; it is the Hopi term for *subjective*. It refers to the state of the subjective, unmanifest, vital and causal aspect of the Cosmos, and the fermenting activity toward fruition and manifestation with which it seethes – an action of *hoping*; i.e. mental-causal activity, which is forever pressing upon and into the manifested realm. As anyone acquainted with Hopi society knows, the Hopi see this burgeoning activity in the growing of plants, the forming of clouds and their condensation in rain, the careful planning out of the communal activities of agriculture and architecture, and in all human hoping, wishing, striving, and taking thought; and as most especially concentrated in prayer, the constant hopeful praying of the Hopi community, assisted by their exoteric communal ceremonies and their secret, esoteric rituals in the underground kivas – prayer which conducts the pressure of the collective Hopi thought and will out of the subjective into the objective. The inceptive form of *tunátya*, which is *tunátyava*, does not mean "begins to hope," but rather "comes true, being hoped for." Why it must logically have this meaning will be clear from what has already been said. The inceptive denotes the first appearance of the objective, but the basic meaning of *tunátya* is subjective activity or force; the inceptive is then the terminus of such activity. It might then be said that *tunátya* "coming true" is the Hopi term for objective, as contrasted with subjective, the two terms being simply two different inflectional nuances of the same verbal root, as the two cosmic forms are the two aspects of one reality.

As far as space is concerned, the subjective is a mental realm, a realm of no space in the objective sense, but it seems to be symbolically related to the vertical dimension and its poles the zenith and the underground, as well as to the "heart" of things, which corresponds to our word "inner" in the metaphorical sense. Corresponding to each point in the objective world is such a vertical and vitally *inner* axis which is what we call the wellspring of the future. But to the Hopi there is no temporal future; there is nothing in the subjective state corresponding to the sequences and successions conjoined with distances and changing physical configurations that we find in the objective state. From each subjective axis, which may be thought of as more or less vertical and like the growth-axis of a plant, extends the objective realm in every physical direction, though these directions are typified more especially by the horizontal plane and its four cardinal points. The objective is the great cosmic form of extension; it takes in all the strictly extensional aspects of existence, and it includes all intervals and distances, all seriations and numbers. Its *distance* includes what we call time in the sense of the temporal relation between events which have already happened. The Hopi conceive time and motion in the objective realm in a purely operational sense – a matter of the complexity and magnitude of operations connecting events – so that the element of time is not separated from whatever element of space enters into the operations. Two events in the past occurred a long "time" apart (the Hopi language has no word quite equivalent to our time) when many periodic physical motions have occurred or accumulate magnitude of physical display in other ways. The Hopi metaphysics does not raise the question whether the things in a distant village exist at the same present moment as those in one's own village, for it is frankly pragmatic on this score and says that any events in the distant village can be compared to any events in one's own village only by an interval of magnitude that has both time and space forms in it. Events at a distance from the observer can only be known objectively when they are "past" (i.e. posited in the objective) and the more distant, the more past (the more worked upon from the subjective side). Hopi, with its preference for verbs, as contrasted to our own liking for nouns, perpetually turns our propositions about things into propositions about events. What happens at a distant village, if actual (objective) and not a conjecture (subjective) can be known "here" only later. If it does not happen "at this place," it does not happen "at this time,"; it happens at "that" place and at "that" time. Both the "here" happening and the "there" happening are in the objective, corresponding in general to our past, but the there happening is the more objectively distant, meaning, from our standpoint, that it is further away in the past just as it is further away from us in space than the here happening.

As the objective realm displaying its characteristic attribute of extension stretches away from the observer toward that unfathomable remoteness which is both far away in space and long past in time, there comes a point where extension in detail ceases to be knowable and is lost in the vast distance, and where the subjective, creeping behind the scenes as it were, merges into the objective, so that at this inconceivable distance from the observer – from all observers – there is an all-encircling end and beginning of things where it might be said that existence, itself, swallows up the objective and the subjective. The borderland of this realm is as much subjective as objective. It is the abysm of antiquity, the time and place told about in the myths, which is known only subjectively or mentally – the Hopi realize and even express in their grammar that the things told in myths or stories do not have the same kind of reality or validity as things of the present day, the things of practical concern. As for the far distances of the sky and stars, what is known and said about them is suppositions, inferential – hence, in a way subjective – reached more through the inner vertical axis and the pole of the zenith than through the objective distances and the objective processes of vision and locomotion. So the dim past of myths is that corresponding distance on earth (rather than in the heavens) which is reached subjectively as myth through the vertical axis of reality via the pole of the nadir – hence it is placed *below* the present surface of the earth, though this does not mean that the nadir-land of the origin myths is a hole or cavern as we should understand it. It is *Palátkwapi* "At the Red Mountains," a land like our present earth, but to which our earth bears the relation of a distant sky – and similarly the sky of our earth is penetrated by the heroes of tales, who find another earthlike realm above it.

It may now be seen how the Hopi do not need to use terms that refer to space or time as such. Such terms in our language are recast into expressions of extension, operation, and cyclic process provided they refer to the solid objective realm. They are recast into expressions of subjectivity if they refer to the subjective realm – the future, the psychic-mental, the mythical period, and the invisibly distant and conjectural generally. Thus, the Hopi language gets along perfectly without tenses for its verbs.

---

33   On the Very Idea of a Conceptual Scheme

Donald Davidson

Philosophers of many persuasions are prone to talk of conceptual schemes. Conceptual schemes, we are told, are ways of organizing experience; they are systems of categories that give form to the data of sensation; they are points of view from which individuals, cultures, or periods survey the passing scene. There may be no translating from one scheme to another, in which case the beliefs, desires, hopes, and bits of knowledge that characterize one person have no true

From *Proceedings and Addresses of the American Philosophical Association*, 47 (1974), pp. 5–20. By permission of the American Philosophical Association.

counterparts for the subscriber to another scheme. Reality itself is relative to a scheme: what counts as real in one system may not in another.

Even those thinkers who are certain there is only one conceptual scheme are in the sway of the scheme concept; even monotheists have religion. And when someone sets out to describe 'our conceptual scheme', his homey task assumes, if we take him literally, that there might be rival systems.

Conceptual relativism is a heady and exotic doctrine, or would be if we could make good sense of it. The trouble is, as so often in philosophy, it is hard to improve intelligibility while retaining the excitement. At any rate that is what I shall argue.

We are encouraged to imagine we understand massive conceptual change or profound contrasts by legitimate examples of a familiar sort. Sometimes an idea, like that of simultaneity as defined in relativity theory, is so important that with its addition a whole department of science takes on a new look. Sometimes revisions in the list of sentences held true in a discipline are so central that we may feel that the terms involved have changed their meanings. Languages that have evolved in distant times or places may differ extensively in their resources for dealing with one or another range of phenomena. What comes easily in one language may come hard in another, and this difference may echo significant dissimilarities in style and value.

But examples like these, impressive as they occasionally are, are not so extreme but that the changes and the contrasts can be explained and described using the equipment of a single language. Whorf, wanting to demonstrate that Hopi incorporates a metaphysics so alien to ours that Hopi and English cannot, as he puts it, 'be calibrated', uses English to convey the contents of sample Hopi sentences.[1] Kuhn is brilliant at saying what things were like before the revolution using – what else? – our post-revolutionary idiom.[2] Quine gives us a feel for the pre-individuative phase in the evolution of our conceptual scheme',[3] while Bergson tells us where we can go to get a view of a mountain undistorted by one or another provincial perspective.

The dominant metaphor of conceptual relativism, that of differing points of view, seems to betray an underlying paradox. Different points of view make sense, but only if there is a common co-ordinate system on which to plot them; yet the existence of a common system belies the claim of dramatic incomparability. What we need, it seems to me, is some idea of the considerations that set the limits to conceptual contrast. There are extreme suppositions that founder on paradox or contradiction; there are modest examples we have no trouble understanding. What determines where we cross from the merely strange or novel to the absurd?

We may accept the doctrine that associates having a language with having a conceptual scheme. The relation may be supposed to be this: where conceptual schemes differ, so do languages. But speakers of different languages may share a conceptual scheme provided there is a way of translating one language into the other. Studying the criteria of translation is therefore a way of focusing on criteria of identity for conceptual schemes. If conceptual schemes aren't associated with languages in this way, the original problem is needlessly doubled, for then we would have to imagine the mind, with its ordinary categories, operating with a language with *its* organizing structure. Under the circumstances we would certainly want to ask who is to be master.

Alternatively, there is the idea that *any* language distorts reality, which implies that it is only wordlessly if at all that the mind comes to grips with things as they really are. This is to conceive language as an inert (though necessarily distorting) medium independent of the human agencies that employ it; a view of language that surely cannot he maintained. Yet if the mind can grapple without distortion with the real, the mind itself must be without categories and concepts. This featureless self is familiar from theories in quite different parts of the philosophical landscape. There are, for example, theories that make freedom consist in decisions taken apart from all desires, habits, and dispositions of the agent; and theories of knowledge that suggest that the mind can observe the totality of its own perceptions and ideas. In each case, the mind is divorced from the traits that constitute it; an inescapable conclusion from certain lines of reasoning, as I said, but one that should always persuade us to reject the premisses.

We may identify conceptual schemes with languages, then, or better, allowing for the possibility that more than one language may express the same scheme, sets of intertranslatable languages. Languages we will not think of as separable from souls; speaking a language is not a trait a man can lose while retaining the power of thought. So there is no chance that someone can take up a vantage point for comparing conceptual schemes by temporarily shedding his own. Can we then say that two people have different conceptual schemes if they speak languages that fail of intertranslatability?

In what follows I consider two kinds of case that might be expected to arise: complete, and partial, failures of translatability. There would be complete failure if no significant range of sentences in one language could be translated into the other; there would be partial failure if some range could be translated and some range could not (I shall neglect possible asymmetries.) My strategy will be to argue that we cannot make sense of total failure, and then to examine more briefly cases of partial failure.

First, then, the purported cases of complete failure. It is tempting to take a very short line indeed: nothing, it may be said, could count as evidence that some form of activity could not be interpreted in our language that was not at the same time evidence that that form of activity was not speech behaviour. If this were right, we probably ought to hold that a form of activity that cannot be interpreted as language in our language is not speech behaviour. Putting matters this way is unsatisfactory, however, for it comes to little more than making translatability into a familiar tongue a criterion of languagehood. As fiat, the thesis lacks the appeal of self-evidence; if it is a truth, as I think it is, it should emerge as the conclusion of an argument.

The credibility of the position is improved by reflection on the close relations between language and the attribution of attitudes such as belief, desire, and intention. On the one hand, it is clear that speech requires a multitude of finely discriminated intentions and beliefs. A person who asserts that perseverance keeps honour bright must, for example, represent himself as believing that per-severance keeps honour bright, and he must intend to represent himself as be-lieving it. On the other hand, it seems unlikely that we can intelligibly attribute attitudes as complex as these to a speaker unless we can translate his words into ours. There can be no doubt that the relation between being able to translate someone's language and being able to describe his attitudes is very close. Still, until we can say more about *what* this relation is, the case against untranslatable languages remains obscure.

It is sometimes thought that translatability into a familiar language, say Eng-lish, cannot be a criterion of languagehood on the grounds that the relation of translatability is not transitive. The idea is that some language, say Saturnian, may be translatable into English, and some further language, like Plutonian, may be translatable into Saturnian, while Plutonian is not translatable into Eng-lish. Enough translatable differences may add up to an untranslatable one. By imagining a sequence of languages, each close enough to the one before to be acceptably translated into it, we can imagine a language so different from Eng-lish as to resist totally translation into it. Corresponding to this distant language would be a system of concepts altogether alien to us.

This exercise does not, I think, introduce any new element into the discus-sion. For we should have to ask how we recognized that what the Saturnian was doing was *translating* Plutonian (or anything else). The Saturnian speaker might tell us that that was what he was doing or rather we might for a moment assume that that was what he was telling us. But then it would occur to us to wonder whether our translations of Saturnian were correct.

According to Kuhn, scientists operating in different scientific traditions (within different 'paradigms') 'work in different worlds'.[4] Strawson's *The Bounds of Sense* begins with the remark that 'It is possible to imagine kinds of worlds very differ-ent from the world as we know it.'[5] Since there is at most one world, these pluralities are metaphorical or merely imagined. The metaphors are, however, not at all the same. Strawson invites us to imagine possible non-actual worlds, worlds that might be described, using our present language, by redistributing truth values over sentences in various systematic ways. The clarity of the con-trasts between worlds in this case depends on supposing our scheme of con-cepts, our descriptive resources, to remain fixed. Kuhn, on the other hand, wants us to think of different observers of the same world who come to it with incommensurable systems of concepts. Strawson's many imagined worlds are seen or heard or described from the same point of view; Kuhn's one world is seen from different points of view. It is the second metaphor we want to work on.

The first metaphor requires a distinction within language of concept and content: using a fixed system of concepts (words with fixed meanings) we de-scribe alternative universes. Some sentences will be true simply because of the concepts or meanings involved, others because of the way of the world. In describing possible worlds, we play with sentences of the second kind only.

The second metaphor suggests instead a dualism of quite a different sort, a dualism of total scheme (or language) and uninterpreted content. Adherence to the second dualism, while not inconsistent with adherence to the first, may be encouraged by attacks on the first. Here is how it may work.

To give up the analytic-synthetic distinction as basic to the understanding of language is to give up the idea that we can clearly distinguish between theory and language. Meaning, as we might loosely use the word, is contaminated by theory, but what is held to be time. Feyerabend puts it this way:

> Our argument against meaning invariance is simple and clear. It proceeds from the fact that usually some of the principles involved in the determinations of the meanings of older theories or points of views are inconsistent with the new . . . theories. It points out that it is natural to resolve this contradiction by eliminating the troublesome . . . older principles, and to replace them by principles, or theorems, of a new . . . theory. And it concludes by showing that such a procedure will also lead to the elimination of the old meanings.[6]

We may now seem to have a formula for generating distinct conceptual schemes. We get a new out of an old scheme when the speakers of a language come to accept as true an important range of sentences they previously took to be false (and, of course, vice versa). We must not describe this change simply as a matter of their coming to view old falsehoods as truths, for a truth is a proposition, and what they come to accept, in accepting a sentence as true, is not the same thing that they rejected when formerly they held the sentence to be false. A change has come over the meaning of the sentence because it now belongs to a new language.

This picture of how new (perhaps better) schemes result from new and better science is very much the picture philosophers of science, like Putnam and Feyerabend, and historians of science, like Kuhn, have painted for us. A related idea emerges in the suggestion of some other philosophers, that we could improve our conceptual lot if we were to tune our language to an improved science. Thus both Quine and Smart, in somewhat different ways, regretfully admit that our present ways of talking make a serious science of behaviour impossible. (Wittgenstein and Ryle have said similar things without regret.) The cure, Quine and Smart think is to change how we talk. Smart advocates (and predicts) the change in order to put us on the scientifically straight path of materialism: Quine is more concerned to clear the way for a purely extensional language. (Perhaps I should add that I think our actual scheme and language are best understood as extensional and materialist.)

If we were to follow this advice, I do not myself think science or understanding would be advanced, though possibly morals would. But the present question is only whether, if such changes were to take place, we should be justified in calling them alterations in the basic conceptual apparatus. The difficulty in so calling them is easy to appreciate. Suppose that in my office of Minister of Scientific Language I want the new man to stop using words that refer, say, to emotions, feelings, thoughts, and intentions, and to talk instead of the physiological states and happenings that are assumed to be more or less identical with the mental riff and raff. How do I tell whether my advice has been heeded if the new man speaks a new language? For all I know, the shiny new phrases, though stolen from the old language in which they refer to physiological stirrings, may in his mouth play the role of the messy old mental concepts.

The key phrase is: for all I know. What is clear is that retention of some or all of the old vocabulary in itself provides no basis for judging the new scheme to be the same as, or different from, the old. So what sounded at first like a thrilling discovery – that truth is relative to a conceptual scheme – has not so far been shown to be anything more than the pedestrian and familiar fact that the truth of a sentence is relative to (among other things) the language to which it belongs. Instead of living in different worlds, Kuhn's scientists may, like those who need Webster's dictionary, be only words apart.

Giving up the analytic-synthetic distinction has not proved a help in making sense of conceptual relativism. The analytic–synthetic distinction is however explained in terms of something that may serve to buttress conceptual relativism, namely the idea of empirical content. The dualism of the synthetic and the analytic is a dualism of sentences some of which are true (or false) both because of what they mean and because of their empirical content, while others are true (or false) by virtue of meaning alone, having no empirical content. If we give up the dualism, we abandon the conception of meaning that goes with it, but we do not have to abandon the idea of empirical content: we can hold, if we want, that *all* sentences have empirical content. Empirical content is in turn explained by reference to the facts, the world, experience, sensation, the totality of sensory stimuli, or something similar. Meanings gave us a way to talk about categories, the organizing structure of language, and so on; but it is possible, as we have seen, to give up meanings and analyticity while retaining the idea of language as embodying a conceptual scheme. Thus in place of the dualism of the analytic-synthetic we get the dualism of conceptual scheme and empirical content. The new dualism is the foundation of an empiricism shorn of the untenable dogmas of the analytic-synthetic distinction and reductionism – shorn, that is, of the unworkable idea that we can uniquely allocate empirical content sentence by sentence.

I want to urge that this second dualism of scheme and content, of organizing system and something waiting to be organized, cannot be made intelligible and defensible. It is itself a dogma of empiricism, the third dogma. The third, and perhaps the last, for if we give it up it is not clear that there is anything distinctive left to call empiricism.

The scheme-content dualism has been formulated in many ways. Here are some examples. The first comes from Whorf, elaborating on a theme of Sapir's. Whorf says that:

> . . . language produces an organization of experience. We are inclined to think of language simply as a technique of expression, and not to realize that language first of all is a classification and arrangement of the stream of sensory experience which results in a certain world-order . . . In other words, language does in a cruder but also in a broader and more versatile way the same thing that science does . . . We are thus introduced to a new principle of relativity which holds that all observers are not led by the same physical evidence to the same picture of the universe, unless their linguistic backgrounds are similar, or can in some way be calibrated.[7]

Here we have all the required elements: language as the organizing force, not to be distinguished clearly from science; what is organized, referred to variously as 'experience', 'the stream of sensory experience', and 'physical evidence'; and finally, the failure of intertranslatability ('calibration'). The failure of intertranslatability is a necessary condition for difference of conceptual schemes; the common relation to experience or the evidence is what is supposed to help us make sense of the claim that it is languages or schemes that are under consideration when translation fails. It is essential to this idea that there be something neutral and common that lies outside all schemes. This common something cannot, of course, be the *subject matter* of contrasting languages, or translation would be possible. Thus Kuhn has recently written:

> Philosophers have now abandoned hope of finding a pure sense-datum language . . . but many of them continue to assume that theories can be compared by recourse to a basic vocabulary consisting entirely of words which are attached to nature in ways that are unproblematic and, to the extent necessary, independent of theory . . . Feyerabend and I have argued at length that no such vocabulary is available. In the transition from one theory to the next words change their meanings or conditions of applicability in subtle ways. Though most of the same signs are used before and after a revolution – e.g. force, mass, element, compound, cell – the way in which some of them attach to nature has somehow changed. Successive theories are thus, we say, incommensurable.[8]

'Incommensurable' is, of course, Kuhn and Feyerabend's word for 'not intertranslatable'. The neutral content waiting to be organized is supplied by nature.

Feyerabend himself suggests that we may compare contrasting schemes by 'choosing a point of view outside the system or the language'. He hopes we can do this because 'there is still human experience as an actually existing process'[9] independent of all schemes.

The same, or similar, thoughts are expressed by Quine in many passages: 'The totality of our so-called knowledge or beliefs . . . is a man-made fabric which impinges on experience only along the edges . . .';[10] '. . . total science is like a field of force whose boundary conditions are experience';[11] 'As an empiricist I . . . think of the conceptual scheme of science as a tool . . . for predicting future experience in the light of past experience.'[12] And again:

> We persist in breaking reality down somehow into a multiplicity of identifiable and discriminable objects . . . We talk so inveterately of objects that to say we do so seems almost to say nothing at all; for how else is there to talk? It is hard to say how else there is to talk, not because our objectifying pattern is an invariable trait of human nature, but because we are bound to adapt any alien pattern to our own in the very process of understanding or translating the alien sentences.[13]

The test of difference remains failure or difficulty of translation: '. . . to speak of that remote medium as radically different from ours is to say no more than that the translations do not come smoothly'.[14] Yet the roughness may be so great that the alien has an 'as yet unimagined pattern beyond individuation'.[15]

The idea is then that something is a language, and associated with a conceptual scheme, whether we can translate it or not, if it stands in a certain relation (predicting, organizing, facing, or fitting) to experience (nature, reality, sensory promptings). The problem is to say what the relation is, and to be clearer about the entities related.

The images and metaphors fall into two main groups: conceptual schemes (languages) either *organize* something, or they *fit* it (as in 'he warps his scientific heritage to fit his . . . sensory promptings'[16]). The first group contains also *systematize, divide up* (the stream of experience); further examples of the second group are *predict, account for, face* (the tribunal of experience). As for the entities that get organized, or which the scheme must fit, I think again we may detect two main ideas: either it is reality (the universe, the world, nature), or it is experience (the passing show, surface irritations, sensory promptings, sense-data, the given).

We cannot attach a clear meaning to the notion of organizing a single object (the world, nature etc.) unless the object is understood to contain or consist in other objects. Someone who sets out to organize a closet arranges the things in it. If you are told not to organize the shoes and shirts, but the closet itself, you would be bewildered. How would you organize the Pacific Ocean? Straighten out its shores, perhaps, or relocate its islands, or destroy its fish.

A language may contain simple predicates whose extensions are matched by no simple predicates, or even by any predicates at all, in some other language. What enables us to make this point in particular cases is an ontology common to the two languages, with concepts that individuate the same objects. We can be clear about breakdowns in translation when they are local enough, for a background of generally successful translation provides what is needed to make the failures intelligible. But we were after larger game: we wanted to make sense of there being a language we could not translate at all. Or, to put the point differently, we were looking for a criterion of languagehood that did not depend on, or entail translatability into a familiar idiom. I suggest that the image of organizing the closet of nature will not supply such a criterion.

How about the other kind of object, experience? Can we think of a language organizing *it*? Much the same difficulties recur. The notion of organization applies only to pluralities. But whatever plurality we take experience to consist in – events like losing a button or stubbing a toe, having a sensation of warmth or hearing an oboe – we will have to individuate according to familiar principles. A language that organizes *such* entities must be a language very like our own.

Experience (and its classmates like surface irritations, sensations, and sense-data) also makes another and more obvious trouble for the organizing idea. For how could something count as a language that organized *only* experiences, sensations, surface irritations, or sense-data? Surely knives and forks, railroads and mountains, cabbages and kingdoms also need organizing.

This last remark will no doubt sound inappropriate as a response to the claim that a conceptual scheme is a way of coping with sensory experience; and I agree that it is. But what was under consideration was the idea of *organizing* experience, not the idea of *coping with* (or fitting or facing) experience. The reply was apropos of the former, not the latter, concept. So now let's see whether we can do better with the second idea.

When we turn from talk of organization to talk of fitting we turn our attention from the referential apparatus of language – predicates, quantifiers, variables, and singular terms – to whole sentences. It is sentences that predict (or are used to predict), sentences that cope or deal with things, that fit our sensory promptings, that can be compared or confronted with the evidence. It is sentences also that face the tribunal of experience, though of course they must face it together.

The proposal is not that experiences, sense-data, surface irritations, or sensory promptings are the sole subject matter of language. There is, it is true, the theory that talk about brick houses on Elm Street is ultimately to be construed as being about sense data or perceptions, but such reductionistic views are only extreme, and implausible, versions of the general position we are considering. The general position is that sensory experience provides all the *evidence* for the acceptance of sentences (where sentences may include whole theories). A sentence or theory fits our sensory promptings, successfully faces the tribunal of experience, predicts future experience, or copes with the pattern of our surface irritations, provided it is borne out by the evidence.

In the common course of affairs, a theory may be borne out by the available evidence and yet be false. But what is in view here is not just actually available evidence; it is the totality of possible sensory evidence past, present and future. We do not need to pause to contemplate what this might mean. The point is that for a theory to fit or face up to the totality of possible sensory evidence is for that theory to be true. If a theory quantifies over physical objects, numbers, or sets, what is says about these entities is true provided the theory as a whole fits the sensory evidence. One can see how from this point of view, such entities might be called posits. It is reasonable to call something a posit if it can be contrasted with something that is not. Here the something that is not is sensory experience – at least that is the idea.

The trouble is that the notion of fitting the totality of experience, like the notion of fitting the facts, or of being true to the facts, adds nothing intelligible to the simple concept of being true. To speak of sensory experience rather than the evidence, or just the facts, expresses a view about the source or nature of evidence, but it does not add a new entity to the universe against which to test conceptual schemes. The totality of sensory evidence is what we want provided it is all the evidence there is; and all the evidence there is is just what it takes to make our sentences or theories true. Nothing, however, no *thing*, makes sentences and theories true: not experience, not surface irritations, not the world, can make a sentence true. *That* experience takes a certain course, that our skin is warmed or punctured, that the universe is finite, these facts, if we like to talk that way, make sentences and theories true. But this point is put better without mention of facts. The sentence 'My skin is warm' is true if and only if my skin is warm. Here there is no reference to a fact, a world, an experience, or a piece of evidence.[17]

Our attempt to characterize languages or conceptual schemes in terms of the notion of fitting some entity has come down, then, to the simple thought that something is an acceptable conceptual scheme or theory if it is true. Perhaps we had better say *largely* true in order to allow sharers of scheme to differ on details. And the criterion of a conceptual scheme different from our own now becomes: largely true but not translatable. The question whether this is a useful criterion is just the question how well we understand the notion of truth, as applied to language, independent of the notion of translation. The answer is, I think, that we do not understand it independently at all.

We recognize sentences like ' "Snow is white" is true if and only if snow is white' to be trivially true. Yet the totality of such English sentences uniquely determines the extension of the concept of truth for English. Tarski generalized this observation and made it a test of theories of truth: according to Tarski's Convention T, a satisfactory theory of truth for a language L must entail, for every sentence *s* of L, a theorem of the form '*s* is true if and only if *p*' where '*s*' is replaced by a description of *s* and '*p*' by *s* itself if L is English, and by a translation of *s* into English if L is not English.[18] This isn't, of course, a definition of truth, and it doesn't hint that there is a single definition or theory that applies to languages generally. Nevertheless, Convention T suggests, though it cannot state, an important feature common to all the specialized concepts of truth. It succeeds in doing this by making essential use of the notion of translation into a language we know. Since Convention T embodies our best intuition as to how the concept of truth is used, there does not seem to be much hope for a test that a conceptual scheme is radically different from ours if that test depends on the assumption that we can divorce the notion of truth from that of translation.

Neither a fixed stock of meanings, nor a theory-neutral reality, can provide, then, a ground for comparison of conceptual schemes. It would be a mistake to look further for such a ground if by that we mean something conceived as common to incommensurable schemes. In abandoning this search, we abandon the attempt to make sense of the metaphor of a single space within which each scheme has a position and provides a point of view.

I turn now to the more modest approach: the idea of partial rather than total failure of translation. This introduces the possibility of making changes and contrasts in conceptual schemes intelligible by reference to the common part. What we need is a theory of translation or interpretation that makes no assumptions about shared meanings, concepts, or beliefs.

The interdependence of belief and meaning springs from the interdependence of two aspects of the interpretation of speech behaviour: the attribution of beliefs and the interpretation of sentences. We remarked before that we can afford to associate conceptual schemes with languages because of these dependencies. Now we can put the point in a somewhat sharper way. Allow that a man's speech cannot be interpreted except by someone who knows a good deal about what the speaker believes (and intends and wants), and that fine distinctions between beliefs are impossible without understood speech; how then are we to interpret speech or intelligibly to attribute beliefs and other attitudes? Clearly we must have a theory that simultaneously accounts for attitudes and interprets speech, and which assumes neither.

I suggest, following Quine, that we may without circularity or unwarranted assumptions accept certain very general attitudes towards sentences as the basic evidence for a theory of radical interpretation. For the sake of the present discussion at least we may depend on the attitude of accepting as true, directed to sentences, as the crucial notion. (A more full-blooded theory would look to other attitudes towards sentences as well, such as wishing true, wondering whether true, intending to make true, and so on.) Attitudes are indeed involved here, but the fact that the main issue is not begged can be seen from this: if we merely know that someone holds a certain sentence to be true, we know neither what he means by the sentence nor what belief his holding it true represents. His holding the sentence true is thus the vector of two forces: the problem of interpretation is to abstract from the evidence a workable theory of meaning and an acceptable theory of belief.

The way this problem is solved is best appreciated from undramatic examples. If you see a ketch sailing by and your companion says, 'Look at that handsome yawl' you may be faced with a problem of interpretation. One natural possibility is that your friend has mistaken a ketch for a yawl, and has formed a false belief. But if his vision is good and his line of sight favourable it is even more plausible that he does not use the word 'yawl' quite as you do, and has made no mistake at all about the position of the jigger on the passing yacht. We do this sort of off the cuff interpretation all the time, deciding in favour of reinterpretation of words in order to preserve a reasonable theory of belief. As philosophers we are peculiarly tolerant of systematic malapropism, and practiced at interpreting the result. The process is that of constructing a viable theory of belief and meaning from sentences held true.

Such examples emphasize the interpretation of anomalous details against a background of common beliefs and a going method of translation. But the principles involved must be the same in less trivial cases. What matters is this: if all we know is what sentences a speaker holds true, and we cannot assume that his language is our own, then we cannot take even a first step towards interpretation without knowing or assuming a great deal about the speaker's beliefs. Since knowledge of beliefs comes only with the ability to interpret words, the only possibility at the start is to assume general agreements on beliefs. We get a first approximation to a finished theory by assigning to sentences of a speaker conditions of truth that actually obtain (in our own opinion) just when the speaker holds those sentences true. The guiding policy is to do this as far as possible, subject to considerations of simplicity, hunches about the effects of social conditioning, and of course our common-sense, or scientific, knowledge of explicable error.

The method is not designed to eliminate disagreement, nor can it; its purpose is to make meaningful disagreement possible, and this depends entirely on a foundation – *some* foundation – in agreement. The agreement may take the form of widespread sharing of sentences held true by speakers of 'the same language', or agreement in the large mediated by a theory of truth contrived by an interpreter for speakers of another language.

Since charity is not an option, but a condition of having a workable theory, it is meaningless to suggest that we might fall into massive error by endorsing it. Until we have successfully established a systematic correlation of sentences held true with sentences held true, there are not mistakes to make. Charity is forced on us; whether we like it or not, if we want to understand others, we must count them right in most matters. If we can produce a theory that reconciles charity and the formal conditions for a theory, we have done all that could be done to ensure communication. Nothing more is possible, and nothing more is needed.

We make maximum sense of the words and thoughts of others when we interpret in a way that optimizes agreement (this includes room, as we said, for explicable error, i.e. differences of opinion). Where does this leave the case for conceptual relativism? The answer is, I think, that we must say much the same thing about differences in conceptual scheme as we say about differences in belief: we improve the clarity and bite of declarations of difference, whether of scheme or opinion, by enlarging the basis of shared (translatable) language or of shared opinion. Indeed, no clear line between the cases can be made out. If we choose to translate some alien sentence rejected by its speakers by a sentence to which we are strongly attached on a community basis, we may be tempted to call this a difference in schemes; if we decide to accommodate the evidence in other ways, it may be more natural to speak of a difference of opinion. But when others think differently from us, no general principle, or appeal to evidence, can force us to decide that the difference lies in our beliefs rather than in our concepts.

We must conclude, I think, that the attempt to give a solid meaning to the idea of conceptual relativism, and hence to the idea of a conceptual scheme, fares no better when based on partial failure of translation than when based on total failure. Given the underlying methodology of interpretation, we could not be in a position to judge that others had concepts or beliefs radically different from our own.

It would be wrong to summarize by saying we have shown how communication is possible between people who have different schemes, a way that works without need of what there cannot be, namely a neutral ground, or a common co-ordinate system. For we have found no intelligible basis on which it can be said that schemes are different. It would be equally wrong to announce the glorious news that all mankind – all speakers of language, at least – share a common scheme and ontology. For if we cannot intelligibly say that schemes are different, neither can we intelligibly say that they are one.

In giving up dependence on the concept of an uninterpreted reality, something outside all schemes and science, we do not relinquish the notion of objective truth – quite the contrary. Given the dogma of a dualism of scheme and reality, we get conceptual relativity, and truth relative to a scheme. Without the dogma, this kind of relativity goes by the board. Of course truth of sentences remains relative to language, but that is as objective as can be. In giving up the dualism of scheme and world, we do not give up the world, but re-establish unmediated touch with the familiar objects whose antics make our sentences and opinions true or false.

Notes

1   B. L. Whorf, 'The Punctual and Segmentative Aspects of Verbs in Hopi', in *Language, Thought and Reality* (Cambridge, MA: MIT Press, 1956).

2   T. S. Kuhn, *The Structure of Scientific Revolutions* (Chicago: University of Chicago Press, 1962).

3   W. V. Quine, 'Speaking of Objects', in *Ontological Relativity and Other Essays* (New York: Columbia University Press, 1969), p. 24.

4   T. S. Kuhn, *The Structure of Scientific Revolutions*, p. 134.

5   P. Strawson, *The Bounds of Sense* (London: Methuen, 1966), p. 15.

6   P. Feyerabend, 'Explanation, Reduction, and Empiricism', in *Scientific Explanation, Space and Time* (Minneapolis, MN: University of Minnesota Press, 1962), p. 82.

7   B. L. Whorf, 'The Punctual and Segmentative Aspects of Verbs in Hopi', 55.

8   T. S. Kuhn, 'Reflections on my Critics', in *Criticism and the Growth of Knowledge*, ed. I. Lakatos and A. Musgrave (Cambridge: Cambridge University Press, 1970), pp. 266, 267.

9   P. Feyerabend, 'Problems of Empiricism', in *Beyond the Edge of Certainity*, ed. R. J. Colodny (Englewood Cliffs, NJ: Prentice-Hall, 1965), p. 214.

10 W. V. Quine, 'Two Dogmas of Empiricism', in *From a Logical Point of View* (Cambridge, MA: Harvard University Press, 1961), p. 42.

11 Ibid.

12 Ibid., p. 44.

13 W. V. Quine, 'Speaking of Objects', p. 1.

14 Ibid., p. 25.

15 Ibid., p. 24.

16 W. V. Quine, 'Two Dogmas of Empricism', p. 46.

17 See D. Davidson, 'True to the Facts', in *Inquiries into Truth and Interpretation* (Oxford: Clarendon Press, 1984).

18 A. Tarski, 'The Concept of Truth in Formalized Languages', in *Logic, Semantics, Metamathematics* (Oxford: Clarendon Press, 1956).

34 How to Tame a Wild Tongue

Gloria Anzaldúa

"We're going to have to control your tongue," the dentist says, pulling out all the metal from my mouth. Silver bits prop and tinkle into the basin. My mouth is a motherlode.

The dentist is cleaning out my roots. I get a whiff of the stench when I gasp. "I can't cap that tooth yet, you're still draining," he says.

"We're going to have to do something about your tongue," I hear the anger rising in his voice. My tongue keeps pushing out the wads of cotton, pushing back the drills, the long thin needles, "I've never seen anything as strong or as stubborn," he says. And I think, how do you tame a wild tongue, train it to be quiet, how do you bridle and saddle it? How do you make it lie down?

"Who is to say that robbing a people of its language is less violent than war?"

Ray Gwyn Smith[1]

I remember being caught speaking Spanish at recess – that was good for three licks on the knuckles with a sharp ruler. I remember being sent to the corner of the classroom for "talking back" to the Anglo teacher when all I was trying to do was tell her how to pronounce my name. "If you want to be American, speak 'American.' If you don't like it, go back to Mexico where you belong."

"I want you to speak English *Pa'hallar buen trabajo tienes que saber hablar el inglés bien. Qué vale toda tu educación si todavía hablas inglés con un* 'accent,' " my mother would say, mortified that I spoke English like a Mexican. At Pan American University, I and all Chicano students were required to take two speech classes. Their purpose: to get rid of our accents.

Attacks on one's form of expression with the intent to censor are a violation of the First Amendment. *El Anglo con cara de inocente nos arrancó la lengua.* Wild tongues can't be tamed, they can only be cut out.

Overcoming the Tradition of Silence

> *Ahogadas, escupimos el oscuro.*
> *Peleando con nuestra propia sombra*
> *el silencio nos sepulta.*

En boca cerrada no entran moscas. "Flies don't enter a closed mouth" is a saying I kept hearing when I was a child. *Ser habladora* was to be a gossip and a liar, to

From *Borderlands/La Frontera: The New Mestiza.* San Francisco: Aunt Lute Books, 1987, pp. 53–9. Copyright © 1987 by Gloria Anzaldúa. By permission of the publisher and author.

talk too much. *Muchachitas bien criadas*, well-bred girls don't answer back. *Es una falta de respeto* to talk back to one's mother or father. I remember one of the sins I'd recite to the priest in the confession box the few times I went to confession: talking back to my mother, *hablar pa' 'tras, repelar. Hocicona, repelona, chismosa*, having a big mouth, questioning, carrying tales are all signs of being *mal criada*. In my culture they are all words that are derogatory if applied to women – I've never heard them applied to men.

The first time I heard two women, a Puerto Rican and a Cuban, say the word "*nosotras*," I was shocked. I had not known the word existed. Chicanas use *nosotros* whether we're male or female. We are robbed of our female being by the masculine plural. Language is a male discourse.

> And our tongues have become
> dry   the wilderness has
> dried out our tongues   and
> we have forgotten speech.
>
> Irena Klepfisz[2]

Even our own people, other Spanish speakers, *nos quieren poner candados en la boca*. They would hold us back with their bag of *reglas de academia*.

Oyé como lada: el lenguaje de la frontera

> *Quien tiene boca se equivoca.*
>
> Mexican saying

"*Pocho*, cultural traitor, you're speaking the oppressor's language by speaking English, you're ruining the Spanish language," I have been accused by various Latinos and Latinas. Chicano Spanish is considered by the purist and by most Latinos deficient, a mutilation of Spanish.

But Chicano Spanish is a border tongue which developed naturally. Change, *evolución, enriquecimiento de palabras nuevas por invención o adopción* have created variants of Chicano Spanish, *un nuevo lenguaje. Un lenguaje que corresponde a un modo de vivir*. Chicano Spanish is not incorrect, it is a living language.

For a people who are neither Spanish nor live in a country in which Spanish is the first language; for a people who live in a country in which English is the reigning tongue but who are not Anglo; for a people who cannot entirely identify with either standard (formal, Castillian) Spanish nor standard English, what recourse is left to them but to create their own language? A language which they can connect their identity to, one capable of communicating the realities and values true to themselves – a language with terms that are neither *español ni inglés*, but both. We speak a patois, a forked tongue, a variation of two languages.

Chicano Spanish sprang out of the Chicanos' need to identify ourselves as a distinct people. We needed a language with which we could communicate with ourselves, a secret language. For some of us, language is a homeland closer than the Southwest – for many Chicanos today live in the Midwest and the East. And because we are a complex, heterogeneous people, we speak many languages. Some of the languages we speak are:

1. Standard English
2. Working class and slang English
3. Standard Spanish
4. Standard Mexican Spanish
5. North Mexican Spanish dialect
6. Chicano Spanish (Texas, New Mexico, Arizona and California have regional variations)
7. Tex-Mex
8. *Pachuco* (called *caló*)

My "home" tongues are the languages I speak with my sister and brothers, with my friends. They are the last five listed, with 6 and 7 being closest to my heart. From school, the media and job situations, I've picked up standard and working class English. From Mamagrande Locha and from reading Spanish and Mexican literature, I've picked up Standard Spanish and Standard Mexican Spanish. From *los recién llegados*, Mexican immigrants, and *braceros*, I learned the North Mexican dialect. With Mexicans I'll try to speak either Standard Mexican Spanish or the North Mexican dialect. From my parents and Chicanos living in the Valley, I picked up Chicano Texas Spanish, and I speak it with my mom, younger brother (who married a Mexican and who rarely mixes Spanish with English) aunts and older relatives.

With Chicanas from *Nuevo México* or *Arizona* I will speak Chicano Spanish a little, but often they don't understand what I'm saying. With most California Chicanas I speak entirely in English (unless I forget). When I first moved to San Francisco, I'd rattle off something in Spanish, unintentionally embarrassing them. Often it is only with another Chicana *tejana* that I can talk freely.

Words distorted by English are known as anglicisms or *pochismos*. The *pocho* is an anglicized Mexican or American of Mexican origin who speaks Spanish with an accent characteristic of North Americans and who distorts and reconstructs the language according to the influence of English.[3] Tex-Mex, or Spanglish, comes most naturally to me. I may switch back and forth from English to Spanish in the same sentence or in the same word. With my sister and my brother Nune and with Chicano *tejano* contemporaries I speak in Tex-Mex.

From kids and people my own age I picked up *Pachuco*. Pachuco (the language of the zoot suiters) is a language of rebellion, both against Standard Spanish and Standard English. It is a secret language. Adults of the culture and outsiders cannot understand it. It is made up of slang words from both English and Spanish. *Ruca* means girl or woman, *vato* means guy or dude, *chale* means no, *simón* means yes, *churro* is sure, talk is *periquiar pigionear* means petting, *que gacho* means how nerdy, *ponte águila* means watch out, death is called *la pelona*. Through lack of practice and not having others who can speak it, I've lost most of the *Pachuco* tongue.

Chicano Spanish

Chicanos, after 250 years of Spanish/Anglo colonization have developed significant differences in the Spanish we speak. We collapse two adjacent vowels into a single syllable and sometimes shift the stress in certain words such as *maíz/maiz, cohete/cuete*. We leave out certain consonants when they appear between vowels: *lado/lao, mojado/mojao*. Chicanos from South Texas pronounce *f* as *j* as in *jue* (*fue*). Chicanos use "archaisms," words that are no longer in the Spanish language, words that have been evolved out. We say *semos, truje, haiga, ansina, and naiden*. We retain the "archaic" *j* as in *jalar*, that derives from an earlier *h* (the French *halar* or the Germanic *halon* which was lost to standard Spanish in the 16th century), but which is still found in several regional dialects such as the one spoken in South Texas. (Due to geography, Chicanos from the Valley of South Texas were cut off linguistically from other Spanish speakers. We tend to use words that the Spaniards brought over from Medieval Spain. The majority of the Spanish colonizers in Mexico and the Southwest came from Extremadura – Hernán Cortés was one of them – and Andalucía. Andalucians pronounce *ll* like a *y*, and their *d*'s tend to be absorbed by adjacent vowels: *tirado* becomes *tirao*. They brought *el lenguaje popular, dialectos y regionalismos.*[4])

Chicanos and other Spanish speakers also shift *ll* to *y* and *z* to *s*.[5] We leave out initial syllables, saying *tar* for *estar, toy* for *estoy, hora* for *ahora* (*cubanos* and *puertorriqueños* also leave out initial letters of some words). We also leave out the final syllable such as *pa* for *para*. The intervocalic *y*, the *ll* as in *tortilla, ella, botella*, gets replaced by *tortia* or *tortiya, ea, botea*. We add an additional syllable at the beginning of certain words: *atocar* for *tocar, agastar* for *gastar*. Sometimes we'll say *lavaste las vacijas*, other times *lavates* (substituting the *ates* verb endings for the *aste*).

We use anglicisms, words borrowed from English: *bola* from ball, *carpeta* from carpet, *máchina de lavar* (instead of *lavadora*) from washing machine. Tex-Mex argot, created by adding a Spanish sound at the beginning or end of an English word such as *cookiar* for cook, *watchar* for watch, *parkiar* for park, and *rapiar* for rape, is the result of the pressures on Spanish speakers to adapt to English

We don't use the word *vosotros/as* or its accompanying verb form. We don't say *claro* (to mean yes), *imagínate*, or *me emociona*, unless we picked up Spanish from Latinas, out of a book, or in a classroom. Other Spanish-speaking groups are going through the same, or similar, development in their Spanish.

Linguistic Terrorism

Deslenguadas. Somos los del español deficiente. We are your linguistic nightmare, your linguistic aberration, your linguistic *mestisaje*, the subject of your *burla*. Because we speak with tongues of fire we are culturally crucified. Racially, culturally and linguistically *somos huérfanos* – we speak an orphan tongue.

Chicanas who grew up speaking Chicano Spanish have internalized the belief that we speak poor Spanish. It is illegitimate, a bastard language. And because we internalize how our language has been used against us by the dominant culture, we use our language differences against each other.

Chicana feminists often skirt around each other with suspicion and hesitation. For the longest time I couldn't figure it out. Then it dawned on me. To be close to another Chicana is like looking into the mirror. We are afraid of what we'll see there. *Pena.* Shame. Low estimation of self. In childhood we are told that our language is wrong. Repeated attacks on our native tongue diminish our sense of self. The attacks continue throughout our lives.

Chicanas feel uncomfortable talking in Spanish to Latinas, afraid of their censure. Their language was not outlawed in their countries. They had a whole lifetime of being immersed in their native tongue; generations, centuries in which Spanish was a first language, taught in school, heard on radio and TV, and read in the newspaper.

If a person, Chicana or Latina, has a low estimation of my native tongue, she also has a low estimation of me. Often with *mexicanas y latinas* we'll speak English as a neutral language. Even among Chicanas we tend to speak English at parties or conferences. Yet, at the same time, we're afraid the other will think we're *agringadas* because we don't speak Chicano Spanish. We oppress each other trying to out-Chicano each other, vying to be the "real" Chicanas, to speak like Chicanos. There is no one Chicano language just as there is no one Chicano experience. A monolingual Chicana whose first language is English or Spanish is just as much a Chicana as one who speaks several variants of Spanish. A Chicana from Michigan or Chicago or Detroit is just as much a Chicana as one from the Southwest. Chicano Spanish is as diverse linguistically as it is regionally.

By the end of this century, Spanish speakers will comprise the biggest minority group in the U.S., a country where students in high schools and colleges are encouraged to take French classes because French is considered more "cultured." But for a language to remain alive it must be used.[6] By the end of this century English, and not Spanish, will be the mother tongue of most Chicanos and Latinos.

So, if you want to really hurt me, talk badly about my language. Ethnic identity is twin skin to linguistic identity – I am my language. Until I can take pride in my language, I cannot take pride in myself. Until I can accept as legitimate Chicano Texas Spanish, Tex-Mex and all the other languages I speak, I cannot accept the legitimacy of myself. Until I am free to write bilingually and to switch codes without having always to translate, while I still have to speak Spanglish, and as long as I have to accommodate the English speakers rather than having them accommodate me, my tongue will be illegitimate.

I will no longer be made to feel ashamed of existing. I will have my voice: Indian, Spanish, white. I will have my serpent's tongue – my woman's voice, my sexual voice, my poet's voice. I will overcome the tradition of silence.

Notes

1   Ray Gwyn Smith, *Moorland is Cold Country*, unpublished book.
2   Irena Klepfisz, "*Di rayze aheym*/The Journey Home," in *The Tribe of Dina: A Jewish Women's Anthology*, Melanie Kaye/Kantrowitz and Irena Klepfisz, eds. (Montpelier, VT: Sinister Wisdom Books, 1986), 49.
3   R. C. Ortega, *Dialectología Del Barrio*, trans. Hortencia S. Alwan (Los Angeles, CA: R. C. Ortega Publisher & Bookseller, 1977), 132.
4   Eduardo Hernandéz-Chávez, Andrew D. Cohen, and Anthony F. Beltramo, *El Lenguaje de los Chicanos: Regional and Social Characteristics of Language Used by Mexican Americans* (Arlington, VA: Center for Applied Linguistics, 1975), 39.
5   Hernandéz-Chávez, xvii.
6   Irena Klepfisz, "Secular Jewish Identity: Yidishkayt in America," in *The Tribe of Dina*, Kaye/Kantrowitz and Klepfisz, eds, 43.

35   Language as Boundary

Wole Soyinka

I have chosen the above title for this paper largely because of recent events of a familiar pattern which have again occurred on this continent – I refer to the expulsion of Nigerians and other nationalities from countries in Central Africa. It is the same as the title of a paper I delivered in Dar es Salaam in 1971 and the contents overlap in some aspects. I feel it is time to go back to the subject – or more accurately – to this specific approach to the question of language because what happened in the Republic of Congo brings up once again the question of boundaries on this continent, and one of my contentions, any time that the problem of a continental belonging is raised directly or indirectly, and in any form whatsoever, is that of all of the forms of boundaries known to man, encountered by him as an act of Nature, created by him for reasons or unreasons of his own, or imposed upon him through the innate conditions of his own struggle for development and fulfilment, language as boundary is one of the most persistent, insidious and tragic. It is not through a wish to sound portentous that I ignore the comic and ludicrous effects of the linguistic boundary; it is simply that they are only good for belly-laughs and, once that is over, humanity finds itself face to face with the vengeful other side of that comic coin. In short, the need for a solution, for corrective strategies, never recedes.

Now, certain shades of ideological opinion prefer to insist that class as boundary is even far more dehumanizing and socially dangerous. I agree. Indeed it is impossible *not* to agree. But it seems to me that even in societies where boundaries in their class colouring have been erased near-totally, or at least blurred to indistinction, the separation syndrome crops up time and time again, and in increasingly bitter forms. Contemporary reality – and I am speaking here not in any time-slack sense but of *now*, today, this very moment – this contemporary reality, manifested in societies as ideologically apart as the United States and the Soviet Union, teaches us very simply that, for reasons which cannot be totally explained, man's linguistic self-affirmation and separation refuse to go away, resurface even after the harshest repressions and must be confronted. Not so many years ago the greatest ambition of the Puerto Rican was to merge with his larger American society so thoroughly that he tried to speak American like John Wayne. Today, not only does he retain his Latin accent, he has compelled the state to broadcast radio and television programmes, regularly, in his native Spanish. Similarly, two or three years ago, the Bretons virtually went to war with France over their demands that their native language become the educational and official language of their region. You are quite familiar with the Welsh movement. You need only drive into Wales to see how fully the Welsh language has been resuscitated and integrated into both the mundane and elevated activities of that society. What you may not recall is the amount of violent political activities that won it official recognition. Canada is on the brink of secession, thanks once again to the language issue. Of course, there are related factors. The class cleavage in that society appears to correspond more or less with the linguistic division, just as, in Northern Ireland, it corresponds for historic reasons, to the religious. Those crucial elaborations must be noted. Yet it needs to be equally asserted that linguistic solidarity in Quebec cuts across class stratifications; that it was a middle-class, more than affluent leadership which led the 'secessionist' Parti Québecois to victory; and that its very first major act on achieving power was to legislate that French become the official language of education. This in a county which carried the policy of bilingualism to such an extent that even notices in public utilities such as 'Please flush after use' are printed in French and English. The Québecois, a minority people among all of Canada, have put up determined barriers even as the central parliament had all but effectively removed them. Let me round up the rough survey with the case of Russia which, a few years ago, succumbed to pressures from the Ukraine, Georgia and one or two other Soviets whose names I forget, and granted them their own linguistic autonomy. Today, the business of those Soviets is conducted in their own languages; literature, the arts in general have, it was noted, flourished noticeably under the new dispensation. No slackening has been reported in the struggle for the triumph of socialism in the Union.

Back to our own continent, after barbaric usage from the bankrupt, 'dialogue' government of Busia, after the even more horrendous experience of Nigerian workers and other migrants at the hands of the black Count Dracula, Macias Nguema, after falling scapegoat to the unabashedly capitalist and corrupt government of Mobutu Sese Seko, after . . . after . . . after . . . the Nigerian, in company of other unfortunates from other countries from West Africa, is bewildered to find himself once again at the receiving end, this time from a progressive, self-avowed socialist people's republic – The Congo! Now, let me avoid any possible misunderstanding. Whatever was the cause of this brutal expulsion of fellow Africans, it was *not* the probable inability of the expelled persons to speak French. It was not even the possible fact that they had failed in the meantime to speak the local languages. But I think we will all agree that those social handicaps, and the fact that, among themselves, they very likely speak their own languages, did mark them out as alien. Audibly at least. Visibly, they probably also looked different, especially if they had tribal marks on their faces. But verbal communication is the most penetrating means of identity within a community. A non-verbal man, except of course those very remarkable and exceptional individuals who, as we say, literally radiate the force of their personality by their very presence, a non-verbal man is equivalent, roughly, to a piece of inert utensil. I exaggerate of course but I'm certain you will concede some measure of truth in this. When it comes to those reacting attitudes within community large or small, it is largely what we hear that defines, that marks out and identifies the alien. 'Be seen, not heard' just about sums it up. To conclude: the degree of linguistic assimilation of any group within a community inversely affects the level of potential animosity which the community can evoke against itself for whatever reason: success in trade, monopoly of social positions, etc., and thereby lessens the probability of hostile action by the community.

Just one example to buttress my rating of this aural dimension. The Ibadan accent is, I know, to many Yoruba the butt of many linguistic jokes. It is certainly an accent and a dialect that you notice. In 1952 – I remember the details because I had gone to collect scholarship forms – I was at the Ibadan Secretariat when I heard a man speak to someone in the furthest-out Ibadan accent I had ever heard. I turned round involuntarily and was surprised to find no sign of the speaker. I continued along the corridor when the same voice resounded. I turned; again no one, yet the voice could have come from nowhere except from that corridor. As I stood pondering the strange phenomenon, the voice rang out a third time; only then did I notice the white man leaning over the balcony, giving orders to someone below. He was a full Caucasian, not even tanned. I found out his name and have never forgotten it – one Mr Kitto. I think he had lived in Ibadan for ten, twelve years – I forget that detail. Well, that is how effectively aural perception colours the visual – not surprisingly, since both forms of signal are interpreted by the same brain. And while no one would claim seriously that the policies of government are governed by the audiovisual sensors of officials, the truth is that the data which are fed into their basic statistical machines are gathered by human beings and coloured by their attitudes to 'aliens' which of course presuppose the process of group-identification. And, more pertinently, the executors of government decisions are the very members of the community whose subjective definition of aliens has been created by this very process. I sometimes encounter a Ghanaian who witnessed the summary expulsion of his or her neighbour Nigerians. Even when that Ghanaian has defended the policy of his government, he has been astonished and embarrassed at the gleeful participation of the local Ghanaians in the rounding up and expulsion of Nigerians of even a generation's next-door familiarity. Clearly, the triggering decision is not of one moment but of the entire length of their co-existence – the implantation, that is, of a mutual separate identity. At the very least, language is *one* of the key factors in embedding that separatist definition of social consciousness. The result, whenever the excuse is afforded from whatever direction, is the breakdown of the tenuous links of daily cohabitation, and the sudden resurrection of boundaries between linguistic groups.

We will not dwell on the lessons to be derived from our own internal experiences, only insist that it would be an extremely foolish or merely mischievous mind which fails to take our recent history into consideration in the mapping out of national linguistic strategies. Now, we must move from the realms of catastrophe and tragedy to some light relief – a very brief excursion into tragicomedy.

Five or six years ago, in the capital of a French-speaking West African county, a group of black statesmen-intellectuals gathered themselves together to confer on ways and means of preserving the purity of French language and culture. Black, African leaders of self-styled independent African countries. They came together with a representative of the French government and one or two members of the Académic Française. It is not clear what overriding fears, motives, ambitions or principle of self-denial created this urge to spring to the defence of an imperial tongue, especially one with a long history of cultural repression, one whose cultural vanity and linguistic superiority were already considered over-inflated even by her fellow European nations. That gathering met again recently, and on the same subject. I believe that one or two of those leaders did come to their senses in the meantime and dropped out. However, the question must be examined – what are their motivations? Could it be simply a fear of linguistic domination by yet another group of language-borrowers – the Anglophone Africans? I had begun to imagine that the message had become clear to all the world that the majority of English-speaking nations regard the language they speak as being nothing more than a tool of convenience, to be discarded whenever something more self-belonging was made viable. What was particularly ironic about the more recent conference was that the French visitors were at great pains to point out that the initiative for the conference had come from the African leaders themselves. Maybe they were embarrassed at this persistent anachronism or merely wanted to put the French-Afros in their place. Maybe they were anxious to assure the world that, on their part, the French had given up on cultural imperialism. (By the way, they have not, as we shall come to see in a moment.) However, the conference did take place, has taken place twice in the last five years, and will probably recur once more in this decade. It only remains, I suppose, for the ex-Portuguese, the ex-English colonies, the ex-

Spanish to appeal in retaliation to our former colonial masters to sponsor or attend 'rival' linguistic conferences on their own languages for the madness to become entire, making several *cordons sanitaires culturels* zig-zag their way across the continent. And now to melodrama.

That language is incorrigibly political in addition to anything else was very crudely illustrated by the recent election into the West African seat of the Security Council, our own Nigerian being one of the two contestants. I was in New York during the preceding week of feverish campaigning; I had business with a UN Agency there, so I am able to provide you a first-hand eye-witness ear-glued summation of the lines of division between the two factions: it was simply – language. Sure, from time to time the contest spilt over into ideological persuasions and power bloc alliances. But I can testify that the most frantic, feverish and unscrupulous campaigning was done by – I shan't name the specific embassies, we'll just call them – the champion of the French-speaking zones and the champion of the English-speaking zone. I was curious to know on which side Canada was. Now Canada was in a very interesting situation. As I have already admitted, there were other lines of division apart from the linguistic – there was for instance the French Community and the Commonwealth. Now Canada, with her split linguistic personally: which way would she fall? Well, before I left, I heard a representative from our own Embassy let out a howl of outrage at Canada's defection to the Froggies – as the French are called in diplomatic language. Maybe Canada was won back later for the English side, I never did find out. If you want the final details I shall simply add that the OAU was, as usual, hopelessly split.

The foregoing will do to remind us of *actualities*, to recall us to the fact that, theorize how we will, language is a *lived* phenomenon, acted upon by human beings and acting in turn upon human beings – individually and as community – in millions of ways from the most banal to the sublime; with a simplistic directness and with the uttermost complexity. And in looking critically at part of the complex nature of language, we come up against its boundary characteristic which, on an embattled continent like ours, cannot be allowed the same luxury of indulgence as those other societies we have pointed at – France, the United States, the Soviet Union, etc. I have already gone on record as advocating the adoption of Kiswahili as a continental language. What is constantly ignored, suppressed, or simply not understood is that I have just as fervently advocated the conservation and creative enrichment of all, repeat ALL existing African languages. Both commitments are complementary parts of a linguistic strategy of total liberation; they do not contradict each other.

Recent reports on the pages of *West Africa* and *New Nigerian* very conveniently afford me the opportunity of clarifying this strategy further. I read to my astonishment in *West Africa* a statement credited to Alhali Akilu Aliyu that Hausa youths in Nigeria appear reluctant to speak Hausa. The Alhali is supposed to have said further that this language is neglected by education policy planners. Now, as I said earlier, I find this claim astonishing. I appear to have been living with the exact opposite impression, that is, in Nigeria especially and certainly in most African countries of my knowledge, the indigenous languages receive massive encouragement by officialdom and are indeed the first choice of today's youths in daily communication. As for Hausa (same as for Yoruba, Efik, Igbo, etc.), I would have thought that the pattern was – where two or three Hausa are gathered, there would Hausa be spoken. And that includes all the new élite I regularly encounter. However, accurate or not as the Alhaji's claim might be, the formation of the Hausa Arts Writers Association is not only a welcome addition to the language-promotion societies and institutions in the county; it is a model which should be followed by all linguistic groups in the county. What is more, it should link up with similar associations in West Africa, thus playing its role in dissolving the artificial boundaries foisted on us by the colonial powers in so arbitrary and greed-oriented directions.

Not so positive however is my reaction to the other report, this time in *New Nigerian* (26 October 1977) which goes further and advocates Hausa as a national language. I must repeat here what I have said elsewhere. In the politics of this continent, I have no patience with any national strategy which in any way, overt or covert, solidifies the meaningless colonial boundaries which have created and are still creating such intense havoc on the continent among African nations and peoples. With C.L.R. James, the radical historian, author of *The Black Jacobins*, I believe that 'the nation state, as an ideal, belongs to the last century'. To consolidate untenable geographical boundaries with the linguistic is not merely stagnating in essence and effect; it is sterile and retrogressive. Obviously this is a standpoint from which my concepts of a linguistic strategy stem. There is no value in contesting related issues which take a contrary standpoint since this, to me, is basic.

A profound examination of the activity of liberation demands an uncompromising look into that phenomenon of man's condition which is rendered, to borrow an American expressive form, as: 'where one is at'. I find this triggers off allied considerations such as 'where one is against' and uncovering, in the wake of squalor, inequality, exploitation, oppression, etc. – boundaries! As a language-user on more than the merely utilitarian level, it becomes intolerable that that favoured medium should constitute yet another boundary, on any level, between the peoples of a continent in search of a common identity. It is inevitable, confronted by retrogressive events such as earlier remarked, that we find ourselves asking questions which probe the very definition of boundary and its actualities: what it encloses, who it keeps apart, what it conceals and what it exposes. And ultimately: whether, specifically for us, language does not signify a wasteful extension of the boundary instinct.

In the process, it may be that we discover that boundaries – geographical, political, economic, cultural or linguistic – are walls of straw, that specifically in Africa, they were eaten long ago by the termites of black discontent, that they are held together only by the inheritors of white empires. Such an awareness makes instant demands on itself. Unfettered by past acceptances, it reaches down to the roots of society, rediscovers eternal causes for human association and proceeds to build new entities held together, not by artificial challenges but by a recognisable identity of goals. It is a process of the mind which transcends the emotional content or separation of unification, and forges, in whatever field it can, the psychological, cultural and political tools for a healthy social entity.

One such weapon of entity restitution is, of course, language. It is not as emotive or utopian as such a goal is often made out to be. We can argue that it is not a priority, but then we are compelled to ask whether or not any mass consciousness in a people which will go some way towards assaulting the acceptance and practice of social differentiation is not in itself a priority. And whether tools and activities which go some way towards creating binding consciousness among peoples are not worthy of a prior place in social programming. Let me however anticipate some basic objections.

We should begin by moving away from, or at least re-examining, the traditional habits of accepted linguistic theories. Such an exercise is not designed to upset these, merely to use the pertinent data to clarify whatever decision which any community of peoples make for their own linguistic future. It is true for instance that language is itself the repository of a people's history and culture, but we cannot afford to agonize unnecessarily over the suspicion that the new African nations, because of the diversity of languages within their boundaries, may not actually possess a unified culture. (Amilcar Cabral was quite definite in denying the existence of one unified African Culture.) We shall waste as much time damning the artificiality of the existing national boundaries as bemoaning the fact that such boundaries have no cultural validation. These nuisances are more than compensated for by yet another fact – that neither history nor culture is static. It is possible therefore, given the necessary historic motivation, to create a new unifying culture from the uneasy amalgam of diversified ones. And where language is involved, we have at our disposal evidence of the revolutionary use to which the language of the oppressor has been used in oppressed societies: DuBois, Frantz Fanon, Nelson Mandela, Agostinho Neto, Nkrumah, Malcolm X, Eldridge Cleaver, Angela Davis, Imamu Baraka, etc., etc. – an unending list through the history of colonial experience. This brutal reversal of the enslaving role of language – prophesied by that unusual Elizabethan, Shakespeare – tells us all we wish to know about the possibility of creating a synthetic revolutionary culture in place of the bastardised or eradicated indigenous culture of the colonized. The unaccustomed role which such a language is forced to play turns it indeed into a new medium of communication and simultaneously forges a new organic series of mores, social goals, relationships, universal awareness – all of which go into the creating of a new culture. Black people twisted the linguistic blade in the hands of the traditional cultural castrator and carved new concepts onto the flesh of white supremacy. The customary linguistic usage was rejected outright and a new, raw, urgent and revolutionary syntax was given to this medium which had become the greatest single repository of racist concepts.

The recognition of strategic options, through language, for African self-liberation has long preoccupied politicians, artists and intellectuals in the long history of colonialism. From Mahatma Gandhi to the modern colonial or ex-colonial poets and bureaucrats both on the mother continent and in the Diaspora, the same dismay has been voiced at the linguistic trap in which the colonial product finds himself. Each has sought his solution firstly in the conversion of the enslaving medium into an insurgent weapon; then in the search for a new medium of identity, indigenous, if not to him, then at least to others with whom he could claim a bond of kinship; often he has adopted both approaches simultaneously. David Diop wrote: 'If Africa were freed by compulsion, no (African) writer would even consider expressing his feelings and those of his people in anything other than his own, rediscovered, language.' And at the Second Congress of Negro Writers and Artists in Rome, 1959, this resolution was passed:

(i)   that free and liberated black Africa should not adopt any European or other language as a national tongue
(ii) that one African language should be chosen . . . that all Africans would learn this national language besides their own regional language
(iii) that a team of linguists be instructed to enrich this language as rapidly as possible, with the terminology for expression of modern philosophy, science and technology

This resolution was taken at the same conference in which the Malagasy poet Rabemanjara, in a mixture of self-disgust *and* triumph at the linguistic cleft in which the colonial writer found himself, declared:

> Truly our conference is one of language thieves. This crime, at least, we have committed ourselves. We have stolen from our masters this treasure of identity, the vehicle of their thought, the golden key to their soul, the magic Sesame which opens wide the door of their secrets, the forbidden cave where they have hidden the loot taken from our fathers and for which we must demand a reckoning.

The ambivalent, even extreme reactions of the modern user of colonial language should be seen therefore as a natural, even positive result of a realistic view of history. For we must not underestimate the attitude of the original owner himself, one which understood the fatal consequence of this acquisition of his own weapon of oppression, a fear, often disguised under a veneer of the benevolent policy of separate development, lest the oppressed peoples prove as skilled as the oppressor has been in the exploitation of the now common medium. South Africa is the obvious example, and Paul Hazoume, an ethnologist from Dahomey (now Benin Republic), at the first Congress of Negro Writers and Artists ripped the veil off such pretensions in the following words:

> Westerners seem today to regret having imposed the study of European languages. They are anxiously asking whether it would not be better to go back, as quickly as possible, on what they now take to have been an error on their part in the task which they had set themselves of educating the Africans, and to start teaching them their own languages. As an African, I cannot help wondering if the reasons used by westerners to justify their decision to teach Africans in their own language alone do not hide the real motives which they are ashamed to admit: motives of sordid, personal interest, presage, fear of competition which they dare not allow

to grow in face of the rapid development of the African elite, brought up until now without distrust of the same humanism as themselves. Some partisans of education in the vernacular have even suggested somewhat timidly, that their culture might produce social and even mental disturbances in Africans fed on it.

This accurately sums up the rationale of the South African Bantu education policy. And with this final concession to the argument for the principle of mastering whatever skills have contributed to the subjugation of millions, whether those skills be linguistic or technological, we turn now to give a little more attention to the alternative school of thought. Not alternative in the sense of being mutually exclusive, but simply as a proposition which, for multiple reasons – the least of which is not the reality of Africa's phenomenal self-advancement – demands that some attention be paid to the second phase of self-liberation: the creation of a continental language as an instrument of the continuing continental struggle.

We cannot – again it is necessary to approach this desirable goal realistically – we cannot immediately destroy the physical, colonial boundaries on the continent. That they will be destroyed is inevitable. That we need to destroy them is, I trust, equally unarguable, and not for any sentimental reasons. The need for their destruction arises from the simple fact that the work of rebuilding a new society, of the essential internal revolution which must follow the colonial liberation, this task is hampered by the physical existence of boundaries which have come to signify power separatist principles and reactionary bastions. What they mean to the masses is entirely separate from what they mean to their rulers. For the latter they are sacrosanct definitions of private ponds within which power can be made manifest. The principle of boundary for us at this moment is therefore allied to the principle of power and privilege, and its erosion becomes a long-term project whose realization can however be hastened by the erosion of symbolic and quasi-symbolic boundaries. By now I hope that we are in agreement that language belongs at the very least, in effect, among the quasi-symbolic boundaries.

A concern with language is fraught with many dangers. But none more serious than those which are posed by the *national* language alternative. Precisely because there is a predictable resistance to all forms of changes which threaten the sectarian and hegemonic mentality, the cry for a national language, where several already exist, is one which has been taken up in the most unlikely places. We have heard it in recent times from the mouths of the most abjectly worshipful colonial aristocrats on the coast of West Africa as stridently as from the genuine nationalist and even revolutionary idealists. When Nigeria was still split up in twelve states, one military governor decided unilaterally to impose on his state educational system the study of one of the Nigerian languages, this being one which he and a number of others believe is the obvious choice of a Nigerian national language. That it was and still is a highly controversial choice, open even to dangerous political misinterpretation, counted for nothing. The national language debate erupts periodically in Nigerian newspapers with as much passion as in neighbouring countries such as Sierra Leone and, I believe, Ghana.

True, some of those who espouse this cause are genuine believers. At the same time, experience teaches one to beware of the fomentors of chaos in society whose business it is to create diversions and divisions while they get on with the business of political manipulation. The harrowing lessons of other nations – India is one example – in their attempt to unify their peoples through the policy of a single language, are not lost upon them. The jealousies, the perennial fears of tribal domination, the possibilities of civil conflict merely encourage their championing of the national chauvinist cause. The resulting internecine conflicts leave them unscathed, wealthier and more securely entrenched in the keypoints of control; for these social predators therefore the question of language is only one of many tactical weapons of discord. And one of the justifications for a sense of urgency on the linguistic question is very simple – to anticipate the situation of chaos which might ensue from the manoeuvring of such people. The attempt to impose a single language within the constrictions of petty nationalities, riven by internal dissensions, is a clearly explosive one and is ultimately negative.

Within the larger framework of a continental accord, however, the subjective resistance is diffused; the motivation is clearly presented as the attractive ideal of the coming together of a continent; the atavistic suspicions cannot be focussed on any single tribe within a politically claustrophobic, and therefore explosive social capsule. Quite simply, we defuse the linguistic bomb and take its control away from scheming little opportunists.

Once again, attention must be called to the fact that our present national boundaries are colonial, that the cultural orientation is therefore still predominantly colonial, that the linguistic boundary is even more critical than the geographical because it is culturally divisive, but also that to replace such boundaries with several nation-linguistic boundaries is to enshrine for all time the principle of colonial fragmentation. Without actually waving the banner of the dream of the early Pan-Africanists who envisaged a United States of Africa 'without passing the middle-class chauvinistic nation phase' (Fanon) it is permissible, one hopes, to declare that the reverses which that dream has suffered so far do not validate the continuation of colonial boundaries, geographical or symbolic. This abstracted solace, even if it is all that is left of the dream, can be exploited to boost the present state of expedient compromise into the ultimate concrete direction of the original idea.

None of the foregoing precludes the continued use, development and enrichment of original languages in the fulfilment of their present functions, or the continued exploitation of colonial languages in order to, as Jean-Paul Sartre warned, 'shatter them, destroy their traditional associations and juxtapose them with violence'. Or even to use them routinely, as a tool of communication which is what language primarily is. The logical development of, or complementary phase to the revolutionary assault on the colonial language is however the creation of a new common medium of communication. The first stage of African liberation has been externally directed; it was the phase of liberation *from*. The conversionary use of the colonial language was logically related to this phase. The second stage, the positive, creative phase of liberation is the one which we are, with the exception of Southern Africa, currently engaged upon; the phase of internal reconstruction. The place of language should relate to this phase in as logical a manner as the first, namely by the adoption of a language of symbolic and practical unity.

All languages are prime candidates for the continental choice. I can only re-affirm and put forward that of my own reasoned choice which also happens to be the choice of several groups and individuals, including the Union of Writers of the African Peoples. I may add that when the paper of this very title was first read in Dar es Salaam, it mentioned no specific language. On my own part, I already felt that Kiswahili provided the sanest choice; I was however still engaged in examining the candidature of other languages. If it is any consolation to that writer whose essay-review appears on the pages of the *New Nigerian* of 26 October 1977, I share with him all the enthusiasm which he expresses for Hausa. It is a graceful, lyrical language; it is also widely spoken in West Africa. In opposition to the European and Arabic authorities which he chooses to cite however, I hope he will concede that there are even more numerous European and Arabic scholars who advocate the suitability of Kiswahili as an international language. Of these I shall cite here only the earliest within my knowledge: R. W. Cuit who, in 1896, declared, in his study of African languages, that Kiswahili not only was one of the eight most important languages in the world but was destined to become recognized as the most suitable language for the African continent. I hope, with that, we can dispense with the authority of foreigners. What do African writers and scholars, teachers and all say on the subjects? Pursuing the same goals as other gatherings of black writers, scholars and artists since the last two decades of the last century, the Accra meeting of African writers declared:

> This Union finds it regrettable that twenty years have been wasted since the Second Congress of African Writers in Rome recommended the adoption of one language for the African peoples. Resolved to end this state of inertia, hesitancy and defeatism, we have, after much serious consideration, and in the conviction that all technical problems can and will be overcome, *unanimously* adopted Kiswahili as the logical language for this purpose.

That meeting was by no means unanimous on the subject to begin with. Nor was the later Congress in Dakar which ratified that decision last year. What we are saying is that it is not something plucked out of some exotic hat with a wave of a magic wand or as in a lottery. Only a handful of Swahili speakers attended either conference, but nearly all are familiar with the socio-history of most African languages, several were language experts and their analyses were objective in detail.

I shall cite as further example and authority the case of Professor Cheik Anta Diop, director of the IFAN research laboratory in the University of Dakar, who, to prove the adaptability of African languages, has written several learned scientific papers and a scientific text-book for schools in his native Wollof. This giant intellect is also an ethnologist, a linguist and historian; when it came to his choice of language for continental adoption he unreservedly chose Swahili. If arrangements proceed without any hitch, the country may be fortunate to listen to Professor Cheik Anta Diop this year or early next at the first full Congress of the Association of Researchers and Scientists of the Black World.[1] The promoter of partisan interests in the *New Nigerian* essay who equates objectivity with the trotting out of indifferent authorities who happened to have been civil servants of the colonial empire in Northern Nigeria will have the opportunity to exchange ideas – if he has any of his own – with Cheik Anta Diop. Only the worst type of colonial enslavement could lead anyone to use the 1975 MA Thesis of some putative scholar from an American University as *basis* for resolving the linguistic dilemma of the entire African continent! May I remark however – lest I be misunderstood (I shall be *deliberately* misunderstood anyway but no matter) – there will be as many favourites as there are languages, and every individual is at liberty to express and promote an opinion. We merely ask to be spared the kind of opportunism and slapstick 'reasoning' such as is exhibited in the article I have referred to. This is not a subject for partisanship or bonded interests, but of commitment and vision. I wish to end by referring to the linguistic experiences of Togo and the Cameroon. In the latter especially, during a mere half-century, its official language changed from English to French to German and French or English again – not necessarily in that order. The people of the Cameroons had no choice but to follow the whims of imperial fortune. Several other peoples on this continent have undergone degrees of the same experience. And so, from those who say, but why should we take the trouble to learn or promote another official language, we can only demand: why does the power of the gun so easily compel you to serve the interests of aliens, but never an act of political will the cause of your own self-interest?

There are no miracles involved. The All-Africa Teachers Union, meeting in Algiers in 1975, has also called for the adoption of one language for the whole of the African continent, and named Kiswahili one of their three first choices. They should know. On them falls the burden of implementing their own resolution. Even modest beginnings in the form of Swahili teaching in universities, as already practised by Ghana, Senegal and Gambia are actions of a positive nature. Most of East and Central Africa already speak and write this language. The real place to begin is the secondary school. Primary education, I believe, should *always* be given in the child's mother-tongue. On that principle, there should be no compromise. But the teaching of Swahili, just as a school subject, begun now, already promises a transformation of the linguascape of the continent within the next twelve years. The rest follows naturally, part of it even simultaneously – Swahili courses on national networks, the same as we now have for French, English, German etc. The mood throughout the continent today is to explore that continent and become acquainted with what the various modes of boundary have kept away from each of us – that mood was reflected in the government's directive to civil servants, urging them to spend their vacations on the continent. Sticking out of their pockets when they visit East Africa will be Swahili phrase-books. In twenty years, the phrase-books will not be needed. The Army of Liberation to the front-line states, what language will they communicate in? A babble of Ibo, Hausa, German, Wollof, French, Ga, Yoruba, Portuguese, Twi, English etc? Is it not more rational to move our minds where history is pointing and teach our mouths to form the language of that moment? We must not, in this phase of the continent's coming-in-being, contract our sights within boundaries of pettiness, insularity and narrow chauvinism.

Note

1 It is sad to relate that Professor Cheikh Anta Diop died suddenly in June 1986 of a heart attack. (W. S.)

INDEX

Valuable Resources in Philosophy of Language

A COMPANION TO THE PHILOSOPHY OF LANGUAGE
Edited by Bob Hale and Crispin Wright
0-631-16757-9 hardcover

TRUTH AND MEANING: AN INTRODUCTION TO THE PHILOSOPHY OF LOGIC
Kenneth Taylor
1-57718-049-6 paperback
1-57718-048-8 hardcover

THE CHURCHLANDS AND THEIR CRITICS
Edited by Robert N. McCauley
0-631-18969-6 paperback
0-631-18968-8 hardback

REALISM, MEANING AND TRUTH
Crispin Wright
0-631-17118-5 paperback

AN INTRODUCTION TO PHILOSOPHICAL LOGIC
Third Edition
A. C. Grayling
0-631-19982-9 paperback
0-631-20655-8 hardcover

THE RISE OF ANALYTIC PHILOSOPHY
Edited by Hans-Johann Glock
0-631-20086-X paperback

THE FREGE READER
Edited by Michael Beany
0-631-19445-2 paperback
0-631-19444-4 hardcover

DIRECT REFERENCE:
From Language to Thought
Francois Recanati
0-631-20634-5 paperback

THE LANGUAGES OF LOGIC:
An Introduction to Formal Logic
Samuel Guttenplan
1-55786-988-X paperback

THE WITTGENSTEIN READER
Edited by Anthony Kenny
0-631-19362-6 paperback

TO ORDER CALL :
1-800-216-2522 (N. America orders only) or
24-hour freephone on 0500 008205
(UK orders only)

VISIT US ON THE WEB : http://www.blackwellpublishers.co.uk

CPSIA information can be obtained at www.ICGtesting.com
Printed in the USA
BVOW06s0526160114

341850BV00004BA/49/P